THE DAY
THE FEDS
CAME CALLING

THOMAS FOLEY

Fulton Books
Meadville, PA

Published by Fulton Books 2024

ISBN 979-8-89221-187-1 (paperback)
ISBN 979-8-89221-188-8 (digital)

Printed in the United States of America

To my dear wife, Sonia, and to my sons, Thomas J. Foley IV and Jake Patrick Foley.

Had I not met Sonia when I did, I would not be alive today. Sonia, I thank you for showing me that the events of the past cannot and will not define who I am as a human being. Thank you, Sonia, for holding me tight when my nightmares wake us in the middle of the night. I dedicate not only this book to you but also my heart and soul for as long as the good Lord allows me to stay on earth. I love you, Sonia.

Thomas and Jake, you need to know one thing. Without you being in my life, I would not have survived one day in prison. Not a day behind the walls of prison went by without me talking to you both through prayer. I love you both with all my heart, and I will do my best to be the father that you both deserve.

CHAPTER 1

It has been well-documented throughout history that people from around the world have come to America in search of a better way of life. Aaahhhh, America, land of the free and home of the brave. I believe that at some point in every American's life, the thought of achieving the American dream seems like a very obtainable goal—fame, fortune, freedom, family. Everyone has their own version of what the American dream is. The strong and determined stop at nothing to achieve their goals, while the weak and lazy make lame efforts filled with excuses as to why they were destined to fail. My name is Thomas J. Foley III. I chose to be relentless in the pursuit of my version of the American dream. I put the pedal to the metal and drove with determination. Failure was not an option. Yes, my efforts toward the American dream were blessed beyond my wildest dreams; that is, of course, until the day the feds came calling.

As I look out of my window, I am taken in by the breathtaking view. I can see the port of Miami with huge cruise ships setting sale for exotic destinations. I can see South Beach with all its luxurious high-rise buildings. I can see the intercoastal waterway alive with speedboats and luxurious yachts. Finally, I can see parts of downtown Miami with its huge business skyscrapers gleaming in the sun. People from around the world pay millions of dollars for this exact view, but from the eleventh floor of the Miami Federal Detention Center, I get this view for free. So who's better than me?

I have a story that needs to be told. This is a true story about my life and how I wound up in federal prison. At this very moment, life sucks for me, but how I got here is a whole 'nother story. Is *'nother* even a real word? Who gives a shit? It's my book, and in my book, *'nother* is a real word. Okay, grab yourself a cocktail, kick back, and read about the rise and fall of an average Joe who had nothing, got everything, and then butt heads with the United States of America. Here's a book disclaimer: Kids, don't try this at home.

I promised myself that if I ever did write a book about my life and how I wound up in prison, I would tell the truth, the whole truth, and nothing but the truth, so help me God. I am not proud of many stages of my life or the fact that I shit on a lot of people. Some of the memories that I am going to share with you are humiliating to me. Some of the memories I am about to tell you will hurt people that are very close to me. Some of the memories I am about to share with you are so painful that I cried the whole time I put them on paper. So why do it then? Because my family and friends that have supported me my entire life deserve to hear the truth come out of my mouth, once and for all. For once in my life, I will not tell lies. The world deserved better from me. So I dedicate the rest of my life to make this crazy world a better place to live. Please don't get me wrong. I like who I am. I have done plenty in the past to help other people on this planet. I just know that I could have and should have made better choices in my life. As the great Robert Dinero said in the movie *A Bronx Tale*, "There is nothing worse than wasted talent." That's how I see myself at this point, a guy who chose to waste his talents. I would also like to apologize in advance for the awful words and phrases that I use from time to time. I truly mean nothing by it. I use words like *fag, bitch, cunt, fuck, shit, retard,* and *dickhead*; well, you get the point. I tend to make fun of everyone, including myself, but at the end of the day, I have no enemies. I am not a racist, and I do not discriminate against people because of their race, religion, ethnicity, political views, or sexual orientation. Certain people tend to piss me off in life, and what comes out of my mouth when I describe those people cannot be controlled. I like to get my point across in a very harsh manner sometimes. If stuff like that offends you, then I suggest you stop reading at this point; you are probably some tightly wound ass wipe that has never gotten laid in any place other than a bed. Go get yourself some therapy. I hope this book acts as a wake-up call for some of you. If I can stop even one person from following down the path that I chose in life, then this book was worth writing. I can't possibly tell you every crazy event in my life in one book; it would be like trying to read the entire *Encyclopedia Britannica* at one time. For now, the major events that shaped my life are in this book, and trust me, that is enough for now.

CHAPTER 2

I grew up on the south shore of Long Island, New York. The town I grew up in was a small town called Massapequa, home of the Chiefs. Massapequa's claims to fame? Well, how about Joey and Mary Jo Buttafuoco, Amy Fisher (the Long Island Lolita), the Stray Cats, the Baldwin Brothers, Brian Kilmeade from Fox News, and that retard that the movie *Born on the Fourth of July* was based on? Oh, I almost forgot, Massapequa is home of some well-known members of the Mafia. Oh, that's right, the Mafia doesn't really exist. Wink. Wink.

Anyway, I was raised in what most people would call an average middle- to lower-class household: Mom, Dad, two older sisters, and a cat. My mother and father stayed married until the day my mom passed on. They never beat or molested me, so I can't use those as excuses for why I wound up the way I did. Both of my parents worked to make ends meet, and in my eyes, neither of them was very ambitious. Please don't get me wrong here. This great planet of ours was built by people like my mother and father, and I have nothing but respect for them. My dad worked for Castrol Motor Oil for almost thirty years. He worked his way up through the ranks with hard work and many long hours. My mother, God rest her soul, worked retail almost her entire life. My parents put a roof over our heads, kept food on the table, gave clothes on our backs, and put me through college. What my parents did for me and my sisters was honorable to say the least. But in my eyes, it was also complacent, boring, and 100 percent not the life I wanted for myself. I mean, for God's sake, we get one life on this planet. I just feel that you have to shoot for the moon and hopefully land somewhere among the stars. You see, there I go with my opinions again. People, I guess what I am saying is that if my parents' dreams were to be an oil salesman and a retail worker, then who am I to say that's wrong? My parents lived a good honest life of mediocracy. Good for them, but no, thank you. That's not for me. I wanted to see how far I could push myself, my mind, my body, and my God-given soul.

Okay, back to my family. As I said, I have two sisters. Paula is now forty-six, and Lisa is fifty-two years old. They were raised to be average nobodies in search of men that could take care of them for the rest of their lives. Neither of my sisters were any good at that one task, and I will surely elaborate on that throughout this book.

Now back to me. This fuckin' book is about me, damn it. I was the ambitious one of the family—the hustler, the troublemaker who was always able to lie his way through any situation. To be honest with you, when I look back on my life, I should have been dead by the age of twenty. My physical statue has not changed much over the years. I have always been tall and thin with a big nose and hair that has been falling out of my head since my mid-twenties. I always participated in sports. Massapequa was big on soccer, and I played for a good ten years. My dad was never one to really encourage me to play sports, and I don't blame him because my talents were limited. That's my way of saying I sucked. I ran on my high school track team and was pretty good at the high jump, but I realized my one true sports talent during college when I played division 1 volleyball for three years.

I always had a lot of friends growing up. In fact, I have known most of my friends since elementary school. I consider my friends in New York to be some of the greatest people on this planet. I would take a bullet for anyone of them, including the friends who abandoned me when the feds came calling.

There are many times that I curse myself for moving out of New York, but I have never been one to play Monday morning quarterback with my life. I made my choices, and I will live with those choices. You will find as you read on that I am my own biggest critic, and I believe that attitude is what makes me strive to be the best that I can be. Okay, so let's get the show on the road. I am going to take one deep breath before I continue on. This is not easy for me to share.

Let me start with my early childhood. The neighborhood that I grew up on always had a ton of kids playing in the streets. Video games were still in their early stages of development, so street games like kickball, whiffle ball, tag, and bicycle racing occupied my time. What I believe separated me from the other "normal" kids was this internal fire that I had—a voice inside of me that just wanted me to be noticed. I wanted to be heard; I wanted to be a leader. For whatever reason, I couldn't figure out why. I convinced myself at that early stage that I could accomplish these inner needs and dreams by simply being funny and becoming wealthy.

Being funny always came easy to me. I was dubbed the class clown by every teacher I ever had. My parents gave me many lectures about that, but I never listened. Now making money, that came even easier to me.

CHAPTER 3

I still remember my first endeavor as a businessman. It took place during the third grade. When I was growing up, it was still safe for a kid to walk to school without your parents. Nowadays, these child-abducting pieces of shit are everywhere, so things are much different. My sister Paula and I used to walk to elementary school almost every day. There was a luncheonette on the way called Sol's that we would stop at to buy the hottest new candy to hit the streets of America: Now and Later. Every kid in our school was hooked on these chewy treats, and one fine spring morning, I came up with a grand idea. On this special day, I saw a supply truck delivering boxes and boxes of candy to the luncheonette, and of course, Now and Later were part of the delivery. I wrote down the address that was on the truck and looked it up on a local map. The following weekend, I told my parents I was going to take a bicycle ride to a local park with friends (a big fat lie). Instead of the park, I rode my bike about ten miles to the candy distributor located in the lovely town of Amityville. Yes, Amityville as in the movie *The Amityville Horror*. That house from the movie is really there, and the last time I checked, it was still abandoned. For the record, I am not racist. I would bang a black chick just as quickly as a white, brown, yellow, red, or semi-retarded chick. I love all people, but Amityville is no place for a white, skinny third grader. Anyway, I get to this warehouse that appears to be deserted. It's the weekend, you moron, and people back then relaxed on the weekends. I walked around the entire building and finally found a loading dock that was open. On the dock was a rugged-looking man stacking huge boxes of exactly what I had come looking for—the holy grail of candy, Now and Later. This guy was about six feet tall, probably weighed around three hundred pounds, and the walls appeared to shake when he spoke. I was scared to death, but a mission is a mission. I explained to Giganture that I was entering a contest and needed Now and Later for a fundraiser that I was going to hold at school (another lie). This guy apologized, acted annoyed, and started with this "I can't" crap because of licensing crap and blah blah blah, the bottom line being, "Get out, kid! I am busy." I responded like any other American entrepreneur would respond: I cried. It was not just a little whimper with tears. No, this was a cry like a woman that had just gotten her period on her wedding dress. I could see instant panic on the big man's face.

> Giganture: Calm down, young man. Calm down,
> for God's sake, calm down. Okay, what the
> heck. I guess I could help a young business-
> man earn a good grade in school.

I purchased a full case of Now and Later, one hundred packs, for just five cents per pack. (That's $5 for you, mathematically challenged readers.) That was also one-fifth of the store price of $0.25 cents. Score! My first legitimate supply purchase was a success; this was great. Now being the absolute moron that I was, I quickly remembered that I rode my bicycle there, and this box was huge. I probably wiped out around two hundred times on the way home, but I was determined and stupid. That following Monday, I threw ten packs of Now and Later into my backpack, and off to school I went. My marketing strategy was simple: break the packs of candy up and sell individual pieces for five cents each. I would gross fifty cents per pack. The kids at school went absolutely wild. I literally had lines of kids waiting for me wherever I went; some even spent their entire lunch allowance on my candy. Within my first three days of business, I sold out the entire case. I made a net profit of $45. Mind you now, I was in third grade in 1973. Forty-five dollars back then was probably equal to $215 today. From that week forward, I made weekly trips to the candy warehouse for supplies. I got smart and pulled a red wagon behind my bicycle so I could buy more than one case at a time while also preventing my near-death riding experience I had on my first trip. Now I ask you, folks, who the hell came up with the phrase "All good things must come to an end"? That guy is a dick, but damn, he was right on the money. You see, what I did not know was that my mother was cleaning my room one day and happened to stumble upon over $200 that I had saved from my candy sales. Quick side note: sock drawers are not good hiding places.

Being the trusting parents that raised me, they somehow came to the genius conclusion that I was selling drugs. I was in third grade for Christ sake! So what did Mom and Dad do? They called the police. It was my first experience of being ratted out to the authorities but not my last, that's for sure. The cops and my parents decided they should follow me, catch me in the act, and hopefully get my supplier at the same time. This should have been an episode of *Geraldo*, like when he opened that safe on live TV, and there was nothing in it. Ooops! The "Big Bust" wound down on a Tuesday. School had just ended, and a group of kids had formed around me for their last fix of the day. Now picture this: I suddenly see two uniformed police officers charging at me with my parents right behind them. What the hell was going on here?

> Police: Nobody move! You (pointing at me) drop the bag.
> Me: (not a single word could come out, but pee was close to coming out.)
> Mom: Just do as they say.
> Me: (scared to death, not a single word could come out, but pee started to come out.)

The cops dumped my backpack out onto the grass along with the last of the candy and a good $10 worth of change. The cops checked all the kids' hands and found nothing but candy and coins.

> Police: Where are the drugs, young man?
> Me: (silent but thinking, *Drugs? What are drugs?* then more pee)

Finally, one of the other kids told the police officer that I was selling them Now and Later.]

> Police: Oh! (then hysterical laughter from both
> of them.)
> Mom: Oh, thank God! I knew he was a good kid.
> Me: I have to pee really bad.

You would think that my parents and the cops would have apologized, but they didn't. I think my old man was just pissed because I was making more money than he was. The principal came out at the end of this event and was filled in by the cops about what went down. The principal was a dickhead by the way. He made it very clear that selling anything on school property was not allowed. I got a week of detention. Life sure can have a sick sense of humor sometimes.

CHAPTER 4

As the years went by, events unfolded in my life, some of which would haunt me for the rest of my life. In the fifth grade, I had a teacher by the name of Mrs. Benson. Mrs. Benson was always nice to me. She seemed to go out of her way to praise my work and would have conversations with me about life, not just boring school talk. She was a big woman, and if I had to guess, I would say she was around 5'4" tall and weighed in at around 280 pounds. Her everyday ritual was also very strange. Every day, as she was teaching our class, she would peel a raw union and eat it like it was an apple.

One day while erasing the blackboard, Mrs. Benson stopped, looked right at me, and fell to the floor. She had suffered a massive heart attack and died right there in front of us. While we waited as a student ran to get help, I held Mrs. Benson's head in my arms. I will never forget her last words.

Mrs. Benson said, "Tom, you have a twinkle in your eyes. It's nice."

Then she was gone. I cried for days. You would think the school would have provided some grief counseling for the kids, but back then, it wasn't part of the protocol like it would be today. The school replaced her and hoped that the kids would forget what happened. But that moment would be one that I will never forget. I truly believe that moments like that really fucked with my mind. I don't think the mind fucking was all bad though. A lot of what I experienced by way of tragedy motivated me to be the best that I could be.

CHAPTER 5

A year or so after the death of Mrs. Benson, another landmark event occurred in my life, one of the moments that I would change if I could turn back time. By now, most people in this world have seen the movie *A Christmas Story*. This is the movie where Ralphie wants a Red Rider BB Gun for Christmas, and the whole world keeps telling him that he will shoot his eye out. Well, in sixth grade, as Christmas was approaching, I was on a quest to get a BB gun like Ralphie. I put it on my list, hounded my parents, and I even threatened Santa Claus: "Look, you fat fuck, a BB gun, or I will come to the North Pole, kill your reindeer, and violate Mrs. Claus." Well, the reindeer are still alive, and Mrs. Claus was able to relax because on Christmas Day, my dreams were answered. Under the tree was a beautiful Crossman BB pistol. Dirty Harry, get the fuck out of my way, I am living large. At the time, my best friend was a kid named Ray. We did everything together. As you may have noticed, I do not use a lot of last names in this book. I have chosen this path because a lot of the people I am writing about hate my guts, and this is my way of giving them their closure. So Ray came over on Christmas morning, and we headed out into my backyard to do a little target shooting. The Crossman came with some paper targets that Ray and I hung on the fence. I would say it took me about ten minutes before I was bored to death. I told Ray I was bored, and I was going to shoot the next bird that I saw. Ray went off on me, but I ignored him and shot at the first bird that landed in my backyard. The damn bird dropped out of the tree like a lead balloon. Ray really freaked this time. As he walked out of my backyard, he told me he was going to tell my father. I knew that upon hearing this, my father would take the BB gun away, so I decided to stop Ray. How? I shot him. I shot my best friend Ray right in the back. BANG! Ray hit the ground like a sack of potatoes, a screaming, crying, sack of potatoes. Holy shit, did I fuck up or what? As Ray was screaming for help, I remember panicking and trying to figure out how to help him. I got down on the floor and told him how sorry I was. I will never forget how Ray looked at me and said, You are such a faggot."

I stood up as it took a second to process that. Here I was trying to apologize, and he called me a faggot. That was just wrong. This is the stupid shit that sometimes goes through my head. I decided to prove to him that I was not a faggot, so I shot him again. What the hell was I thinking? At this point, my father was approaching to find out what the screaming was all about. Dead man walking, ladies and gentlemen, dead man walking. I will not get into how I was punished, but mark my words, I was. I never saw that BB gun again, but I think that was for the best. Ray never spoke to me again, and if you are out there reading this, Ray, I am sorry. I truly am sorry.

CHAPTER 6

Junior high was when I really started to blossom. I almost always had straight As. My comedy routines were constantly getting me in trouble. I was approaching six feet tall and had connected with an awesome group of friends. I would like you to now meet what I considered to be my inner circle at that point of my life (that's a Hollywood term).

Donny L was of medium height and very skinny. Athletics were not his cup of tea. He was one of my earliest childhood friends and introduced me to most of the friends that I grew up with. He was a funny, funny kid who loved practical jokes. He was raised by a single mom and lived in a waterfront house in Massapequa, had a boat that we got to use all the time, and was willing to try almost anything. I would consider Donny to be one of the most loyal friends a guy could have.

John T was the cool-looking Italian stud. He was a real ladies' man as far back as I can remember. John grew up in a waterfront house in Massapequa in a stable household anchored by his mother and father. He was a real speedster on the track team, very athletic in his early years, and a wild man capable of almost anything at any time. I will always remember his beat-up old Chevy Nova that was his pride and joy.

Arthur L: Arthur was a Norwegian male whore. He was always a looker, with the hottest girlfriends. He was raised in a waterfront house in Massapequa with his mother, father, and sister. He was the party animal of the group, and you had to constantly be on your toes around Artie. Expect the unexpected. I consider him to be one of my best and most loyal friends at that point of my life.

Patrick R—although a madman back in the day, I would consider him to be one of the most stable guys I have come to know. Pat lived in Eastern Massapequa and was raised by his mother, father, and had two brothers. He was very athletic and always seemed to have a steady girlfriend. Pat was a very loyal friend who could be trusted to be there in a time of need.

Alfred M or Al was also one of my earliest friends and an all-around great guy who had a laugh that could make you piss in your pants. When he laughed, you couldn't help but join in. He was raised in South Massapequa by his mother and father. He had a sister and an older brother Joe that my group loved to hang out with. And unlike the rest of us who were bums, Al always had a steady job.

Jimmy H was the oldest of the group. I believe he was around five years older than us. Jimmy lived in a waterfront house in Massapequa and was raised by his mother and father. He was an awesome ice hockey player and was a strong doofy and very nice guy. Jimmy was a shitty dresser and always had pigs for girlfriends. I wanted to sugarcoat that one, but it is simply impossible to do. He was a very loyal friend, and I have nothing but respect for him, except for the woman thing.

Lenny W was an all-around great guy. He was the only one in the group that did not drink. He had a great laugh and always had a steady girlfriend. Lenny also lived in south Massapequa and was raised by his mother and father. He was always very business-minded and bypassed college to go into business for himself. Nice job, Lenny.

Tommy P did not hang out with us as often as the rest, but I do consider him to be a part of the crew. Tommy grew up in a waterfront house in Massapequa, and if I remember correctly, he was raised by his mom and stepdad. His mom spoke with a heavy German accent, and no one could understand a fuckin' word she was saying. Tommy also had a sister with big tits. Sorry, Tommy, it's true.

So that was the inner circle. I mentioned things like their households because I want you to realize that I grew up around friends with good upbringings, and most of my friends' families were much wealthier than I was. Regardless of all that bullshit, I miss them all and sometimes wish I never moved out of New York.

CHAPTER 7

As any freshman will tell you, entering high school is like starting life all over again. Everyone seems to be older than you, more mature, and physically more developed. All my close friends except Al and Donny were at least a year older than me. High school was filled with strangers; strangers divided into the following groups called cliques: the geeks, the jocks, the burnouts, and the misfits. Every freshman needed to figure out which group they wanted to be a part of and set a course that would allow them to be accepted by that group.

When I look back on high school, I would say that I never chose one particular group. My friends and I were a true combination of all of them. We fit in with everyone like the true chameleons that we were. This can pretty much be said for my entire life. I could fit in with anyone at any time if I chose to, and people tended to accept me without much effort. It's not like I am an egomaniac or anything like that. I just have a gift that allows me to read almost any situation and blend in accordingly. It was usually when I chose not to blend in that all hell broke loose.

Several events from high school are forever embedded into my mind and have affected me through my entire life. I don't know how many people will be able to relate to these events because I am convinced that this shit only happens to me, but you be the judge.

The end of my freshman year was approaching, and the walls were covered with signs and posters advertising the upcoming senior prom. I was hanging out by my locker one day talking to friends when a girl approached me and asked if she could talk to me in private. Now that did not happen to me very often. To Artie? Yes. To John? Yes. But not me. The first problem I had at that moment was that I could not take my eyes off her tits. They were just perfect.

16

She had an all-around nice body, but God help me, those tits were awesome. As my friends shuffled off in awe, I realized that she was still talking to me. I managed to divert my gaze away from her chest long enough to look her in the eyes. It was not the greatest face that I have ever seen, but who cares? A senior, yes, a senior with nice tits was talking to me.

Me: I'm sorry. Did you say something?

I had to ask that stupid question because those damn tits made me temporarily deaf. Her reply knocked me for a loop.

> Nice Tits: I would like to know if you would go
> to the senior prom with me.
> Me: I'm a freshman. You do realize that I'm a
> freshman.
> Nice Tits: (smiling) Yes, I do know you're a fresh-
> man. Is that a yes?
> Me: You bet your… Yes, I would love to go.

Her name was Janice. I love you, Janice. My friends were in shock. How in God's name did I of all people get invited to the senior prom by a semi-hot chick with great tits? One of my wiseass friends came to the conclusion that she must be a guy. Thanks, guys. Thanks a lot. It did not take long before I convinced myself that I was in way over my head, but I said yes, so it was time to man up.

Our school had a tuxedo company come in to do the fittings for the big event. Janice met me at the fitting and picked out a white tuxedo with tails and a black vest. I thought that it made me look like an anorexic penguin. Janice insisted on paying for everything: the tux, the prom tickets, the limo, the pictures, everything. I felt like a male whore. What a great feeling! (Guys, I highly recommend you try it.) Janice informed me that we would be sharing the limo ride with two other couples. I was introduced to them during lunch one day. I had recognized them from the school hallways, and they all seemed nice enough. None of them gave me shit about being a freshman; that was a relief. One of the guys, Rich, pulled me aside and asked me if I drank alcohol or did any drugs. Well, that was a real icebreaker there, Rich. Thanks for not making me feel too uncomfortable.

> Me: I drink when the opportunity arises.
> Rich: What's your poison?
> Me: What?
> Rich: What kind of liquor do you like?
> Me: Oh, I drink vodka most of the time.
> Rich: (laughing) Okay, killer, then vodka it is.
>   I will bring some for you on prom night.
>   Cool?
> Me: Cool.

I know I made an ass out of myself. I could just tell. Vodka? I was fifteen years old. What the fuck do I know about vodka? I drank beer once or twice before, and that made me into a drunken idiot. Like I said earlier, I was in way over my head. I was a freshman going to the senior prom with Nice Tits and Vodka Rich. Lord, help me.

I had absolutely no intention of telling my parents that I was going to the senior prom. My plan was to lie of course and tell my parents that I was sleeping over my friend's house. I did not need any more pressure that I was sure my parents would apply. And I definitely did not want to hear about some ridiculous curfew.

I forgot to cover my tracks, and my retarded sister Paula ran home to tell my parents the big news. Thanks, Paula. Paula always had a heart of gold, but her mouth definitely did not wait for her brain to warm up in the morning. Much to my surprise, my mom actually seemed impressed, and my dad asked me if Janice was retarded. Such a vote of confidence. "No drinking, no drugs, no funny business, and get your ass home by one a.m." were the rules set by my parents. Not bad, not bad at all, but also not possible.

I can't even begin to tell you what I went through over the next few weeks leading up to the prom. My friends were just having way too much fun with this whole ordeal. They were experienced, and they knew I was sweating this one.

By the time prom night came around, I had been given at least a dozen condoms from all of them. A dozen? What was she, a hooker? I was so worked up that I almost shit my tux twice. I took a couple of antidiarrheal pills and prayed on my knees in my bathroom. Please, Lord, please don't let me make an ass out of myself. I beg this of you.

The limo arrived a short while after my bathroom prayer group ended, and I could hear my parents greeting Janice at the door. As I walked out into our living room, I got my first look at prom-ready Janice. Wow. Holy shit. Wow. Janice was wearing a short black cocktail dress that showed off legs I was not ready for. And of course, her great tits were also being shown off; those I was ready for. Folks, I believe the name "cocktail dress" was developed by a guy that was in my situation. It was a dress, and one part of my body was affected by it. Enough said. After about two minutes of small talk with my parents (but it felt like ten years), Janice and I headed for the door. I turned and looked at my parents for their approval, and what did I see? It was my dad trying to catch a peek at Janice's tits. My dad realized I was looking at him and turned this funky shade of red. Got ya, Dad. I finally saw a side of you that wasn't screaming, "I'm the pope." Dad, deny it all you want. You know it's true!

So now we are in the limo, and rule number 1—no drinking— was about to go to shit. Rich made good on his promise and produced a bottle of vodka for me. "Screwdrivers" would be the drink for now, so let the drinking begin. I would say that about halfway through my first drink, I started to unwind. As the hour-long drive went on, Janice was looking better and better, and the drinks went down easier and easier. Not good, not good at all.

The prom was being held at the Sands Atlantic Beach, Long Island, and by the time the limo arrived at the Sands, I was absolutely shit-faced. Thank God, Big Man on Campus (BMOC) Rich noticed my condition and took control. He escorted me to the men's room and told me to throw some cold water on my face. Now I am not a sloppy drunk, but my biggest problem when I drink is that I laugh uncontrollably, I speak my mind, and I am relentlessly funny (or at least I think I am).

I threw some water on my face as Rich suggested, and when I got my head out of the sink, I noticed that Rich had spread some nice white powder out on the shelf above the sink. Yes, folks, no need to guess, it was cocaine. Rich looked me right in the eyes and told me I must trust him on this one. He took a rolled-up dollar bill and snorted a long line of coke into one side of his nose and then did the same using the other side. Rich handed me the rolled-up bill and told me to do the same. Sorry, Mom and Dad, rule number 2—no drugs—just went down the shitter. People, I have never drank vodka before. I have never snorted cocaine before, but here I was in one moment in time catching up quickly. Two snorts completed as instructed by Captain Rich and Holy Mary Mother of God, and the Promised Land had arrived. For you, readers, that have ever done coke before, you know what I am talking about. I was instantly pumped up. I was still way drunk but wide awake, light-footed, and ready for action. *Thanks, Rich, I will take it from here.* I looked over at Rich, and I could tell that he was scared to death at what he had just created. But he kept his cool, shoved a bag of powder in my tux, grabbed my shoulders, and said, "Just don't fuck up, okay?"

No problem, young squire, no problem. I slapped Rich's face, gave him a wink, and did my best impression of the moonwalk as I left the bathroom.

Out in the catering hall, Janice and I were having a blast. We danced to every song, we laughed, we snuck a few more drinks in, and we laughed some more. I know at some point in the night they served food. I couldn't tell you what it was, but I could tell you that I did not eat a bite. My body was filled with vodka and cocaine. And that, my friends, was all that my freshman body needed to survive that night.

About halfway through the night, the band played a series of romantic slow songs. I grabbed Sweet Tits and walked her out to the dance floor. We danced close, and as I held her tight, I could hear her breathing in my ear. This was just a little more than I was prepared to handle. Then it hit me. I had a hard-on right there on the dance floor, and this bad boy was just not going away. I will venture to guess that all of you guys that have done coke and gotten aroused know exactly what I was talking about. Oh, shit. Did she notice? Did she? Did she? Yes, folks, Janice noticed quite quickly. I am shitting pickles here, folks. Janice looked up at me, smiled, and then laughed. Not that she was laughing at me but in the way that said, "I got you, big boy. I got you." Okay, confession time, folks. I was fifteen years old, and I was a virgin. I was also drunk and coked up and just about to lose it when Janice took me by the hand and escorted me off the dance floor. Thank God for women like Janice. She proceeded to walk me right into the lady's bathroom and right into one of the bathroom stalls. Sorry again, Mom and Dad. Rule number 3—no funny business—was about to go right down the toilet. Janice took over from there. She was so into this moment that I barely had to do anything. Thank you, Lord, for hooking me up with a trained professional for my first time. Oh, yeah, and thank you to all of my friends for the dozens of condoms that you gave me. All in all, Janice and I made three trips to the lady's room that night; each trip was better than the one before.

The limo ride home was just a pile of bodies using one another as human pillows. I can't even remember what time my body crashed that night, but I wasn't the only one that was zonked out. Rule number 4—get my ass home by one a.m.—was also broken that night. All I remember is Big Rich carrying me into my parents' house at 4:00 a.m. and sleeping for the next day and a half. But I think my parents were just glad that I was alive because they didn't really give me any shit about it.

Janice, if you are out there reading this book, thank you for making my first time a memorable one. Rich, if you are not dead—and by the way you party, you probably are dead—thanks again for an awesome night.

CHAPTER 8

Let's now take a small step forward in time to my second year in high school. It was an event that seemed to be a precursor of things to come for me. The school halls were buzzing with rumors about a student that had punched a female teacher right in the face. As the story went, the student was asked by the teacher if he had a hall pass. When the student could not produce a pass, the teacher attempted to escort him to the main office for discipline. Nobody knew why, but the student snapped and punched the teacher in the face and then simply walked away, leaving the teacher lying on the floor.

About halfway through the school day, two teachers entered my science classroom and asked for Mr. Thomas Foley to please stand up. I was caught completely off guard. My heart appeared to skip a beat or two as I rose up out of my chair. All eyes in the classroom were fixed on me.

> Me: What's going on?
> Teacher 1: Just grab your things and come with us.

I complied and grabbed my belongings as requested. On the way to the main office, I tried to make conversation several times with these two mutes, but not a word came out of their mouths. Both teachers seemed to look at me in complete disgust.

As we entered the main office, I was escorted directly into the principal's office; that is never a good thing. In the office stood my mother and father, and the one thought that came to my pea brain was that someone must have died. As I looked at my mother, I could tell that she had been crying. I went to console her, and then came shock number 2. My father hit me right in the face with a semi-open fist. Now listen, my father is 6'2" tall and weighed around 230 pounds. I was pushing 6'3" and weighted around 170 pounds. My point is that he was a big guy, and his upward swing at my jaw caught me completely off guard. My bottom teeth crashed into my upper teeth from the impact, and I thought they were going to fall out of my mouth.

Me: Are you fucking crazy?

That was all that I could manage to get out of my throbbing mouth. The principal then stepped between my father and I. My mother screamed my father's name, but no one seemed to give a shit that I just got whacked.

Me: Can someone please tell me what the hell is going on? Holy shit!

And yes, that actually did come out of my mouth. That is when a uniformed Nassau County Police Officer stepped into the office.

Police: Is this the one?
Principal: Yes.
Policeman: (looking at my parents) Are you his parents?
Dad: Yes, we are, Officer.
Me: Hey, people, what the hell is going on?
Policeman: You shut your mouth, Mr. Foley, or I will shut it for you, tough guy.
Me: What a dick.
Policeman: I am going to bring in the victim to ID this punk.
Me: Holy shit, he knows my name.
Policeman: (looking out of the office door) Miss, will you please come in? Don't worry, he can't hurt you anymore.
Me: What?

Into the office walked one of our home economics teachers. I never took home economics, but I recognized the teacher immediately. She looked like a train had hit her. She had dried blood on her shirt, a huge welt on her face, and her bottom lip had been split wide open.

As she walked into the room, she had the look of a frightened animal on her face and then took a scan around the room to see who was present.

> Victim: Okay, I am ready. Bring him in.
> Policeman: (pointing at me) He's right there.

Now I still didn't quite get what was going on here, but let me digress for one moment. I have watched a lot of TV in my days, and usually when a victim is asked to ID a criminal, the cops don't usually point him out. In fact, there are usually a couple of potential suspects present, and the victim then IDs the right one. I just needed to get that point across so you can see just how ridiculous this whole situation was.

> Victim: That's not the boy that hit me.
> Mom: Oh! Thank you, Lord.
> Dad: What's going on here?
> Me: Hey, fuck you, Dad. Thanks for the punch.
> Policeman: (yelling out the door) Bring in the eyewitness.

Into the room walked a female student.

> Principal: (pointing at me) Is this the person that you saw strike the teacher?
> Witness: No, sir, that's not him.
> Principal: You told me you saw Tom Foley punch the teacher.
> Witness: No, sir, I told you I saw Tim Foley punch her.
> Side note: Tim's last name was spelled Foli.

Ooopss! Tim Foli was a junior at the time and a real badass. The room fell dead silent, followed by this.

> Principal: Sorry for the misunderstanding, Mr. and Mrs. Foley. We will straighten this whole mess out.
> Policeman: Someone go find this Tim Foley thug.
> Dad: You people need to get your act together. My wife and I both work, you know.
> Mom: Well, thank God it was not TJ (my family nickname).
> Principal: (to me) You can return back to your class now, Mr. Foley.
> Me: What? Are you people nuts? How about, "Sorry, Mr. Foley?" How about, "Sorry I punched you, son." How about, "Sorry I called you a punk, Mr. Foley." This is a freakin' joke.
> Policeman: (with his had extended to shake my hand) No harm, no foul, kid. No harm, no foul.
> Me: You're a dick.

I left the office and decided I had earned the rest of the day off from school. As I walked home that day, I played the day's events in my head and couldn't help but laugh. Things like this only happens to me. As word spread around school about the mishap, my friends could not help but get some good laughs at my expense, and looking back, yeah, it was funny.

CHAPTER 9

My junior and senior years of high school were good ones for me. I had great grades with minimal effort, I got thrown off the track team for calling the coach a fag, and I met what would turn out to be a very special woman in my life.

On the weekends, my crew would always hang out together. We would drink, sometimes smoke pot, play sports, and do whatever was needed to meet as many women as possible. One evening, I received a call from my friend Al, and he told me that he had been out "cruising for chicks" (an eighties slang word) and that he had met a group of girls from the nearby town of Wantagh. Al told me that he had met them at Burger King, and they invited him and as many friends as he wanted to bring to a house party on Friday night. Since he had met them at Burger King, I was compelled to ask him if they were pigs. He assured me that they were not. I will give Al credit where credit is due. He always had good taste in women.

Friday night rolled around, and the crew agreed to gather together at Artie's house. Now I need to sidetrack for a moment. It's my opinion that my friend Artie grew up in one of the coolest and strangest environments that I have ever seen. Artie's mom was a sweetheart, and I considered her to be a second mother to me—a mom away from home (God rest her soul). This woman would just roll with the punches, and believe me, having Artie for a son was no easy task. Arthur's mom and dad could drink with the best of them, and they usually tied one on during the weekends. It was like spring break every day in that house. When we would go pick up Artie, we would usually all pile into Arthur's parents' bed while he got ready. He was always the last person to get ready. Why you ask? You see, Artie and his dad could sit around the house all day doing nothing but shooting the shit together, then five minutes before we were ready to go out, his dad would ask him to do a chore. The chore, whatever it might have been, had to be finished before he went out.

Artie's dad would say, "Hey, Artie, before you go, could you cut up the firewood out back?"

No shit, that was the most popular of the chores. But Artie had nothing but respect for his old man and would never refuse. To this day, I still bust his balls about that shit.

So anyways, it was Friday night. The firewood was cut, and we headed out to party with the Wantagh women. We stopped at a local beer distributor on the way (back then, the supermarkets did not sell any alcohol), and my friend Jimmy bought us a couple of cases of beer for the ride over. We arrived at the house of a girl whose name was Cheryl (it is very possible that I misspelled her name, tough shit), and I noticed a few things right off the bat—a keg on ice in the backyard, good music playing, a few bottles of liquor on a table with shot glasses, a very distinct smell of pot, and best of all, the hot Wantagh women. As we introduced ourselves to the women, something struck me as odd. We were the only guys at the party. You have a house party filled with hot chicks and not one guy except for me and my friends. Not that I was complaining. It just struck me as weird that not one of them already had a boyfriend or brother or something. Most of the early evening was spent on introductions and cute one-liners. We played some drinking games, told some jokes, and just had an all-around great time. These women were great to hang out with. Around an hour after we arrived, a second group of women arrived. One of the new arrivals caught my attention immediately. Maybe it was the cheerleading outfit that she was wearing, or maybe that she was taller that the other women, but I believe to this day that it was her eyes. I had never seen such beautiful eyes in my life. Her name was Denise, and she had large green eyes that also had a touch of brown to them. I introduced myself to Denise and apologized to her. I told her that if I had known this was a costume party, I would have dressed appropriately. I got a laugh out of her the first time we spoke, so that was a good start. She explained to me that she had just finished cheering at a high school football game and did not have time to change. Please, no need to change. She looked great. I made a quick inquiry to make sure that some football steroid junkie was not on his way to meet her. No, Tom, you are clear to engage. We did not leave each other's side for the rest of the night, and it felt like we had known each other for years. We exchanged phone numbers, and before we parted ways, I managed to sneak in a quick good night kiss. I left that party on cloud nine.

Now I must tell you, I believe that Nice Tits Janice caused a serious defect in my brain when it comes to what I should expect from women in the early stages of a relationship. Not that I am complaining about my experience with Janice. For God's sake, I'm no idiot. But as I look back, I realize just how shitty I have treated some of these women. No, I have never abused a woman in my life, and for those scumbags out there that do, I think you should rot in hell. No, I consider myself to be a very nice guy when it comes to women, but when it comes to ending a relationship, I could definitely use some counseling.

Denise and I dated steadily for several months. We had our share of alone dates, but a lot of our together time was spent with groups of our friends. The gathering place quickly became Denise's house in Wantagh. She grew up in a very strange environment as a teenager. If I were to describe Denise's upbringing in one word, the word that comes to mind would be *dysfunctional*.

Denise, her sister Laura who was only one year older, and her brother Richard approximately five years younger lived in a high ranch-style house without any parent supervision. Her mother and father divorced several years before I had met her. Since their divorce, Denise's mother was running around thinking she was Bo Derek or something chasing men with money in hopes of finding a sugar daddy to take care of her (no offense to the real Bo Derek) with little regard for her kids' well-being. Her father had moved to Florida after the divorce and helped run an investment company to send money to the kids to pay for the house bills. These three kids were basically left to raise themselves, and I must say, they did a pretty good job at keeping their lives together.

Anyway, here we all are, high school students dating hot chicks hanging out and partying in a house with no adult supervision.

Things could not be any better. Now remember earlier when I mentioned the dickhead and his phrase, "All good things must come to an end." I will admit that this time, the bad ending was 100 percent my fault.

My friend Al had been dating Denise's good friend Christine the same time that Denise and I were going out together. So we decided to go out together for a nice dinner on Valentine's Day. Earlier that day, I had roses sent to Denise's house, and she called to tell me how much she loved them. Around an hour before the time that Al and I were supposed to pick up the girls, Al called me on the phone and informed me that he was sorry, but he decided to break up with Christine and would not be going to the dinner. I told Al that I was sorry to hear that and asked him how Christine had taken the news. That was when Al hit me with the shocker. He told me he had not told her, and he was just not going to show up. *Hey, buddy? Chum? Pal of mine? That kind of puts me in a tough spot, doesn't it?* Al apologized, but he just did not want to deal with a messy breakup, so this was his "easy way out." Now I had to take a few moments and imagine in my pea brain how this ugly evening was going to play out. Absolutely no good scenarios entered my head. The girls would curse Al, Christine would be crying, Denise would take sides, and I would be fucked. No, thank you.

> Me: So what are you going to do tonight?
> Al: I think I'll go to the mall and buy some shirts.
> Me: Ah, screw it, come pick me up. I'll go with you.
> Al: Really?
> Me: (joking) Yea, I can't let you be alone on Valentine's Day.

Yes, readers, I did go shopping with Al, and I did blow Denise off on Valentine's Day. Don't hate me. I was young, obviously immature, and very stupid. According to my mother, Denise called my house at least a dozen times that night, and each time, she had more choice words picked out for me. I took an entire night's worth of shit from my mother. She was disgusted by what I had done, and the next day, I called Denise to apologize. I let her go off on me because I deserved it, and that was the end of that. Now I know what I did was terrible and unforgiveable, and I have no excuses. Denise did not deserve to be treated like that. To this day, I am still embarrassed that I treated another human being so poorly, and with that all said, I would like to make one claim in my own defense. I place some of the blame on Nice Tits Janice. I know, it's lame, but at the time, Denise was not willing to sleep with me, and that damn Janice had just set the sex bar so damn high, or was it low? Anyway, you get the picture. To be 100 percent honest, I sent those roses and planned the Valentine's Day dinner as a last-ditch effort to get Denise into bed. If Valentine's Day had not resulted in a trip to the sack, then I would have hit the road for good anyway. Oh, stop it, all you haters. You know it, and I know it that sex is a very important part of any relationship. For all you people shaking your head and saying that it's just not true, I will bet money that your partner is probably getting it from someone else. Listen, what I did was inexcusable, cruel, and cowardly, so, Denise, I am truly sorry. You deserved better.

I would like to do a quick shout-out to all the Wantagh women: Chris, Christine, Kathy, Cheryl, Teresa, and Jemma. You guys were great to hang out with and good all-around people. I hope life has treated all of you well.

As I close out my memories from high school, I can't help but stop and think about how good those times really were. I had great friends, and we partied like rock stars: beach parties, ski trips, house parties, and women. It was such carefree living. We truly pushed our young lives to its limits, and I could probably go on for months about the crazy times I had with my friends, but I have bigger things to discuss now. So shout-out to the Brew Crew from Massapequa. I love you, guys, and I miss you dearly. Thanks for the memories.

CHAPTER 10

My departure from high school was rapidly approaching, and I had no real path or plan for my future. I had absolutely no interest in going to college, but my parents insisted that I was going to be the first Foley to graduate college and forced me to apply to colleges across the country. My friends on the other hand were going to the local colleges, some worked part-time or full-time, and my friend Lenny dropped out of school in his first semester to start his own business. Lenny's route seemed to be the most appealing to me, but my parents would not entertain that idea at all. I will say that I thank my lucky stars that my parents won that argument. It would have been a shame for me to miss out on a great education and experiences had I not gone to college. I was accepted to plenty of schools across the country, but I chose the place that I felt I would have the best time (being that I did not want to go to college at that time). I enrolled in Daytona Beach Community College. That's right, folks, home of spring break, the Daytona 500, and biker week. I had been to Daytona Beach several times with my friends for spring break, and I loved the town in general. I figured, at the very least, it would be a cool place to hang out and figure out what path I wanted to take in life. I will never forget the day my parents left me in Florida. After getting settled into an apartment and getting registered at the school, it was time for Mom and Dad to fly home. My mother cried like I was dying or something, and just after my father hugged me goodbye, I saw a tear in his eye. They really did care about me, and that was a great feeling. Although I felt bad about leaving them, my friends, and home state, it was something that I knew I had to do. It did not take long for me to realize that I was all alone, so my first year of college was dedicated to my studies. I really gave it an all-out effort to see if I had what it took to make the grades. I declared my major to be business management with economics as a minor. Only a week into my classes, I quickly realized that this was something that I was going to love. I aced every test, every assignment, and I actually looked forward to going to my classes. In my downtime, I hung out at the beach and played golf. Tim, a guy from Kentucky, taught me how to surf and how to work out. He was also starting point guard on our school's basketball team and made sure I was invited to every party on and off campus. In return, I helped him with his study habits and test preparation. Tim was what you might call educationally challenged (not that bright, get it?).

At the end of my first semester, one of my management professors announced that there was a nationwide business transfer scholarship contest that we could enter. DBCC was only a two-year college, and anyone that wanted a bachelor's degree would have to move on to a four-year college to do so. The scholarship rules were simple: each applicant had to write an essay about a company that made a large impact on its industry. I chose to enter the contest, and I wrote a very abstract paper on the marketing programs used to promote Cabbage Patch Dolls. Cabbage Patch Dolls went through a period in time where it seemed like an entire world had to have one, and there were never enough to go around. That supply shortage was the focus of my paper. My application of the supply-and-demand theories made me one of several scholarship winners nationwide. I was awarded a $2,500 per semester scholarship to the university of my choice, granted that I qualify academically and was accepted to the university that I applied to.

CHAPTER 11

When my first year of college ended, I decided I wanted to transfer back to New York. I missed my friends, and I missed my family. So I applied and was accepted into a small private college located in Southampton, Long Island—the summer playground for the rich and famous. Soon after I began attending, Southampton merged with Long Island University, and its name was changed to Long Island University–Southampton Campus. My graduating class of 1987 was the last class to receive diplomas that read Southampton College.

Although my parents never said anything to me, I knew they always struggled to pay my tuition. My grades were always good, which motivated them more. They really wanted me to be the first Foley to graduate college. In order to help out financially, I applied for and was hired as a dormitory head resident. The basic duties involved making sure that the students complied with all dorm rules and regulations, handling student requests to university staff for dorm maintenance, assigning new students to rooms, handling disputes between students, student counseling, and coordinating monthly recreation programs. It was a great job to have. In return for being a head resident at my assigned dorm, the university paid for my room and board, which was a huge financial relief for my parents.

Once I settled in at Southampton, I met some very special friends named Roger and John. They turned out to be my party friends, and man, could these two party. College brought my drinking experiences to a whole new level, and I could probably fill an entire book with ridiculous college party stories, but I will save those for another day.

Besides Roger and John, I also met a very special woman at Southampton. She was a freshman named Karen, and I fell for her the first day we met. Karen and I dated for my entire stay at Southampton, and had it not been for the fact that she had one more year at school after I graduated, I could've definitely seen myself marrying her. I tried to maintain our relationship after graduation, but it just did not work out. (In other words, she dumped me.)

I decided to try out for the school's volleyball team and made the squad on my first try, and let me tell you, folks, playing a college sport in front of a screaming crowd of students is one of the most awesome feelings that I have ever experienced. What a rush, the thrill of victory, the agony of defeat, and playing for nothing but school pride!

CHAPTER 12

I was a junior in college; I had great grades, great friends, and a steady girlfriend; I was head resident; and I was playing a sport I loved. Things for me had never been better. Queue the dickhead: all good things must come to an end. Fffffuuuuuccckk!

Now this moment in my life is no joking matter. What I am about to tell you scarred me for the rest of my life, and I believe that this chain of events helped to hurl me toward the fate I am suffering today.

It started on a Wednesday night. I was responsible for watching over three other dorms apart from my own, and every two hours, I was required to walk through all four dorms to make sure all was well. Turns out that students were having a victory party following a successful basketball game in one of the dorms I was assigned to. I tried to ignore the party for as long as I could up until around midnight when I received a call from campus security informing me that the party was out of control and wanted me to try and calm things down. They were usually pretty good about things like this as they understood that college kids sometimes needed to release some energy. Having a head resident intervene before security had tended to resolve the issue without conflict between security and students. Upon arriving at the party, it was obvious that things were way out of control. There was broken butcher-block furniture in the common areas and broken beer bottles on the floor, the music was blasting at an unbearable level, and there was an awful smell of puke and alcohol in the air.

In an attempt to get everyone's attention, I decided to unplug the stereo. Big mistake. A group of students led by the starting center of our basketball team, Andre, immediately got in my face. I told them that security had sent me and that the party was now over. Andre, who stood around 6'9" and weighed around 280 pounds, made it very clear that the party was not over and that I was not welcome there. I tried to explain to him that I was doing them a favor since the incident would go unreported by just ending the party. Andre laughed at me, plugged the stereo back in, and the party went on like I wasn't even there. Now I am no pussy, but a drunk Andre is not the guy you want to mess with. No, thank you. So I left the building, and security was waiting outside for me. I informed them of what had taken place, I filled out an incident report, and then security went in and shut the party down. At my college, once an incident report is issued, the students involved must give security their ID cards and have to pick them up the next business day at the head of housing's main office. Three starters on the basketball game, including Andre, were suspended from playing in the next scheduled game. Freshmen that were caught drinking received tickets with hefty fines, and all the partygoers had to pay for the damaged furniture. Let's just say that I was not loved at that moment, so I decided to stay in my room and lay low on Thursday.

About halfway through the day, I received a call from Arthur, one of my friends from Massapequa. He told me that some of the guys were going to take a road trip to Niagara Falls for the weekend and wanted me to come with them. Talk about perfect timing. Why not escape for the weekend and let things cool down. I told him I would leave first thing Friday morning and that I would be at his house no later than 10:00 a.m. After we hung up, I was feeling much better about the upcoming weekend away from campus.

Later that same day, my friends John and Roger came by my room and told me that they were going to an off-campus party that night. They did not ask me if I wanted to go; they just told me that I was going, which didn't matter because I rarely turned down a party invitation.

We arrived at the party at around 8:00 p.m. It was a typical off-campus event—a rented house, loud music, kegs on ice surrounded by thirsty students, dancing, drinking games, and coeds making out. I was in the middle of a conversation with Roger when a heavy hand tapped me on the shoulder. I turned around to find Andre and his boys standing in front of me. Shit, shit on a fucking stick. I listened to him rant for about thirty seconds in which he called me a rat, pussy, ass-kisser, and so on. The smart thing to do was to take the abuse and walk away, but that is just not my style. I am an Irish/Hungarian mutt, and I couldn't just walk away from a bully with a big mouth. Much to Andre's surprise, I told him to get his ass outside, and we would settle this like men. Some retarded part of my brain thought he would not follow me. What was I thinking? I wish I could tell you guys that I kicked Andre Jolly Green Giant's ass, but that would be a lie. I was proud of myself though. I held my own in the fight and could see that the other partygoers respected me for not backing down.

In my opinion, there is nothing worse than a bully. To all that are reading this book, don't put up with it, don't just watch an innocent person get bullied, and don't be afraid. Bullies are cowards and can ruin people's lives if they are not stopped. There are people in this world that I have seen get bullied, and they asked for it. I have no sympathy for those people. It's the innocent that simply do not have the heart or courage to stand up for themselves that need your help. That's all I have to say about that.

The next morning, I woke up a little battered and bruised but still felt really good about myself. I popped a couple of aspirins, packed some clothes for the weekend, and headed out to the student parking lot toward my car. The only words I could manage to get out of my mouth when I saw my car were, "No fucking way, man! No fucking way!" All four tires were flat. It was not that they were slashed; someone had actually taken the tine to deflate all four tires. Pretty much, I was going nowhere.

I went back to my dorm to call Artie and tell him about my car and last night's events. Artie cheered me up and gave me a speech about sticking up for myself and said his goodbye. The guys would be going to Niagara Falls without me. I was pissed. Southampton College was a very small campus. Rumors and information tended to spread quickly. So did last night's events and what had happened to my car, which several people told me that Andre and his friends had

37

taken credit for. No shit. It doesn't take a genius to figure that out. I decided that enough was enough and defused the situation by doing nothing in retaliation.

Saturday night came around, and my intramural deck hockey team had a game. They were held in our basketball arena and usually drew a larger crowd than an actual basketball game. I had planned on missing the game because of my trip, but the trip was off, so game on.

It was the middle of the second period, and the game was really starting to heat up. Players were running everywhere, and students were screaming in the crowd. The place was filled with so much energy. All of a sudden, the game came to a sudden halt, and the crowd went quiet. As I looked around to see what the holdup was, I saw two campus security guards on the hockey floor accompanied by the campus chaplain, the campus nurse, and my girlfriend, Karen, who was crying. The security guards pointed at me and waved at me to come over to them. I thought my body was going to explode between the adrenaline from the game and now this heart-pounding moment. I was escorted out of the building with the chaplain's hand on my shoulder, and you could hear a pin drop in the arena.

> Me: What's wrong?
> Chaplain: Your parents have been trying to reach you, Tom. You need to call them.
> Me: Why? What's going on? For God's sake, just tell me.
> Chaplain: I am sorry, Tom. There has been an accident.

I will never forget the sad faces of the campus staff, the soft voice of the chaplain, and my girlfriend's arms around me as he told me that my friends back in Massapequa had been in an accident on the way up to Niagara Falls. Karen knew my friends very well and told me that Donny and John were both killed in the accident. Artie was in critical condition at an upstate New York hospital; his chances of survival were slim. *There is no way that this had happened* was all I remember thinking. I called the chaplain a liar and was in complete denial. I ran back to my dorm room and called my friend Al. Unfortunately, Al confirmed what I had already been told. Shock set in along with an indescribable sadness and emptiness that I had never felt before. In one brief moment, my life had changed forever. The next morning, I packed a bag and left for home. Campus security took care of my tire problems and were true professionals during this awful time in my life. I was going home to bury two of my best friends.

I would like to take a quick moment here to thank the people that were there for me on that tragic night. Karen, without you, I would not have made it through the night, never mind the next few years to come. To the staff at Southampton College, you were all wonderful, true professionals and humanitarians, and for going above and beyond your job description, I will never forget your compassion. Last but not least, I would also like to thank you, Andre. If you were not the asshole that you proved yourself to be, I would not be alive today. You flattened my tires, but you saved my life. Let's call it even.

CHAPTER 13

Over the next few days, I realized what a great family I really had. They supported me with lots of love and compassion, and I would not have made it through the week without them. My mother and I have always had a great relationship, but at this rather difficult time, our mother-and-son bond developed into something special. God bless that woman. She would stay up with me for countless hours of the night as we cried together, laughed together, and sometimes we just sat in silence, her loving arm on my shoulder as she assured me that life would go on.

I buried my two best friends that week. I cried with their parents, I cried with my friends, and I said my goodbyes to two of the greatest friends a guy could ask for. I was raised in a Catholic household, and I do not question the good Lord's motives or actions, and I understand that everything happens for a reason. But dear Lord, in my opinion, the world was a better place before this tragic moment.

By the grace of God, Artie recovered from some serious physical injuries. His physical rehabilitation was long and painful, but it was the emotional recovery that would take a lifetime. As the months after the accident went by, I tried to spend as much time with Artie as I possibly could. We had several heart-to-heart conversations about that night, and I could tell that Artie was hurting deep inside. I believe it was either guilt, the need to tell me the truth, or that Artie was finally releasing a repressed memory from the back of his mind, but he broke down in tears one night. It was believed by all involved parties that John had been behind the wheel on the night of the accident (Artie's original story to us and the police), but John and Donny had both drank themselves to sleep. Artie told me he lied to us all and that he was the driver on that terrible night. He killed two of our best friends and lied about it to save his own ass from going to prison. (Yes, he was drunk and high and driving). Can you imagine, John's parents not only lost their son, but for almost a year, they thought their son was responsible for killing another individual and himself while driving drunk. I made Arthur tell John's parents the truth. He did, and in a true Christian act, they offered him their forgiveness, but truth be told, I could see the disgust in their eyes.

I blame my friend Arthur for that accident, the death of our two friends, and it really bothered me that he lied. With that being said, the truth is that John and Donny died doing what they enjoyed doing, what we all enjoyed doing at that time, partying with life-long carefree friends without fear or reservations. I thank my lucky stars that none of us hurt some innocent bystander with our reckless actions; that would truly be a sin.

Rest in peace, John. Rest in peace, Donny. Out of the ashes the phoenix rises.

CHAPTER 14

Students and staff alike at Southampton greeted me back with open arms. It was great to have such overwhelming support, but the extra attention just reminded me of what I had just been through. I most certainly should have gotten professional counseling, but I did not. I returned to school in order to finish my studies and graduate. It was not easy to concentrate, but I managed to keep my grades up. I had this new level of recklessness about me. I was willing to try anything to test my fate, as if I were going to die at any moment. This new attitude eventually caught up with me, and it cost my parents dearly. There was no excuse for my next lapse in judgment.

In the winter months, Southampton is a cold, snowy, and windy environment. Few people on campus venture outside unless it is for class or maybe to the chow hall for mealtimes. Students tended to find ways to entertain themselves within their dorms. I was on head resident duty when my buddies John and Roger dropped by my room on one of these weekends. They told me that another student had a friend visiting, and he had brought blotter acid with him. I had no idea what that was, but just the name of it scared me. Roger said that it was a hallucinogenic drug that looked like a piece of paper that was taken orally. Just great. I was on duty, and now half of the campus was going to be tripping on acid. I thanked the guys for the heads-up, which only resulted in their laughing at me.

Roger said, "No, you idiot, we bought some for the three of us to try tonight."

Were they serious? I was on duty. But like I said earlier, I was in reckless mode, and after a very quick three-minute debate, I decided to try the acid with them as long as they stayed in my room and did not let anyone know. No one had to say it. That was the stupidest idea in the world. How did I even think I was going to control myself and two other guys while tripping on acid? What a fucking moron.

I remember taking the acid and laughing a lot. I remember Roger telling me to never look in the mirror while on acid, but I did it anyway, and I remember being totally freaked out while looking in the mirror. But that is all I remember.

The next morning, I was dazed, confused, and freezing. Being that I was on a bench in the middle of Central Park in Manhattan, it made sense. Holy shit! For those of you that are not familiar with Long Island or Manhattan, Southampton is about a three-hour train ride to Manhattan, and you have to change trains twice to get there. During the day, Central Park is a beautiful place to visit, but at night, not even the police feel safe there.

So as I tried to get my bearings, I looked around to find Roger lying on the ground about twenty feet away from me in some bushes. I was just glad he was alive. When we were both fully awoke, we couldn't stop hysterically laughing. We looked like two fucking idiots freezing to death in the middle of Central Park. Then it hit me. Holy shit, where was John? Holy shit, I was on duty back at school.

There was no sign of John anywhere, so Roger and I decided to go back to the train station as quickly as possible. New York is just too big of a city to try and find one person. We just hoped and prayed that John never left campus. Now remember, folks, this was 1986. Cell phones were not a mainstream item yet, so communication was very primitive in comparison to today. After a grueling walk to the train station, we began to defrost, and our heads began to clear. I checked my pager that the school provided for me for duty weekends in hopes that no one had tried to contact me last night. No such luck, not even close. Twenty-six pages from security and the head of housing. I was so screwed.

Roger and I arrived back on campus around 1:00 p.m. and headed directly to John's dorm. Thank God he was there. Okay, problem 1 fixed. The three of us were alive, not a bad start. My celebration was short-lived when John told me that everyone from my girlfriend to the campus security to the actual head of housing was looking for me.

Dave, the head of housing for the university, was a very cool guy. He liked me and my friends and would even go out with us from time to time. When I arrived at his office, I decided to tell him the truth out of respect for the man, which was very rare for me, and he was such a good guy about the whole ordeal. He was willing to bury the whole incident and take the heat for me. He said that he would tell the head of security and the dean of students that he had forgotten to assign a head resident for the weekend. This was his career on the line, his livelihood. He knew it, and I knew it. Southampton was a small campus, and too many people knew I was on duty and left campus that night, so I chose option B. I apologized to the staff at Southampton and relieved myself of head resident duties. I thought the problem was solved, but I was wrong. I received a phone call from my parents a week later after they received a bill of over $5,000 for my room and board. This expense was usually covered in exchange for being a head resident. Instead of telling the truth and getting my ass handed to me along with maybe some psychological help, I apologized to them. I told them that the head resident duties were interfering with my studies, so I had to quit. It was a totally shitty thing to do to them, but how were they going to argue with me supposedly trying to protect my education? I know that the bill put a lot of added stress on them, and I wish I wasn't such a moron back then. Sorry, Mom. Sorry, Dad. You guys deserved better from me.

CHAPTER 15

At the ripe age of twenty-two years old, I was able to repay my parents back. Well, let's call it a partial payment that came in the way of graduation from Southampton College. I received a bachelor of science in business management and a minor in economics. I have never seen my family with such pride on their faces. After celebration was over, I realized that it was now up to me to get out there in the business world and stake my claim. Look out, world, here I come.

I came back to Massapequa where my parents built me an apartment in the basement of the house that I grew up in, and I was so grateful. Looking for the right career opportunity turned into quite a chore; not having to pay rent was a huge advantage for me.

My plan of attack was to look for a large corporation with a management training program that would give me the opportunity to work my way up the corporate ladder. I didn't want to work for a company that I could only advance through seniority. I wanted to prove myself and advance through my merits and performance. What I found out rather quickly was that I just really sucked at working for other people.

I landed some jobs with some large corporations, but they were just so damn set in their ways. Middle management was too scared to present upper management with new ideas. Everyone seemed to be okay with covering their asses instead of putting their asses out on the line in the name of progress. I just did not fit in with this type of attitude and work ethic. I became frustrated quickly and found myself quitting jobs left and right. If I remember correctly, my record time for quitting a job was eighteen minutes into orientation. That was all the time it took to tell my team leader at a major Wall Street firm to go fuck himself. So much for working my way up that corporate ladder.

CHAPTER 16

I felt like I needed a change in my life—a fresh start. I convinced my friend Artie that he and I should move out of our childhood homes and find an apartment together. My parents were disappointed to say the least. At that time, I had just landed a management position at a milk processing plant in Brooklyn, New York, and Artie was working nearby in Queens. As fate would have it, a friend and coworker of my father's was retiring and moving to upstate New York. He just happened to have a rent-controlled apartment two blocks away from my job and told us that he would sublease the apartment to me. What a score. The apartment was two thousand square foot, three-bedroom, two-bathroom layout with a balcony that overlooked the Manhattan skyline for only $500 per month, including utilities. What a serious, serious score. But like everything else in my life, there was a catch to this fantasy bachelor pad. The apartment, like the milk plant that I worked at, was located in the war zone known as Starrett City in Brooklyn. I can describe it in these three words: New Jack City. No kidding, this was one badass neighborhood. Living here was asking for trouble. Once again, folks, I am not racist, but Artie and I were the only two white people in the building, maybe in the whole city.

We moved in immediately and made the place into a real bachelor pad. One of the coolest things we did was purchase a fully operational Pepsi Cola machine and placed the "soda" machine right in the middle of the living room. The best part, we filled it with our favorite beer and programmed the machine for a zero-dollar vend. All we had to do was push a button, and an ice-cold beer would come out. Artie and I also turned our third bedroom into a workout center complete with an incline bench and tons of free weights. The people below us hated us every time we worked out. At this point in my life, I was more focused on women and good times than I was on obtaining my career goals. The milk plant paid well, the work was fairly routine, and my living expenses were low, so that left plenty of time and money for fun.

I must digress for a moment and tell you a funny story. Arthur and I drank almost every night, sometimes casual, but usually to get shit-faced drunk. If you think about it, why else do people drink? The great taste of alcohol? Please spare me. Anyway, one night, we arrived back to New Jack City around 2:00 a.m. after a serious drinking fest night. Arthur and I were very big on betting each other who was better than who at anything from sports to ridiculous physical and mental challenges. On this particular night, I bet Arthur I could run up the stairs to our apartment faster than he could. Please keep in mind that walking was a challenge at this point, and we lived on the twelfth floor of a high-rise filled with people that did not like white people. Challenge accepted by Arthur. Our building had two sets of stairs. I took the east staircase; Arthur took the west staircase. First one to touch our apartment door would win. Ready, on your mark, get set, go! We both took off. I would guess that I probably tripped and fell on the stairs at least a dozen times and stopped to throw up at least twice. In my drunken pea brain, I was running like the wind. I was an Olympian, for sure. I got to our apartment door, and there were no signs of Artie. Yes, I was victorious, or was I? Did he get there first and go inside? I fumbled my apartment keys out of my pocket and tried to open the door. What the fuck, my keys did not work. That bastard, he did beat me. Not only did he beat me, but he messed with the lock to lock me out. Maybe he even changed the lock. Yes, folks, this was the stupid shit that was going through my drunken head. Now I was pissed off. I started yelling at Arthur to open the door. I punched and kicked the door with bad intentions. No luck. That door was solid. I decided to remove one of the hall fire extinguishers to help me gain entry into my apartment, and then Arthur and I would be duking it out. This was bullshit. As I screamed my final obscenities and threats of breaking the door down, a weird thing happened. A voice came from behind the door. It was a woman's voice. What the fuck? She said she called the police. She must have been looking through the peephole in the door because she called me a crazy white boy.

> Woman: You crazy-ass white boy, I called the cops. I have a gun. I warn you I will shoot you if you don't leave.

A moment of brief sobriety set in from the threats. I looked around as confused as could be.

> Me: Who are you, and why are you in my apartment?
> Woman: This ain't your apartment. Its mine. What's wrong with you?

Then it hit me. I was on the eleventh floor, not the twelfth floor where I lived. Opppss! You would think that the GIANT number 11s printed on the hallway walls or the fact that the number on the apartment door that I was in the process of destroying started with 11 and not 12 would have alerted me, but no, I was just a drunken moron.

I said, "Oh, sorry about that. Tell Artie I beat him. Have a good night."

Yes, that just shows you how messed up I was. I still thought Artie was inside her apartment. The next morning, I built up the courage and went back down to the woman's apartment and slid an apology note under her door. I did not knock as I was afraid she would surely shoot me. As a brief side note, Artie had passed out in the stairwell he was climbing, so just for the record, I won the bet.

CHAPTER 17

Now for all you bachelors across America, if you ever get a chance to date a woman from Brooklyn, I highly recommend it. These women are pretty, extremely loyal girlfriends that really know how to party. I feel compelled to warn you at this time that if you decide to date a Brooklyn babe, just know that at some point in their lives, they have dated Brooklyn guys. Those guys are total dickheads. Sorry, guys, but it's true. Unless you plan on getting that piece of ass away from Brooklyn, you will someday find yourself face-to-face with a jealous Brooklyn steroid junkie who is not big on the talking.

Okay, so for the women that I was dating, I would always have a nickname picked out for them. They of course never knew about the nickname until it came time to break up with them. That was when the gloves usually came off. Let's see, there was Debbie the Bitch who was hot and a total animal in bed, but this witch was the crabbiest bitch ever put on this earth. My friends hated having Debbie around, and to be honest with you, I hated being around her too, except when we were having sex, of course. I dumped Debbie in the middle of a fancy restaurant on her birthday after she went off on an innocent waiter. I got up and left the restaurant by myself to a standing ovation.

There was Mary Ellen the Psychopath. Mary Ellen was beyond hot and great in the sack, but this chick was out of her fucking mind. I decided one day to take a trip down to Florida for a week to visit my oldest sister, Lisa, and her second husband and go to Disney World for a couple of days. I needed some time to unwind. Now don't ask me why, but I decided to ask Mary Ellen, whom I had only been dating for a couple of weeks, to go with me. For God's sake, I met this whore in a bar just a couple of weeks ago, and now I was taking her on vacation. What a moron.

The first two days I stayed at my sister's house was fairly uneventful. Mary Ellen was very normal. I left my sister's and checked into a hotel inside of Disney World. That first night, Mary Ellen and I went to a bar in downtown Disney to drink, dance, and see the fireworks. One minute I was having a good time, and the next minute, Mary Ellen dragged me to the bathroom (no, not a Janice moment, I wish). She started hyperventilating and screaming.

Mary Ellen the Psychopath said, "They found me! They found me!"

I said, "What the fuck are you talking about? Who found you?"

She went on to tell me that there had been these men following her for the past several years and that she was in danger(oh, boy). Of course, she couldn't find them when I asked her to point them out, but she continued to tell me that we must leave town and hide at once. Hmm, let me think about this for a moment. No problemo there, sweetheart, no problemo.

I excused myself to go to the bathroom and decided to take off when she wasn't looking. See you, nutjob. I checked out of that hotel and checked into another one down the road. I had a great time for the rest of my vacation. Yes, I stayed in Disney and finished my vacation. I must tell you though, the shit really hit the fan on the flight back home. I changed hotels, but I did not change my flight. I figured that Mary Ellen would have left town already. What a flight home. The flight was full, and I was stuck sitting next to psycho. I cannot tell you how many times I called her a psycho during the entire flight. It was an absolute miracle that we weren't thrown off before taking off. You guys on Delta Air, you're all right in my book.

CHAPTER 18

Next on my list of women was Jenny the Nanny from Idaho, which wasn't really a nickname. Her name really was Jenny, and she was a nanny, and she was from Idaho. I guess the fact that Jenny did not have a real nickname was a sign that I really liked her. We really hit it off when we met in a club in the Bronx. Jenny was a very simple person. She wasn't gorgeous but was nice to look at. She was not skinny but also not fat. She had nice large breasts and was athletically fit, but her number 1 trait was definitely her personality. I fell in love with this girl's simplicity and lack of life experience. Before moving to New York, she had never left her small town in Idaho. Everything was new to Jenny; everything was an adventure. I loved watching her expressions and hearing some of the silly questions she would ask. My friends thought Jenny was retarded because she really was that simple. But no, she was genuine, real. The kicker was that she also loved to play volleyball and was pretty good at it. At the time, I played in a coed volleyball league on Wednesday nights. Jenny would meet me there, and after volleyball, we would go out for drinks.

As our relationship progressed, Jenny would spend almost every weekend at my place in Brooklyn. I can't say it enough. I loved spending time with her. Unfortunately, what I did not know at the time was that Jenny's refusal to work weekends caused her to lose her nanny job. Had I known that Jenny and her employer were at arms, I would have tried to work around her schedule. We just enjoyed each other's company, so much that she chose not to tell me. Jenny arrived at my apartment on a Friday, sat me down, explained to me that she had been fired, and then hit me with a revelation: she was in love with me.

She continued by asking to move in with me in hopes that we could spend the rest of our lives together. She really put her feelings out there, way out there, and was hoping I would pull her in and embrace the idea. Sorry, guys, but I panicked. I just was not ready for that sort of commitment. It was crazy, I tell you. Here was a woman that I loved to spend time with and made me happy. Now she came to me with open arms, and I rejected her. Why did I reject her? I told her that I cared for her but that I was not ready for a live-in girlfriend or anything more for that matter. Jenny was crushed, in a big city, without a job, a home, and now without the life partner that she so badly wanted. She was completely lost. I offered to let her stay until she could find a new job, but she refused and left that night and moved back to Idaho. I never saw her again. Cue the song "If I Could Turn Back Time." Thanks, Cher.

Chapter 19

As I tried to overcome my stupidity with the whole Jenny ordeal, I met Tricia the Virgin. Pat, my close friend, had married a sweet woman named Doreen, and Tricia was Doreen's best friend at the time. Tricia was a great girl, and I enjoyed spending time with her. She was always good to me and was a very loyal girlfriend for the months that we dated exclusively. The only problem was the whole concept of sex with Tricia. I am not the guy that you should lose your virginity to. I didn't want that responsibility because, in my eyes, a woman who was still a virgin at the age of twenty-four was looking to commit to a special someone for life. We came close a few times, but again, the whole situation was just too much for me. I was immature at the time, and like I had just told Jenny, I was not ready for the big commitment. I'm not proud of this, but I waited until a week before Christmas to dump her. I was a total scumbag about it, and I wish I could take back the way I treated her. The ugly breakup caused some waves between me, Pat, and Doreen, which was understandable. But time would prove to heal our friendship, so I asked them to apologize to Tricia for me. I was told she accepted the apology.

CHAPTER 20

Following the messy breakup, I happened to be at one of my Wednesday night volleyball games when I noticed a familiar face walk in. It turned out to be Cheryl from Wantagh, the girl who had the house party where I initially met Denise. We went out for drinks with my friends and had a great time catching up on one another's lives. The following Wednesday, Cheryl showed up again, except that this time she was not alone. You guessed it, Denise was with her too. When she walked in, I couldn't help but notice how great she looked all dressed up. Her hair had grown out, and she had lost some weight since the last time I saw her, but of course, she still had those pretty eyes. We went out for drinks after volleyball, and believe it or not, Denise did not hate me. I know it had been seven years, but for God's sake, I dumped her on Valentine's Day. Well, after some liquid courage, I got up the nerve to ask Denise out on a date. I promised her I would show up, and that got a chuckle from her. She accepted. Game back on.

On our first date, Denise and I talked for hours about where we had been for the last seven years. It turned out that Denise's mother had finally landed her sugar daddy, and Denise was living with them in the exclusive town of Oyster Bay. She was not happy about her mother's new husband. His name was Lenny. Lenny was an alcoholic who had inherited millions when his father died but managed to piss off most of his inheritance. Lenny was now waiting for his mother to die so that he could get the final motherload so he could piss that away too.

Denise and I managed to pick up right where we left off seven years ago, and this time, we did end up sleeping together right away. Although she hated where I lived in Brooklyn, she started spending entire weekends at my place to stay away from her mother and Lenny the Drunk. Things were looking up again with Denise back in my life. I was finally happy again, unaware that my life was about to take another dramatic change.

CHAPTER 21

One Sunday morning, Denise and I were planning to go out for breakfast. On our way out to my car, I was stopped dead in my tracks. We were surrounded by police officers, and the lobby was partially covered in yellow police tape. There was a chalk etching on the floor in the shape of a person and dried blood on the floor and walls along with bullet holes. We were told that a woman had been sexually assaulted by a gang the night before, and the rival gang came back to the building to settle the score. There was a shootout, and one man died. Denise was freaked out to say the least. I can't blame her for that.

After that, Denise refused to spend the weekends at my place anymore and started pressuring me to move back to Long Island. She hated that I lived so far away. It just so happened that a few weeks after the lobby incident, I received a call from the guy who was sub-leasing the apartment to me and Artie. He told me that he was trying to get a mortgage on a new house, but the apartment was killing his debt-to-income ratio, so he had to give it up. Artie and I were given two months to move out.

Well, for starters, I could tell that Denise was very happy about me losing my apartment. She was happy for all the right reasons, but then she hit me with a doozy: she suggested that we should find an apartment on Long Island and live together. I shit you not, folks, when she suggested that, I was driving and almost killed us both. I pulled the car over to the first bar I could find, and by pull over, I really mean cut across three lanes of traffic without looking. Considering my past relationships, I just wanted to think it through and hopefully not say the wrong thing. My solution? Go to a bar, have a few drinks, and talk things out. She enjoyed seeing me all nervous and vulnerable and got a pretty good laugh at my expense.

I concluded that fate had indeed brought us back together, so why not make the commitment and see where it would lead us? So we decided to get a place of our own to see if we were meant to be.

CHAPTER 22

At this point in my life, a lot of things were happening all at once. I was moving out of New Jack City; I was leaving my good friend and roommate, Artie; I was making a commitment and moving in with Denise; my parents decided to retire and move down to Palm City, Florida; and I decided to quit my job at the milk plant in order to start my own home milk delivery business. That was a freakin' full plate where I came from.

Denise and I found an apartment in my hometown of Massapequa. It was a dump, but it was affordable. I also helped Artie move into an apartment in one of his coworker's homes and helped him settle in, giving him the soda/beer machine as a parting gift.

Saying goodbye to my parents after they sold our house in Massapequa was harder than I thought it would be. I was happy for them, but at the same time, I was losing the support crutch that had always been close by. I will never forget one of the last things my mother said to me before they left. Now keep in mind that my mother had a great sense of humor, but she was very emotional as she said, "People move to Florida to die. I guess I am on the list."

I laughed it off, gave them hugs, and watched as they drove away.

One of the things they did before leaving for Florida was give me a business loan. I loved my parents' loans. They lend me money, I promise to pay them back with interest, but I never actually pay back a single dime. It's a better deal than I could find at any bank in the country. Sorry, Mom. Sorry, Dad, but it's not like you didn't know me.

So over the next few months, I multitasked my ass off. I was really pumped up and ready for this company to get off the ground with a bang. Between my social life, my new business venture, and Denise, I was finally in my true comfort zone. I was feeling really, really good.

It's now time to cue the dickhead again, "All good things must come to an end." FUCK ME RAW!

CHAPTER 23

This event that I am about to tell you is one of the darkest moments in my life. It was this event that brought my whole family to its knees. It is a tragedy that I do not like to relive, not even for the purposes for this book. But in order for anyone to understand why there is a fire that burns inside of me and drives me even to this very day, this moment must be told. Even as I put this moment on paper, I can only shake my head and wipe tears from my eyes.

It was September 17, 1992. I was twenty-seven years young, and I was preparing to take the bull of life by the horns and stake my claim on this world. After an intense day consisting of running around to business supply companies, advertising agencies, and a hundred other miscellaneous errands, I returned to my apartment to organize the rest of this week's other business needs. I saw a note on my door from my sister Paula's fiancé.

Paula met a guy named Alan, and after dating for some time, they became engaged to be married. I describe Alan as a fraternity guy who graduated college but never left that fraternity life behind. He liked to drink, smoke pot, gamble, and party with his friends. And with my often-immature nature, I fit in pretty good with him.

The note on my door said, "Call me ASAP, Alan." My head began to buzz with possible reasons why Alan would take the time to travel to my apartment, only to leave me such a generic note. My immediate reaction was that something must be wrong with my sister, but why not call? Why come to my apartment? I checked my answering machine, and sure enough, there were over a dozen messages from Alan all telling me to call him as soon as I got in. With my hands shaking and my heart pounding, I made the call. Alan picked up on the first ring, and I could hear my sister crying out loud in the background.

> Me: Alan, what the hell is going on?
> Alan: Where are you? Where the hell have you been?
> Me: I'm at home now. What the hell is going on, Alan?

In the background, I could hear Paula yell to Alan.

> Paula: For God's sake, tell him, Al.
> Me: Tell me what? What happened?
> Allan: I am sorry, TJ. There was an accident. Your mom was in a car accident. She didn't make it.

I don't remember hanging up the phone. I don't remember very much except that my body was numb, maybe even in shock. I was not crying. I just simply stood in my bedroom and stared at the walls. I do remember at one point talking to my mother as if she were right in front of me. "This can't be. You just retired. I need you. I need you in my life. I need you to be alive. I have so much that I want to accomplish in life for you and all of the love and support you have given me. Please, please don't go."

I don't know how long I stood in the bedroom for, but I was brought out of my daze when I heard Denise yelling my name. Denise found me in our bedroom. She had already heard the news from Al. She put her arms around me and held me tight. Memories of my mother and our life together flashed through my head, and suddenly I was able to cry. The reality of what had happened started to set in.

That night, as the news spread throughout my inner circle, my friends came over in small groups to offer their love and support. They all knew my mother well, and their faces reflected the same sadness that I was feeling. I spoke briefly on the phone to my sister Paula, and my older sister Lisa's husband, Burt. Lisa was unable to come to the phone herself. Burt told me that my father was staying with them, and he was a complete mess. It was a blessing that my parents had chosen to retire in the same town that Lisa and Burt lived in. At least they were not alone during this tragic time.

Thank God that I had Denise in my life. She was a true rock for me during this tough time. She made all the arrangements to get us to Florida the next day and gave me the love and support I so desperately needed. I would like to be able to tell you details of that week in Florida, but I simply can't. That week in my life was and still is a blur. I do remember seeing my father cry uncontrollably, I do remember all the friends and extended family that flew in to see my mother laid to rest, and yes, I do remember talking to my mom as she rested in peace at her wake. I said my final goodbye to one of the greatest women that God ever placed on this earth.

Rest in peace, Louise Regina Foley, rest in peace.

Like everyone else in this world knows, we all must die at some point. I knew that someday my parents would pass on to their next more glorious lives, but I believe that what made this tragic event even worse for my family was the way it occurred. My mother was still relatively young, she was not sick, and she had just retired from a lifetime of hard work. Here one day, gone the next, we were just not prepared for this.

My father has blamed himself for my mother's death for a long time. As the story goes, my mother had been having headaches for weeks and made a doctor's appointment with her general practitioner. My father was going to drive my mother to the doctors that day but decided at the last minute not to go. My mother was an extremely independent person, so it was no big deal or unusual for her to drive around by herself. What my mother obviously did not know was that her headaches were the result of an aneurysm in her brain. As my mother crossed the Port Saint Lucie Bridge, the aneurysm exploded. Her car veered into oncoming traffic and collided head-on with another vehicle.

I guess my father figured that if he had gone with her, if he were driving, my mother would still be alive today. Well, Dad, that simply is just not true. You know it. I know it. First of all, the doctors made it very clear that my mother died from the aneurysm and not from the car accident. Second, life is not ours to take or give. We are here on God's time, and when he decides that it is our time to leave this life, then it is our time. It was not your fault, Dad. You were a good husband to Mom. You guys lived a good life together filled with happy memories. As a family, we always called you the Pope because of your strong faith. These are the times to practice what you preach, and someday, you guys will be reunited in heaven.

CHAPTER 24

As I arrived back home from Florida, I was lost and unmotivated. It was causing me to doubt my abilities to start a business. At this point in my life, I needed someone to come along and slap me in the face. I needed to be woken up. I needed a life-changing pep talk to shake all this negative shit out of my head. The person that I would normally turn to had just been laid to rest.

I am not some weak helpless pussy, but sometimes, everyone, and I mean everyone, needs a boost, a helping hand, a shot of confidence. I turned to my girl Denise in hopes that she would step in and build me back up to the spark plug that I was before. I needed that fire to be relit under my ass, but unfortunately, that was just not what Denise was all about.

As I mentioned earlier, Denise and her siblings were basically abandoned as teenagers and left to raise themselves. She did manage to go to college and graduate, but upon graduation, Denise found herself homeless. Her father was nowhere to be found, and her mother was still only concerned about her own well-being. She spent her postcollege life shuffling from one friend's house to the next, supporting herself with decent jobs and the goodwill provided by her friends' families, not being able to save any serious money for her future. When you couple her early years as a teen with her fight for pure survival after college, your result is a young lady with severe insecurities.

This was simply not a person capable of motivating a maniac like me with such big dreams. If opposites do attract, then Denise and I were meant to be together. I decided that I needed to get some security of my own to get my life back in order. I was in love with Denise, and she needed to be a part of that life.

One week after burying my mother, I decided to ask Denise to marry me. I was sure that I could help her get over her insecurities and at the same time hoped that my new family would rekindle my fire. I had planned on proposing to Denise at a romantic dinner celebrated with champagne after the special moment. But a funny thing happened one night in our apartment. It was the middle of the week, and Denise and I were folding laundry together (yes, I know folding laundry is lame). I just remember that our eyes locked on each other in a way that had never happened before. I could see deep into her soul at that moment, and I believe she could see deep into mine. I could feel some of her childhood pain and her need for love. It was at that very moment that I wanted her to know how much she meant to me. I went to our bedroom where I had hidden an engagement ring and made my way back to the living room. She had not moved an inch. I got down on one knee and asked Denise to be my wife. Denise did not hesitate. She accepted me with open arms. That moment felt so good, so natural. Things were going to be all right.

CHAPTER 25

Over the next few months, I made an absolute lame effort to make my new business venture a success. Although I had accumulated over 150 customers and I had developed my first complete delivery route, I needed to be honest with myself. I just was not into the business as a whole. My heart was not in my work, and that makes for a miserable environment. I guess I never really thought through the process of what my responsibilities would be if I had succeeded at building a delivery route. For example, I would have to drive a delivery truck from 10:00 p.m. until my deliveries were completed at around 8:00 a.m., and I would have to do that six days a week. That schedule basically meant that I would be awake while everyone else was sleeping and vice versa. After a few frustrating months, I decided to sell my newly developed business—the dairy that I was purchasing, all my delivery products, my customer base, and my equipment. I made a couple of dollars on the sale, but I was not happy with my poor planning or the fact that I was now unemployed. I needed to plan for my future, especially since I had just committed to starting a new life with Denise. So I decided to take the "stable" route and once again seek a job in management.

I was always good getting jobs. I consider myself to be an artist during interviews. Just put me in front of a recruiter, and I will land the job. I have always been good at freelancing conversations, and I can honestly say that I have never been nervous during an interview. I guess I just went into interviews with the attitude of "the worst that can happen is that I don't get the job, big deal." I never really wanted a "job," but sometimes in life, you must take a step backward in order to see clearly and go forward.

I ended up landing a job with Hertz Rent A Car at LaGuardia Airport in New York. Hertz hired me based on my previous job at the milk processing plant, which, like Hertz, was a union shop. I was hired as a shift manager. I was initially put in charge of the union that ran the courtesy buses that circle the airport and pick up arriving or drop off departing customers. The job definitely had its benefits. First of all, management had to be ready to take over union jobs in the event that a strike took place, so my first task was to train for a commercial driver's license.

That took me all but a few weeks, and I passed the test on the first try. Since Hertz also took care of management's core expenses, I received a company car, free car insurance, free gas, free health benefits, and got issued the required Hertz brand suits along with free dry cleaning. Wow, now take all those benefits and add a very decent starting salary, and what you get is a pretty good employment package. There was only one problem with that job though: I fuckin' hated it. A third-grade special-needs child could do my job; there was absolutely no challenge at all. New ideas were immediately shut down by a middle management that simply wanted to put in their time and go home. Upper management was just concerned with covering their asses so they could just get through the year and get a small bonus. I still doubt that my direct supervisor had a heartbeat. I went to work each day and looked for a reason not to shoot myself, but don't worry, I stuck it out for a while.

CHAPTER 26

Denise and I had settled on a wedding date for October 15, 1993, and that was less than a year away. I convinced myself to stay with Hertz due to the stability that it offered, so I hung in there. I was miserable at work but happy with my personal life. I guess that was a decent trade-off.

The apartment that Denise and I were living in turned out to be an absolute nightmare. We started having problems getting hot water, had to battle an ant infestation, and the guy that lived above us smoked pot every day, and the smell of it was constantly coming through our vents. We decided that it was time to move. But as I started looking for apartments again, Denise, the love of my life, without my knowledge, decided to ask her mother and husband if we could move into the apartment in their house. Now picture this, I came home from work one day, and Denise had most of our stuff already packed. She told me she found a place to live, and guess what, it was free. Now listen, folks, you know it, and I know that nothing in this world is free—nothing. That was when she sprung the news on me about my new residence at her mother's house. Ring the bell, it was fight time. I reminded her that she moved out of that house because she was so miserable, but now she wanted to bring me into that mess. No, thank you. After cooler heads prevailed, Denise laid the cards on the table. First of all, her mother's husband was in AA and had been sober for months. Second, we were getting married in less than a year, and we could save a lot of money. Third, it was closer to my and her place of employment. This was one time in our relationship that Denise had me dead to rights. I mean, how can you argue with that sane logic? I agreed to give it a shot, so off to Oyster Bay Cove we went.

Living in Oyster Bay was not so bad at first. I mean, this is the place where the true rich and famous live. I enjoyed being around the constant smell of money. My entrepreneurial juices began to flow from the first day that we moved in.

Now Denise's mother was a complete psychopath. There was not a day that went by that she did not have a new house project or renovation that she wanted complete. I actually felt bad for her husband. One of the many projects that came to light when we first arrived there was the demolition of their beautiful built-in swimming pool. Denise's mother wanted to fill in the pool and make a garden.

During my high school and college years, I worked for a swimming pool construction company, and that was one dirty job that I always enjoyed. So I figured that since I was living there rent-free, I would offer my help. Big freakin' mistake, folks. Big freakin' mistake. The two hammerheads decided that I was capable of doing the entire job without hired help—Just me and Lenny, the almost-sober drunk. Talk about taking advantage of someone. I worked on that project at night and on weekends, and I will tell you, the job came out perfect. I mean, you would have no idea that there was a swimming pool in this yard once we finished. I felt this sudden sense of pride and accomplishment that I had not felt in a while. It felt really good.

CHAPTER 27

My brain was beginning to awaken from the graveyard that Hertz had turned it into, and I decided to start a swimming pool maintenance and repair business. I went through my normal routine of calming Denise down after pitching the idea.

I told her, "Don't worry, sweetheart. I am just going to take jobs on the weekend. It will be good extra money."

Now it was my turn to have her dead to her rights. How could she argue with that sane logic?

So while I was at Hertz doing squat shit all day, I formed a corporation, I purchased a mailing list of residents in target areas that have swimming pools, I developed advertisements and business cards, and I sent out a bulk mailing. I did not purchase anything major except for a business telephone line, phone, and answering machine. I figured I would see if anyone responded and act from there. Folks, I will tell you, fate is a very, very scary thing. You see, one of the bulk mailers that I sent out arrived at a home of a woman whose pool I used to clean in high school. High school! I had named my company Foley Swimming Pools, and this woman, whom I will call Mrs. B for now, recognized my last name. She called to see if it was actually me that was soliciting her, and after a brief conversation, Mrs. B hired me to repair her broken pool filtration system. That, my friends, was the beginning of something that I was surely not expecting.

The job at Mrs. B's house was perfect. I replaced an entire pool filtration system and decided to clean Mrs. B's pool and deck tile as a free bonus. She was overjoyed. I made a net profit that day of over $1,500. Not bad for a side job.

Let me tell you all something about New York. In-ground swimming pools are a major expense up there. You can only use them for around six months out of the year, and toward the end of each summer, they must be covered and winterized in order to prevent pipes from freezing and cracking underground. In the spring, the pool needs to be properly uncovered, and filtration systems need to be reassembled. So most of the pool owners in New York use professional companies for those openings and closings, as well for weekly maintenance and repairs. The people of Long Island pay through the ass for good-quality pool services. The season is just too short to take a chance on doing it themselves. The only thing is that most Long Island pool companies close down in the winter. I guess you could say that a pool company has the exact opposite schedule of a schoolteacher.

So after a job well done at Mrs. B's house, I decided to try a new networking promotion with the few customers that I picked up from my first bulk mailer. I offered people like Mrs. B one week of free pool cleaning service for each person that they referred me to. That is, as long as the referred person signed up for an entire summer of my cleaning service. I figured it was worth a shot. After all, I would be trading $60 worth of service in order to gain over $1,400 worth of business. Like I said, folks, fate is a scary thing. I was slammed with new business, and I mean slammed. Mrs. B sent me over twenty people on her own, and people were calling me for cleaning services, repair work, chemicals, pool toys, new equipment. You name it, they wanted it. My phone was ringing off the hook. My small "side business" was quickly becoming a growing beast. I now found myself working on pools after I left Hertz at night and all weekend too. I was exhausted after a few weeks, so it was definitely time for a new plan.

CHAPTER 28

It was spring of 1993, and summer was rapidly approaching. I decided to start easing Denise into the idea of quitting my job at Hertz and working on pools full-time. All I kept hearing from her was about the security that Hertz offered, and she reminded me repeatedly about the milk route that I had failed at. I must be honest, I was hurt. I was hurt by the lack of confidence that my future bride-to-be had in my business abilities. I mean, I was making double the money working on pools part-time compared to what I was making at Hertz, and that was only a few weeks in. I needed this woman to believe in me—to grab my shoulders and tell me to go for it. Do you know what I mean? I was not meant to work with a bunch of half-dead douchebags. But I did not want to fight with her, so I stuck it out at Hertz for one more week, and then good old fate stepped in again. This time, fate came in the form of a New York Yankee baseball player. For the purposes of this book, I will call him Bernie W. You baseball fans know exactly who he is every time he trots to the outfield; you non-baseball fans can look up who he is.

It was Friday afternoon, and my shift was rapidly ending at Hertz. Up to this point, my day was filled with mundane bullshit. I think I even fell asleep at my desk once that day. I had two houses that I needed to stop at on my way home in order to do repair estimates. Meanwhile, my weekend was booked solid. One of the Hertz bus drivers radioed me that he was inbound to my location with an unscheduled Platinum Club member that needed a car for the weekend. Now Hertz Platinum Club is not an easy club to become a member of. It was basically set up for the rich and famous. Normal protocol for a Platinum member requires a manager like myself to drive a car to the airport terminal and give the member the car right there. The manager then takes a Hertz bus back to the rental location. Now this was an unscheduled Platinum rental, so protocol had not been breached at this point. I met the bus as it arrived at my location, and off the bus walked none other than New York Yankee Bernie W. I recognized him immediately, not because I am a Yankee fan but because I am a New York Met fan, and I hate the Yankees. I decided not to hold that against him though. I said hello to Mr. W., and he informed me that he was just getting back from spring training and did not arrange to get picked up at the airport, so he would need a car until Sunday. No problemo, Bernie, I will have you on your way in no time.

Now remember, it was Friday afternoon, and that happened to be our busiest day of the week, so our location was packed with renters. I walked Bernie over to an unmanned reservation terminal, logged in, and pulled up Bernie's Platinum Club account. Platinum Club members had all their information stored in the Hertz system, including name, address, driver's license number, and credit card and billing information. All I had to do was assign him a car from our lot and print out a rental agreement. That was it, piece of cake, no problem, right? Wrong. I tried and printed out Bernie's rental agreement, and the system would not allow me to rent him a car. An error code was displayed on the terminal informing me that Bernie's credit card on file was declined. In fact, the code on the screens required me to confiscate his card. Now what the fuck do I do? Ask him for his card and then keep it? I don't think so. I took a more sensible approach.

I said, "I'm sorry, Mr. W. For some reason, our system is unable to process the credit card that you have on file with us. Do you have another card?"

I could have been a total dick about the situation, but don't you think I worded that well? I guess Bernie didn't think so because he handed me another credit card but gave me a real attitude. Bernie looked at my name tag (for the record, I fucking hate name tags) and told me, "You know, Shift Manager Foley, I can rent a car any place I choose. Perhaps you can keep that in mind when dealing with me."

I replied, "Yes, I realize that, Mr. W. Thank you for your patience. I will get you out of here in just a few minutes." (Translation: Go fuck yourself, you deadbeat Yankee bitch.)

I swiped Bernie's second card, and fuck a duck, I got the same damn denial code. For God's sake, it was the end of my shift, dear lord. I just wanted to get out of there.

> Me: (Very quietly in an attempt to preserve his integrity) My apologies, Mr. W, but I can't use this card either. Would you like to use a phone in my office and call your credit card company?
>
> (Bernie lost his shit.)
>
> Bernie: Are you kidding me? I'm Bernie W. I play for the New York Yankees. You know who I am. I just need one of your piece-of-shit cars for the weekend. What's your problem? Listen, forget the credit card. Just give me a car, and I will pay for it on Sunday when I return it.
>
> Me: Sorry, Mr. W. I can't let a car leave this lot without a form of payment to secure it. Like I said, we can go into my office, and you can call your credit card company if you would like.
>
> Bernie: Look, you are the location manager. I am sure it is well within your discretion to just give me a car based on who I am. I am not going to steal the damn thing. You need to work on your customer service skills. You are not very good at your job.

Folks, that was more shit than I have ever taken in my life without smacking the shit out of the guy saying it. I kept telling myself, "Just keep your cool, Tom. Just keep your cool."

> Me: I am sorry you feel that way, Mr. W. I am trying my hardest to help you here. I ask that you put yourself in my position. I

mean, could you imagine if I showed up at the Yankees Stadium and went to the ticket window to purchase some box seats for the game, and my credit card was denied. I doubt I would get the tickets even if I promised to return in two days to pay for them. Don't you agree?

Bernie: That's different. You're not me. Everybody knows who I am. Okay, listen, I will tell you what I will do. Not only will I pay for the car on Sunday, I will also give you four box seats to our home opener. What do you say?

Me: I just can't do it. I would get fired for sure.

Bernie did not say another word. He just stormed out of the building, and I never saw him again. I could not help but laugh about the whole ordeal. I told all my friends about my encounter with the superstar, and everyone got a real kick out of it.

CHAPTER 29

I put the whole incident behind me and pressed on with my weekend. I worked my ass off, and on Monday, I went to work at Hertz like a good little boy. Upon my arrival at work on Monday, I was greeted by my boss who escorted me into his office. Waiting inside was the guy who had recruited me for the job and some suit from corporate headquarters that smelled like freakin' mothballs. Really, this guy stunk. I found myself holding my breath and only breathing through my mouth; it was so bad. Any old hoot, these three numb nuts informed me that they received a complaint over the weekend from a Platinum Club member, and I needed to run them through what had taken place. Bernie, what a fag! Now I consider myself to be a pretty sharp guy that can read people well, and I could just tell that none of these guys were listening to a word I was saying. In one ear, out the other. I was midsentence several times and was cut off by Captain Smelly. That really pissed me right the hell off. After a few minutes of hearing "my side of the story," I got the message loud and clear: Mr. W, the prima donna, had complained about me and blah blah blah blah blah. Fuck him. So the Three Stooges come to the conclusion that I was not sensitive to Bernie's needs, and on top of that, I should have confiscated his credit cards. Now I am no genius, but how in the hell does that make sense? I don't know. Anyway, they decided that I needed some procedural retraining and, get this one, sensitivity training. Oh, please spare me for God's sake.

> Smelly Suit: So that's my recommendation, Mr. Foley. Two weeks of training should be sufficient, then we can reevaluate Mr. Foley at

that time. Let this be a lesson learned, Mr. Foley. The customer is always right.

(My Irish Hungarian blood hit its boiling point.)

Me: I tell you what, stinky. Yes, you smell just awful. I am going to pass on your sensitivity training and reevaluation. This job sucks. I hate working here, and I believe that I will never come back. That's my recommendation. Oh, and by the way moron, if a customer can't pay for a product, he is not a customer. You are taking that customer is always right bullshit way too literally. It was a pleasure.

And that was the end of that. As I walked out of Hertz, I felt a huge weight lifting off my shoulders. I was free, free again, I... Oh, shit, I had no way of getting home. Do you think they could rent me a car for the week? Ah, who cares. I felt great!

CHAPTER 30

The news of my departure from Hertz did not go over well with Denise. Once again, I found myself disappointed that my fiancée saw me as an irresponsible, immature person who was dreaming his way to nowhere. I just did not understand the lack of support. At that time, I probably should have had a heart-to-heart with myself to reevaluate whether Denise was truly the right woman for me. I knew I loved her, but maybe it was for the wrong reasons. Maybe I wanted to be her savior more than her husband. In my eyes, Denise deserved a better hand than life had dealt her so far, and I wanted to be the man to give her the better life. I also got the feeling at that time that if our wedding was not so damn close, Denise would have dumped me. Part of the tension between us also came as a result of her mother. Denise's mother was embarrassed that her future son-in-law not only couldn't hold down a job, but now he wanted to clean pools for a living. Yes, folks, I heard Denise and her mother having several conversations like that. They just did not get what I was really after in life. In my opinion, it does not matter what you do for a living. It's what you make that job opportunity into that counts. Big job titles and prestigious careers are worth shit if you are not enjoying what you are doing.

Anyway, I decided to take my licks and ignore the negativity around me. I had a vision, and now I needed to properly act on that vision. The only way to prove yourself in the business world is to perform, put up, or shut up. And now that my fire was back in my belly, I felt I was ready to prove my true business capabilities to all.

I started off my now full-time venture by purchasing transportation in the form of an old beaten-up Dodge Charger Hatchback. My future mother-in-law and her husband were so embarrassed by this car that they made me put a cover on it whenever I parked in the driveway. Two fucking snobs. Look, the car had a good engine, got great gas mileage, and had plenty of room for my equipment. That was good enough for me. I purchased a brand-new set of tools and swimming pool maintenance equipment, and I was ready to rock and roll. Let me tell you one thing about being a true sole proprietor: you really need to have the discipline to structure your day, and you need to be highly self-motivated. It was a very strange feeling when your alarm clock goes off in the morning, and now you must create your day. I had no office to go to, and I had no employees to consult with or a boss to report to. It was all up to me. I don't know. It was just a very strange feeling especially since I did not have any support on the home front.

CHAPTER 31

Now up until this point, Denise was working for a company in Manhattan that manufactures men's specialty boxers (underwear). I knew deep down inside that Denise hated her job, especially the daily commute on the Long Island Railroad, but she had her security, didn't she? I often got the feeling that Denise was actually jealous at the way that I walked the earth with such a carefree mannerism. But that's part of the American dream when you work for yourself. It's scary, but you make the rules, you make the hours, and you make the decisions that could either make or break your dreams. To me, it's just the greatest feeling. It's a high that no drug can ever duplicate.

My phone was just exploding, business was pouring in fast, and my multitasking skills were being challenged every day. I sometimes found myself on the phone more than I was performing money-generating work. Now that was not a totally bad thing, but it was also not a good thing. Yes, answering customer calls is important, but at some point, it's the work that pays the bills.

I arrived home after a ridiculous fourteen-hour schedule; I was hungry, I was dirty, I was exhausted, and I still had calls to return that I was just not able to answer during the day. As I walked into my kitchen, I found Denise sitting in a chair, crying. Now what? She informed me that she had been fired from her job. I swear to God, people, I wanted to stand up and laugh my ass off. How's that for security? But no, I did not say that to her, which goes to show how different Denise and I really were. I could have made her feel like shit. I could have returned the attitude that she gave me when I quit Hertz. I mean, she got fired for poor sales performance. At least I quit with pride, on my terms. I offered her nothing but support and love. I held her tight and convinced her that it was their loss and not hers.

I laid some pretty thick bullshit on her, but the point was that it was the right thing to do. That's what you're supposed to do when a loved one is hurting. It's not brain surgery, folks.

So I took a shower, had some dinner, and I began to get my shit in order for the next few days. Then it hit me, Denise was the organizing queen. There was not a more organized person than Denise. She could help me while she was unemployed. I sat her down and explained to her how she could help, and even though she would never admit it, I saw a twinkle of excitement in her eyes. I knew she did not want to go back to the grind of working in Manhattan.

Now it was obviously going to take Denise some time to learn the technical side of my business, but having her with me answering the phone, setting appointments, and doing some billing was an absolute godsend. Within a week or so, Denise was an absolute pro. We were an unbelievable team out in the field. The customers just loved us working as a couple. As the summer rolled in, I actually got the sense that she was starting to understand why I wanted to work for myself. I mean, we had so much flexibility and freedom that there was no way she didn't get it. Now with Denise and I working together all day, we were able to discuss and finalize wedding plans. We had already set the date for October 15 (that was just a few months away), but now we had to pick a church in Oyster Bay for our ceremony, a catering hall for our reception, limos, photographers, an entertainment company, and even a company to videotape our special day. I also chose Aruba for our honeymoon.

CHAPTER 32

One weird thing had happened over and over again when I would mention her father and ask why he was not attending our wedding. Denise would blow me off each time I mentioned him. I assumed for a while that it was because she had hard feelings toward him because of her upbringing, or lack thereof, but that just did not make sense to me. Her father supported her financially when she lived with her siblings in Wantagh, and she told me that he paid for her college education. On the other hand, Denise's mother abandoned her as a child, yet she was still talking to her.

I decided to press the issue one day, and sure enough, Denise broke down and told me the truth. Now when I say broke down, I mean broke down as in crying. She composed herself long enough to tell me that her father was incarcerated in a federal prison. It's funny. One minute she did not want to talk about him, and the next she was defending him. She told me what a great person her father really was and that he had gotten involved with some crooked investment company. Basically, he worked at the wrong place at the wrong time. I could see in her eyes and hear it in her voice just how much this man meant to her. I did not prejudge her father. I did not think any bad thoughts about him at all. My theory on life is that you never will know the truth about anything until you do some looking yourself. I mean, how many times have you heard on the news about men convicted of murder or rape, and then decades later, they are found to be innocent through DNA? Anyway, I asked Denise to always be upfront with me. I wanted to have an open, honest relationship and to be able to trust each other. From her hugs and kisses, I would say Denise was relieved with my reaction to her news. If she loved her father, that was good enough for me.

Now I know that I had done some shitty things in previous relationships, but I am honestly an old-time romantic. I love to romance and court a woman that I have feelings for, and after hearing about Denise's father and his predicament, I decided I needed to meet him and officially ask him for his daughter's hand in marriage. No, that is not corny; it's traditional, so shut up.

Denise's father, Richard, was in the federal prison camp in Jesup, Georgia. I decided to spend a weekend down there, and Denise arranged with her father to have me put on his official visitors' list. To this point in my life, I had never had to visit anyone in any sort of prison, so I had no idea what to expect. A prison camp is the lowest-level security facility in the federal system, and the visiting rules and regulations were pretty lenient. Now for those of you that have never been to Jesup, Georgia, and I will assume that is everyone reading this, Jesup, Georgia, is a tiny, tiny Southern town in the middle of nowhere. The best way for me to describe Jesup would be by comparing it to the town from the movie *My Cousin Vinny*. If you have not seen that movie, then you are an idiot. Anyway, I went to Jesup and spent the weekend visiting Richard in prison. I liked him from the minute I met him, and I believe he liked me. Richard is a handsome, charismatic Italian man with a great outlook on life. We spoke for hours that weekend, and on Sunday, we hugged and said our goodbyes. Richard made it clear that I was officially welcomed into his family. It made me sad that he would not be able to give his daughter away at our wedding. I could tell how much it bothered him. He was in the middle of a five-year sentence, and nothing was going to change that. I had a good feeling that I would be seeing a lot more of Mr. T (that was the nickname I called him; the *T* is short for his last name). And I looked forward to the day when he would be a free man and back in Denise's life.

CHAPTER 33

The summer of my first year with the pool business came to an end, and I would call that summer a complete success. I ended the summer by winterizing all my customers' pools, and I offered every customer a small discount if they signed advanced service contracts for the next summer. Every single customer signed new contracts. I decided that I did not want to spend all the money that I had saved that summer, so I signed on with an oil company to drive a truck during the winter. This company specialized in home-heating fuel, and they hired temporary drivers for their busy winter season. I already had a commercial driver's license thanks to Hertz, so I took a quick DMV test and received my HAZMAT and Tanker endorsements that allowed me to drive a truck that carried heating oil. I set a starting date for the week after I was to return from my honeymoon. The guys that interviewed me for the driving job seemed to be cool, and I was able to make my own schedule. The job required me to be out driving most of the day, so I saw it as still having plenty of freedom. I could have very easily just hung out all winter, but I wanted to save money and hopefully buy a house for me and Denise. So what the heck, I would give it a try, but first thing first, it was time to get married.

October 15, 1993, I married Denise, my onetime high school sweetheart. The ceremony was beautiful. Denise and I chose friends and family to be our ushers and bridesmaids. Denise's sister Laura was her maid of honor, and my best friend Artie was my best man. Everyone was there, my father and sister Lisa flew up from Florida, I had relatives present from everywhere, and so did Denise. Everyone dressed their best.

I was scared to death saying my vows. I did not want to screw it up, and I didn't. Denise and I were asked to kiss, and that was that. I was now a married man. What a rush!

The reception was a party like no other wedding reception that I had ever been to before. Denise and I wanted this to be more fun than formal, and damn did we succeed. I can't remember more than one or two moments that we were not dancing. The DJ was incredible, the professional dancers were hot, and everyone drank their asses off. When it came time for the night to end, nobody would leave the catering hall.

Now I know this is probably going to seem funny. I mean, it was my wedding night, and I just finished having one of the best nights of my life. I just got married to the woman I loved, but I have to do it. Please cue the dickhead: "All good things must come to an end." Yes, sorry, folks. Just a couple of hours after my wedding reception ended, and I have to cue the dickhead. This part sucked.

Denise and I booked the newlywed suite at a beautiful hotel in Garden City, Long Island. We were leaving for our honeymoon the next day, and Denise's sister had volunteered to take us to the airport in the morning. Now I envisioned my wedding night to be like the ones you see in soap operas, you know, two newlyweds making love all night until they fall asleep in each other's arms. Well, evidently, Denise is not a big soap opera fan. Instead of making love all night, she decided she wanted to open all the gift envelopes that people had given us. Are you fucking kidding me? Who gives a shit about money and gifts right now? Let's get naked. It never happened, folks. Really, I mean, what the fuck? My new bride and I did not have sex or make love or whatever the fuck you want to call it. Guess what, it got worse. I decided to help myself to the hotel minibar while I sat around with a hard-on and Denise opened envelopes. As she progressed through her chore, she started to get offended at the amounts of money that some of our relatives gave us as gifts. She started cursing at first and then eventually started crying. She started with some whining shit about how this was supposed to be our jump-start in life and how the wedding cost more than what we received as gifts. I did my best to console her, but the reality was that I wanted to knock her ass out and then maybe have sex with her unconscious body. Did she get married and have a wedding to make money? I just didn't get it. I hated that night with a passion. The next morning, I had a talk with Denise about life and all that crap, but I am telling you, that damn insecurity trait that she had just drove me crazy. I don't want to wait around and expect people to provide and care for me. If you want something in your life, go out and get it. Stop looking for handouts and stop with the bullshit that people owe me from the past. I hate that.

I tried to take refuge in the fact that I was on my way to Aruba for a week of fun in the sun and hopefully a sweet honeymoon with Denise. Now Denise gets panic attacks when she flies. I knew this for a long time, and I had learned to deal with them. But I found them annoying and embarrassing. If the plane is going to crash, what the hell is hyperventilating and throwing up going to do? Nothing, absolutely nothing. Denise and I spent an entire week in beautiful Aruba. I highly recommend it as a vacation destination. The sand in Aruba is pink, it never rains, there is always a breeze, the locals are great, and the scuba diving is awesome.

With all that being said, I was ready for a divorce by the end of the week. In the seven days spent in paradise, I got my wife to make love to me once—once, what the fuck. I got so sick of hearing her excuses that I just stopped trying. Yes, for all the wrong reasons, I will never forget my honeymoon.

CHAPTER 34

The winter of 1993 was brutal. It felt like we got a snow or an ice storm every day. I was driving around Long Island carrying five thousand gallons of fuel oil. I came home every night smelling like oil shit, but the driving was challenging, and I loved a challenge. I did a lot of planning for my pool company that winter, and I decided that once the summer came around, I was going to hire someone full-time to take over my cleaning route and free my time up for new customers and repairs. Denise got tired of sitting around the house that winter, and she was hired by a company based on Long Island that published a computer magazine. We received full medical benefits from her job, so that was a big plus.

Things between Denise and I seemed to smooth itself out, but the reality was that I just decided to push our issues aside for now. Maybe she just needed a little time to adjust to being a married woman. Whatever.

The summer of 1994 was approaching quickly. I quit my driving job in February in order to give myself time to hire an employee and find a vehicle for him to drive. The oil company was totally cool. They gave me an open invitation to return the next winter, and they even gave me a bonus in my last paycheck. They were good people in my book.

I would like to take a quick moment to clarify something. I was a very happy man at this point in my life. Denise and I had some intimacy issues to hash out, but we were a happy couple. My sister Paula had married Alan the month after we got married. All my best friends were either married or engaged to be married, and Denise and I would spend our weekends hanging out at either barbecues, dinner parties, or by ourselves for a night out on the town. Denise and I smiled and laughed a lot when we were together, and that was always a good thing.

CHAPTER 35

Okay, back to business. I placed a help wanted ad in a local Long Island newspaper, and I had high hopes of finding an experienced pool man to join my company. When the ad ran, I did not get many calls, but I did get one very promising call from a man named Nick. I had a good all-around feeling during my phone conversation with Nick. He had been in the pool industry for over twenty years. He had recently been divorced and sounded like he was down on his luck, so he was looking to rebuild his life again. I decided that I needed to meet Nick face-to-face, so I arranged to meet him for breakfast at a diner close to where he lived. We agreed on 10:00 a.m. the next day. When I arrived at the diner, Nick was waiting for me outside. He was early. That was a good sign. I cannot stand people that are late for anything. That just drives me crazy. Anyway, Nick's physical appearance left a lot to be desired. Nick was around 5'6" tall, and he probably weighed 110 pounds soaking wet. His clothes appeared to be dirty and wrinkled, and I would say it had been quite some time since he shaved or had a haircut. He also carried a backpack over his shoulder that looked like a truck had run over it. My first impression was not a good one. In fact, when I first saw Nick, I was starting to think of excuses for me to get the hell out of there already. There was no way I could send a guy that looked the way Nick looked to my customers' homes. I have to give credit where credit is due, he could definitely talk the talk. He knew everything there is to know about swimming pools. I decided to be honest with Nick and talked to him about his appearance. I wanted to know why he would show up for a job interview looking the way he did. Nick cleared the air for me pretty quickly. Nick was homeless. He went on to tell me about his divorce six months ago and how he became depressed and lonely. He could not get himself motivated to find work and was soon unable to pay his bills. Nick had been on the streets for three months and spent his nights sleeping in a local industrial park. I was speechless and stared at Nick with the heaviest of hearts.

Now let's talk about fate again. Nick saw my help wanted ad as he used the local newspaper as a blanket to keep himself warm at night. Come on, folks, that's sick stuff. So here I was sitting across this poor soul that just spilled his guts out to me, and the only thing this man wanted was to get to work and earn a living. We live in a country that helps people all around the world with financial aid and resources, yet we still have people like Nick in our own backyards. I just never understood that.

I decided to put my money where my mouth and heart were and decided to help Nick change his life. We came to an understanding that I was going to restart him back on the path to regaining his independence, and in return, I needed him to give me his best work in the upcoming summer. We shook hand that morning, and "Project Nick" began.

CHAPTER 36

I started Project Nick by checking him into a cheap efficiency motel. I gave Nick money to get a haircut and a shave and for food to put in his motel refrigerator. I went to a local pharmacy to purchase him toiletries and then stopped at a discount clothes store to pick him up some clean clothes. Nick and I had a small ceremony one night in which we burned his backpack and all his old clothes. Within a week, Nick looked like a new man.

Over the next few weeks, I found a small apartment for Nick inside of a person's home. I set up a phone account for him, and I even took him to my doctor and dentist for checkups. All the while, Nick gave me many thanks and hugs. It felt really good to help another human being. I spent some time researching and hunting for a good used van and ultimately settled on a Ford Econoline F150 van to hold all the equipment he would need for the summer. And when the time was right, I handed Nick the keys. I could just see a sense of pride in this man's face. What a marvelous site. I took the time to drive Nick to every customer's house that he would be servicing along with a map highlighting all his stops in case he needed a reminder. I took several days to go over with Nick how I serviced stops and the high standards that I was expecting him to follow. The summer was here, and we were ready for action.

Nick and I worked together for the first month and a half opening swimming pools. That tends to be a two-man job. Besides work, Nick and I would have some great conversations about life and the dreams we were hoping to one day achieve. I could not help but feel proud of what I had done for this man. One day, he was sleeping in a park, and a few months later, he was telling me about his dreams of a bright future. That was so cool.

Summer was now in full bloom; my pool openings were finished, and it was time to set Nick out onto his cleaning route while I concentrated on repairs and new business. Once again, things were looking good. Things were looking really good. Sorry, folks, I have to do it. Trust me, I don't want to do it, but this is my life story, so cue the dickhead: "All good things must come to an end."

CHAPTER 37

The call came around 10:00 a.m. on a Monday morning three weeks after Nick had been out on his own. Mrs. B, one of my first and most loyal customers, was hysterically crying and begging for me to get over to her house. I didn't ask questions. I dropped what I was doing and shot over to see what was going on. What I saw when I arrived would leave a lifelong haunting image in my brain. Mrs. B lived in a very exclusive upscale neighborhood. All the homes were seated on several acres of nicely manicured property, and Mrs. B's house was no exception. The scene that I was looking at was just not real to me. There were tire tracks on her front lawn, her cast-iron mailbox was crushed, and the van that I had given Nick to drive was sticking through a retaining wall that surrounded the property. What the hell happened? Mrs. B was crying and yelling at the same time.

Mrs. B yelled, "How could you? How could you send someone like this to my home?"

It was then that I spotted Nick lying face down on Mrs. B's lawn; he was not moving. I ran to see if Nick was alive, and as I rolled him over, the god-awful smell of alcohol hit me. Nick was not hurt; he was passed out drunk. It got worse, of course. As I tried to calm down a hysterical Mrs. B, letting her know that I would get a landscaping company to fix her lawn, mailbox, and retaining wall, she then asked me, "What about my house?"

She grabbed me by the arm and walked me into her house and then down a flight of stairs into her basement, leaving a drunk Nick on the lawn, and then wow, holy shit, I could not believe my eyes. A basement that had been fully renovated into an entertainment room complete with a pool table, bar, and projection TV was now submerged in four feet of swimming pool water. Everything was ruined. What the fuck did he do? I needed some time to figure out what the hell happened. After walking the property and checking the swimming pool equipment, I realized that drunk Nick had properly cleaned the filtration system but never changed the filter setting from rinse to circulate when he was done. Once the holding tank that the dirty filter water drained into became full, it resulted in the continuous overflow of water into Mrs. B's basement. And Mrs. B had a very large swimming pool. The entire 38,000 gallons of water drained from the pool into her basement. Not good, not good at all.

Mrs. B told me that when she heard the water rushing into her basement and ran outside to tell Nick, he panicked and ran for the hills. The remaining damage on Mrs. B's property was caused by Nick's ridiculous escape attempt. When I returned outside, the police had already arrived. A semi-awake Nick was handcuffed, and the police searched the van and found a completely empty bottle of Jack Daniels and several beers on ice. It was ten in the fucking morning. Are you kidding me? Oh, and here is the funny part. Nick had turned the van glove compartment into a cooler. It was lined with plastic and filled with beer on ice. The whole situation was just a freakin' nightmare. I apologized over and over again to Mrs. B, but I could tell it was in one ear and out the other. I had lost her confidence and her business. I made good on my word to fix the damage that Nick had caused. A whopping bill that was well over $18,000, and no, folks, I did not have the proper insurance to cover those damages. That was a huge hit for me to take at that time. Not only did it hurt me financially, but now I was in the middle of my summer rush, and I no longer had a worker. Oh, and let's not forget that I had to inform my always understanding young bride about this financial downfall. I got the same negative bullshit from my wife about how "this is what you get" when you work for yourself crap. It's funny that when things were going good in my business life, all I got was support and pride from my wife, but when something would go wrong, it was like I was the Antichrist in her life. One more of my theories, folks. When you are the person who is always putting your neck out on the line, when you are the one that people turn to in their times of need, when you are the one who takes chances to help others, then you are going to be the only one to take a beating when things go bad. It does not matter how good your intentions were or how much others have benefitted from your action; it just takes one step backward for certain people to point their fingers at you and turn on you. In my eyes, that is just total bullshit.

Once again, I took my licks like a man. I still had a business to run, and I needed my customers to be happy. The damage to my van was minimal, and I needed to find someone to replace Nick as soon as possible. I placed a help wanted sign on the outside of my van in hopes of finding a new employee. As luck would have it, I scored, or did I?

CHAPTER 38

While picking up supplies at a distributor's warehouse, I was approached by an older gentleman about my help wanted sign. This man was well into his sixties and the job inquiry was for his son. I spoke to the old man for about half an hour. He was a retired union construction worker that had a son that dreamed of being a rockstar. His son, John, played in a band on the weekends and needed a full-time job for his weekdays. The old man told me that his son had worked on swimming pools before and was currently looking to get back into the industry. I agreed to meet with John.

Now you will have to take my word on this. John was one big boy. He stood around 6" tall and weighed in at a good 240 pounds (all muscle). John had tattoos all over both of his arms and very long curly red hair. The first time that I saw John, I was honestly scared to death. You know the old saying, "Don't judge a book by its cover." Well, that is a very good rule to live by. After an hour-long conversation with John, I realized that he was a pussycat. For real, this rock-and-roll wannabe was about as nice of a guy that I have ever met. I hired him on the spot.

I took the time to run the cleaning route with him so that he could get familiar with the stops. I also wanted to be there the first time John met each of my customers. I did not want these people freaking out when they saw him. I also decided to make John more "presentable" by having company shirts made. I figured that would help my customers identify the tattooed beast in their backyard.

John turned out to be a godsend. He knew the business, he was nice to my customers, and for an entire summer, I did not receive one complaint about his work. The Lord sure does work in mysterious ways. Setting aside the major disaster that Nick had created, the summer of 1994 turned out to be a good one. John and I winterized all of my customers' pools at the end of the summer. I gave him a sweet-ass bonus in his final paycheck, and John told me he would be back the following summer. I took the time to go see John and his band perform that winter. All I will say is that he really needed the pool job. There would be no recording contract for him anytime in the future. Sorry, John.

My winter was uneventful, which I guess is a good thing. I did go back to the oil company and drove all winter. Denise was still at her job with the publishing company, and I would say that we appeared to be on cruise control. Foley Pools had proven itself to be sustainable and profitable, even in the face of disaster. The best part was that I really enjoyed what I was doing.

CHAPTER 39

The summer of 1995 rolled on in, and sure enough, John returned for work. Foley Pools had made a name for itself and continued to grow, so I started putting plans on the drawing board for a second cleaning route.

Now Denise and I were doing fine together even though we still had the same issues. Denise just did not have a need for an overly intimate relationship, but I did. Our solution for our troubles, one that many couples use to try and solve marital issues, we decided to try and have a baby. I know. That makes absolutely no sense. But hey, in order to have a baby, we had to have sex, and lots of it. Right? Wrong.

As the great George Costanza proclaimed in the series *Seinfeld*, "My boys came swim, my boys came swim." Denise became pregnant the very first time we tried. It was July of 1995, and my wife was officially pregnant. I was going to be a father. Folks, I always wanted to be a father. I dreamed of one day handing over the reins of whatever company I had grown to my child or children. This was a very exciting time for me and Denise. It's funny how things work out sometimes. My sister Paula found out the month before that she was also pregnant. Denise and Paula spent a lot of time together that year planning for our new arrivals. I turned our second bedroom into a nursery. Denise and I did most of the work on our own. Neither of us had obviously ever been through this before, so we were both nervous nellies for the next nine months.

March 7, 1996—it was the middle of the night, and we were in the middle of a late-season ice storm. It was simply a miserable night as far as weather was concerned, and as luck would have it, Denise's water broke. We had practiced for months on what we were going to do when this day arrived, but in one quick moment, I forgot everything, including my own name. I ran around the house like an idiot for a good ten minutes. It was at this time that Denise's mother had one of her few shining moments. She calmed us both and got us on our way. I drove Denise to the hospital in the middle of that treacherous storm, and after almost twenty hours of labor, we welcomed Thomas Joseph Foley IV into the world. I was a father, and I had a son, a beautiful and healthy son. I was the proudest parent that God had ever put on the face of this earth. I prayed that night and thanked God. It was at this moment that I also spoke out loud to my mother. "I wish you were here, Mom. I wish you were here to see your grandson." Life now had a whole new meaning to me. I had a family to provide for, and that is what life is really all about, folks. Here's a brief side note: Denise made it through labor just fine.

CHAPTER 40

I adapted to being a father like a true professional. I could not spend enough time with my son. I insisted on taking most of the middle-of-the-night feedings, and Denise definitely had no problem with that. When I was not working, I was on the floor playing and laughing with little Thomas. I even got used to changing those stinky-ass diapers. The three of us were bonding like one happy little family. Denise took a few months of maternity leave from work, and when it was time for her to return to work, Thomas was able to go into a day-care center right inside of Denise's building. Things just seemed to be falling into place.

Denise and I started to get the feeling that we were wearing out our welcome at her mother's house. The hints were getting more and more obvious, and we had been there for several years already. Thomas did some serious crying at night, and that seemed to be an issue for Denise's mother and husband. Sorry, that's what babies do, Grandma (translation: JACKASS). Anyway, Denise and I were adults. We were a family of three now, and it was time to start planning for a place of our own.

For those of you who do not live in Long Island, let me give you some insight on the housing market. It is brutal. There is some new construction on the island, but that tends to be for people that are very wealthy. Most homes being sold are anywhere from twenty to eighty years old, and there are a lot of fixer-uppers available for the handy home buyer. At this point in time, I am neither wealthy, nor have I ever been handy. On top of this, the property taxes in Long Island are just ridiculous. Denise and I were making good money at the time, but when it came to finding a home that would be affordable, we hit a brick wall. Denise and I had both been to Florida to visit friends and family. My father lived by himself in Palm City, my oldest sister Lisa and her family now lived in a small town outside of Fort Lauderdale called Weston, and Denise's sister, Laura, and her husband also moved to Weston. Denise's father, brother, aunt, and uncle all lived in the Tampa/St. Petersburg area, and Denise had friends from college that lived in Boca Raton. We were always amazed at how affordable housing in South Florida was. I mean, at the time, a young couple could build a brand-new three-bedroom, two-bathroom home for under $150,000 with property taxes of less than $1,000 per year—a brand-new home for a quarter of the price of a Long Island fixer-upper. I decided to bounce the idea off Denise to see if she would consider leaving New York and moving to South Florida. I was surprised by her openness to the idea.

There was a lot to think about if we were going to make this big move. What about my business? What about employment in Florida? What about leaving my sister Paula and all my close friends? And where in Florida would we move to?

Listen, life hits us with some tough decisions. There are major forks in the road of life, and the best you can do is to make educated decisions with the information in front of you. There are many uncertainties in life, and sometimes you have to take a risk. Denise and I did just that. We sat down, we evaluated our current position in life, and we decided that Florida was the right place for the Foley clan to continue on its journey.

Planning the move to Florida was not as difficult as I thought it would be. I sat down with my sister Paula, and I explained to her my intentions. Paula was sad, but she understood my reasons for leaving. Paula was now a proud mother of a beautiful daughter named Erica. Her in-laws had recently retired to Florida and were able to sell Paula and her husband their house and business at affordable terms. Paula would be fine. My friends also understood why I was leaving, but that did not make it any easier for us to say goodbye. We had been through so much together, and they were all brothers in my eyes.

Denise did have one requirement for our move to Florida. She needed to be close to her sister. No problem there. Denise's sister and my sister Lisa sent us package after package of housing opportunities for Weston, Florida. I decided to put my business up for sale immediately since the summer would be the best time to sell that type of business. Our plans included using the proceeds of the business sale for a down payment on a Florida home. I had planned on getting back into the swimming pool business after our move, but Denise's employment situation wound out to be a home run. Denise was assigned an area in Northern California. So I started thinking, *Why does she need to be in an office in New York, when her sales rep and territory are in California?* I told Denise that instead of just quitting, she should inform her company about her intentions to move and ask them if she could continue her job from a home office. I mean, all she needed was a phone, a fax machine, and a computer.

I put a short presentation together for Denise to give to her company. The presentation included things like her past work reviews that showed that Denise was a valued employee and that she was capable of working in an unsupervised environment. I included a few articles from major US companies that had already implemented work-from-home programs that saved them millions, and I included a short list of materials and equipment that Denise would need to get a home office started. Denise made the pitch to her company, and they loved it. Her company agreed to provide her with all the necessary office equipment. They would pay for a dedicated business phone line to be installed where we moved to, and they agreed to keep Denise at her current New York-level salary and benefits package. What a huge score that was. You see, you just never know what people are willing to do unless you ask. Now it was up to me. I needed to sell my business, and I needed to sell it for a good price.

I decided that the right thing to do first was to call John and inform him of my intentions to sell the company. John had been a valuable employee, and I did not want him to find out that I was selling the company from anyone else but me. I knew that John needed the job, and I needed John to work the cleaning route until I found a buyer. When I told him, I could see the disappointment in his eyes, not because he needed the job but because he enjoyed working and helping me build the business. I assured John that I would try my hardest to convince the buyer to keep him on board. I could tell that he appreciated that. I did the right thing by John, and it felt good. He was not in the dark about my intentions, and he decided to continue to work his ass off for me.

A few days after having my talk with John, I received a call from John's father. He requested to meet with me for lunch. He told me that it was important, so I agreed to meet with him. That meeting wound up to be the answer to my final moving need. John's father wanted to buy my pool business. I could not believe what I was hearing. Like I mentioned earlier, John's father was a retired union construction worker. What I did not know up until that point was that his father was no ordinary union man. Back in his day, John's father was a union big shot, and unions take care of their own when it comes time to retirement. John's dad told me that this was the first time in his life that he was able to not worry about his son. He told me how much John had changed since coming to work for me. His son was suddenly motivated and had a sense of direction in his life. His father did not want that to end for him, in fear that if John lost his job, then the days of rock-and-roll fantasies would return. It amazed me how much love this man had for his son. That is the type of father I saw myself being. It did not take long at all. I met with his father's accountant and lawyer. We hashed out a fair price and put a transition program on paper, and that was that. I received a multiple five-figure settlement at the beginning of the summer, I agreed to work the business with John and his father for the whole summer of 1996, and at the end of the summer, I received another multiple five-figure check. Foley Pools had been sold. Yes, I was sad to give my business up, but it served as a huge stepping stone for me and my family. The Foleys were ready to move to Florida.

CHAPTER 41

At the end of the summer, I decided to take a trip down to Weston in order to get a firsthand feel for the area and to start looking for a home. At that time, Weston was a small town that was booming with new construction. The town's one claim to fame was its superstar resident, former Miami Dolphins quarterback Dan Marino. Weston was being built up by a construction/management company called Arvida. The town was being billed as "upscale" with a family atmosphere. Arvida was offering preconstruction home prices ranging from the low $100 thousand mark all the way up to $10 million. I quickly realized that there were way too many housing options, and choosing a new home without Denise would be impossible. I found a nice apartment complex right in the heart of town, and I leased a three-bedroom two-bath apartment. It made all the sense in the world to rent a place; this way, Denise and I could take our time choosing a new home, and it would take almost a year to build the home once we made a choice.

The logistics of moving my family from New York to Florida was not that complex. It was decided that I would drive a U-Haul truck down to Florida with all our worldly possessions and tow Denise's car behind me. Denise and Thomas would fly down to Florida after I got our furniture and things moved in. I had sold my van and the beat-up old Dodge Charger with the business, so I decided to buy a car once we were in Florida. So off I went. It was November of 1996. I drove the moving truck nonstop to Florida, and with the help of family, I moved into the apartment. Denise and Thomas arrived in Florida two days later. The Foleys were now Floridians.

CHAPTER 42

It was a very strange feeling once we were all together in Weston. I had lived in New York for thirty-one years, and now I was in Florida. It was the middle of November, and I was wearing shorts and a T-shirt. I guessed that it was just going to take some adjusting until we felt like Florida was actually our home. For the first few months, it felt like we were on vacation. Although, Denise would disagree with that statement. She set up her home office and began to work immediately. I purchased a brand-new Ford Escort wagon. Yeah, I know I really went for it with that big purchase. LOL. Anyways, I was not sure about work yet, so I tried to be very budget-conscious. Denise and I would spend the weekends looking at new home developments, and I spent the weekdays feeling out the Florida swimming pool industry. I did not like what I found. Unlike New York, Florida pool companies were a dime a dozen. These companies cut one another's throats with ridiculously low prices and used unskilled illegal immigrants to do their cleaning work. At the time that I was looking, the average home was being charged no more than $30 per month for a full cleaning service. Up in New York, I was charging no less than $60 per week for the same service. Plus in Florida, there were no opening and closing pools, so again, there was much less revenue. What a nightmare. I needed to come up with something better than that. I am not a person that is capable of providing shitty service and doing the churn and burn with customers. That is not my idea of a growing business that I could one day pass over to my children.

Now a huge benefit of moving to Florida was the fact that I love to play golf. In New York, golf has a short season. It is expensive, and the courses are overcrowded. In Florida, I could play on a different course every day if I so chose to, and the courses were cheap and empty. Now don't get me wrong, there are some very exclusive golf courses in Florida that are costly to play at. Weston even had a country club, but the membership fees were way out of my league.

One day, I decided to play at a nearby course called the Bonaventure Country Club. It's a nice place, it has great Florida residence prices, and a nearby luxury hotel has a deal that allows its guests to play on the course at a discounted rate. While paying for my round at the pro shop, I met a guy by the name of Mark.

Mark just looked like a golfer. He was several years older than me, tanned from head to toe, and just had this "I am having a good time" aura about him. Mark asked if I wanted to join him since we were both playing alone. Why not? Okay, first of all, I was wrong. Mark was probably one of the world's worst golfers. He may have looked the part, but this guy was a walking train wreck out on the golf course. It didn't matter though. Mark was a talker, a schmoozer, just an all-around happy person.

As we worked our way around the course, Mark and I traded stories of who we were, where we were from, and what we wanted out of life. I found it incredibly easy to talk to this man. (No, he was not gay, not that there would be anything wrong with that if he was.) Mark was from California. He was in the process of moving his family to Weston, and he owned a company that built and sold photo booths. You know, like the ones that you find in a shopping mall or an arcade (four Polaroid pictures on a strip). Mark was in Florida that week because he was in the middle of moving his entire operation from California to Florida, but only a small handful of Mark's employees were making the move with him, so he came in advance to hire a new staff and to set up a new corporate facility. When he heard where I was from and that I was not employed yet, Mark asked me if I would be interested in interviewing for a job with his company. Sure, why not? You just never know. Mark offered to pick me up that same evening for an interview over dinner with him and his newly appointed vice president whose name was John. We had dinner at P. F. Chang's that evening, and I listened as Mark and John gave me a summary of where Photo Vend International Inc. (PVI) had been and where the company was heading in the future. Mark and John sounded like they had given the speech at least one hundred times. I mean, it just flowed off their tongues without effort. John was an ex-New Yorker who left his job with the Polaroid Corporation several months ago to work with Mark. Polaroid was the company that provided an exclusive bar-coded film for all of PVI's photo booths. These two guys were a real trip. They ordered food and wine like they were being sent to the electric chair the next day. I have never seen two guys in such shape eat so much food at one meal. I was just going with the flow. When we finally started to talk about me and the actual interview started, I was already half-shit-faced from the wine. They asked questions, and I blurted out answers. They laughed out loud, and I gave them each a few slaps on their shoulders. It was just a freaking funny situation. So dessert showed up, and Mark pulled an envelope out of the inside pocket of his sports coat, and he handed me the envelope.

> Mark: Listen, Tom, you seem to be all right in my book. After playing golf with you today, I could tell that you would fit right into my company. I prepared a job offer for you. It's in the envelope. This dinner isn't really an interview. It is more of a welcome aboard celebration.
> (John reached over and shook my hand.)
> John: Congrats, Tom, welcome aboard.
> Me: Okay, time-out here, boys. This is getting way too weird right now. I don't even know what I am interviewing for. I mean, no offense here, but I may not want your job.
> Mark: (looking totally confused) Why wouldn't you want the job?
> Me: (laughing) You guys are freaking me out.
> John: (laughing) Read the offer, moron.

Okay, I had known these two guys for less than a day. I played golf with one of them, got drunk at dinner with both of them, and now one of them just called me a moron. I love these guys. I decided to open the envelope and read the offer.

So I was reading the offer, and Mark and John started to mimic me.

> Mark: (in a child's voice) I may not want the job.
> John: (copying Mark's child voice) I don't know what you're talking about.

Both of these guys were just cracking each other up it was like a skit from a sitcom. I was finally able to read through the job offer, and I suddenly found myself to be surprisingly sober. I was being offered an unbelievable opportunity: director of operations for PVI, third in command with a salary that was larger than what I was making in New York. There were also added benefits like a car budget, a travel expense account, a company credit card, and the freedom to make operational decisions with minimal oversight. I was being asked to find a Florida home base for PVI and then make it operational; soup to nuts. I put the offer back in the envelope and placed it in my coat pocket. I sat there for a minute in silence.

> Mark: Hey, John, I think dumbass is on board.
> John: What do you say, Tom? Are you in or out?
> (I called our waiter over to the table.)
> Me: We will be needing a few rounds of tequila shots. Feel free to bring some for yourself.
> Mark: You see, John, that's what I'm talking about right there. That's the guy that I was planning on.

We did several rounds of shots that night, and yes, the waiter joined us for more than one. You see, I had a round of golf to clear my mind, and look at what it led me to. Just step back for a moment and think about what had to take place between my life and Mark's life to bring us together on that faithful day. It's just mind-boggling to me. When something is meant to be, then it is meant to be. So I was starting off 1997 with a new career and an old problem.

CHAPTER 43

It would appear to anyone on the outside looking in that Denise and I had it all going in the right direction. We were living in beautiful South Florida, we had good jobs making great money, our son Thomas was approaching his first birthday and was healthy and happy, and we started construction on a new home. So what was the problem? Well, folks, I still was having trouble getting Denise interested in a steady sexual relationship with me. Seriously, if we had sex once a month, that was a banner month in the Foley household. I just did not get it, and after a while, I got tired of the excuses. I was a dedicated father, and as far as I could tell, I was being a good husband to Denise. Denise was a great mother to Thomas and a good wife as far as taking care of our meals, laundry, cleaning, and providing financial support to the cause. But to be honest, I wanted a soulmate, a lover, a best friend, not a maid. So I convinced Denise to go to marriage counseling with me.

We found a marriage counselor right in our hometown. She had been practicing for over twenty years, and I had high hopes of solving our little problem. Listen, this meant a lot to me. I needed to know why my own wife was not interested in being intimate with me. The counseling lasted for two whole sessions. Denise did not like to open up to the counselor, and she did not like what the counselor was suggesting. The counselor suggested that perhaps there was a hormone issue with Denise, or perhaps the fact that Denise was abandoned as a child affected her ability to be intimate. Denise never gave the counseling an open, honest chance. She cried during the session and kept saying, "I guess that I am just a bad wife," over and over again. I assured Denise that she was not a bad wife and that I loved her very much. I tried to get her to continue the marriage counseling just so we could put this issue to rest once and for all. Denise would have no part in any additional sessions. She promised to be more aware of my needs and begged me to leave it at that. I felt horrible. I did not want Denise beating herself up over this. My intentions were to try and better our relationship. I decided to honor her wishes, and I stopped asking her to go to counseling. Denise did keep true to her word. I could see her making an effort to be more of a lover in my life, and that felt good. I don't know how the subject came up again, but out of nowhere, Denise and I decided that it was time to try and have a second child. I know what you're thinking—that was not the answer to our problems. But we were happy parents. We were both thirty-one years old, and we both wanted more than one child. If not now, then when? Once again, folks, bull's-eye on the first attempt. No shit, the very first attempt and Denise gets pregnant again; I could not have been happier. As the days went by, Denise and I grew more and more excited about our growing family. We started to send Thomas to a local day care so that he could interact with other children. It was at this day care that we met one of the nicest human beings that God had ever put on this earth. Her name was Susan. She was the woman assigned to care for Thomas at the day-care center. She was a mother of four, including twin teenage girls, and she was just the most good-hearted person that I had ever met.

Denise and I decided to hire Susan to watch Thomas on the weekends if we wanted to go out. Susan would often bring her daughters Shellie and Stacie with her to watch Thomas. They were good people, and I knew that they would be a big help once our second child was born.

CHAPTER 44

We finally got the word from the builder. Our new home was finished and ready for us to move into. It was a very exciting time for us—our first real home. The house was a four-bedroom, three-bathroom two-story model that was located inside of a gated community called the Ridges. The development was planned to hold several hundred single-family residences that surrounded a swimming pool complex. The pool area included a massive free-form pool with a small waterpark, a clubhouse for parties, basketball courts, and even a roller hockey rink. It was a real family atmosphere. Denise and I were settled into our new home and introduced ourselves to neighbors as new houses were completed.

One of the first people that I met was a guy by the name of Rob. Rob was originally from New Jersey. His wife was from Long Island, and they had a daughter the same age as Thomas. Rob was an investment portfolio manager for a company in Weston and was one of those guys that was always probing you for business. He was a nice enough guy, but he just could not stop trying to get me to invest money with his company. I was never big into financial planning. I was just not ready to start thinking of retiring yet. Anyway, that was Rob, and despite his constant sales pitch, we became friends.

As families started to pour into our new development, Denise and I decided to have a block party and get all the new people together for some fun. It was a great day. We barbecued, played sports in the street, had music playing, and drank beer. I met a guy named Chuck that day. He had purchased the home three doors down from ours. Chuck had a wife, two teenage boys, and he worked in management for our local sanitation department. Once again, Chuck was a nice enough guy, and we became friends. It seemed like the baby boom all over again. Everyone I knew had kids popping out. My sister Paula up in New York had her second child, a boy named Jonathan. My sister Lisa who now lived in our neighborhood had two kids, Marissa and Jeffery. Denise's sister Laura and her husband, Fidel, had a son named Antonio. And all the families in our neighborhood either had kids or had kids on the way. It seemed like a perfect place to live. Unfortunately for Denise and I, the dickhead arrived yet again: "All good things must come to an end."

CHAPTER 45

It was a very sad day for us. Denise had been having stomach cramps, and her doctor decided to do a sonogram and check on our unborn child. The news was not good. The doctor could not find a heartbeat for our child. Denise had suffered a miscarriage. I can't describe the emptiness that I felt. It just did not seem real. One moment we were preparing for a second child, and the next moment, that dream was over. I guess it was not meant to be at that time. I believe in God, and he is the one that decides when the time is right. The doctor scheduled Denise for a procedure the following week, and he told us that we could try again in a few months.

Denise was strong during this tough time. I don't know how she did it. I went to the hospital with her the next week, and I offered her all the emotional support that was humanly possible. A very strange event took place while I was in the waiting room of the hospital.

I was trying to keep my mind off what Denise was going through that day, and I decided to watch the local news for a little while. I could not believe what I was saying. The local investigative reporter was doing a story on sexual predators in South Florida, and up on the TV screen popped up a picture of a man that looked all too familiar. The man on the screen was my neighbor Chuck. I could not believe my eyes. Chuck was a three-time convicted child molester. That's right—three separate groups of children at two different middle schools had been sexually molested by this animal. I felt sick to my stomach. This man had been in my house, and he held my son in his arms. I was enraged to say the least. When Denise was finished in the hospital that day and I went to the recovery room to get her, she instantly knew something was wrong. Denise told me I looked worse than she did.

On our way home, I told Denise about Chuck, and I tried to assure her that everything was going to be all right, but the truth is that our perfect little life had just taken two hits. It is times like these that a person can judge themselves and see what they are made of. Some people brush their problems under a rug, and others choose to hit life's challenges head-on. I am definitely a head-on type a guy. Upon arriving home, it was obvious that the news was already spreading about Chuck. There were several police cars in front of Chuck's house, and a crowd of neighbors had gathered outside also. Chuck was going to come out and make a statement. I brought Denise inside to rest and went outside to join my fellow neighbors waiting for Chuck to come out and address the neighborhood. I wanted to knock his fucking teeth down his throat from the minute I saw him. Chuck was looking for sympathy and forgiveness. He claimed that "most" of what he was convicted of was a misunderstanding on the kids' part. He claimed he finally agreed to plead guilty to save his family further embarrassment and heartache. Ahhh, what a nice guy. I could not believe what I was hearing from my other neighbors. People were hugging him and telling him that the Lord forgives all that seek forgiveness and all this horseshit. I just lost it. I yelled to Chuck, and I threatened to kill him if he came near my family. I told the rest of the gathered crowd what sick fucking people they were. Yeah, I would say that the days of block parties were over for me. One of the police officers took hold of me and walked me back to my house. He insisted that I calm down, and I complied. I will never forget what he told me next. Now keep in mind, folks, this was a detective with a sex crime unit. This was no ordinary cop. The detective informed me that he dealt with Chuck in the past and that Chuck was a true predator. Chuck would strike again at some point in his life; he simply could not stop himself. I could not believe my ears. The law is the law, and Chuck had complied with the law since his last sexual attack. Then the detective looked me in the eyes.

> Detective: I can see that you are an emotional
> young man. I would protect my family the
> same way that you were trying to protect

yours, but don't do something stupid and
find yourself in jail instead of him. The law
is the law, and you cannot attack another
individual. With that being said, if you
ever find yourself in a situation and you do
attack him, make sure you drag him into
your house or at least onto your property.
You have a right to defend your home and
your family. Do you understand what I'm
telling you?

Me: Yes, I understand.

Detective: (smiling) Good, because I never told
you that. Stay cool.

I kept my cool that day, and Chuck kept his distance from me
and my family, but I still would never feel the same about the neighborhood. This was not an easy time in my life, and the good Lord
decided to throw one more wrench into my life just for kicks, I guess.
Denise's mother and husband, Lenny, decided to sell their house in
New York to move to Weston. Now I don't really blame God for that
one, but I can't believe that I just lost my 1,300-mile buffer. The
wicked witch and drunk were moving to our town. I decided the best
thing to do was to bury myself into my work.

CHAPTER 46

I had done one hell of a job setting up the new corporate headquarters for PVI. I mean, I really took the bull by the horns and attacked this one. I found a 20,000-square-foot facility and turned it into a beast of an operation. I had construction crews separate the building into specific departments: executive offices, customer service, technical support, sales, and billing. I purchased an entire phone system, a computer network, networked fax, and copy machines—you name it, right down to basic office supplies. After the facility was loaded and ready to be occupied, it was time to conduct interviews. Now on the technical side of the business, I was lucky enough to have one of the employees from California come to Florida and train me. By the time he was done with me, I could take apart and rebuild an entire photo booth in my sleep. John had already taken care of hiring a sales team. He hired over twenty people for the sales department; I became close friends with two of them. Their names were Jim and Andy, and they were true sales professionals. Either one of them could sell ice to Eskimos, but there was definitely a shady side to both of them. During business hours, John and I watched Jim and Andy like a pair of hawks. They wanted to earn huge commissions, so they were capable of saying just about anything to make a sale. At night, well, that was a different story. Jim, Andy, Mark, John, and I would go out and turn the town upside down. Dinners, drinks, bars, and strip clubs were enjoyed by all. Now Mark and I were the only married guys in the group. Mark could give a shit about his wife. I have never seen such a cheating playboy in my whole life. I hung out with the guys and definitely enjoyed myself, but when things got out of hand and the guys started paying for sex, I hit the road. I know it sounds funny, but I did. I was still committed to my wife, and I had a child that I loved very much.

Anyway, I got way off track here. I started to interview potential employees, and I decided to break the interviews down by department. Customer service was first. Now I am not a sexist guy, but I am definitely prone to hiring women. I don't think it's a sex thing. I just believe that women tend to be more responsible and easier to train. That's just my opinion. The very first group of women that I interviewed for customer service positions totally blew my mind. I had four interviews scheduled at thirty-minute intervals, yet all four women showed up together. As it turned out, they not only all knew one another, but they were two pairs of a very openly gay woman. Picture two pairs of women entering a conference room holding hands. I thought John and Mark had played a prank on me, but no, they were here to apply for jobs. I could hardly resist. I had to ask.

> Me: Are you women together?
> Lesbians: Yes.
> Me: What's with the hand-holding?
> Lesbians: I am dating her / And I am dating her.
> Me: Sorry, you guys just caught me off guard.
> Lesbian: Is this a problem for you?
> Me: No, I love lesbians.

What a stupid thing to say. Thank God they all laughed. They were young women, not overly attractive but funny as shit. I did not read one of their résumés. I had such a good time talking to them that I hired all four of them. The lesbians were on board. When I told Mark and John about the lesbians, they did not believe me. After I finally convinced them that I was serious, they started to act like two little schoolboys. Guys are funny when it comes to lesbians. We all think that at any given time, lesbians will just start having sex with each other no matter where they are. I am pretty sure that is why I hired them. Next was technical support and shipping and receiving. I hired a total of eight people to cover those departments. Ron and Kim S are worth telling you about.

Ron was a punk kid that was attending college at night. He needed a full-time job to cover his tuition. Ron was a computer genius. He ran several websites of his own that were aimed at fighting racism. Yes, Ron was going to help save the world. I will never forget Ron's interview because he showed up with his mother. When I say showed up with his mother, I mean she came into the interview room with him to ask questions. How messed up was that? That was a first for me. It's not easy to ask somebody's mother to please leave the interview. I mean, that is not something that they train you for in college now, is it? Ron definitely knew his technical computer shit, so I hired him, but I did not hire his mother. I believe she understood why. Ron's mother did give me a hug and kiss on the cheek; I promised her that I would watch over him and make sure that he ate his lunch. As weird as that interview was, Ron's mother was a good woman that simply cared about her only son; it was nice to see.

Kim S also applied for a position in technical support. Kim was my age and had a real tomboyish look and attitude. Although Kim had no experience in technical support, I got a really good feeling about her abilities to learn quickly and her actual need for a job. I hired Kim, and she quickly became one of my favorite employees. For a long time, the employees at PVI were convinced that Kim S and I were having an affair. Kim and I spent a lot of time hanging around each other at work, talking and joking, and yes, I did give Kim some favorable treatment. The truth of the matter is that I was married, Kim was married, and nothing sexual ever took place between the two of us. I have another theory on life, my friends. I don't believe that men and woman can just be friends. I know that sounds ridiculous, but my feeling is that at some given time, with the right circumstances, a man and woman will always test out the next level of a relationship. It's just human nature. I would have done the same with Kim, that I guarantee you. I am being honest here. But to prevent that from happening, I simply did not interact with her anywhere outside of work. Work was a safe zone, end of story. You doubters out there can lie to yourselves all you want, but this "he or she is just a friend" is absolute bullshit.

CHAPTER 47

At any given time, I would say that PVI employed between thirty and thirty-five workers. As 1998 rolled around, PVI decided to manufacture a new-style photo booth called the Sticker Club. The Sticker Club was a stand-up photo booth that took a person's picture and then allowed the photographed person to place a vanity border around their face. The picture with the border would be printed on sixteen individual stickers. This type of sticker photo booth was already a huge success in China and Japan, and PVI wanted to introduce this to the United States. To me, this seemed like a perfect second product for PVI to promote.

Now I will tell you, I originally took the job at PVI because of Mark and John and the great salary and benefits package I was offered. Once on board with PVI, I liked the company even more because they had a great business model. PVI would mass-produce photo booths at a very low-cost structure. They would then sell the photo booths at trade shows to arcade owners, vending route owners, malls, and party planners. PVI did not make a killing with the initial sale of the photo booth; they made their money off film sales. All PVI photo booths used a barcoded film that was manufactured by the Polaroid Corporations, and PVI had exclusive rights to the film. Basically, as long as PVI kept the booths operating out in the field, they would have a growing lifetime residual income. It was a great business model.

CHAPTER 48

In the first quarter of 1998, I started to notice changes at PVI, and I did not like what I was seeing. I was responsible for maintaining an inventory of Polaroid film at PVI, and I worked with a fairly tight budget. Out of nowhere, I found my orders being ignored or changed. I would order one hundred cases of film, and Polaroid would send me a tractor trailer filled with maybe one thousand cases of it. I also noticed that the payment terms on the bills of lading had changed from net ninety days to "upon request." In other words, PVI no longer had to pay for its film purchases within a ninety-day period. They now had no payment time frame attached to the order. The problem was that this type of film has a shelf life stamped right on the package just like a carton of milk does in a supermarket. The shelf life for this film was usually six months. Why the hell were we getting all this film, and what the hell were we going to do with all of it?

I voiced my concerns to John and Mark during a Sticker Club production meeting, and I did not like what I heard. John informed me that Polaroid was not doing well as a company, and they were quickly losing market share to companies like Sony. Some of John's old Polaroid friends had contacted him and offered him a "win-win situation." Polaroid would ship PVI large quantities of film toward the end of each quarter in order to boost their sales numbers, and in return, PVI would receive a discounted price and could pay for the film as they sold it. It was an honor system plan. Now John and Mark decided that this would be a great way to pay for the Sticker Club's manufacturing costs. They would sell the film to photo booth owners on a COD (cash on delivery) basis at a discounted price and use that money to pay for Sticker Club's production costs. Basically, they just took their whole business model and threw it down the drain.

PVI survived on the profit from the film sales, and now they just cut that revenue stream in half. On top of that, they were going to use that film revenue to pay for other manufacturing costs of another product instead of paying for the film. How in the hell were they going to pay for the film? I pleaded with them to reconsider what they were doing, but my pleas fell on deaf ears.

The next massive change came to light at our first Sticker Club sales meeting. The meeting included me, Mark, John, Jim, and Andy. The marketing presentation that I listened to just totally blew my mind. Now before PVI, Jim and Andy had owned a business opportunity company together that was shut down by the Florida attorney general's office due to massive customer complaints. That should give you an idea of how hard Jim and Andy were willing to push the envelope in order to get sales. As a general business model, business opportunity companies make all their profits off the initial sale of their products because the chance of the purchaser actually making money with their products are slim to none. Let me give you an example of how most of these companies operate. Okay, so Jim and Andy were selling bulk candy vending machines (like gumball machines). The machine would cost the company $40 to purchase. Jim and Andy would sell the machines in packages of, let's say, twenty machines with locations to place the machines in for $10,000 ($500 per machine). Jim and Andy would then send the customer his or her twenty machines directly to their house and advise their new customer that a "professional locator" was contracted to place their machines in "profitable locations." The customer was also sent back $1,200 to pay the location company. This would ensure the "fastest" placement of the machines into the marketplace. The customer would receive his machines at his home and signed for then as being received. What the customer did not realize was that by signing for the machines and accepting the $1,200 to pay the "professional locator" themselves, Jim and Andy had just cut themselves out of the loop and no longer had any responsibility to the customer. Jim and Andy would make around $7,400 and could move on to the next sucker. The real deceit takes place during the sales process. Potential customers are fed more bullshit than you can imagine. The company gives potential customers "references" of people that supposedly owned these products; their references were fake, of course. The customer talks to the locating professionals who are also on Jim and Andy's payroll. Everything seems great to the potential buyer until it comes time to make money. The locating companies do call the new machine owners, and they request their locating fees upfront. Sometimes they locate the machines, and sometimes they don't. Regardless, the machine owner usually makes absolute shit from the machines. At the price that they paid for the equipment, it would take a lifetime or longer to recoup their investment. After company complaints build up, the company simply closes their doors and opens up under another name. It is just a disgusting thing to do to another human being. So what does this all have to do with PVI? Well, PVI decided that they were going to sell the Sticker Club as a business opportunity, but not to worry, this company was going to do it in a legitimate fashion. Now I am not in a position to call the company owner and its vice president liars. But I am in a position to question the company's change in business strategy. Sticker Club was supposed to be marketed like the Polaroid photo booth, low pricing (around $2,000), and we would make our profits from proprietary sticker sales.

Now I was being told that the Sticker Club was going to be sold for no less than $10,000 each, and the stickers would be the same brand used in the Japanese models. In other words, a machine operator could buy stickers from any distributor worldwide. Once again, I voiced some serious opposition to this plan, but I was once again shot down. In my head, I had already started to prepare an exit strategy. This company was on a one-way ticket to bankruptcy.

CHAPTER 49

Now there were also some changes being made back on the home front. On March 28, 1998, my father at the ripe old age of sixty-seven decided to get married again. He had met a younger woman by the name of Sandy and decided it was time to remarry. I can tell you that this did not go over well with either of my sisters. I guess they saw it as my father trying to replace my mother, but I did not see it that way at all. Yes, it was going to be weird to see my father with another woman, but no one could ever replace my mom. Besides, it made me feel good that my father would not be alone during his golden years. I welcomed Sandy into our family with open arms.

The other big news in my personal life came in July of 1998. One shot, Tommy strikes again, Denise was pregnant gain. I was scared to death. I just did not want to go through what we had gone through last time, but that was not up to me now, was it? I did everything within my power to keep Denise comfortable and stress-free. I never told her about the problems that I saw coming with the company I was working at, and I suggested that she quit her job that was starting to stress her out. Denise did quit and was now a stay-at-home mom and a mother-to-be. One other positive thing in my life was my growing relationship with Denise's father. He was released from prison just before we moved to Florida, and we took turns visiting him in Tampa and him coming to stay with us. We enjoyed each other's company, and it made me feel good to see Denise and Richard together with my son Thomas. Richard was one proud grandpa.

CHAPTER 50

My fears about PVI unfortunately started coming true. As the Sticker Club was introduced as a business opportunity, customer complaints seemed to arrive immediately. Machines were not being located in a timely fashion, customers that had machines placed were not making money, Polaroid started asking for payment on advanced film sales, and Mark and John started to scramble for answers. Now I am not an "I told you so" type of person. I don't rub salt in people's wounds, but I did take offense when I was asked to take part of the solution that Mark and John came up with. It was a joke of a solution. In early 1999, Mark and John decided that we needed to cut operating costs. Their cuts came in the form of firing employees. Good, honest, hardworking employees were going to be let go, and as director of operations, I was assigned the ugly task.

As shitty as the situation was, I needed to be there. I had a growing family to provide for, and until I could produce something better, I would have to stick it out. Yes, I was working on an exit strategy.

The first to go were the lesbians; that was yet another silly decision on Mark's part because they were the lowest-paid employees, and they were the buffer between pissed-off customers and management, and yes, I would be assigned to take over the pissed-off customer complaints. Thanks again, guys. The next cuts came at the expense of technical support and shipping personnel. I let everyone go except for Ron and Kim. John reduced the sales operation to include just Jim and Andy. PVI was now a twenty-thousand-square-foot ghost town.

It would not seem possible, but things did get worse. Polaroid completely cut off PVI from purchasing film. I mean, go figure. You take huge shipments of film, you spend the money generated from that film, and you can't figure out why you were just cut off. Sadly, Mark turned out to be a fucking retard. I will say one more thing about the whole PVI mess. In my eyes, Polaroid was just as much to blame for this mess. They had no right to try and dump film on companies just to try and project false quarterly numbers. It would not be long before they got their share of misery.

CHAPTER 51

On March 23, 1999, the world became a better place. Jake Patrick Foley entered into my world. Jake was born a happy and healthy baby just like Thomas. I was once again a proud pop. I had two children, a wife, and a house. The home front was awesome, but I needed to get my employment situation straightened out.

In April 1999, I began to put my PVI exit strategy into action. I had put a lot of time and thought into this plan, and I knew that it included risks and hopefully great rewards. My plan was to go back to being an entrepreneur again. No, that would not go over big with Denise, but I had to do what I had to do. I formed a Florida corporation that I named Global Vending Inc. My plans for Global Vending were going to initially be twofold. I would not start operating my business until PVI either released me or went belly up. This was a last-resort exit plan, but it sure did appear that it would be open sooner rather than later. Anyway, my business plan was as follows: First, I would provide technical support, parts, and repairs for all existing PVI customers. Second, I would initiate a buyback program for any PVI customers that no longer wanted to operate their photo booths or Sticker Clubs. I would refurbish the used equipment and resell it to new customers. The new customers would be contracted to buy film or stickers from me. I had already come up with a solution to making the Sticker Club an exclusive product. I was sure that if people purchased Sticker Clubs from me, they would still shop around for cheaper stickers from Japanese distributors. So I planned on installing a computer into each Sticker Club with a counter that would count the number of vends per month. This way, I could send the customers stickers free of charge. Dial into their machine once a month through a program called PC anywhere and bill them for the number of stickers used each month. Not bad, huh? The Polaroid film would be tougher, I did not have time to try and work out a deal directly through Polaroid, nor did I think that they would want to do business with a former PVI employee. I decided to take a different approach.

Several months earlier, PVI's largest customer came to Florida to meet with Mark and John about the sudden film issues. His name was Carrol, and he owned a huge vending company out in Greenville, South Carolina. Now Carroll had been in photographic vending his entire life, and he already purchased other films directly from Polaroid. Carrol's only business with PVI was for the one specific photo booth film. I decided to approach Carroll and propose a partnership. My proposition was for Carroll to contact Polaroid and become their new photo booth film distributor. I would provide technical support and parts for the photo booth customers. I would give Carrol 50 percent of my net revenue each month, and he would give me 50 percent of the net film revenue each month. This plan would keep the photo booths from becoming dinosaurs. Plus both Carrol and I would make equal revenue. I put that proposal on paper and kept Carroll's phone number handy. As fate would have it, PVI went bankrupt before the year ended. I was out in the street, so it was time to spring Global Vending into action.

CHAPTER 52

I said my goodbyes to Kim S, Jim, and Andy, but I asked Ron if he would be interested in working for me once I was set up. Ron agreed, even without asking his mother. Ron and I had become pretty good friends at PVI, and I would need someone with his knowledge on the technical support side of the business. I made the phone call to Carroll. He actually remembered who I was, and at his request, I faxed him my partnership proposal. Within twenty-four hours, Carroll called me back, accepted my proposal, and even faxed me a copy of his new distributor agreement with Polaroid. Game on. I quickly found a small office/warehouse combination in nearby Sunrise, Florida. I set up a phone and fax number and sent all my information to Carroll. Things had to happen fairly quickly. We did not want the photo booth customers to think that once PVI was gone that the equipment was useless, or possibly pull the equipment from their locations all together. I sent Carroll a copy of PVI's customer list that somehow wound up in my briefcase. Go figure. Carroll was going to send out a letter to all the customers advising them where they could now get photo booth film, parts, and technical support. He even had magnets made up with our information for the customers to keep inside of their equipment. Carroll sent out the mailers and magnets, and we waited. Bang, our phones started to ring—mine for parts and support, and his for film purchases. It actually scared me at how smoothly things got started. I put Ron to work immediately, and folks, that was how Global Vending Inc. was born. I figured I would need a couple of months to settle in, and then I could plan for the future. I must admit, I patted myself on the back a few times that month.

It was amazing. My first month's check from Carroll was almost $10,000, and my first month's check to Carroll was for almost

$5,000. Now keep in mind that the customers had not had access to film or technical support for a few months, so I anticipated that this would not be a typical month. But hey, that was a hell of a jump start. I introduced the buyback program to the entire customer base, and that program took off also. The good news was that the only people looking to sell their booths back to me were the ones that had not purchased any film or parts. That meant that these booths were dead out in the field. I repurchased Polaroid photo booths for $100 to $500 per unit depending on what kind of shape they were in. Customers initially paid PVI $1,000 to $2,500 per unit. I would resell these units for $1,500 after I rebuilt them. The Sticker Clubs were a totally different animal. Customers initially paid a minimum of $10,000 for these units, and I was repurchasing them for $500 as is. Some of these units had never been used. It was unreal. Since I wanted to make most of my money off the film and sticker sales, I resold the Sticker Clubs for $2,500 each. While Ron stayed busy rebuilding booths and doing telephone technical support, I started to hit the road with Carroll. We decided to hit the trade-show circuit to promote our new venture, sell booths, and look for new ideas on how to grow in the industry. Carroll and I went to trade shows in Florida, Texas, Ohio, California, and of course Las Vegas. Folks, I fell in love with Las Vegas. I think it is one of the single greatest towns in America to visit. I highly recommend it. The amusement industry is constantly changing. I mean, as soon as a new arcade game came out, there were versions 2, 3, and 4 on the way. But not so much when it came to photo booths. Yes, there were new gimmicks that came out at every trade show we attended. But people still loved the old-style four-picture booth. We had no problem regenerating the refurbished booths back into the marketplace. Carroll and I quickly became the talk of the photo booth industry.

After I would return from each trade show, I started to notice more and more that Ron was getting overwhelmed. I mean, I left him with the phones to answer, booths to rebuild, parts needed to be shipped out, and orders needed to be placed for new inventory. I was asking a little too much from this kid, so I started to put plans on my blackboard for Global's next growth stage.

CHAPTER 53

I received a visit one day from PVI's old sales reps Jim and Andy. I had not seen or heard from them in months. Jim and Andy had bounced around to a few other sales organizations and had not found a solid opportunity, so they decided to try and get back into business for themselves again. This time would be different according to them. This time, they were going to produce what they promised to customers, or so that was their plan. They saw that I had an entire office that was not being used and asked me if they could rent the space from me. Why not? For now, it was unused space, and lowering my rent obligation could never be a bad thing. I must admit, I was also a little short on friends at the time, and these two were always good for a night out on the town. Carroll and I had become good friends, but he lived in South Carolina, so getting together usually took place on the road. Jim and Andy moved in and began to sell their candy vending machines again. Ron and I did our thing, and I promised Ron that help was on the way.

Things on the home front settled down especially after Denise realized just how much money Global Vending was making. I decided it was time to upgrade my life a little and enjoy the spoils of my early business victory. I traded in my Ford Escort wagon for an S 500 convertible Mercedes.

Yes, I realize that it is a ridiculous exchange, but things were good, and I always wanted a top-of-the-line sports car. Denise and I also realized that it was time to get out of our neighborhood and put some distance between Chuck and our family. Once again, I do not make small changes; it's just not in my personality. Denise and I picked out a four-thousand-square-foot home on a lake inside of Weston Hills Golf and Country Club. The house was a spec home and several months away from completion, so Denise and I were still able to customize it. One huge change that I made to the house was a huge custom-made pool that I designed with the builder. This pool was incredible. I placed lion heads along a retaining wall that were actually fountains. I built a children's play area right inside of the main pool area that required you to go into the pool and then make three steps up into the play area. The play area only had eighteen inches of water in it, but the pool itself was six feet at its deepest point. I also had a 10' × 10' hot tub built into and raised above the pool with the waterfall that ran from the hot tub into the main pool. I've been surrounded the pool with a three-thousand-square-foot cool deck patio. It was just an unbelievable site.

CHAPTER 54

Toward the end of the year 2000, the facility that I was in was no longer big enough for my needs. I needed to hire more help, I needed more office space, and I needed a lot more warehouse space. It was time to shit or get off the pot. I chose to take a big huge shit. Part of my growth plans called for the hiring of a sales force, so I decided to bounce the idea off Jim and Andy to see if they would be interested in working for me, on my terms, of course. Yes, these two were slick ricks, but I figured I could oversee their sales and stop problems before they started. Jim and Amy both signed on. I had no trouble finding a perfect building to rent. In fact, the new building belonged to the same landlord that was renting me my current space. The new location was exactly that, brand-new. I loved that. It was almost fifteen thousand square feet. It already had a main reception area, and the landlord agreed to build out office space according to my needs. When it was completed, I had roughly four thousand square feet of office/common space and almost eleven thousand square feet of warehouse space with two raised loading docks attached. Ron and I took care of wiring the place for a computer network, and I hired a company to come in and install an elaborate phone system. I also purchased brand-new office furniture with high black leather reclining seats at each desk. The place looked very high-tech when you walked in. Now that the facility itself was ready to be moved into, I needed to settle in and do some hiring. I decided to hire a receptionist first. I figured having one person to handle and route all initial calls would be a great help to Ron, me, and the sales force, and having a friendly face at the front door would not hurt our cause. I did one round of interviews, and I hired a home run by the name of Susan (no, not the same Susan that watched Thomas). Susan was an older woman

131

in her early fifties and was an absolute knockout; yes, that was part of the reason why I hired her. The other reason I hired her was because of her experience and personality. Susan was the lifetime secretary/receptionist. She was highly skilled, and her personality was off the charts. Next, I made a call to my old friend from PVI, Kim S. Kim was unemployed and thrilled to hear from me. I hired Kim S as a second technical support person and warehouse worker; it was great to have her back. That would have to be enough for now. I did not want my payroll to get out of control. The additions I made were quality hard workers. I knew we would be all right for a while with this staff. Jim and Andy went to work on leads that Carrol and I generated at our most recent trade show, Kim jumped into the mix with Ron, and Susan held down the front office. Things progressed nicely.

It seemed that as soon as moving day was finished with the new office, it was time to move into our new home. That was one exciting day. Denise stayed busy with the movers and kept tabs on the kids. I enjoyed just watching all the activity and energy that the move seemed to have pumped into my family. As I looked around at Denise; Thomas; Jake; Denise's sister Laura and her husband; my sister Lisa and her husband, Burt; and even Denise's mother and husband, Lenny, I only saw smiles. It was as if everyone knew that something special was beginning to happen. I did not have a lot of time to celebrate our new home. I had a growing business to attend to; I had a monster to unleash.

CHAPTER 55

Unfortunately, the good times did not roll for long. Yes, you guessed it, folks. Cue the dickhead: "All good things must come to an end." Aren't you just getting sick of that shit? I surely was. You see, when the shit hits Tom Foley's fan, it sometimes hits on more than one blade. My life was about to get messy. First things first, trouble hit me on the home front. No, it was not Denise and I having an argument about sex. This time, it was the youngest man of the house, Jake. Jake was approaching two years old and was a very active little guy. He loved to pull himself up and to make daredevil attempts at walking and even seemed like he wanted to run; he was a real handful. One morning before leaving for work, I noticed something very scary about Jake. As he sat in his playpen, Jake would attempt to stand up and then fall right back down; this was not like him. I stood Jake up again, and I realized he was favoring his right leg. In fact, he would not put any weight on his left leg at all. I assumed that Jake had somehow twisted his leg while playing, but to play it safe, we took Jake to his doctor. The doctor took X-rays and saw something that he did not like. He scheduled a CAT scan for Jake the next day at the Children's Hospital. The CAT scan revealed that Jake had a bacterial infection on his right knee that was literally eating away at his leg. It scared the living hell out of Denise and me. The hospital recommended immediate surgery; I could not believe what I was hearing. Denise and I okayed the operation, and before we knew it, this poor little soul was prepped for surgery and then sedated. You could just see his eyes. Jake was afraid, and so were we. The operation lasted several hours, and thank the good Lord above, the doctors were able to remove the entire infection. I thank them all for all that they did for my son. Our pediatrician was told by the surgeon that had we not caught the infection when we did, Jake very easily could have lost his leg. How's that for a reality check? Folks, always follow your gut instincts and try never to hesitate in life. Procrastination can be devastating.

CHAPTER 56

So we got Jake home, and that little angel healed like a champion. Nobody said that being a parent would be easy. I returned back to work after missing only two days, and Susan, my new receptionist, handed me mail and messages that needed to be returned. I noticed several were from Carroll, and they were marked ASAP. I called Carrol first and spent a few minutes on small talk about Jake and his recovery. Carrol was very sympathetic, and you could tell that he really cared about my family. I cut to the chase and asked Carroll what I could do to help, and that was when he laid it on me now. Carrol had a soft-spoken Southern drawl when he spoke, and everything always sounded better when Carrol said it. Unfortunately, there was no sugarcoating this nightmare. He informed me that his sales rep at Polaroid had contacted him with bad news. Polaroid was in deep financial trouble; bankruptcy was being considered and a very likely scenario. On top of that, the film that Polaroid was producing for our photo booth was being discontinued as part of their budget cuts. Like it or not, within a year, the photo booth film would be gone. You have got to be fucking kidding me!

I ran options through my rattled brain, trying to solve this devastating development. I convinced Carroll to contact higher-ups at Polaroid and possibly making the film ourselves. The executives at Polaroid were all for it. In fact, they asked Carroll and me to come to Boston and negotiate a price for the machine that produced our film. Now let me just interject something here before I continue. The executives at Polaroid were a bunch of fucking assholes. I mean, they knew the size of business that Carroll and I ran; they sold us the film. So what am I talking about? Well, Carroll and I flew up to Boston to meet these retards, see the equipment, and talk about pricing and moving the equipment to Florida or South Carolina. Here I am before I left for Boston with a tape measure and notepad figuring out just how much extra space I had in my warehouse. Carrol did the same with his warehouse. Upon arriving in Boston, we were escorted to one of Polaroid's production buildings, and there it was, our film machine. The fucking machine covered two full city blocks, it weighed several hundred tons, and Polaroid estimated the machine itself would be sold for $30–50 million. I looked at the sketch that I made of my warehouse and showed it to Carrol; in return, he showed me his. I swear we stood there and just started to laugh hysterically. I could not catch my breath at one time. "Carrol, we are going to need a bigger boat." That almost made Carroll piss his pants. What a waste of time and money that trip was, but what a great laugh we had for many years to come.

With all laughing aside, this was not a funny situation. My company revolved around that film revenue. I needed to refocus and find a new direction. I decided to hold a company meeting and see what my crew could come up with. Hey, you never know where the next great idea will come from. I saw a few concerned faces at that meeting. I guess I was not hiding the seriousness of the situation very well. Look, we had some time to deal with this, but I am just not one of those people that has a lot of patience with uncertainties, especially with business. For business, I plan, then adjust. Then I plan some more. Every successful business has a short medium- and long-term plan. My medium- and long-term plan had just been shot to hell. My employees promised to put some thought into our dilemma. I did not expect much, but at least I was keeping my employees informed. A few days after my big think tank meeting, I was approached by one of the sales guys, Jim. Jim handed me some literature on a new-style ATM machine and thought it would be worth looking into for our company. The ATM machine that Jim presented to me was called a scrip ATM. The difference between a scrip ATM and a normal bank-style ATM is that a scrip ATM does not dispense cash; instead, it dispenses a receipt that the user brings to a location cash register and receives his cash. I didn't know shit about ATM machines. I was not even aware that individuals could own ATM machines. I thanked

Jim and told him that I would do some research. Now I have to tell you, the more I thought about the idea, the more I liked it. I mean, everyone uses ATM machines. Maybe it could be the next-generation machine for Global Vending.

CHAPTER 57

I spent the first few months of 2001 researching the ATM industry. The more I researched, the more that I fell in love with the industry. I looked at scrip versus cash machines, how transactions were processed, the average cost of each machine, the average usage of a typical ATM machine, the best place to put an ATM machine, and industry trends from the past fifty years. One thing became very clear: the number of transactions that ATMs produced increased every year exponentially, and the owners of these machines were cleaning up. I decided to change Global Vending's business plan to revolve around the operation of ATMs.

Now don't get me wrong. I was still making great money from the photo booth business, and I would ride that out until the end. My plan was to slowly inject ATMs into Global Vending's revenue arsenal.

First things first, the product. I needed to decide which brand ATM machine we were going to operate. My research revealed that Triton Industries located in Mississippi was the largest manufacturer of scrip ATM machines in the country. Triton's products had great industry reviews, so I decided that it would be my initial ATM brand. After a few phone calls, I discovered that my initial purchase needed to be made through one of Triton's authorized distributors. There was a rather in-depth process to becoming an authorized distributor for Triton. But I would visit that animal at a later date. Triton provided me with a list of authorized distributors, and I began my search. After some serious long hours in front of my computer, I decided to contact a company located in Las Vegas named ATM Merchant Services (ATMMS). ATMMS was one of Triton's largest distributors, but what I liked about ATMMS was that they were also a national processing company that offered one-stop shopping. In other words, I could buy my equipment there, have it programmed to operate there, and ATMMS could handle the processing of my ATM's daily transactions once they were placed in locations. Every ATM machine that any of you have ever used is hooked up with the banking networks through processing companies. Without these companies integrating with the banking networks, your ATM card would be denied every time you try to use the machine. The processing company also sets up the electronics software that divides up the ATM surcharges so that the owners of the machines gets paid for every transaction. As you probably have experienced, when a person uses an ATM machine that does not belong to his bank, that person is usually charged a fee. This fee is known as a surcharge. The owner/operator of each specific ATM machine decides how that surcharge will be and if the surcharge will be divided up with a location. For example, let's say a machine charges a $2 surcharge. The ATM owner may have promised the location that houses the machine $0.50 of that fee, with the machine owner getting the remaining $1.50. These surcharges are collected every time someone uses the machine, but the fees are paid out to ATM owners on a monthly basis. Processing companies have software that tracks this monthly activity and then settles each account at the end of every month.

ATMMS also offered operators like me free online tracking of all machines that I placed in the field. That means that at any given time during the day, I could log on to the website of ATMMS, enter my specific login information, and I could see how many times each of my machines had been used that day. I just like the overall package that I was being offered. I set up an appointment to meet with the owner of ATMMS, whose name was Bart. I could tell that he thought I was completely off my rockers when I discussed how many machines I wanted to operate. Why? Doesn't everyone want to place ten thousand machines in the marketplace over the next five years? Anyway, I flew out to Las Vegas and met with Bart. He was truly one of the nicest, most genuine individuals I have ever met. I felt very good about the decision to go with his company. Bart and I hashed out a multilevel purchasing and processing contract. The more I purchased and processed, the lower my machine prices would become. In other words, put up or shut up time, Mr. Ten Thousand Units. Bart was a realist; he consistently reminded me that I was missing one key piece of the ATM puzzle: where was I going to place these machines?

I said, "Uh, I'll have to get back to you on that one, sir."

That was of course a hell of a question that would require a lot of thought. For now, though, I needed to better understand my product. I wanted to know ATM machines as good as I knew photo booths. I needed to be able to rip apart and rebuild them with my eyes closed. I also needed to know what these machines were actually capable of doing and not doing. God, was I excited! Bart had provided me with a list of technical classes that Triton offered to ATM operators; I signed up for every class that made sense. I flew to Triton's headquarters in Mississippi and attended tech classes on several different occasions. I learned how to repair ATM machines, how to properly install them, how to do preventative maintenance, and how to grow revenue through added machine software options. I also sent Ron and Kim to tech classes at Triton. I purchased a few machines and practiced taking them apart and putting them back together. I love knowing my products. It is the true key to any sale: never let your customer know more about your product or industry than you do.

CHAPTER 58

Although I envisioned Global Vending Inc. as an operator of ATM machines, I did have to develop a marketing plan so that Jim and Andy would have something to sell. They needed a way to make a living also. I consider myself to be an extremely fair person, and I knew that without Jim, the idea of ATM machines would not have been on the blackboard. I owed him. Besides my owing Jim, I figured that my profits generated from actually selling machines to the public would help me finance additional machine purchases for Global to operate. As it stood, I had enough money set aside for my first twenty-five ATM machines. Yes, I had a shitload on my plate at this time. I could no longer avoid the last piece of the ATM puzzle. I needed to figure out where I was going to place the machines. I racked my brain, I bounced the question off all my employees and even family members, and I received very few legitimate suggestions.

What makes a good ATM location? Well, you need a place with a lot of foot traffic (at least five hundred people per day). You would prefer locations that did not accept credit cards as a form of payment, and of course, you needed to find locations that did not already have an ATM machine on-site. It started to seem impossible. These things were everywhere. Perhaps that was why Bart was laughing at me. Anyway, I decided to try a new approach. I placed a large marker board in my office, and I started to write down every place I went through an entire week. I listed the location, why I went there, and whether an ATM machine was available at that location. My hopes were to uncover an overlooked ATM market. Folks, sometimes I amaze myself. I mean, I am one of those people I can truly look outside of the box to solve a problem. Sure enough, there it was: my golden goose had presented itself. As I analyzed my week's worth of activity, I saw the answer: fast-food restaurants! I had lunch that week at three different fast-food restaurants, and not one of them had an ATM machine, not one of them accepted credit cards, and all of them were packed with customers. He shoots, he scores! Remember, folks, this was 2001. Fast-food restaurants were different back then. It was unheard of to see a credit card machine at a fast-food location. Cash was king. Well, my dream locations have been identified. Now what?

Let me tell you how excited I was at this very moment; I grabbed the picture of the Triton ATM machine, hopped in my car, and drove to my local McDonald's. I had no sales pitch planned, no idea what to say, but I had to bounce this idea off one location and see what kind of initial reaction I would get. I got to McDonald's, ran into the store, and insisted on speaking to a manager. Within minutes, I was face-to-face with Mandy, one of McDonald's finest managers. I started to explain my reason for the visit, and Mandy quickly turned from Sweet Mandy into You Have to Be Shitting Me Mandy. Okay, readers, fast-food restaurant rule number 1 is do not try a sales presentation during the lunchtime rush. Big fucking mistake. I looked at my surroundings and realized that the place was packed, employees were scrambling to fill orders, alarms were sounding on deep fryers, and like an idiot, I was trying to pitch ATM machines to this poor overworked Mandy. Sorry, sweetheart, my bad. I apologized to Mandy, who was nice enough to point me in the right direction. Mandy informed me that most of the McDonald's were not individually owned; instead, they were part of a group of stores that were managed by a corporation. Mandy gave me a business card for the corporation that owned her location, and I was sent on my way. The least I could have done was buy lunch there, but no, I just walked out with my new information. Oh, well.

Okay, so now I had some direction. I put some computer hours in, and I found that some McDonald's locations were actually owned by corporate McDonald's, while others were owned as franchises like Mandy had informed me. I found this to be true about almost every fast-food chain being operated in America. I really needed to organize a plan of attack for this beast. I mean, how do you approach every fast-food restaurant in America with a new product? Here's the answer: very slowly.

I decided that while I was putting together my attack on the fast-food industry that I would run a few small sales ads in nation-wide newspapers and see if the general public had any interest in owning ATM machines. My first few ads ran in the *USA Today* and the *Wall Street Journal*, and they were as simple as could be:

OWN ATM MACHINES
TURN KEY OPERATION
MINIMUM INVESTMENT $17,995.00
Call !@# #$% !&*(

You get the idea. The goal was to see if there was a general inter-est. I have nothing to offer for sale yet, but at least we could build up some qualified leads. Let's just see what happens.

CHAPTER 59

The business gods must have been looking after me because the few small ads that I ran brought instant results, and I mean instant results. Jim and Andy started to field calls from prospective ATM customers, and you could just feel the excitement in the air. We had hit on something very special here. I would estimate that in the first week of advertising, we received well over one hundred qualified leads; that was one hundred people that answered our sales ad, were seriously looking to invest in an opportunity, and had the money to do it. I had never seen anything like it, and of course, I had nothing to sell yet.

Besides the calls from prospective customers, sales ads tend to bring in calls from other companies that are trying to sell you their products and services. Those calls were passed along to me. As I flicked through a pile of messages from other companies, one caught my eye quickly. The message was from a woman in Alabama named Kim W. Yes, now you know why I have been using the name Kim S instead of just Kim. Anyway, Kim W's message was to please call her if we needed locations for our ATM machines. HELLO? I called Kim W immediately. The first thing that struck me about Kim W during our phone conversation was her Southern drawl. It was like talking to a female Carroll except that Kim's voice was much sweeter. She advised me that she was in the business selling credit card processing to retail locations across the country. She told me that from time to time, she came across location that were looking for ATM machines. Kim asked me if I would be interested in buying locations from her should she find any in the future. I agreed to buy any locations that met my foot traffic criteria and did not accept credit cards. Kim and I hashed out a per location price over the phone. I asked Kim to fax me a résumé with contact information, and in return, I faxed Kim a contract and a 1099 form to be filled out. I found our conversation to be captivating. This woman was obviously a trained sales pro because she had my attention throughout the entire call. We said our goodbyes, and I wished her luck on her pursuit. A few minutes later, I received her résumé, and much to my surprise, I noticed one of Kim's references. It was Bart, the owner of ATMMS. This was weird. What a small world we truly live in.

CHAPTER 60

So I called Bart to check up on Kim and see what he could tell me about her. Bart had nothing but good things to say about her. He informed me that she was a true performer and a professional saleswoman. That was very encouraging to hear.

A few days later, I received a call from Kim W. Now check this out. I never mentioned to her or anyone else about my idea to place ATM machines in fast-food restaurants. Kim was calling me to see if I would be interested in buying thirty locations in California that wanted ATM machines; these locations were all McDonald's. What?

Wait, it gets crazier. Kim then informed me that the locations were currently running scrip ATM machines with another operating company that was trying to raise cash in order to become a processing company. Come on now, folks. Fast-food restaurants with scrip ATM machines already installed? No, the machines were not Triton machines. In fact, they were a much smaller countertop model that I had seen during my research, but what the heck. When I told Kim that I was interested, she faxed me over transaction reports from the machines' first few months of operation; they were doing pretty darn good. Now a dealer's price for one of these units was around $300. This particular seller was looking for $1,500. Including the location and Kim's fees, that was $45,000 for the whole batch. The transaction surcharge was actually set on these machines for $1.50, and the location was contracted to receive $0.50 per transaction. Not bad. I asked Kim W to have the seller put together a contract for all thirty locations. Problem number 1 was that I only had $25,000 set aside for my first purchase. I wish I had this problem every day. Let's get busy. I returned to Jim and Andy, and they helped me create some sales literature that included pictures of the machines onsite, the transaction reports, industry statistics from the American Bankers Association, and a whole bunch of crap about global, you know, like, member of the Better Business Bureau, consumer affairs, and Dun & Bradstreet. I had already put together a pricing plan for the full-size ATM machines, and I figured I would stick with that pricing. After all, it was all about how much the machines would make, not what they looked like. My pricing was structured as follows:

> 1 machine: $7,995 with Global getting $0.20 per
> transaction for processing
> 3 machines: $17,995 with the same processing
> agreement
> 25 machines or more: $5,000 per machine

I had asked Jim and Andy to hit the phones to find a buyer for the thirty locations that we were about to own. Ladies and gentlemen, we sold those thirty locations in less than two weeks for an average price of $6,000, $180,000 in all.

I was blown away. People were sending us checks via UPS and FedEx ranging from $7,995 to as much as $25,000. Yes, there was some price negotiating involved, but very, very little. This thing was hot. The company that was selling the California locations was called Nationwide Cash Systems, and as it turned out, Kim W had originally been the person to secure the McDonald's locations for them. The entire sale and resale went off with very few problems. Global was now operating thirty ATM machines for six private investors. We had a gross profit of $135,000 and a $0.20 per transaction residual income. What a great start.

CHAPTER 61

I worked out the technical side with Ron and Kim S. We ordered a few of the countertop models like the ones located in California, and they were actually very easy to work on. I worked out an exchange program with the locations in case of a breakdown. Basically, I would overnight them a fully programmed unit with a return UPS receipt, the location would unplug the malfunctioning unit, plug in the new unit that I would send them, and use the UPS return receipt to send the bad unit back to us. Once we received a defective unit back at our location, we would simply troubleshoot it, rebuild it, and put it back into inventory. Nice and easy.

Now how do I repeat this whole chain of events 9,970 more times so I could have my 10,000 operating units? No problemo! I felt my answers lied within the mind of Kim W. She had already done what I was going to do, so why not get some help from her? I called Kim W and convinced her to visit us in Florida. I paid for Kim's entire trip, including her plane ticket, car rental, and hotel. Now Kim W was a married woman and a mother of three kids ranging from grade school to college freshman. I would say that Kim W was about eight to ten years my senior. That would put her at about forty-five years old in 2001. Kim arrived on a Monday morning, and my receptionist, Susan, escorted Kim back into my office. I believe that I made a total ass out of myself for the first five minutes or so of our meeting; Kim W was a true Southern belle, beautiful looks to match her sweet Southern voice. I mean blond hair, blue eyes, fit body in tight business attire that just caught me way off guard. I could tell she knew I was looking, and I could also tell that she was used to it. I managed to get my shit back in order, remembered that I was a married man, and proceeded with our meeting. Over the two days Kim W was in Florida, I went over my visions for Global Vending Inc. as an ATM operator and to show her that it was more than possible to accomplish. I showed her how we flipped the thirty locations that she had just brokered for us. She was blown away.

On Kim's last night in Florida, I decided to go for broke. No, I did not try and jump on her, you pigs. I decided to offer her a full-time job with Global Vending Inc. I knew it would have to be an offer that she could not refuse, but we needed her expertise. I presented Kim W with a job offer that I titled "Head of Business Development." The package I offered her included a six-figure guaranteed salary with possible performance bonuses, full company-paid medical benefits, and Global would pay to have Kim and her family moved from Alabama to Florida. I even offered to pay Kim's first year of rent in Florida so that she did not have to rush to sell her home in Alabama. Now that definitely caught Kim W way off guard. I could tell from her expression that she had never made money like that before. Kim W was in a position to accept the offer if she so chose to. Her husband was unemployed, and the summer was about to begin, so her kids would be finishing up the school year. Kim thanked me for the offer about one million times and asked for some time in order to talk to her husband. Being the patient, easygoing guy that I was, I gave her forty-eight hours to decide. What a sport.

I had my answer within twenty-four hours. Kim called me, all giddy and excited. Global Vending Inc. now had itself a business development officer. Within two weeks of Kim's Florida visit, she was settled into a South Florida apartment and ready to get to work. Meanwhile, Kim's family would make the move to Florida as soon as the school year ended.

CHAPTER 62

I spent many hours in the office with Kim W preparing our plan of attack on the fast-food industry: Oh, rule number 2 when dealing with the fast-food industry, "Never ever call it the fast-food industry." They are called quick-service restaurants. Kim advised me that there were multiple steps needed to sign on quick-service restaurants. First, you had to become a preferred vendor. This required submitting your company information to the corporation headquarters of McDonald's or Burger King or Yum Brands like Taco Bell, KFC, and Pizza Hut. Then if corporate decided that your product may be beneficial to their franchises, they would let you show your products at quick-service restaurant trade show or at company co-op meeting. Now a co-op meeting is when a group of regional restaurant owners get together to discuss general business, problems, new products, business development, and anything else that could help them as a group with a common cause. Co-op meetings were not easy to get invited to. Kim and I decided to put together literature for what I called the big 3 quick-service players: McDonald's, Burger King, and Yum Brands. Becoming a preferred vendor for those groups would be a great start. Now don't get all crazy if your favorite restaurant is not on that list. I would eventually get to others.

The funny thing was that I only placed my sales ads that one time, and a month later, my phones were still ringing with new leads. On top of that, the six customers that already purchased machines from us started to call, looking for more locations for themselves and friends and family. Listen, I shit you not, this thing was for real. I decided to rearrange my business plans and focus more on selling machines and operating them for private investors. Operating company-owned machines would have to wait. This plan of selling machines to private investors would require a larger staff, so off to the help wanted ads I went. I decided to hire an entire customer service crew and a small warehouse staff for shipping and receiving. I also decided to beef up my sales crew just a little. Customer service and warehouse positions filled quickly. I hired Denise's sister, Laura, to work in customer service along with a woman by the name of Nitae. Nitae was such a good person. A single mom who crammed her size 12 frame into size 6 clothes, she was a loyal hard worker with a bubbly personality. I love having her at Global. At the request of my sister Lisa, I hired my nephew Jeff to work in the warehouse. Jeff was in high school and needed a job to help pay for his car expenses. I didn't mind. Jeff was a good kid and a hard worker, so why not keep some of the money in the family. I also hired a friend of Nitae's, George, to work full-time in the warehouse. The place was filling up nicely.

CHAPTER 63

I want to put this on the record now. I treated every employee like family. I wanted my company to be a place where people wanted to work and like their jobs. I was flexible in every possible way. I overpaid every employee and provided them with full company-paid health benefits from United Healthcare. I have read many periodicals about tech companies that created an enjoyable work atmosphere for their employees, and the results were high morale, excellent work performance, and a very low turnover. That was what I was trying to do. I organized company nights out on the town, I brought lunch in for everyone several times a week, and I tried my hardest to develop a personal relationship with each employee. Let me give you some examples. Nitae was having trouble with after-school care for her son, so I would allow her to leave in the middle of the day, pick up her son, and bring him back to Global Vending. I even set up a desk and chair for him so he could do homework or color or whatever. The point was that this was a huge weight off her shoulders, and she showed her appreciation with great work ethic. Ron was still attending college at night, and to keep him motivated, I offered to pay for any classes that he finished with the B or higher—yes, tuition reimbursement. Kim S was my pet project; she really was having a tough life. Kim S was a victim of an abusive husband. I can't count how many times I held her bruised body, and she cried and described horrific beatings. Kim S had made me promise not to call the police, and I honored her wishes. It blew my mind that she was protecting this guy, but she loved him and felt he could change. Her situation got so bad one time that I secretly moved her and her children to a company-paid apartment so that she could not be found. Kim's husband did go for counseling and therapy, and when his doctor decided it was safe, I took him to Kim. Let me sidetrack for a moment. All of you guys that hit women are fucking scumbag cowards. Back to Global. Like I said, I wanted people to come to work not just because they had to but also because they wanted to. I encouraged new ideas and suggestions through open-forum meetings. I held an open forum every Friday afternoon in order to encourage my employees to show me how to build a better mousetrap. Anything, and I mean anything, could be discussed, and I will tell you one thing. It was working. Global was becoming more functional, more efficient, and morale was through the roof.

CHAPTER 64

One of the new ideas and improvements that came out of an open-forum meeting was a suggestion from Ron and technical support. Ron had made the observation on how many times we passed customer files from department to department, and many times, employees had to backtrack to see who and what had actually been done to help a customer. Ron suggested an awesome computer program called ACT. ACT is a program that allows users to form specific databases, enter information on specific accounts, and then share that information with anyone who is granted access to that database. I purchased ACT, and Ron installed it on our server. This was how I made it work: I had Ron set up a separate database for photo booth owners, Sticker Club owners, ATM owners, and ATM locations. Now all customer information must be entered into ACT manually the first time, that is a little time-consuming but worth it. Once everyone's basic information was entered, I had our phone system integrated to be able to work with ACT. The uses were unlimited. For example, say "Mr. Jones" called with a photo booth problem. Susan, the receptionist, would transfer the call back to technical support. Before Ron and Kim even picked up the phone, the customers' information would show up on their computer screen. The tech would then take the call. Let's say that it was determined that the customer needed a part, the tech would enter a work order in to ACT, and ACT would route that order to our warehouse. The order would show up on the warehouse computer, the warehouse worker would confirm with ACT that we had the part, and the customer's credit card would be charged. Once the warehouse worker got an approval code, he would print out the order from ACT and ship the part. Every step of that process was dated, stamped with the employee's name, and time stamped right down to the time that UPS picked up the shipment. There was no paper exchange at all. That information stayed in the system for good. The program was a godsend for us.

CHAPTER 65

Things at Global were shaping up, but not everything was going smoothly. I was having a hell of a time trying to find a third sales representative to work alongside Jim and Andy. The job was not for everyone; it was a commission-only job. And the fact that we were selling to people from the East Coast to the West Coast required the sales guys to come in to work around 11:00 a.m. and leave around 9:00 p.m. or later. The commissions were large. I allowed the sales guys to stay as late as they wanted at night. The good news was that there was no immediate rush to hire a third salesman, but I felt that I would have the same problems in the future that I was having now. I would have to put some thought into that one.

Well, the marketing packages that Kim W and I put together paid off big-time. Global was accepted as a preferred vendor for the three major quick-service restaurant chains. I decided to immediately start running full-page ads in the industry's most popular trade magazine *QSR* (*Quick Service Restaurant* magazine). I also instructed Kim W to put a list together of upcoming restaurant trade shows. It was time to meet the restaurant decision-makers face-to-face.

By the middle of 2001, Kim W and I were traveling trade-show professionals. We flew across the country and proudly displayed our ATM program. We handed out marketing materials, and we collected business cards from interested decision-makers. We even did some wining and dining. Our company name was quickly being introduced to the quick-service restaurant industry.

For those of you that have never had a job that required you to be a road warrior, I will tell you that it is not easy. Travel can be draining, especially when your performance will decide an entire company's fate. On top of that, being away from home and the office can be trying to say the least. I give credit where credit is due. Denise had things well under control on the home front. I missed her and my boys terribly while I was on the road, but I knew it would not be forever.

CHAPTER 66

Back at the office, things were not under control at all, and I will take blame for that. I guess I figured that with all the new hires being trained to do their jobs, with the new computers and ACT software, the place would kind of run itself, but that was not the case at all. My employees were very good at the specific jobs that they were given, but that was where it ended. Nobody was willing to step up and take control of even the simplest of situations. It was very frustrating, but at the same time, I realized that I set the environment up. I realize that I was micromanaging my company, and that is usually a recipe for disaster. I mean, why should the owner and president of a growing company be the one doing the ridiculous tasks like buying toilet paper? I know that sounds stupid, but twice while I was on the road, my employees ran out of toilet paper and called my cell phone to see what they should do. I mean, fuck, really?

My cell phone rang so many times each day that I felt like I was going to explode. It made me realize that I needed to hire more management. I needed someone that could take my place while I was on the road. I needed someone that could open company mail, pay bills when needed, place inventory orders, and keep morale up while I was on the road. I needed a vice president., a decision-maker.

I wanted to offer the position to my best friend Carroll. I mean, think about it. He already knew the photo booth and Sticker Club customers, and he was a smart businessman that could take control. Every instinct told me to pursue Carrol for the job, but I simply could not do it.

When it comes to my family, I am a real softy. I have a huge heart, and someone in my family needed me. I had kept in close contact with my sister Paula, who was still living in Long Island with her husband, Alan, and her two kids. Since Alan's father retired and moved to Florida, Alan was left to run the family quick-oil-change business. During my calls with Paula, she consistently cried about how lonely she was in New York. I mean, our entire family and most of Alan's family moved to Florida. On top of her loneliness, she told me how much trouble they were having making ends meet in New York. Property taxes were skyrocketing, and Alan had to send monthly house and business payments to his father in Florida. They were struggling to survive. Now here I am with a golden ticket opportunity at my company. How could I not offer it to Alan?

It was the right thing to do, so I made the call. Alan was not interested in a job with my company, but he was interested in becoming a partner in Global Vending. Alan asked me to put together a proposal for him to buy into my company. Don't ask me why, but I agreed that would be a good move.

I put a lot of thought into this situation and decided to offer Alan a 45 percent share of Global Vending. The proposal was very basic: Alan would pay $100,000 for a 45 percent of Global Vending Inc. He would be assigned the title and duties of vice president, and he would start at a salary of $100,000 that would adjust throughout the years as the company's profit increases or decreases. I faxed the proposal over to Alan, and he accepted the offer the very same day. Alan and my sister decided to sell their house and business and move to Weston, Florida, as soon as possible. Since Alan had signed the partnership proposal, I hired a Miami law firm to prepare the proper corporate documents and stock certificates for Alan once he arrived. Now I just had to keep things rolling while I waited for my new vice president and partner to arrive.

CHAPTER 67

In anticipation of ramping up Global's ATM sales efforts, I decided to make a few company investments. First, I hired on a website hosting company to work with Ron on developing the website for Global Vending. Next, I hired a printing company to work with Jim and Andy to develop a more professional-looking sales presentation for prospective ATM buyers. I also hired on two additional law firms to research and prepare state-required sales disclosures. You have to send every potential customer a state-specific disclosure that describes the investment opportunity, the company, and the risks involved. Most business opportunity companies don't bother with disclosures because it is expensive to prepare, and the materials inside can sometimes discourage sales. Global was going to do things the right way. Lastly, I decided to have company shirts made for all the employees. I saw it as a sign of unity and professionalism. I had nice polo-style shirts made with Global's name embroidered on the front, pink-and-black shirts for the ladies, green-and-black shirts for the men. They came out great.

I was surprised at how quickly Paula and Alan were able to wrap things up in New York. Their house sold, the business sold, and that was that. My sister was now a Florida resident; it was nice to have her and her family close again. I could not help but think about how happy my mother would have been to see her kids all together again and taking care of one another like family is supposed to do. After a brief settling-in period complete with barbecues and pool parties, it was time to get busy.

I was very excited to have Alan on board, I could see the path we would go down and was very excited about the company's future. Unfortunately, things got off to a horrible start. Alan arrived at

Global Vending. I settled him into his new office and discussed how daily responsibilities would be split up. I introduced him to all the employees and showed him the office layout. After lunch, I presented him with the papers that the law firm prepared for our partnership. I showed him where to sign and gave him his stock certificates that showed him as a 45 percent owner of the company. Everything I was supposed to provide per our agreement was now in his hands. Now Alan needed to read the papers over, sign them, and give me a check for $100,000. In the meantime, I figured the best way to get Alan's feet wet in the business would be to have him spend one full week in each department, learning what the department did and how they did it. This way, he would know everything about Global Vending's operation. Alan agreed that this was the way to go. He spent a week with Kim W in the locating department, a week with Ron and Kim S in technical support, a week in the warehouse with Jeff and George, a week in customer service with Laura and Nitae, a week in sales with Jim and Andy, a week in the reception area with Susan, and finally a week with me so that I could show him finance, marketing, future plans, and goals. Yes, it was a lot to take in, but at least he was introduced to Global as I knew it. Alan insisted every step of the way that he felt good about what he had already learned, and he was confident that he could handle his duties. The man's training was over, and we were closing in on the end of the summer of 2001. I was ready to take a shot at the big times here. But there were two things that were eating away at me. Number 1, every time I asked Alan if he had any questions, he would say no. No matter what I trained him on, he seemed to be yessing me to death just so we could move on to the next topic. On top of that, the man never made any suggestions on how to do things differently, not once. Considering that he ran an entire business up in New York this just concerned me. Second, and more importantly, Alan never gave me a check to buy into Global. I mean, how long does it take to read over a three-page agreement, sign it, and write out a check? It had been almost a month and a half since I gave Alan the papers. I decided to ask him what was going on and called Alan into my office.

Me: Listen, Alan, I think it's time to wrap up the corporate partnership. Is there any problem with the papers that I gave you?

Alan: No, everything was fine.

Me: Okay, why haven't you signed them and giving them back to me?

Alan: I did sign them, and I sent them back to the law firm that you had to prepare the papers.

(Okay, what? So now Alan was a 45 percent owner in Global, and I received nothing in return. I told myself not to worry. This was my brother-in-law, my friend. He was just confused.)

Me: Oh, well, what about the check that you need to give me?

Alan: Well, I was thinking about that, and I came up with a better idea.

(His first suggestion, great! Now he had a better way of doing something.)

Alan: I thought it would be better if you took half of my paycheck every week until you are paid in full.

Did he just say what I thought he just said? I would get paid with my own company's money overtime instead of his money up front? I was instantly fuming. I saw this as a guy who did not want to make any commitment. I saw this as a guy who was suddenly trying to pull a fast one on me, his brother-in-law.

I said, "Let me ask you, Alan, when did you decide this, and when were you going to mention this to me? Never mind. Don't answer those questions. I don't fuck around when it comes to money and business. I will give you until the end of the week to hand me a cashier's check in the full amount, or you're out of here. End of conversation."

Alan got up and left my office. Can you believe it? He was actually mad at me. That very same night, my sister Paula came over to my house to see what had happened. Evidently, Alan had gone home and stirred the pot up there. Now once again, I love my sister, but when it comes to business and finance and, well, almost anything that takes planning, Paula just was not the sharpest tool in the shed. I did, however, take the time to show her the partnership proposal, a copy of what the lawyers prepared, and I explained to her Alan's new "idea." Even she got it, and she was mad as hell that her husband was being such a dick. But I had such a huge knot in my stomach at this point. What the hell was going on here?

The next day, Alan showed up for work with a check in the full amount that was owed to me. I was happy to get the check, but I also had serious issues with the route I had to take to get it. I prayed that this was not a preview of things to come. I let the whole situation go for now. I had a business and family that needed attending to.

CHAPTER 68

September 11, 2001, it's a date that every American has etched into their memory. If you ask the average person where they were and what they were doing at the time that the terrorist rammed those planes into the World Trade Tower and the Pentagon, I bet you most people would have no problem remembering.

I was at work on that ill-fated morning. I always had the *Howard Stern Show* on the radio not only in my office but also in the main gathering area in the office. I remember when Robin from the *Stern Show* initially reported that a small private plane had struck one of the towers. That report was quickly changed to the reality that jumbo jets had struck both towers; it was obvious that this was no accident. As news reports came in about other planes having been hijacked and were being tracked across America, a feeling of helplessness and anger came over me. Thousands of innocent lives were being taken by a bunch of scumbag cowards. I saw the despair and concern on the other employees' faces, and I decided to shut Global down for the day in order to let everyone spend this moment in time with their families. It's times like September 11 that you tend to stop and reflect on life and what is important to you. I spent the rest of that day with my wife and children. I watched the news as the horror unfolded throughout the day, and I prayed for the souls whose lives had been taken. I will never forget standing in my backyard that afternoon and looking up at the sky: nothing, not one plane, not one sound. It was a very eerie silence. For all the brave souls that lost their lives during those terrorist attacks, I pray that you rest in peace. For all the men and women of our Armed Forces, I pray for your safe return home. You are all true heroes. The events of September 11 left me with some strong feelings of unrest. What would my family do if anything happened to me? As it stands right now, if I disappeared, Global Vending would collapse. That is not a big ego talking; it was just reality. I needed to protect my family financially and plan for her future. I made a call to my old neighbor Rob, the financial adviser. Even though I moved out of the neighborhood, Rob and I had remained good friends and still went out on occasion. He had never stop soliciting me to invest with this company, so I guess his persistence was about to pay off. Denise and I went to Rob's office and got to work. We set up a will, a life insurance policy, and I wrote him a check for $50,000 to put into investments for retirement or a rainy day. Can you believe the nerve of this prick. He let me know that I was now his smallest customer, but since we were friends, he would not hold it against me. Fuck you, Rob. Anyway, after that appointment, I took Denise over to the local Chevy dealership, and I purchased a brand-new red Chevy Suburban for her. I saw this as a nice big safe vehicle for her to drive our two children around in. I tell you, it felt good to be able to provide safety and security for my family. Now let's get back to work and see what Global can really do.

CHAPTER 69

Back at Global, Alan actually scored a home run for us. I had told him that I was having a problem hiring a third salesman, and Alan told me that he had someone in mind. Sure enough, his lead paid off. He had an oil sales representative up in New York that had expressed his interest in leaving his current job and possibly moving down South. Alan arranged for me to interview him. His name was Bruce, and Bruce was a keeper. He was funny, charming, a man with one million stories, and get this, he had met my father when my father worked for Castrol Motor Oil. Bruce actually knew almost everyone that my father knew. After a few phone calls to check up on Bruce, I decided he was the man for the job. I made Bruce a job offer that included a draw against earned commission. I wanted him to start off on the right foot with us. Bruce dove right into the mix.

Since Bruce's coming on board, I started to notice a trend developing. Since Alan already knew Bruce from New York, he started to hang out around the sales guys on a regular basis. In fact, before long, Jim, Andy, Al and Bruce were inseparable. They would go out for lunches and dinners together, they would hang out on the weekends together, and they even all purchased season tickets to the Miami Dolphins together. Now what happened outside of the office was none of my business as long as it did not affect things once they came back into the office. I made that point clear to Alan. I warned him to watch his back with Jim and Andy, and I left it at that. Listen, I am not a stick in the mud. I can and would party with the best of them. I just wanted my company to get a fair shot at reaching its true potential. I decided not to distance myself too far from the crowd, so I set up a poker night at my house. Every Thursday was poker night, and there was an open invitation to all Global employees and their spouses. Different people showed up from time to time, but eventually, it became the same players: me, Denise, Alan, Andy, Jim, and sometimes Bruce. My sister Lisa's husband would join us from time to time. For the most part, it was five or six players, and the steaks were raised throughout the night. We always started with a $100 buy-in, but that went to shit as soon as someone started to lose. The big loser was almost always Andy. Andy was a degenerate gambler. He could not fold a shitty hand and did not know when to go home. During our poker nights, he had to be near a TV so that he could keep tabs on his multiple sports bets for the evening. He often gambled money that he did not have. Once again, don't get me wrong. I love to play poker and bet on sports, but you have to know when it's time to call it a night. Poker night was my way of staying a part of the sales crowd. After all, the company was going to rely heavily on these guys and their production. Let's see what happens.

CHAPTER 70

By this time, Global's ads were running in QSR. Kim W and I had a steady flow of leads coming in from restaurants, and we even started to sign on some locations that were not originally targeted. A few gas stations signed on, a few convenience stores signed on, a couple of Subway sandwich shops, and Cicis Pizza.

Our investment ad remained very simple:

Own ATM Machines
Major Fast-Food Restaurant Locations Available
Turnkey Operations inside KFC, Taco
Bell, McDonalds, Burger King
Minimum Investment Required: $17,995.00

That was it! That was the ad that started what I would call an explosion of sales at Global Vending. Within just a few short months, Global had ended the year with a $1M final quarter; that's right, over $1 million in sales on the final three months of the year. I couldn't believe what was happening here. Was I dreaming? Is this what it feels like to finally hit the big times? I was on cloud nine, and I wanted everyone involved to float on those clouds with me. I decided to issue end-of-the-year bonuses in the amount of one month's salary for each employee; no one complained about that one. I also decided to throw the company a holiday party at Jo Roby Stadium. (That's what Dolphins Stadium was called back then.) I rented a luxury suite in a section called the Dolphins Hall of Champions. We had catered food and an open bar all night. We got to watch my New York Jets kick the shit out of the pussy Miami Dolphins. Oh, by the way, I am a huge Jet fan. J-E-T-S: Jets, Jets, Jets. Okay, sorry about the sidetrack thing. It was a great night and a great way to end 2001. I had my boys, I had Denise, and I had a company that was starting to really hit its stride. What could possibly go wrong?

CHAPTER 71

I started 2002 out the same way that I started almost every year off. I traded in my car, no big change, still a two-door convertible S 500 Mercedes. This time, it was white with gray interior. I am obviously a big Mercedes fan. The salesman at Fort Lauderdale Mercedes thought that I was an absolute nutjob. He would try to do the whole sales routine, but I would just ignore him and point when I saw the car I liked. He would then start with all this finance garbage, and I would just write him out a check for the amount of the car. That always caught him off guard. I love not having a car payment; it just gives you freedom to do whatever you want with your own car whenever you want to do it. I highly recommend it for all of you with the ability to just pay for a car in full. No, I am not stuck-up. I have never had money like this before, and I was enjoying myself.

Sales were hopping back at Global, and the Global infrastructure seemed to have control of the situation. So Kim and I hit the road again in order to keep a steady stream of locations coming in. I guess that was when Global started to suffer from what I assumed were growing pains. I'm not going to cue the dickhead because this was not one of those moments, but it was a very frustrating time for me.

I would spend a few days on the road with Kim and then casually hook up with Carrol somewhere on the road for Sticker Club and photo booth promotions. I tried my hardest to keep my travels to less than eight business days; I missed my family way too much, and the office. Now remember, I brought in Alan as a partner due to the fact that every time I went on the road, things went to shit at the office. Well, now Alan was there, and nothing had changed. I would come back from the road, and my desk was covered in unopened company mail. I had dozens of messages from customers that were trying to get problems solved. No bills were paid, no supplies were ordered, and new customers' paperwork littered my desk. What the fuck was going on here? I had many frustrating conversations with Alan. I sometimes wanted to shoot myself during our talks. I mean, I would ask him why he did not open any mail or pay any of the bills, and he would simply tell me that they all had my name on the envelope as the company contact. Really, that's your answer? I'm no fool. I can spot laziness from a mile away, and this was pure laziness staring me right in the face. I assured Alan that I did not get any personal mail sent to the office, and I insisted that he start to open all company mail while I was gone along with paying the bills as they came in. Alan assured me he would. I asked Alan if he needed to be retrained on our accounting system, and he insisted that would not be needed. I instructed him to start returning customer phone calls even if they were asking for me.

> Me: Just call them back Alan and inform them that I am out of the office on business, but you would love to try and help them with their needs. Can you try that?
> Alan: Sure, no problem, Tom.
> Me: Can you also check the warehouse from time to time and order supplies and inventory when we need them?
> Alan: Yes, I can do that, Tom.
> Me: You remember that all of our suppliers are in the ACT system, and it lists what they sell us and how to pay for the product. Do you need me to go over that again with you?
> Alan: No, Tom, I get it.

Well, I would sure as shit hope so. I mean, this guy laid out $100,000 and then just watched from the sidelines? I found myself needing many alcoholic drinks at night after an Alan conversation. Anyway, a new trend was starting to take place with our new customers, and it required a lot more attention than the Alan being lazy issue.

CHAPTER 72

People are funny when it comes to money and numbers. It does not matter how many times you tell people that there are no guarantees of any level of income from an investment. Once they have laid out their hard-earned money, people expect miracles. In Global's case, people started to complain about the money that they were making from their investment. Now they were not complaining about the investment as a whole, but they did complain that not every machine was making them the same amount of money. If one machine was making them $300 per month and one was making them $200 per month, in their eyes, that was a problem.

Okay, rule number 1 in selling a business opportunity: you cannot guarantee any specific level of income. That's the law end of story. I made sure to keep a close ear on my sales guys while I was in the office. The salesman at Global Vending Inc. was not made aware that our phone system allowed me to listen in on their sales pitches. I used that phone feature quite often when I was in the office, and I encouraged Alan to do the same. I did not want anything outside of our set's sales pitch to be promised to potential customers in order to close the deal. I would not allow our company to become one of Jim's and Andy's dumping ground. But that was not what people were complaining about; they just wanted all high-producing machines. The greed factor started to hit them. I needed to solve this growing phenomenon before it got out of control. I initially decided to set a minimum income that I felt was acceptable for each machine. I decided that if the machine was operating for at least three months and was producing less than one hundred transactions per month, then it was an unacceptable machine by global standard. So if a customer called Global and made a complaint about a low-producing machine, I would see if it met the minimum standard. If it was producing above the minimum of one hundred transactions per month, then the customer had to keep the machine. If the machine was producing below the minimum standard, then Global would buy back the machine and assigned the customer a new one. Now I tell you, this was walking a very thin line as far as the Florida state attorney general's office was concerned. Because technically, I just started to offer a minimum level of income. I just wanted to be fair with people, and I felt that this solution was more than fair. The customers seemed to agree with me.

The exchanging of machines seemed simple enough, but man did it cause extreme problems. First of all, we had to redo paperwork for ATMMS so that they knew who to pay for what machines. Then if the transfer occurred in the middle of the month, the customers would complain about getting paid for a partial month on the old machine, so ATMMS had to redo the online tracking for the affected customer. The results? Well, let's just say that I would have been better off just saying, "Too bad," to the customers that were unhappy. The paperwork was slow and sloppy, the transition was mishandled on several occasions, people were paid for the wrong machines, and I had to settle everyone down over and over again. I started to get the feeling that some customers thought we were incompetent, and that bothered the hell out of me. I decided that Global had the staff and the hardware to take a large part in the whole processing side of the business. No, we were not even close to being ready to become a processor. But the monthly payouts, daily machine tracking, and machine programming were definitely something that Global was capable of doing. I worked the numbers out with Bart at ATMMS for ATMs, and then Global received one bulk check from ATMMS for surcharges each month. Customers now tracked their machines' daily activity on Global's website and would receive a monthly check for their ATM surcharges from Global instead of from ATMMS. If a customer needed to exchange a machine, it was now up to Global to do all the paperwork and the machine reprogramming. Yes, people, that did solve the whole recurring problem of people being assigned new machines in a timely fashion and being paid for the right machines. However, it did not solve the initial problem of some locations that were underperforming. The only difference now was that Global was making the transfers happen properly, but the number of transfers being requested began to get out of control. I needed to revisit the location situation as a whole.

CHAPTER 73

Money was still pouring into Global, but I started to get extremely stressed out about the way things were going. I had the location issue, I had Alan that still refused to take control when I was gone, and then I started to have problems with our salesman Andy. While listening in on one of Andy's sales calls, I overheard a potential customer thank Andy for giving him references to talk in order to help him make a decision to purchase. Now at the time, there were existing Global Vending customers that agreed to be references for the company. They were happy with their Global investment and agreed to allow Global to give out their names and phone numbers to potential new customers as references. Getting customers to become references was not an easy task. The law does not allow you to pay them for being a reference, so they have to do it out of pure kindness. I made it clear to every Global reference that their names would be given out sparingly, and yes, I did give them preferential treatment when they had a question or a problem. Anyway, the problem that I had with Andy was that this potential customer mentioned a reference in Arizona; Global didn't have a reference in Arizona. What the hell was Andy doing?

As soon as Andy hung up the phone, I called him into my office and closed the door. I explained to Andy that I overheard him talking to his last potential customer and that I heard them mention of an Arizona reference. I asked him what was going on, and he didn't even try to hide the fact that he was using fake references—people that he had used when he and Jim were selling candy machines. These people never purchased any products from anyone; they were paid by people like Jim and Andy to lie for them. The professional term for a person like that is a shill. I called Jim into the office to see if he was doing the same bullshit, and he assured me that he was not. Andy told me that he decided to do this on his own.

Andy said, "Hey, I took a shot, and I got caught. Sorry." That was typical Andy. "Sorry, I swear it won't happen again."

Andy added, "Please, Tom, I have a wife and kids. Give me one more chance. It will never happen again."

I knew better, but I also had a bit of greed factor going inside me. Andy produced sales, a lot of sales, end of story. I decided to reprimand him with a stern warning.

I said, "If it happens again, you're out. Understood?"

Of course, he agreed that it would never happen again. He slid out of my office with his tail between his legs. I made a call to the potential customer that he gave the fake reference to. I set the record straight and told him what Andy had done, and then I gave him the five real Global references. Andy was fuming with me. Two days later, a check arrived from that customer in the amount of $25,000 with a note attached to his purchase order that read, "Thank you for showing me that there are still honest people in this world. I look forward to a long business relationship with Global Vending Inc." I showed the note to Andy as I handed him a commission check for 50 percent of his normal rate. The rest went to charity.

CHAPTER 74

I decided to lock myself in my office for a few days and brainstorm the problem that we were having finding locations that produced well. I used my erasable marker and board again to create a compilation of data to try and narrow down a common factor that was in all good locations. I just could not come up with a common factor that was present in every high-performing location. It was not the restaurant chain, it was not the foot traffic, and it was not any one geographical area. A good location seems to be a combination of high foot traffic with the added plus of some unique set of circumstances for that particular area. We have plenty of high-foot-traffic locations that were not performing well; we also had plenty of moderate-foot-traffic locations that were performing very well. It seemed that every good location had people that accepted the concepts of an ATM machine in a fast-food restaurant without hesitation; other areas seemed to be reluctant to use the machine simply because it was not common to see an ATM machine in a fast-food restaurant. It was all so strange. I needed to simplify the locating process.

As I gaze at my eraser board over and over again, two things began to stick out. First of all, even the worst-producing locations were profitable if Global was the owner/operator of that particular machine. I mean, our average cost per machine was only $1,000. Our worst-producing machines were producing about $50 per month in revenue, which gave me a breakeven point of less than two years. The second thing that I noticed was that after a ninety-day ramp-up period, machines tended to produce a consistent daily number of transactions. In other words, after three months of operating in the field, we could tell how much a machine was going to produce each month. Then it hit me, that was it. I suddenly saw it; all I had to do was to not assign customers machines until they had proven themselves to be good locations. It seemed so simple now that it was staring me right in the face. After ninety days of operation, I could separate good locations from bad location and just assign customers the acceptable ones. Global would continue to place machines everywhere, assign good locations to customers, and operate the poorer performers as a company-owned machine. That should solve the location problem. It was really that simple.

Well, unfortunately, it was not that simple. I still faced two conflicting stumbling blocks. Number 1, sales were pouring into global: we had done another $1M worth of ATM sales in the first month of 2002. Number 2, locations were pouring into Global, and when a location decided to sign a contract, they wanted the equipment installed yesterday, if you know what I mean. I needed the new sales to help cover the cost of equipment and the cost to run Global's infrastructure. The problem was that I would not have any locations to offer new customers until the locations proved themselves in the field. What a freaking nightmare. I was between a rock and a hard place, yet both the rock and a hard place were great situations. Go figure.

CHAPTER 75

Say what you want to say about my situation. Yes, I could've just stopped all the sales at Global until locations have proven themselves. I could've returned hundreds of thousands of dollars in new business with the promise of us calling the customers back once locations were proven. I could have tried to go to the banking institution and borrowed the money to cover the equipment and operating costs, but none of that was reality. No growing company in its right mind turns down sales in the hope to one day call customers back and ask them for their business again. It's plain business suicide. I would have no part in that; instead, like any real entrepreneur, I got creative. I found a way to create my own in-house financing, retain my customers, and offer them an immediate return on their investment.

Let's go back to my initial vision of how I saw Global Vending making money. Whether it was selling film, selling stickers, of collecting ATM surcharges, Global was going to survive on residual income and not on the sale of the equipment that produced the residual income.

The ATM contracts were structured so that Global was receiving $0.20 per ATM transaction. It did not matter how much the ATM surcharge was set at on the machine; Global would still receive $0.20 for each transaction. If Global was the owner-operator of a specific machine, then Global would receive a full transaction fee minus any portion that was allocated for the location. The average Global ATM surcharge was broken as follows:

Total surcharge: $1.25
The location would receive: $0.25
Global would receive: $0.20
The ATM owner/investor would receive: $0.80

Now on the equipment side, Global was selling ATMs for a minimum of $5,000 each. A countertop ATM would cost Global $300, and a full standing ATM would cost Global $1,700. That gave Global an average ATM cost of $1,000. The company operated an equal number of countertop units and full standing units. Customers did not care which model they received; the important factor was the monthly revenue generated by the ATM. Global had countertop units that outperformed full standing units and full standing units that outperformed countertop units. Anyway, Global's gross profit per ATM sold was $4,000. After running operating expense numbers, I determined that at that current pace that global was selling ATM machines, there was an operating expense of $600 per machine. That $600 included things like payroll, advertising, rent, and electricity. Now I was looking at an average pretax net profit of $3,400 per ATM machine sold. Remember that $3,400 was not part of the original Global business plan; if we made absolutely nothing on the sale of ATM machines, that was fine also. Global would build its residual income revenue stream and flourish off that in due time. Now don't get me wrong, the $3,400 profit was a great bonus, and I had absolutely no problem continuing to collect that money.

Okay, I don't want to get too far off track here. The question here is, how do you continue to take in sales and not offer a return on investment to customers until your locations have proven to be productive? Remember, this was an investment for people across America, nothing more, nothing less. There was no hands-on operation for these people to take place in. They simply sent us money and tracked ATM transactions online. Global operated and managed the machines at all times. The people investing with Global were looking to make money ASAP, and I needed to buy time after each purchase in order to groom good locations. Ninety days was the minimum time to place machines in the field and decide if they were customer-worthy, but even after each ninety-day period, there was no guarantee that Global would have a stockpile of good locations. Like I said, I needed to buy time. I knew good locations existed; we had plenty of them. Just buy some time, and good locations would fall into place. It was a pure numbers game.

CHAPTER 76

The solution that I had developed was exactly what I have been saying. I would actually buy the time that I needed to groom locations. I would buy the needed time from the people whose clock I was on, the customers. So let me tell you how I did just that. First of all, I named the new program the shared location program, and here is how it worked. The shared location program (SLP) was a rebate program. For every month that Global did not have a permanent location for the customers' machines, Global Vending would send the customer back a portion of their investment as a rebate or a purchase discount or whatever you want to call it. We called it a monthly rebate. If it took Global six months to locate the customers' machine, then the customers received back six monthly rebate checks. Now the big question was how much they would get back each month. I decided to let operating ATM machines make that decision for me. Here is how it worked. Let's say Mr. Jones purchased three ATM machines for $15,000. Global would place the new customer on the shared location program and set up an online tracking account for the new customer. Global would then allow this new customer to track three operating machines from the field. Now I would assign three average-producing machines to the new customer's account that at the time was producing around $150 per month each. So for this example, let's assume that each of the three machines that Global assigned this new customer produced $150 per month. At the end of each month, that new customer would receive a rebate check in the amount of $450. Let's say the machines had a better month and produced $600 in ATM surcharges, then the new customer would receive a check for $600 that month and so on. The point is that at an average of $450 per month, Global could afford to make twenty-two monthly rebates to this customer while it groomed locations, and Global would not lose a dime ($3,400 per machine profit × 3 machines purchased = $10,200 profit divided by $450 = 22 months).

The shared location program created a true win-win situation. Global got twenty-two months of free financing to groom locations, and the customer received an immediate return on investment. Once good locations were assigned to the new customer, then they would earn the actual ATM revenue instead of rebates from the shared location program. The pressure was on us to secure and operate as many locations as possible. The faster that we signed good locations to customers, the more money Global would make. I want everyone reading this to remember one thing at this point: the law allowed, and actually insisted, that Global assign locations to these customers, and if they turned out to be shit locations, then too bad for the customers. That is what the business opportunity laws allow companies to do, no promises of success, no guarantees. Take a chance, buyer, and if you don't make any money, well, too bad. The company provided what they said they would: an operating ATM, a location, and processing services. I was aware that I could have done this, but fuck that noise. I did not see it that way. I wanted these people to be successful. There was no reason why they could not get a great return on their investment; it would just take time. The majority of the customers loved the idea of the shared location program. There were some that chose not to participate; that was their choice. The salesmen loved it because it was easy to sell. I loved it because I had solved yet another stumbling block in my business world, and I loved a good challenge.

CHAPTER 77

I needed to be able to track all the new customer money and how much I had to give each of them in the form of rebate checks. I decided to create a profit-and-loss chart for every new customer. I entered the information into the ACT database, and then I made monthly entries into each customer's profit/loss statement to show that month's rebate. This was a very time-consuming process that was assigned to the customer service department, but it was very much needed so we could make sure we did not lose money.

Let me make one more thing very, very clear at this point: in my eyes, my business plan was very safe. I made sure that at any given point in time, Global had enough ATM inventory and cash reserved to purchase every shared location participant their own ATM machine. For example, let's say two hundred new customers were on the shared location program, and those two hundred customers had purchased a total of six hundred ATM machines; Global Vending Inc. would have enough ATMs in our warehouse or cash in the bank to cover purchasing six hundred ATM machines. Customer money was not being spent on other projects or expenses at any time. The previous company that I worked for, Photo Vend International, buried itself by using prepaid film sales for other projects. I would not have any part in that.

So let me make myself clear. If Global suddenly had enough good-producing locations to fulfill its obligations to the two hundred new customers that purchased six hundred machines, Global could immediately fill those locations with ATM equipment. I never knew when the motherload of locations was going to hit. I had to be prepared to satisfy my obligations to my customers at any given time. And prepared we were.

So with the location dilemma seemingly solved, it was back to business, back to sales, back to operating, and back to fine-tuning the beast. I actually started to feel invincible. Nothing could stop us from hitting that ten-thousand-unit mark that I had set as a goal for Global. I was flying high again, but unfortunately, I was about to get shot down from my new high. Life was about to deal me a new blow.

CHAPTER 78

The call came into my office on a Friday afternoon. It was around lunchtime when my receptionist, Susan, told me that I had an urgent phone call from Denise. I picked up the call and heard Denise in a panic. She was talking very loudly, almost screaming through the phone. I could barely hear her. There were sirens in the background that just brought a sickening feeling to my stomach.

Finally, I was able to start understanding what Denise was telling me. She was inside an ambulance and on the way to the local hospital with our youngest son, Jake. Jake was now three years old. Denise was able to tell me that Jake had some sort of seizure, but the details did not make sense. I found out what hospital they were headed to, grabbed my black leather briefcase that never left my side, and ran out of the office. My heart was pounding the entire way to the hospital. How could this be happening? How does a three-year-old healthy child suddenly have a seizure? What did this mean? I pushed the S500 to its limits. I remember several times looking at the speedometer as I shot down the saw grass expressway. It would reach 130 mph once, 145 mph the second glance, but I did not care about anything but getting to my boy.

Upon arriving at the emergency room to the local hospital, a nurse was able to direct me toward my son Jake. As I entered the room, it took every ounce of strengths not to break down and cry. There he was, my little man, in a hospital bed with tubes and wires all over him and an oxygen tube in his little nose. My oldest son, Thomas, was there, and he ran and jumped into my arms. I could tell he was terrified from what he must have seen and from what he was seeing now. I gave him a big hug and kiss, and I whispered in his ear, "Don't be afraid. Jake will be all right, I promise."

I gave Denise a hug and a kiss, and she started to explain what had happened. The boys and Denise were at a playdate at a friend's house. Jake approached Denise and said that he was hungry. Denise said she was looking at Jake when suddenly his eyes rolled to the back of his head. He stiffened up like a two-by-four and collapsed to the ground. Denise was able to catch Jake on his way down. That was when Jake started to have full-body seizures. Our friend called for an ambulance, and there we were, in a hospital. I approached Jake in his bed; he was awake and smiling. Jake always had a smile on his face. Here was this poor three-year-old that just had a seizure and was attached to five different machines that were monitoring him, and as I leaned down to say hello and give him a kiss, Jake looked at me and asked, "Can we still play when you get home from work tonight?"

I couldn't believe the toughness of this little guy. Jake had absolutely no memory of what had happened to him.

Over the next few hours, doctors ran tests on Jake and found nothing to be wrong with him. One doctor actually had the nerve to suggest that maybe Jake did not have a seizure; maybe he was just a little dizzy from running around. Denise set him straight right away. The staff at the hospital decided to do a CAT scan on Jake's head to make sure there was no trauma to his head that they could not see. I could tell that Jake was scared. I explained to him what the machine looked like and what was going to happen once he was placed inside the machine. I promised him that if he closed his eyes and pretended to be asleep inside the machine, then it would be over before he knew it. The doctor told Denise and I that one of us could come to the CAT scan floor. But once the scan started, Jake would have to be left alone. Jake grabbed my hand and asked if I would go with him; I did. I talked to Jake as the nurses rolled his bed toward the scanning room. I wanted him to see me strong so that he would not be afraid. I prayed in between talking. We reached the CAT scan room, and as the nurse rolled him in, I followed. I leaned forward to kiss him and let him know that I would be right outside waiting, and then it happened, right in front of my eyes, his entire body straightened out like a plank of wood, his eyes rolled into the back of his head, and his little body began tremoring with seizures. The nurse grabbed me as I rushed to help Jake.

The nurse said, "Don't touch him!"

She yelled in my face. The nurse ran to the intercom and yelled for emergency assistance and a crash cart. Jake had stopped breathing. As doctors and nurses rushed in, I was pushed out of the way. I could not believe what I was seeing. A tube being placed in his throat, needles being jammed into Jake's little body with anti-seizure medication. How could this be happening? He was fine two minutes ago. I stepped out of the room, and fear ran through my body. I started to cry as I saw Denise starting to approach me. I had to stop her from going into the room where Jake was being worked on. I told her what had happened and what I had seen.

A few minutes later, a nurse came out and told us that Jake was stabilized, and they were going to bring him back into the emergency room to admit him. As they wheeled Jake out, his eyes were still closed, but I took his hand and walked by his rolling bed. There were no further incidents that night.

The very next day, it was decided by the hospital to transfer Jake to a children's hospital for further testing. I rode in the ambulance with Jake, and Denise followed behind us in my car. Jake seemed okay. He even seemed to think that the ride in the ambulance was fun.

Test after test after test were performed on my little guy, and nothing concrete was discovered.

One doctor at the children's hospital blamed the seizures on electrical waves that run through your brain. He concluded that Jake's brain just needed a little development time to catch up with these electrical pulses in his head. There were no guarantees that the seizures would or would not return. After a week of tests, Jake was released from the hospital. Denise and I were issued anti-seizure shots that we would have to carry around with us just in case Jake had more seizures. No matter where Jake went, one of those shots would have to be available just in case. We even had to leave a shot with Susan at Jake's preschool in case he had another episode. After all the flying-high-and-nothing-could-stop-me attitude that I had been experiencing at work, I suddenly felt extremely vulnerable. I love my kids more than life itself. And I could not imagine what I would do if something happened to one of them. Let's hope I don't ever find out.

CHAPTER 79

Traumatic events such as Jake's seizures tend to bring life into perspective a little more than usual. You tend to appreciate what you have a little more than you did before the event. I think that happened to Denise and me after Jake's seizure incident—well, sort of.

One night just a day or two after we got Jake back home, Denise decided to have a heart-to-heart conversation with me. This was very un-Denise-like. She started the conversation by telling me that a few months ago, she was feeling depressed, and she went to see her general practitioner. The doctor concluded that Denise was having small anxiety attacks, and that was leading to depression. My first reaction was along the lines of "Please give me a break," and no, I did not say that, but come on. We had two great kids, a beautiful house, new cars, and plenty of money. Denise was not working and spending her days with friends and family, boo-hoo. Okay, once again, I did not act like that. I was very concerned on the outside. The doctor had started Denise on the antidepressant drug Paxil. I thought it would've been nice to have been informed of that just in case any side effects reared their ugly heads. But what the heck, I was just her husband. So next, the conversation got interesting. Denise started to tell me that she believed that she had figured out why she did not like having sex on a more regular basis, and she would like to try and fix this situation. Now she had my attention. All I heard was "more sex," great. Denise told me that she did not like the way that she looked, she did not like her naked body, and she did not like her overall appearance, and that was why we did not have a steady sex life. Once again, I will not get into what I really wanted to say. I mean, I never had a problem with the way she looked, dressed, or undressed. Denise was my wife, and I loved her. Anyway, her solution to this problem was to get caps on her teeth, a nose job, and a breast job all at the same time. Her logic, if she looked better to herself, she would have more self-confidence and more drive to have sex. Whatever. You wanted new teeth, a new nose, and new tits. Who was I to argue? Knock yourself out.

Just give me a shout-out when that whole sex drive thing kicks in. Love you.

Roughly $9,000 later, I had a wife with perfect teeth, a nice new nose, and big-ass tits. I don't think our kids recognized her for a week or two. Denise of course had to buy new clothes to show off the new package. I encouraged her every step of the way. I mean, for God's sake, she was on antidepressants and just redid her whole appearance. Did she look good? No, she looked great, but like I said, I liked her just the way she was. As far as solving our little intimacy problem, sorry, same shit. different day except now I had these huge tits I could not touch. This sucked!

CHAPTER 80

I needed to get back to work. Jake's seizures and Denise admitting to depression and the need for a makeover were taking a toll on me. I wanted nothing more than to dive back into the mix at work. Sales were still booming, and the office was riding high, except for the fact that Alan still did not want to work while I was gone. I started to get individual complaints about him from the staff. Think about that one. The staff was complaining to me about the lack of effort from the vice president and partner of Global Vending. The receptionist told me that Alan had instructed her on several occasions to tell customers that he was not in the office when he was. Several customers told the receptionist that they were tired of being run around. Run around? At Global? That was just not acceptable to me. The tech crew and customer service crew made similar complaints; they had left several important customer needs on Alan's desk, and he just ignored it. Every employee that came to talk to me told me the same thing. Alan was constantly on AOL instant-messaging multiple people all day. The employees could hear and see this happening, and they were getting sick of being ignored. Alan still had not jumped into the mail or billing issues when I was gone. Nothing had changed in his performance, and that was unacceptable. I needed to address this and fast. As fate would have it, I did not get the chance to speak to Alan about his laziness. While driving home from work one day, I felt a shift in my back like I had never felt before. Something was wrong. By the time that I got home that day, I couldn't even get out of the car. My back was locked in place, and every time that I tried to move, I felt pains shooting down my lower back. I actually thought I was partially paralyzed. Denise heard me in the garage as I was trying to get out and helped me roll—yes, roll out of my car—and I literally had to crawl inside of the house. I crawled up the stairs and into bed and lay there in excruciating pain.

The next day, I lay down in the back of Denise's SUV, and she drove me to see an orthopedic surgeon. The news was not good. I was told that I had two herniated disks in my lower back and that my spinal disks were degenerative (they were thinning). This basically meant that I would be in a world of pain until the disks went back into place. The doctor also told me that I could count on this happening again.

The doctor was a great guy. I thank my lucky stars that I chose him out of the millions of orthopedic doctors in South Florida. He told me that I would have options to consider after the disks were back in place. I could opt for surgery, but that would always be a last resort. I could begin physical therapy to strengthen my back and abdominal muscles in order to help support the weak disks, and I could use pain management during the time of extreme flare-ups like I was currently suffering. The doctor prescribed me three medications: 10 mg/325 mg hydrocodone (a painkiller), Skelaxin (a muscle relaxer), and Celebrex (a sort of joint lubricant). I thanked the good doctor, filled my prescriptions, and headed home.

The very first time that I took the medication was the most unreal thing that I have ever experienced. Although I still had a very tough time walking, and technically I could still feel pain, it didn't matter; I was as high as a kite. This stuff was just kick-ass legalized heroin. In all my days of high school and college, I have never felt a high like this before. It was actually pretty scary. I decided to speed up my recovery process by going to a chiropractor five days a week for electrode therapy and some physical therapy. I needed to get back to the office. I remember how happy I was that I had not yet had it out with Alan; even he was better than nothing at the time. Within a week, I returned to work, except I still could not sit or walk well. I brought a blanket and several pillows from home and made a makeshift bed on my office floor. I answered and returned calls and even held meetings right there on the floor. I think my employees thought I was off my rocker. I also could tell that they were thrilled that I was back in control.

It took almost a full month for my herniated disks to drop back into place. You just don't realize how important good health and being in shape is until something like this happens. Anyway, I remember the day that my painkiller prescription ran out. I was not happy to be losing that wonder feeling that those pills had given me. I am sure it was in my head, but I started to notice my back pain returning almost immediately. I called the doctor for a refill, and he informed me that I would have to come in again before he could renew anything. Like I have time to keep going to the doctor's office. No, I have a much better idea. I remembered seeing a story on *60 Minutes* or *Dateline* about online pharmacies and how easy it was to get prescriptions through the internet. I, of course, ignored the part of the story about it being illegal to purchase prescription drugs online, or was it illegal for people to sell them drugs online? Ah, who cares? I did about a half hour's worth of searching online. I filled out some questionnaires on pharmacy sites, and would you believe that within an hour, my cellphone was ringing. The calls were supposedly from doctors that worked for the online pharmacies, but to be honest, I was more likely to be a doctor than these people were. Once again, I could care less. I just wanted my drugs sent to me so that I did not have to go to my doctor's office. Let me tell you, folks, it was sick just how easy it was to order prescription drugs from these sites. I had no idea if these sites were real or if they were scams, so I placed an order with four different sites and used my credit card as a form of payment. If any of the sites did not ship me the medication, then I would take that up with my credit card company. It sounded like a plan to me. Each online doctor prescribed me a month's supply 10 mg hydrocodone (ninety pills), and each prescription would have two refills. The total cost for each prescription was $190, which included my "telephone consultation." The very next day, Federal Express and United Parcel Service each delivered two overnight envelopes containing my pills. Four orders, each containing ninety painkillers delivered right to my office. I could not believe it; all four online pharmacies filled the orders. I check my credit card balance, and sure enough, I was charged a total of $760 for the four orders. Oopppsss, honestly, I could give a shit about the money. I avoided spending an entire day at the doctor's office, and I received my drugs. Damn, I'm good. Chalk one up for the internet. So I popped a pill, put the rest into my briefcase, and got back to work.

CHAPTER 81

The summer was coming to a close, and Global Vending was firing on all cylinders. I decided to spend some quality time in each department, and I made some minor adjustments here and there. I spent some time with a local packaging/shipping supply company to create a custom shipping box for our full-size ATM machine. The machines came to us in two pieces, and I wanted to be able to shop the unit fully assembled. I made bulk purchases of this new custom box that we nicknamed the Coffin. When the box was fully assembled and packed for shipping, it had an earie look to it; it really did look like a coffin. It was funny, our UPS driver would come at the end of every day for pickups and ask our warehouse guys, "How many coffins do you have for me today?"

There were days at Global where we would have to call our UPS representative and ask for an empty truck for the end-of-day pickups. Yes, we were shipping out that many new ATM machines to locations. What a great feeling.

Next, I decided to spend some considerable time monitoring sales calls; Bruce was on fire with sales, Jim was on fire with sales, but Andy started to struggle a little at one point, and I could tell he was getting frustrated. I decided to listen in on a day's worth of his calls and try to figure out where he was missing his mark. I could not believe that almost immediately I was getting an earful of vintage Andy bullshit. On two consecutive calls, Andy gave potential customers bogus references. I couldn't believe what I was hearing. He promised never to use fake references again, but sure enough, there he was doing it all over again. I was fuming. This piece of shit was putting us all at risk. He was messing with my family's livelihood, he was messing with the livelihood of every Global employee, and he was lying his ass off to potential customers. I had heard enough. I called Alan into my office and told him what I had just heard Andy doing and that I was going to fire his ass right then. Alan did not like to hear that at all. Remember, Alan had befriended Andy. This was his little pal, too fucking bad. Alan reminded me that Andy had a wife and young daughter, and I reminded Alan that Andy had been warned about this bullshit already. Andy had to go. I called Andy into my office and confronted him with what I had just heard him telling customers. Once again, just like the last time, no denial. It was just a shrug of the shoulder and a sorry-ass excuse.

Andy said, "It won't happen again, Tom. Sorry, man, my bad. I was in a slump, and I needed an edge."

I replied, "Yes, your bad, and I agree that it won't happen again. I want you to pack your personal property and get out of the building. You're fired. I don't want you to ever come back. I will give Jim your last check at the end of the week.

Andy said, "You can't be serious."

I told him, "You have five minutes to get out, or I will throw you out."

A few employees heard the yelling and came into the main sales area to see what was going on. I snapped a little and ordered everyone back to work. That was so not me; everyone scattered. Andy left my office, and as he was packing his things, I heard him tell Jim and Bruce that he was fired for absolutely no reason and that I would be begging him to come back once I realized how much I needed him. I don't think so, douchebag.

As soon as Andy left the building, I called for a group meeting of all employees. I needed to be a little tactful with how I worded things because Jim and Alan were still close friends with Andy. I made a brief statement as to why Andy was fired. I made it very clear that Andy would never be back. I made it very clear what Global was all about and that deceiving our customers would never be an acceptable practice. I asked every employee if they had any questions, and none of them did. I apologized for snapping a little earlier when I ordered everyone back to work. I just wanted these guys to know how much the success of Global meant to me and should mean to them. Meeting adjourned.

CHAPTER 82

I decided to hold off on hiring another sales rep right away. Sales were still booming, and the support staff was working at almost maximum capacity. I divided Andy's lead book between Jim and Bruce. I figured Andy's leads along with their own leads would keep them busy enough to forget that Andy was gone. That was some serious wishful thinking.

As it turned out, Global and its employees had no trouble forgetting about Andy. But Andy would not let go of Global or his firing. About a week after I had fired Andy, a call came into the office from a Fort Lauderdale-based attorney named Andrew Cove. Yes, folks, at this point, I am going to start using some last names. Just keep one thing in mind: if I use a last name, it is because the person is truly shit, the bottom of the barrel, a real fucking piece of garbage, and I choose not to protect their feelings, reputations, or families; they don't deserve shit. Okay, sorry about that. So Attorney Andrew Cove called Global, asking to speak with me. I have never heard of Mr. Cove before, but any attorney asking to speak directly with the company president must have a problem, so I took the call. Mr. Cove informed me that he represented a gentleman by the name of Andrew Levinson. That's right—Andy, Global's former sales representative that I just fired. Mr. Cove explained to me that his client, scumbag Andy, was mad that he was fired from his lucrative job at Global Vending Inc., and he was seeking $150,000 in severance pay. Mr. Cove advised me that the severance amount was not a negotiable number. Listen, folks, I tried. I told myself to remain professional, to be courteous, but I just couldn't do it.

> Me: Really, that's what he wants? $150,000 in
> severance pay. Let me ask you something,

Mr. Cove. Is there a Florida labor law that I am unaware of that forces companies to pay severance to employees that get fired for being slick, lying scumbags? If there is, then come on over, and I will cut you a check. If there isn't, then I must ask you to stop wasting my valuable time. I took this call out of respect for the fact that you are an attorney, but that's it. Your client is an asshole, and he is not entitled to shit. Andy was a 1099 employee without any benefits, and he was fired for deceiving customers. He had been warned in the past about this behavior, and he chose to ignore those warnings, so he was fired. End of story.

Scumbag Cove: Wow, that was very entertaining, Mr. Foley, and what you are telling me may be true, but I think you should rethink your position. You see, my client has informed me that you are conducting some highly illegal business practices at Global. My client had prepared a statement that he intends to have me present to the Florida attorney general's office if you do not pay him. Now the statement claims that Global is promising customers a guaranteed return investment, which is not allowed in the business opportunity world, but that's nothing compared to the fact that you are running a Ponzi Scheme over there at Global.

Me: What are you talking about? What the hell is a Ponzi Scheme?

Scumbag Cove: A Ponzi Scheme is when you pay investment returns to old investors with new investor money to make it appear that they are making money. That's illegal.

Me: I don't know what you are talking about.
Your client is a piece of shit, and it sure does
sound like you are trying to blackmail me,
Mr. Cove. Is that common practice nowadays for an attorney to try and blackmail
companies for their clients on? Global
Vending is not breaking any laws, so lick
my fucking balls.

I hung up. I know, I know, "Lick my balls" is not a professional
thing to say, but hey, I was still new at this whole business thing, and
I guess I needed to work on my vocabulary. Anyway, now my brain
was on overload. Why would this guy say that I was running a Ponzi
scheme? I decided to look up that phrase on the internet. I found a
lot of information including where the term originated from. A guy
by the name of Charles Ponzi had duped thousands of investors at
one time by collecting investment money and never investing the
money into anything; he simply started sending old investors decent
face returns as new money came into him. This enticed people to
invest more and more money. The scheme fell apart when he no longer could bring enough money to cover the payments that he needed
to make to investors, so the whole scheme collapsed. What did that
have to do with me and Global? I wasn't paying old people with
new customers' money, and I was purchasing and operating ATM
machines with investor money. My rebates were in no way being
made to encourage more investing; it was simply a way to give a
return on investment while the customers waited for locations. Fuck
this Cove guy and fuck Andy. I had enough of this bullshit. I decided
to tell Alan, Jim, and Bruce about the phone call. Even Jim was a
little taken aback that Andy had gone this far. I mean, if anything
ever happened to Global, Jim, Bruce, and Alan would be out of a
job. Andy surely was not thinking about them when he hired on Mr.
Cove. Jim told me that he was going to have a talk with Andy that
night. He assured me that he would straighten Andy out. I didn't
argue with Jim, but good luck with that one, pal.

CHAPTER 83

I needed this bullshit like I needed another hole in my dick. I started to take my pain pills a little more often to relieve stress; those pills always did the job. The next day, Jim came into my office and closed the door behind him. Ooooooh, very dramatic. Jim informed me that he spoke to Andy and that Andy was very apologetic for having Mr. Cove call and threaten me. Jim explained to me that Andy's little pea brain never comprehended that he might actually get fired for being a scumbag. I mean, he'd been a scumbag his whole life; he didn't know any better. Whatever! Jim told me that Andy had no money saved. He owed a bookie a few thousand dollars, and his electricity at home was about to be turned off.

> Jim: Please remember, Tom, Andy has a wife and little girl at home.
>
> Me: Look, Jim, I'm sorry. Andy is a piece of garbage. He put us all at risk with his bullshit fake references, then he gets a lawyer to threaten me and try to blackmail me for $150,000. I feel sorry for his wife and child, but Andy will never work here again, end of story.
>
> Jim: He understands that, Tom. Do you think that it is possible to just give him a small severance check so that he can catch up on his debts? Andy wants to apologize to you, and you will never hear from him again.
>
> Me: Yea, I've heard that before. I can't believe this. Okay, fine, have him call me.

Within thirty minutes, Susan was transferring a call to me from Andy. He was very apologetic over the phone. He made a valid attempt to sound sincere, but that's what lowlife scumbags do: they try and make you feel sorry for them. I told Andy that I would give him a severance check equal to one month's average pay. I also told Andy that in order for him to get a check from me, he would have to sign a statement that described why he was fired and also described how he hired Mr. Cove to blackmail me. I told Andy that I would prepare the statement, that he could review it and make changes if there were any inaccuracies, and then he would have to sign the statement. I advised him that I would keep the statement in a safe at home just in case he ever tried this bullshit again. Andy insisted that he would never make up lies about me and my company again and that he was finished with Mr. Cove. So it was agreed, Andy would come into the office the next day so that we could put this crap to rest.

I carefully prepared the statement describing the situation. I cut a company check for an amount just over $12,000, and I expensed it as severance pay. I showed the check and statement to Jim and Alan; they both agreed that I was being very understanding toward Andy and that this would end our feud. Deep down inside, I knew that this was the wrong thing to do. I should have called the police and reported Scumbag Andy and Scumbag Cove to the police. I hated this whole idea, but I had agreed to do it, and I needed to let this one go.

Just before Andy arrived at Global, I placed a small tape recorder in a plant next to my desk. I wanted to make sure that I documented this meeting as best as I could. When Susan announced that Andy had arrived, I reached into the planter and turned on the tape recorder; now everything we said would be on tape. Andy came into my office and would not look me in the eyes, a true coward. I felt it necessary to tell him how disappointed I was that he would make up lies about me and my company. I had done so much for this guy in the past. Andy apologized several times and tried to explain to me that he was a survivor, and these are the things that survivors do sometimes. I wanted to puke on this shitbag. Andy agreed that we were not breaking any laws at Global and that he had lied to Mr. Cove in order to get Mr. Cove's help. Oh, well, that makes things better.

I handed Andy the statement that I prepared, and he took some time to read it. He agreed that the statement was accurate; he signed it, dated it, and wrote his social security number on it. I handed Andy the check that I had cut for him and told him that I did not want him back in the building again. I even was able to get myself to wish him good luck in the future. No, I did not mean it. Andy left the office with his check, and that was that.

It made me sick to hand over that check to Andy, but truth be told, I did not want to take the chance of Global being placed on the Florida attorney general's radar. South Florida was in the middle of a business opportunity witch hunt, and I could see them attacking us for offering minimum guarantees. I definitely did not need that added headache. I opened Global Vending Inc. in 1999. We were members of the Better Business Bureau, consumer affairs, and Dun and Bradstreet: we had never had even one complaint made by a customer to any of those agencies, and I wanted to keep it that way.

Now I have to tell you, as hotheaded as I can be, and as immature as I can be, I was pretty proud of myself for keeping my cool and resolving this matter as I had done. It was a peaceful, civil ending to a totally scumbag situation; that was not easy for me to do. I had a business to run here, and I just wanted to move forward. I wanted to forget that Andy existed and concentrate on the ATM program, but if you can believe it, Andy just would not go away. I shit you not, folks, this guy was like a disease that I just kept spreading.

CHAPTER 84

About a week after I last saw Andy, Bruce came into my office. I could tell that he was upset and confused. Bruce explained to me that he had been working with a potential client for the past few weeks, and today was the day that this new client was supposed to be purchasing five ATM machines. Bruce contacted the client today so that he could fax all the paperwork to this client's office, but the client decided to back out of the purchase. Now this happens; people get cold feet all the time. The problem was why this guy decided to back out of the purchase. Bruce's client informed Bruce that he had received a call from another business opportunity company that told him that Global Vending was a scam. The sales rep for the other company told Bruce's client that we were breaking every business opportunity law and that we were going to be shut down by the state of Florida. Yes, folks, you guessed it. The other sales rep was Andrew Levinson formally of Global Vending Inc. But how did Andy get Bruce's client's phone number? Who was this other company he was working for, and what the fuck was going on here? Bruce went on to tell me that Andy tried to sell his client bulk candy vending machines, just like he used to sell. Okay, now my Irish/Hungarian blood had reached its boiling point.

Bruce's client had been nice enough to give Bruce Andy's new business name and phone number. I decided to get to the bottom of this shithole situation. Now Florida has a website called www.sunbiz.org. On this website, anyone can look up any active Florida corporation and review any incorporation papers filed by that company. I was interested in seeing the articles of corporation for Andy's new employer so that I could see who the owners and officers were. It took me all but three minutes to find Andy's new employer on

Sunbiz, and what I found in the articles nearly gave me a heart attack. There it was, in black-and-white, CEO and president Mr. James Fernandez. Yes, Mr. James Fernandez as in Global Vending's current sales rep whom we called Jim. That lowlife piece of shit was competing with me while I employed him. Okay, now it was war. I called Alan into my office and told him what had happened with Bruce, then I showed him the papers that I found on Sunbiz. Alan had very little to say. I questioned Alan to make sure that he did not know about Jim employing Andy, and Alan insisted that this was news to him. I could not control my temper at this point. I hate snakes like this fucking piece of shit. I called Bruce and Jim into my office. Once they were both in my office, I asked Jim to look at my computer screen and to explain to me what was on there. Jim read the papers that I had displayed from Sunbiz and turned a nice shade of red.

> Me: Well, is that your company?
>
> Jim: Yes. But what's the problem?
>
> Me: Are you employing Andy?
>
> Jim: Yes, but that has nothing to do with you or this company. I can do whatever I want to do outside of this office, Tom.
>
> Me: Nice attitude, huh? Anything you want to do, huh?
>
> (I explained to Jim what had happened to Bruce's client today. Jim looked surprised.)
>
> Me: So you feel that you can open a business opportunity company, hire a guy that I just fired from here, become a competitor of the company that is currently paying you over $200,000 per year, and steal our leads so that your new sales rep can bad-mouth us and lose sales for us. You see this as being okay? Really?
>
> Jim: I didn't steal leads. I gave Andy the leads that I considered to be dead, people that did not

want to buy ATM machines from us. I took
Bruce's old leads out of the garbage and gave
those to Andy also.

Bruce: That wasn't a dead lead. I simply rewrote
all of that customer's information on a purchase order he was going to buy from me
today.

Jim: How am I supposed to know that?

Me: Oh my god, you are so fucking stupid. That's
not the point, asswipe. The point is that you
took stuff from Global and gave it to a guy
who's guts I fucking hate so that he could
try and sell them another product, and to
boot, the fucking piece of shit gets ahold
of someone who was about to buy, and he
bad-mouths this company. What is wrong
with you? Why would you take a chance
like this? You know what, I don't care. Get
the hell out of here and don't come back.
Go join Andy in scumbag land.

I walked out of my office and into the warehouse; I grabbed an
old box, walked over to Jim's desk, and dumped all his personal shit
into the box. I walked out the front door and threw the box into the
street. Jim walked out without saying another word. This was just
great; 2002 came to a close, and I only had one salesman left. But
you know what, I didn't care. I will not get fucked over like that.

Can you imagine, with all this soap opera drama going on,
Global Vending still did over $4M in ATM sales in 2002. Global
had placed and was currently operating over eight hundred ATM
machines and still had plenty of locations waiting for equipment to
be installed. As a whole, I was very happy with the year that we had.
Once again, I gave out nice holiday bonuses, and this year, instead
of a holiday party, I took the entire company and their significant
others on a weekend Norwegian cruise line vacation. We had a blast.
We drank, we gambled, we danced, and we enjoyed one another's

company. Everyone thanked me for such a good time. Those were the types of things that I enjoyed most: making other people smile and laugh.

I refused to look back and worry about the firings of Andy and Jim. In my eyes, they were completely justified and unavoidable, they deserved to get fired, and Global's customers deserved better from our employees. I would hire more sales reps when the time was right; for now, Bruce was just ripping the sales up. He was on fire. I gave Bruce Jim's leads and decided to tone down the advertising for a little while to give Bruce a chance to catch up.

CHAPTER 85

The year 2003 started off with a small pleasant surprise. I received a call from a guy named Brett out of Shawnee, Kansas. Brett was a real card. He had seen our advertisement in *QSR* magazine. Brett was an experienced ATM installer, repair tech, and locator. Brett was currently unemployed and told me that he had eight children and really needed to get to work. I liked this guy; I liked him a lot. I decided to fly Brett down to Florida so that I could meet him before I contracted any work with him.

When Brett arrived at the offices of Global Vending Inc., I was a bit taken aback by his physical appearance. Brett was medium height and fairly thin everywhere except he had a beer belly that made him look pregnant; it was the funniest thing I had ever seen, and he made it clear that his belly was from drinking beer. (Brett assured me that he never drank when he worked, but with eight kids at home, well).

Brett also had a bowl-style haircut that reminded me of the one that Jim Carey had in the movie *Dumb and Dumber*, but look, this was not a fashion show; this was an ATM business. Brett proved to be a no-bullshit type of guy. He spoke from his heart, and he definitely knew everything required to repair, install, and locate ATM machines. I liked this guy. Brett was a true diamond in the rough. I hired Brett on an independent contractor basis: Brett would get paid top commission for any locations that he secured, and I worked out a payment schedule for the installation and repairing of ATM machines. I had more than enough work to throw his way, so I gave Brett a supply of Global Vending shirts, an expense check so that Brett could get some needed tools, and I even gave him some money so that he could have a few minor repairs done on his truck. Yes, I took a chance, but like I said, I can read a person fairly well. Brett was a keeper.

CHAPTER 86

My first road trip for 2003 was with Carrol. We decided to display the Sticker Club machines at a huge entertainment expo in Las Vegas. I loved my trips with Carrol; he was such a pleasure to spend time with. Carrol and I always talked good business; I would bounce situations off Carrol, and he would suggest solutions and vice versa. There was little that Carrol and I could not figure out together. At night, we would eat at some of the finest restaurants in town and sometimes sample wines until the wee hours of the night. At one point in this particular trip, Carrol had inquired about the pills that I was constantly taking. I told him what they were, and Carrol expressed some concern for me. The truth was that at this point, I was taking at least twelve pills a day instead of the three a day that I was supposed to be taking. My body was building up a tolerance to the painkillers, but I just ignored it and upped the dosage.

The expo turned out to be a huge success for us. Carrol and I had taken dozens of new orders right there at the expo, which was not a common occurrence. Usually, Carrol would do extensive follow-up work from his office before people placed orders for equipment. On our last night in Vegas, Carrol and I decided to celebrate our good fortune. We got absolutely shit-faced that night. Carrol was not a big drinker, but on that particular night, he was in rare form. I definitely could drink with the best of them, but this night would turn out to be one of the strangest and funniest nights of my drinking life. So check this out; we were drinking in the main bar at Mandalay Bay Hotel and Casino (we were staying there). I had to go to the bathroom at one point, so I left Carrol alone at the bar for about five minutes. When I returned from the bathroom, Carrol was no longer alone. He was in the company of two drop-dead gorgeous women. Now Carrol was not some good-looking suave young man. He was roughly 5'10" tall, he was almost completely bald, he was about eight years older than me, he wore super thick and wide rimmed glasses, and he was shaped like a human bowling pin (he weighed a good 350 lbs.). I guess what I am saying is that Carrol was not the most attractive man in America, yet no matter where we went, beautiful women would approach him. It was the darndest thing. I love Carrol to death, but if I am being totally honest here, Carrol was a womanizer; he completely ignored the fact that he was a married man when he was on the road. Anyway, I got back to my seat at the bar, and Carrol introduced me to his new friends, Wendy and Ashley. Damn, people, these two were freakin' hot. We all drank and laughed until around one in the morning. I was having a great time when, out of nowhere, Ashley announced to the group that she was going to take an ecstasy pill. Go ahead, sweetheart, knock yourself out. Ashley asked Carrol and I if we wanted to take some X also. Carrol completely ignored the question. By this time, he and Wendy were all over each other. Ashley repeated the question directly to me. Man, I was drunk. I had no idea what X was. I already had a good twelve painkillers in me but I said, "Sure, what the heck, I'll try it."

Ashley popped a small pill in my mouth, and I chased it down with a glass of white wine. God, was I a moron.

So a little time passed by, and then BAM, the X kicked into gear. Holy shit, that stuff was just out of control. It was a crazy roller-coaster ride for sure; one minute you are high as a kite, the next minute you feel fairly normal but always pumped up, super pumped. I don't remember doing anything too crazy except maybe yelling to people that I had never met before and buying the whole bar a round of shots, but Carrol decided that he needed to get me away from the general public. Carrol suggested we go back to our suite and order food and drinks from there. The girls had no problem with that, so off we went. It was around 2:30 a.m. by the time we got to the room. Carrol and I had a two-bedroom suite that also had a main living room. We ordered food and drinks and continued to have some serious laughs. At one point, Carrol and Wendy decided that they were going to leave for one of the bedrooms. Carrol, you stud, you. I was tripping my freakin' ass off, and so was Ashley, and soon, Ashley became sexually aggressive toward me. I mean, this woman wanted to get naked, like now. I am sorry to disappoint you, male readers, but even though I was drunk and tripping on X, I could not forget the fact that I was a married man. I know, I know, Denise wanted no real part of any sex life with me, but a vow is a vow. I had told Ashley earlier that I was married, and I reminded her again; she could give a rat's ass about my marriage. After making it very clear that I was not going to sleep with her, Ashley had a few choice words for me, most of them aimed at my sexuality, and then she stormed out of the suite. See you again some time, you little whore. Listen, I felt funny just having a woman in my room, but Carrol was my friend, and every friend needs a good wingman. I was doing my best. Truth be told again, I felt like a complete faggot. Anyway, a few minutes after the whore split, I started to get really bad hot flashes. I mean like menopause-type hot flashes, or at least that was what I imagined menopause hot flashes feel like. They were unbearable, so I decided to start taking some ice-cold showers. I would take a cold shower for a few minutes, dry off, put on a hotel robe, and go back to the living room to drink some more. I had this stupid-ass idea that drinking would make the hot flashes go away. Don't ask me what made me think that.

So after my fourth trip to the shower, I got back to the living room, and Carrol was sitting there slightly slumped forward on the couch. Carrol looked up at me for a brief second and then turned away. I could see that he was very sad; he may have even been crying.

Me: What's wrong, pal? Where's Wendy?
Carrol: She left.
Me: Why the long face, stud? I expected a super happy Carrol to exit from that room.
Carrol: I don't know what happened, Tom. We had a great time in there, and then once we were finished, she got all psycho on me. She was really mean to me.
Me: Mean? What the hell are you talking about? What did she say to you?

Carrol: She said I was old and fat. She said she
    had no idea why she was with me but that
    she was sick to her stomach. Sorry, Tom,
    but that sort of stuff really hurts.
Me: That fucking little bitch, that whore, she
    owes you an apology.

I don't know what the hell was going on in my brain at that point. All I knew was that Carrol was sad, and I was hell-bent on getting this piece of shit to apologize to my friend. Carrol kept telling me to forget about it. I guess he could sense that I was starting to lose my shit right in front of him. I was pacing back and forth in the room like a wild animal. Every time Carrol tried to speak, I would cut him off and start yelling about an apology. Let's just blame it on the drugs and alcohol.

Finally, I said, "Fuck it!" Yes, I actually yelled out, "Fuck it!" I grabbed my room card key and told Carrol that I was going to find her and bring her back to apologize to him. He pleaded with me for a brief second, but I was out the door before he could finish a sentence. I thundered down the hallway toward the elevators. I walked passed a couple in the hall who got out of my way, and I mean in a hurry. The woman looked at me and said, "Oh my god!" The guy she was with said, "Holy shit!" Whatever, I didn't have time for you, freaks. I was on a mission.

I reached the elevators, and I pressed the button like two hundred times thinking that would speed up the elevator's arrival; I think we all know that doesn't work, but who cares, I was pissed. An elevator finally arrived. I jumped in, and I pressed the button for the casino level. Yes, I pressed that button like two hundred times also. My twisted X-infested mind was convinced that this woman would be back at the same bar that we were hanging out at earlier. Don't ask me why. That just seemed to make perfectly good sense to me at the time. As the elevator descended to the casino floor, I remember saying over and over again out loud, "Some nerve, this woman has some nerve."

The elevator reached the casino floor destination, and the elevator doors opened. I started to storm out of the elevator when I ran right into a wall of security guards, six of them to be exact. These guys were blocking me from exiting the elevator; in fact, they walked forward toward me, which forced me to retreat back into the elevator. These guys were huge, and there was no way for me to just simply walk around them.

> Me: Can you guys please move. I am currently on
> an important mission.
> Guard Number 1: I'm sorry, sir, but are you a
> guest of the hotel?
> Me: Yes, I'm a guest. (I showed him my room
> card key.) Now can you move?
> Guard: What is your name, sir?
> Me: Thomas Foley. You guys are killing right now.

The guard called someone on his radio and gave them my name; the person on the other end of the radio responded by confirming that I was a hotel guest and repeated what my suite number was. I almost felt like I was in a movie, and these guys were getting ready to kick the shit out of me for some reason.

> Guard: Mr. Foley, I don't know what's going on
> with you tonight, but we are going to escort
> you back to your suite where I suggest you
> stay for the rest of the night.
> Me: What? What are you, my mother? Look, I
> need to get to your main bar area and find
> this bitch that was rude to my friend. I am
> simply going to bring her back to my room
> so that she can apologize to my friend. That's
> all, okay? Is that going to be a problem?
> Guard: No, that would normally not be a prob-
> lem. The problem is that you are naked, Mr.
> Foley.

What did he just say? I needed a moment to process that one. Did he just say that I was naked? I slowly looked down at myself, and I will be damned, I was stark freakin' naked, not an ounce of clothes on my body. After my last cold shower, I never put my robe back on. I never put any clothes back on. That was why Carrol kept looking away from me. That was why he was yelling at me to come back. That was why the couple in the hall freaked out. Holy shit, I walked out of my room, down a hallway, and into an elevator naked. Then I stood there arguing with security guards over why I couldn't go to the main bar to find a woman that owed my friend an apology. Can you get more fucked up than that?

I said, "Holy fuck, I am naked!"

The guards tried their hardest to keep straight faces, but they could not. On the elevator ride back up to my suite, one of the security guards told me that I was spotted by the hallway and elevator cameras, and they thought that they were going to be confronting some sick pervert or something. As I told them the story about how I got so messed up and what my mission was, they just started to break down laughing. I guess they realized that I was just a harmless fool. Carrol was waiting out in the hall when I got back with my six new friends. Carrol looked scared to death. I shook all the guards' hands, and I even tried to get Carroll to tip them, but I could tell that they just wanted this big dumb wasted naked fool to get into his room and put some clothes on. What a crazy night. I decided not to tell my wife and kids about that little episode. Good idea, huh?

I spent most of the next day recovering from the crazy night. Carrol had an afternoon flight back to South Carolina, and I was taking the red-eye back to Florida. I hopped on the red-eye, I popped a few of my hydrocodone pills, and I passed out. The America West Airline red-eye from Las Vegas to Fort Lauderdale was the best flight to take back from Vegas. It was the only nonstop flight, and by the time the flight arrived in Fort Lauderdale at 7:00 a.m., I was Vegas-detoxed. Those of you who have been to Vegas know what I am talking about. Those of you who have not been to Vegas, well, you need to get your asses over there; it's the single greatest place to visit.

CHAPTER 87

Anyway, I arrived back in Florida, and my routine after a road trip was to normally take the day off and relax at home. On this particular trip, I was returning on a Friday, and I would have the whole weekend to relax. I decided to surprise the employees of Global Vending, and instead of going home, I would work half a day. I stopped at a local diner for some breakfast, and I finally arrived back at the office at around 9:00 a.m.

I wandered into the reception area, and Susan jumped up and gave me her traditional welcome back safely hug; I loved her hugs. I tried to make a little small talk with her about how things were at the office while I was gone, but Susan was a no-bullshit type of person; I loved her for that too. She immediately handed me a stack of no less than twenty messages, all from customers, and all with Alan's name on them. Some of the messages were almost a week old. Susan then handed me a stack of messages with my name on them, and most of these messages were from the same people requesting an immediate callback.

Susan quietly explained to me that Alan had had Susan telling customers all week that he was out of the office and would not be back until the following Monday. She also told me that this had become a standard practice of Alan's when I was away, and she did not care if she got fired for telling me because at this rate, she could see that we would not be in business for a long time anyway. I believed Susan, and I reassured her that Global Vending would be around for a very long time to come. It was time to put an end to these games. I went into my office where, of course, there was a stack of unopened mail, bills, advertisements, you name it. Alan had not opened the mail for a week again. There was also a stack of new customers' contracts and checks on my desk; they had not been touched either. I just could not continue on like this anymore; enough was enough.

I walked over to Alan's office, and I did not bother to knock. His door was closed, but I just opened it and walked in. Alan was at his desk, no shoes on, feet up on his desk, and he was on the phone laughing with someone, obviously a personal call, not a business call. Alan looked shocked to see me. I didn't ask him; instead, I told him to get off the phone. Alan gave some wiseass remark to the person on the phone about how he had to go because the Furor was back in town. As Alan hung up the phone, I immediately noticed a host of AOL instant messaging boxes on his computer screen, and the incoming message chime went off about every six seconds.

> Me: Look, Alan, you need to shut down your little instant messaging chat room so that we can talk.
> (Alan turned to his computer, shut down his America Online screen and turned back to me with a smile.)
> Alan: So how was Vegas?
> Me: Forget Vegas. What the hell is going on in here? I can't handle this bullshit anymore, Alan.
> Alan: What's the problem, Tom? Everything's under control here.
> Me: No, it's not, Alan. No, it most certainly is not. I have a stack of messages from pissed-off customers that want to talk to me immediately because you will not return their calls. What's this bullshit about you being out of town? When did that start? Why haven't you opened up any of the mail? Why haven't you paid any of the bills? Why haven't you entered any of the new customers information into ACT? Why are you sitting here with your feet up on the desk, talking

on the phone, and typing instant messages
to all your friends? You call this under control? I call this absolute bullshit, and I will
not deal with this anymore.

Alan: Hey, listen, Tom, not everyone is like you. I
am doing the best I can right now.

Me: Your best? That is so sad if this is your best.
Look, Alan, I tried everything I know: I
tried to retrain you, I have asked you over
and over again if you needed help understanding what was expected of you, but this
is simple shit. This is just plain laziness, and
I can't deal with this anymore. I am giving
you a choice: you buy me out, or I will buy
you out, but as of this moment, our partnership is over.

Alan: That's crazy. You know I can't run this place
without you. You need to give me another
chance.

Me: No way, Alan, you have had many chances,
and for some reason, you think this is a big
joke. Well, ha ha, the joke is over. Since you
don't feel that you can run this place without
me, then I will buy you out of this business.
I am going to give you back your $100,000,
and I am going to continue to pay you your
current salary for as long as Global Vending
Inc. is in business. I just don't want you here
anymore. Please get your stuff together and
get out.

I stormed out of Alan's office. Once again, employees heard my
yelling and had gathered to listen. I went straight to my office and
closed my door. My heart was racing at a thousand beats a second.
I was just so pissed off that this guy, my brother-in-law, would take
such advantage of me. There was no excuse for his actions, and since

I had tried to work on these problems with him several times before, I did not feel bad at all. As I started to calm down, I saw Alans car leaving the parking lot. Boy, that was fast.

I decided that I had better call my sister Paula and explain to her what had just happened. Paula was at a loss for words. In fact, the only thing she could say to me was that she was sorry for what Alan had put me through. Paula also thanked me for the offer that I had made to buy Alan out of the business. Look, folks, Paula was my sister, and she had two children to care for; my decision to get rid of Alan was obviously not about money, or I would not have offered to continue to pay him his salary forever. If you have a cancer in a company, you need to cut it out before it spreads; that was what I did with Andy, that was what I did with Jim, and now that was what I did with Alan. I would definitely need to make some employee additions before things got out of control.

CHAPTER 88

Over the next few weeks, Alan made several lame attempts to get back into Global. It was just a pitiful site to see this grown man come into my office, close the door behind him, and just sit in front of me and cry. Yes, cry, like a little fucking bitch. Alan never came back to me with a plan on how he was going to improve his work ethics. He never was able to tell me why he was so lazy in the past. He just repeated over and over again that I was not being fair; it was like having a thirty-seven-year-old child in front of me. I had absolutely no respect for him at all.

My sister on the other hand really surprised me. Paula came into work the following Monday and insisted on working for the paycheck that I was going to continue to send home for her. Paula started doing clerical and customer service work for the photo booth and Sticker Club portion of the business. I thought that was very honorable of her to take that position.

Now it was time to regroup and rebuild my staff. I hired a man named Herb to act as director of operations and special projects at Global. Herb was a construction engineer that I had worked with for several years designing and rebuilding our photo booths and Photo Sticker machines. Herb was a smart guy and would play a huge part in the logistics of getting ATM machines to where they needed to get and to make sure that they were installed and online in a reasonable amount of time. I saw Herb as being the number 3 guy at Global. Herb was no slouch; he organized himself and jumped right into the mix. Next, I made the call. I made the call that I should have made a year ago instead of calling Alan. I called Carrol to try and convince him to become Global Vending's next vice president. Here came the crazy fate thing again, folks. I was just with Carrol a few weeks ago,

218

and all appeared to be fine with his personal life, but on the day that I called him to offer him the vice president position, Carrol was moving out of his house. Evidently, Carrol had a rocky marriage for years, and now that his kids were all off to college or employed, Carrol was getting a divorce. He could not believe that I just so happened to call him on that particular day. Carrol had planned on calling me after he was settled in to let me know what had happened. Well, my friend, don't get settled in. You are moving to sunny South Florida. It didn't take much convincing. I simply offered him a job, salary, and benefits that he could not refuse. Amen, Carrol was moving to Florida. I now had an awesome new vice president.

Things were going to be great. It did not take long for Carrol to move to Florida and get settled in. Carrol was a no-nonsense kind of guy when it came to business. I decided to put Carrol through the same training regimen that I put Alan through. Carrol spent a few days with each department in order to familiarize himself with our operation. After training, Carrol almost immediately started to give me suggestions on how we could perform certain tasks more efficiently. God, was that a breath of fresh air. Morale at the office seemed to skyrocket once the old staff got used to working with the new staff. New staff, new customers, new locations—Global was firing on all cylinders again.

CHAPTER 89

Let me tell you a funny thing about success and money; as soon as people realize that things are going good for you, and they see that you are raking in cash, certain people tend to try and ride on your coattail. My situation was no exception to that rule. I already had my sister Paula working for me, my sister-in-law Laura (Denise's sister) was working for me, my nephew Jeff (son of my sister Lisa) was working for me, and soon, more family would be looking to come on board. My guess is that people like Paula, Laura, and Jeff would go home and talk a lot about our continuing growth and success at Global because people outside of Global started to smell the money.

So one day, I received a call from my brother-in-law Burt (my sister Lisa's husband / also father to my nephew Jeff). Burt was calling to see if I would get together with him in order to discuss me possibly employing him. Now I never had any real problems with Burt. Burt was twenty years older than my sister Lisa, and that caused some issues with my parents when they first got married, but hey, that was their deal, not mine. If they were happy, then so be it. Burt was a lifetime engineer at Florida Power and Lights nuclear power plant at Turkey Point, Florida. I knew that Burt had always hated his hour-and-a-half commute to and from work; I also knew that Burt was pushing sixty years old, and he wanted to retire soon. I never in a million years thought that Burt would even consider working for me. Burt was a tight ass, a play-it-safe type of guy, a creature of habit, and he was very opinionated. I will never forget the time that Burt tried to rearrange my mother's refrigerator. He told my mother that her refrigerator was not efficiently organized, and he started to rearrange things inside of it. My mom, God rest her soul, was just like me. She did not like to be told what to do or how to do it, especially in her own home. My mother pushed Burt, gave him a few choice four-letter words, and put everything back into its original place. God, I loved my mother. Burt acted like a little child for the rest of that day; it was freakin' hysterical.

Anyway, so now this guy wanted to work for me at Global? Global was a growing beast that changed on a daily basis. The employees had to be flexible and innovative at times in order to adapt, and this tightly wound nitpicker wanted to work there. I honestly just did not see him fitting in there. Burt would not take no for an answer; he actually played the family card on me, reminding me that he had my sister, niece, and nephew to provide for. Holy shit was I a big softy.

I agreed to sit down and talk to him. Burt and I got together at my house on a weekend. I listened to Burt bitch and moan about his three-hour-long commute and the fact that he was getting too old to keep that pace up and how he needed a change. Burt also told me about some of his retirement investments that had gone bad, and he really needed an opportunity to make some serious money. He had the idea that he would retire from Florida Power and Light, collect a pension from them, and work for Global for five years or so in order to build up a second retirement account. It sounded like Burt already had it all figured out. He also had it figured out that I was a fucking sucker when it came to family. I was raised with the understanding that family always helps family whenever possible. I could not help but think about where that theory got me with Paula and Alan, but family is family, and I felt obligated to try and help. I caved in. I hired Burt to become Global's new head of customer service. I gave him a salary of $100,000 per year plus benefits. That was more money than Burt was making as an engineer. Burt thanked me a million times, my sister Lisa thanked me a million times, and although it felt good to help yet another family member, deep down inside, I was worried about this one. Within a week, Burt was settling in and training at Global. Welcome aboard.

CHAPTER 90

In 2003, it seemed like every time that I turned around, Bruce had another new customer for us. Each new sale also appeared to be larger than the last; heavy hitters were starting to show up. On the locating side, Kim W had branched out her search for new locations, and she was currently pursuing Dollar Store chains across the country. Kim W had come up with the idea of adding dollar stores to the list of potential locations, and I agreed with her that they would be a great addition to our location portfolio. I also decided to beef up our nationwide advertising campaign for new customers. I was still placing ads in hundreds of newspapers across the country, but I decided to hire on a production company to make a TV commercial for Global. I paid the production company to make a thirty-second commercial, a sixty-second commercial, and a sales video that we could include in all our sales packages. I purchased bulk airtime on cable channels like the Golf channel, the Weather Channel, the TV Guide Channel, the Food Network, TNT, TBS, and several other odd stations. Upon the airing of our commercial, sales immediately kicked up another notch. I could not believe how much money was flying in the door, and I do mean flying. Most clients would fly down to Florida in order to check out our operation before they purchased. Each visitor received a tour of the facility from Bruce, and then I would sit down with them, answer questions, and close deals. After business was over, I made sure to entertain our newest customer. Some customers wanted to play golf, so I would take them to my country club. Some liked fine dining, so I would take them down to South Beach and wine and dine them. Others wanted sex and woman, so I would take them to strip clubs. The point is, I would make sure that the customer always left Florida with a smile on their face.

Now this is no lie, folks. I had a 100 percent closing ratio in 2003 for fly-in customers. Every single person that flew down to check Global out purchased ATM machines from us. That, my friends, is just simply unheard of in sales, but in this case, it was true. I made a decision that it was time; it was time to start living the life that I had always dreamed of. I wanted the best of the best for my family. I wanted to help people in this world that were less fortunate. I wanted to build an empire that I could one day turn over to my sons for them to carry on my legacy.

I placed my boys in a private Catholic school that was attached to the church that we attended. The name of the school and church was St. Bonaventure. The church was in the process of building an entirely new building, and I quickly became a major financial contributor to that cause.

I suddenly found myself invited to charity events and fundraisers that were sponsored by sports legends like Dan Marine, Jason Taylor, and the Roby family that used to own the Miami Dolphins. I played in charity Pro/Am golf events, attended charity balls and auctions, and I always made sure to leave a big fat check behind when I left an event. That part of my life was very gratifying to me; these were worthy causes that were doing good humane work, and I was part of it.

On the home front, it was time to enjoy the fruits of my labor. I decided first to pay my house off in full; less than two years into my mortgage, I paid for my house and now owned it free and clear. That was so cool. I made sure to treat my wife like a queen; Mother's Day, her birthday, Valentine's day, Christmas, whatever the occasion, I sent her to spas for days of relaxation and pampering. I also purchased her what she loved the most—diamonds, diamond earrings, a diamond tennis bracelet, a diamond cocktail ring, the best of the best. I spent over $400,000 at our local jewelry store that year. Sorry to say though, folks, none of those purchases got me more sex. Well, I tried, didn't I?

It was funny how my investor friend Rob started calling me a heck of a lot more during 2003; I wonder if it had to do with the fact that I was sending him fifty to one hundred thousand dollars a month to put into my retirement account. Yes, I am sure that was why he was calling. He invited me out to meet the partners of his company, cigar clubs, diners, his kids' birthday parties. Whatever the occasion, my phone was suddenly ringing. Since I fired most of my poker buddies, I decided to start playing poker at the Seminole Hard Rock Hotel and Casino in Hollywood, Florida. The Hard Rock had great no-limit Texas hold 'em tournaments. I played once or twice during the week at night and at least once a weekend. Denise would always come with me on the weekend where she played regular-limit Texas hold 'em ring games. Denise and I had a great time together on the weekends; we would pick a nice restaurant for dinner and then go to the Hard Rock for some poker. Susan and her daughters would watch my boys, and there was no one that I trusted with my children more than Susan and her girls; they were like family to me.

I next decided to do a little car shopping again. I would say at this point that I was semi out of control, but I was having a great time. It is an unreal feeling to be able to write a check and not have to worry if you have enough money to cover that check; this was the first time in my life that I had that luxury. So anyway, I was off to Fort Lauderdale Mercedes again. My sales rep there had called, and he told me that just got in a new Roadster that I had to see. Man was this car hot. It was a 2004 AMG SL55 convertible, black on black, 600 horsepower of pure sports car that came with a sticker price of $145,000; I'll take it. I felt a little funny buying myself a car that day, so I also purchased Denise a 2004 Gold S 500 sedan. Yeah, she should like that, another $80,000.

On the way home that day, I passed a Cadillac dealer, and I saw this beautiful pearl white Escalade SUV. Fuck it, I will take that too. I went home, got Denise's Suburban, and traded it for the Escalade plus about $30,000.00. Oh, well, it was worth it.

I could not forget about my kids, of course. I purchased them each Florida college prepaid accounts. I know that they were a long way from going to college, but at least I did not have to worry about that anymore. I also took my boys on an awesome trip to the Bahamas. Denise still did not like to fly, so it was a boys' weekend at the Atlantis Hotel. I flew over to the Bahamas on Chalk Airline, which flies air/seaplanes to Paradise Island several times a day. It was so cool. We landed right in the water in front of the hotel.

For those of you who have never been to, or heard of the Atlantis, I can tell you that it is just one of the greatest places on this planet to visit. The Atlantis is the type of hotel where you can do something twenty-four hours a day or do nothing all day; it was up to you. They have amazing sea exhibits, with stingrays and sharks; they have huge waterslides and lazy rivers; and the beach is just awesome. At night, the Atlantis has a world-class casino, a nightclub, and five-star restaurants; it's just an all-around great place to go. My boys and I had an unbelievable good time together there.

I wasn't finished buying shit quite yet. Don't ask me why, but all of a sudden, Denise and I decided that our house was a little too small for us, so we started to knock around the idea of finding a larger home. Now the man that Denise's mother was married to, Lenny the Drunk, had decided to get his Florida real estate brokers license, so I put him on notice to let me know if anything nice came on the marketplace. In the meantime, I decided to check out the newspapers and some local real estate magazines.

One Sunday morning while dicking around with the local newspaper, I spotted an ad for a new high-rise condominium that was being built in a section of Fort Lauderdale called Las Olas. The description and the artist rendition of the building got me all excited. The building was going to have high-end retail stores on the street level, its own parking garage, its own entertainment club complete with billiards room and movie theater, its own exercise gym, and there would be a swimming pool complex on the roof. I decided to drive down to the sales center that day. I hopped in the new Roadster and dropped the hammer. God, I loved this car, especially with the top down on I595 doing 160 mph or so.

Anyway, I got to the sales center, and this freakin' totally hot-ass babe welcomed me. I was a fucking dead man; this chick could sell me dog-shit perfume if she wanted to. Okay, so truth be told, I loved the building layout and amenities, but the units were laid out like shit. I just didn't get it, and even though Hot Pants was hanging out of her clothes and giving me unreal fantasy thoughts, I decided to pass. I walked out to my car, not realizing that the sales hottie was still watching me, and when I reached my car, I could see that I suddenly caught her attention. This babe ran, not walked, but ran out of the sales office to my car. She bounced in all the right places, Lord. Thank you, Lord. The saleswoman apologized to me, but for what? Well, she got honest with me. She judged me by what I was wearing and how I was acting, and sales babe told me that she did not bother to show me the best units available because she simply did not think I could afford them. I guess the Roadster made her realize what a huge mistake she had made. Never judge a book by its cover, folks. Okay, so I go back inside with her, still convinced that this place was not for me. That was until she showed me the layout for penthouse number 2.

The unit was on the top floor, of course. It was over three thousand square feet, and best of all, I could design the layout. There were almost no limitations to what I could do. Now I was not looking at this place for a primary residence. I wanted my kids to grow up with a huge yard to play in and such. No, this was going to be an investment and a place to hang out on the weekends. So Sweet Pants hit a home run with this one; the unit was $750,000, and it would be completed sometime during the summer of 2005. I'll take it.

Now let me tell you the type of guy that I am; while filling out the contract, I listed Lenny as my real estate agent. That entitled Lenny to a 3 percent commission on a $750,000 sale, and he never even showed up at the place. Come on, that was nice of me, don't you think? I had not yet found a new primary residence, but I decided to put my current house on the market for a ridiculous price just to see if there was any interest out there. Yes, I gave the listing to Lenny, and he went to work.

A couple of days later, I was driving to the Hard Rock to play poker, and there was an accident on I595 heading east, which was my route to the Hard Rock. I was diverted off I595, and I decided to take a side road the entire way to the Hard Rock. The Hard Rock was located on the corner of 441 and Stirling Road, so I decided to use Stirling Road the whole way.

So I am putting along Stirling Road when my eye caught a huge real estate sign that was announcing an open-model home for sale located on five acres of property. Screw it, I had plenty of time, so I decided to turn down the road and have a look. The street was called Stallion Way, and I could tell that its name reflected the area; this was horse country. Stallion Way was a dead-end road that ended with a circular cul-de-sac. There was only one home built on this road, and it was the model that was being advertised. The entire property was surrounded by a wall made of cobblestone and black iron. The property was sprawling and manicured beautifully.

The house, holy cow, what a house, a huge brand-new ranch with a four-car garage facing the street. The house itself was set back from the street at least half an acre. I pressed a button on the security box in front of the property, and after I mentioned that I wanted to look at the house, the black iron gates began to swing open. This was so cool; there were security cameras everywhere. I parked my car in front of this six-foot-high water feature that was located right in the middle of a circular driveway. I was greeted by a salesman that welcomed me to Sterling Ranch Estates; that was the name of the development to be built on this block. As it wound out, the man that I met with was the actual builder. I did not read the part of the sign that said "Shown by appointment only," but once again, the SL 55 did the door opening for me. Rick was the builder, and he seemed like a nice enough guy. He informed me that he would be building a total of four homes on the entire block, homes like the one that I was about to enter.

The house was just over ten thousand square feet under air; it consisted of six huge bedroom suites, eight bathrooms, an office/library, a family room, a movie theater, a great room with wet bar, a formal dining room, a gourmet kitchen with a butler's pantry, and separate maids' quarters. The master bedroom was just a ridiculous-size room. It was currently furnished with a king-size bed and two large sofa chairs with tables. The master bathroom had a huge raised Roman-style tub that you had to walk up three steps to get into; it also had a walk-in car wash-style shower big enough for at least eight people to stand in (that would be fun), his and her toilets, his and her sinks and vanities, and his and her walk-in closets that were each larger than my current bedroom. The great room was large enough to land an airplane in, I would say roughly 2,500 square feet with four sets of French doors that opened up to the pool area. There was a natural gas fireplace in the great room along with a huge black granite wet bar that housed a wine refrigerator as well as a regular refrigerator. The ceilings were twenty-five-foot-high cathedral-style ceilings, and the floors were either marble or limestone—fossil tile. The library/office had a natural gas fireplace, dark mahogany floors, and light shelving with enough space for over three thousand books. The formal dining room had a huge crystal chandelier that hung over a glass top formal dining table and chairs that could fit fourteen people. The gourmet kitchen had all subzero commercial appliance, two ovens, a grill for frying or barbecuing, an island prep area, a butler's pantry complete with a warming station, and a food pantry that could hold enough food to feed a small army. The family room had floor-to-ceiling buildouts with huge sectional sofas and a billiards table. The movie theater had a projector that dropped down from the ceiling and a surround sound system that could blow your ears off. Every inch of the house had high ceilings, tons of windows and French doors, and first-class lighting fixtures and appointments. Even the four-car garage had a refrigerator and twenty-foot ceilings. The house was a palace fit for a king. In the backyard, there were thousands of square feet of covered patio. There was a barbecue station complete with a commercial-size gas grill, a wet bar, and a prep island with a refrigerator. The patio was also fine tile with fifteen-foot ceilings that had fans attached everywhere. The swimming pool was twenty feet by forty feet and had a huge raised hot tub with a waterfall that flowed into the pool. There was a raised cobblestone path that you could use to drive from the front of the house directly to a barn located in the far backyard. The barn was over three thousand square feet and had four huge stalls and a two-bedroom one-bath apartment that was intended for a groundskeeper to live in. The apartment had its own small living room, laundry room, and a full kitchen. Even the barns apartment was covered in top-of-the-line marble and granite. The grounds that the house and barn sat on were just beautiful: green grass as far as the eye could see, wide-open space with enough room for any recreational activity. I could not believe how perfect this place was. I fell in love with it instantly. This was the type of house that I had always dreamed of owning.

After the tour, I asked Rick how much the house was selling for. Rick informed me that this particular house was not yet for sale but would be in around a year. Rick estimated the house would be put on the market for around $3.8 million. Rick was showing this house because he was in the middle of building another development nearby that would offer this same exact house, except in a scaled-down version. The other development would have about fifty houses at about half the size of this one. I had absolutely no interest in any other house. I shook hands with Rick that day and told him I would be in touch. I decided that this house was going to be the Foleys' next residence; no one was going to tell me otherwise. People, I strongly believe that everything is for sale in this world. It's all just a matter of reaching a price that is acceptable to the seller or, in this case, the non-seller. I decided to skip the Hard Rock that day. Instead, I called Lenny and asked him to meet me at his real estate office. Upon arriving at Lenny's office, I told him about the house that I had found that was currently not for sale. I asked Lenny to put together an offer sheet for that house. Lenny thought I was completely off my rockers.

Lenny said, "You can't make an offer on a house that is not for sale. That's not how things work in real estate."

Sure it is. Who writes the rules of life? We do. Now let's get to work.

I made Lenny type up a onetime nonnegotiable offer for Rick to consider. I made a purchase offer of $3.2 million for the house, and to show that I was serious, I wrote out a check for $650,000 as a down payment. I gave Lenny Rick's business card, and we faxed over the offer to Rick. Let's just see what was for sale and what was not for sale. Lenny received a call from Rick within thirty minutes. Rick could not believe that I was trying to purchase his model home that wasn't even for sale, but Rick was a businessman, and a smart one at that. He accepted my offer, and that was that. Not for sale my ass.

I have to tell you that I forgot one small detail in this whole house-purchasing escapade: my wife. I just purchased a house for $3.2 million, and I never even let Denise see it first. Fuck it. Who could possibly not like this house? I asked Lenny to keep his mouth shut so that I could break the news to Denise. If Lenny was to tell Denise's mother, the whole town of Weston would have known before I was able to break the news. Lenny had just earned a $90,000 commission, so I guess he could afford to shut his mouth for a day or two. I shot home and rounded up Denise and the boys. I told them that I wanted them to look at a house that I had just seen. Denise knew something was wrong already. I had missed a poker tournament, and that was just not like me. Denise finished straightening up the house. She told me that a real estate agent was coming by that night to show our house to someone for a second time. Hey, Lenny, thanks for telling me, you moron.

Okay, so I called Rick and asked him to meet me so that I could get a key to the house and the code to get into the front gate. Rick told me that I had some set of balls, not only because I bought the house the way that I did but because I did not even tell my wife about it. He agreed to lend me a key and the security codes until we closed on the house. While Denise was finishing her cleaning, I ran out and met Rick. By the time I returned home, Denise and the boys were ready to roll. I gave them a quick description on the way over, but I really downplayed the actual size of the house. I wanted them to have the same first experience that I had when I entered the house. As we pulled up to the property, Denise started to laugh at me.

Denise said, "You are such a dreamer. Let's go get some dinner and stop wasting time."

Can you believe it, she thought the house was way out of our means and that I was wasting her time by showing her this house. My boys on the other hand were just dying to see the house and the yard. I entered the security code, and the grand iron gates swung opened. Already, Denise started playing detective.

Denise said, "How did you get the security code?"

I replied, "Don't worry, Denise, the builder has temporary codes that he gives out for the day."

That was the best lie that I could come up with at the time. I parked in the same place as the last time, right in front of the fountain.

We got to the front door, and I did the old, "Are you ready? One, two, three, and then I unlocked and opened the door. My boys went flying into the house, and as they disappeared into the massive house, I could hear them saying, "Wow, this is cool! Wow, look at that." Denise just stood in the foyer with her mouth opened. She was shocked at the pure size and luxurious layout of this castle. I gave her the grand tour from one side to the other. I walked her and my boys outside and showed them the pool area and the barn. When we were done with the tour, Denise actually had a look on her of being overwhelmed.

> Me: Well, what do you think?
> Denise: It's beautiful, definitely something that dreams are made of.
> Me: Is this the type of house that you could see us moving into?
> Denise: (sarcastically) Yea, let's get our stuff and move in tonight.
> Me: Well, we can't move in tonight. We have to go to the closing next week.
> Denise: You're an ass.
> (I took a copy of the offer out of my pocket and handed it to Denise.)
> Me: I bought it, Denise. I bought this house for us today. We can move in after the closing next week. For real, this is our new home.

It took some real effort to convince Denise that I was not joking. My boys were jumping up and down and ran back into the house to pick out their new bedrooms. Denise asked me over and over again how we could possibly afford this house.

As we walked back through the house again, we talked about life and how good things were going at Global. Denise never had any interest in my company or what we actually did there, but now she realized just how good things were going. We hugged and kissed, and that was that. The Foleys were moving to Stallion Way.

CHAPTER 91

I have mentioned fate on several occasions already, and I believe that it was fate for me to find our new house: the accident that led me to the house, the fact that Rick the builder was at the house instead of a salesperson, and as fate would have it, my current house was about to be sold the very same day. Can you believe it?

That night, I returned home, and my house was being shown to these two gay guys that had looked at the house once before. These two guys were a trip, acting like an old married couple, arguing over what would go where if they were to buy the house. The real estate agent that had brought them was a total asswipe. Sorry to all of you, real estate agents, out there in the world, but the majority of you just don't get it. Try and do some selling sometime, and stop with all your descriptions. Sales are about convincing the buyer that this is the product for them. Learn who your clients are and adapt a sales pitch to their needs. Stop with the stupid readings from the listing and the boring descriptions. Anyway, I walked along with Mary Number 1 and Mary Number 2, and I listened to what they were saying. They wanted the fucking house, no doubt. They were just a little short on the down payment. That was all that they were talking about. I decided to step in and end this shit. I can be such a loose cannon sometimes.

> Me: Listen, gentlemen, I don't mean to bud into
> your business. You like the house, right?
> Mary Number 1: Yes, we love the house.
> Me: Is the only thing stopping you from buying
> this house the fact that you are short on the
> down payment?
> Mary Number 1: Yes, that's it.

232

Me: Do you mind me asking you how short you
    are on the down payment?
Mary Number 2: $5,000.
(Mary Number 2 was obviously the moneyman,
or woman.)
Me: Okay, so here is what I am going to do. I am
    going to drop the price of the house so that
    your down payment will go down $10,000.
    This way, you will have enough for the
    down payment and an extra $5,000 in your
    pockets. How does that sound?

Well, you would have thought that I just told one of them that they had won the lottery. They smiled, they hugged each other, and they even hugged me. Don't worry, I was cool about it. The real estate agent had this puzzled look on her face, like, what just happened. It's called sales, sweetheart. You should try it some time. Old house sold, closing next week on both houses, all in a day's fun for me. That, my friends, is how I would like to live my life forever: people negotiating in good faith without outside influences, cut out all the bullshit, and get down to business. Life is way too short for anything else. Let the good times roll. I want you to know that I am no fool. Remember that I jacked up the price of the house to see what kind of interest there was out there in the marketplace. Denise and I still netted over a $300,000 profit on the house, and we only lived there for two years. Not bad if you ask me. We also did our neighbors one hell of a favor by increasing the projected prices in the neighborhood.

Anyway, it was time to call the movers and settle into paradise. I can't even tell you how excited we all were about moving. I kept wondering if things could possibly get any better.

The closings on both houses went off without a hitch. The movers showed up on time and packed us up. It was funny how our existing furniture got lost in this huge new house. I had decided to purchase some of the model furniture that was in the house, and Denise hired an interior decorator to handle the rest. That should keep her busy for a while.

The first few nights in the new house were very strange; here we were out in the middle of nowhere in ten thousand square feet of house. It took some time to get used to all the new house noises. One of the things that were hard to get used to was the fact that the boys' rooms were on the complete opposite side of the house from the master bedroom. The rooms all had intercoms, and I showed the boys how to use them, but they were only four and seven years old, and I found myself walking over to their rooms in the middle of the night to check up on them. I don't know what I was so worried about. The house had a security system that you would probably find at the White House, inside and outside motion sensors, video cameras around the entire perimeter of the house along with motion-censored lights, smoke detectors, heat sensors, carbon monoxide detectors, and everything was hardwired to the local police and fire stations; anyway, I guess I was just being a dad.

One of the cool things that the new property also had was wildlife. We had an owl living in our barn, wild peacocks, raccoons, possums, and even a Florida bobcat showed up from time to time. I loved being outside on the new property; it was so peaceful. I rallied up the boys every chance I could; whether it was to go swimming in the pool or play a game or sport outside, I just loved being out there.

I decided to purchase some toys for the property; I went to our local Honda dealership and purchased two four-wheel ATVs and a dirt bike. I also purchased matching gloves and helmets for the whole family. I had everything delivered to the house, and man did we have a blast riding those things around the yard. Denise and I would each grab an ATV and take the boys for rides all over the place. When no one else wanted to come outside, I would fire up the dirt bike and fly around the yard. There was just so much room; it was incredible. Every time that we had people over to the house, we would break out the ATVs for some high-speed fun. I even managed to get my seventy-three-year-old father to take one for a spin. These were definitely the good times for the Foley family.

CHAPTER 92

I wish I could say that things were good for everyone in my family, but that was just not the case. Since my partnership broke up with Alan, my sister's marriage was hitting some tough times. I could not help but feel responsible for their troubles, but I did feel that I was left with no choice when I broke our partnership up. Alan was working at a local ten-minute oil change; he smoked pot constantly and spent most of his nights going out with Jim and Andy. He was completely ignoring Paula and their children. There were many occasions when Paula would come to me in order to vent and cry about how bad Alan was treating her. The breaking point of their marriage unfortunately came from a confrontation that I had with Alan. Alan decided one day to try and "pull an Andy" on me. Alan called me one day demanding a lump sum of $2 million in place of the weekly checks that I was giving to Paula. Alan's threat was the same as Andy's: "Give me the money. or I will make sure that your company gets shut down." I found myself at a loss for words. I mean, this was my brother-in-law. I kept repeating that to myself, my own freakin' brother-in-law was threatening me for money. I managed to muster up three choice words for Alan: "Go fuck yourself."

The whole situation really sucked. I had no choice at the time. I had to tell Paula what a piece of shit her husband was. Paula had heard enough. Paula and Alan split immediately, and when all was said and done, Paula was left with no home and two kids to care for. Let's place Alan Nudelman at the top of the scumbag list for now. I could not believe how much this guy wanted to hurt my sister. He could care less that his kids had no place to live. He just wanted Paula to be miserable. I would have none of that. I once again called on Lenny to put his real estate cap on and find a place for my sister and her kids to live. My sister was very grateful for the help that I gave her. She wanted a town house if at all possible. She just did not want to have to deal with the upkeep of a regular house and yard.

Within a week, Lenny found my sister a new three-bedroom two-bathroom townhouse right in the middle of Weston. I wrote out a check for $240,000, which paid for the townhouse in full. I told my sister that some day when her credit was better, and her life was settled down, she could repay me. The truth of the matter is that I never wanted any money from my sister. I just wanted to make sure that she saved money and planned for her own future. Paula told me that Alan was pissed off when he heard about the townhouse. Fuck you, Alan. You should rot in hell for what you did to your own family.

CHAPTER 93

For a guy as strong-willed as I am, and for a guy that seemingly had the world by its short hairs, I sure did manage to get myself into one ugly situation. My only problem at this point of my life was that I could not stop taking these damn painkillers. By the middle of 2003, I had a $2,000 per month habit. The money was not the problem; the problem was that I was taking at least twenty 10 mg hydrocodone pills a day, and I still was not getting the "high" that I used to get from one pill. My body had obviously built up a tolerance to the pills, and I was completely addicted to them.

I made a decision to detox my body of this poison. I had had enough of running around with pockets full of pills. Now for anyone who has ever been hooked on opioids, you will understand exactly what I am talking about. Going cold turkey after years of abusing painkillers like hydrocodone or Percocet is a very painful experience. Like I said, I have always considered myself to be a physically and mentally strong individual, but withdrawing from the painkillers simply brought me to my knees. I started the detox process by doing a lot of online researching; I wanted to know what I was getting myself into.

What first hit me was the amount of information, websites, chat rooms, and public forums that were dedicated to people that were going through or had finished painkiller detoxification; this was obviously a huge problem across the country. The more I read about what I was about to go through, the more afraid I became of the process. I was about to enter into hell. The detox process took around two weeks to complete, with the worst withdrawal symptoms occurring in the first seventy-two hours. After the first seventy-two hours, the withdrawal symptoms would slowly disappear. As I read on, I found out that I could expect severe body and muscle aches, cold sweats, headaches, involuntary muscle spasms, an intense craving for the drug, a runny nose, diarrhea, restlessness, and sleepless nights. The whole thing just sounded horrible. In fact, I thought that most of the sites were exaggerating.

I decided to tell Denise about my addiction and what I was about to do to end it. I truly expected her to feel sorry for me, hug me, and support my courageous effort to rid myself of this addiction; instead, I was belittled. Denise just went off on how people who have addictions are weak, and they use the word *addiction* as an excuse to keep doing drugs or whatever their addiction might be. She made sure that I knew how disappointed she was in me. I felt like a real loser; I definitely did not want to hear that kind of talk out of my wife. The funny thing about this situation was that she was taking Paxil and Xanax for years to help with her depression and anxiety attacks. I mean, give me a fucking break. I never made her feel like any less of a woman or human being for that. Anyway, I am me, and she was her. We were two different types of people, and I just needed to get myself healthy again.

I decided to move into one of our guest rooms on the kids' side of the house while I went through the detox. I did my best to hide this whole situation from my kids; I simply told them that I was sick, and I did not want to get Mommy sick, so I would stay in that room until I was better.

The detox was a living hell: everything that I had read about and a whole lot more. The worst part for me were definitely the sleepless nights. I actually remember having hallucinations from the lack of sleep and the lack of drugs. I can remember several times during my first three nights when I fell to my knees and asked God to simply end my misery. I would be better off dead than feeling that kind of torturous pain and suffering. Thankfully, God spared my life. I had pinned a calendar on the wall to track the number of detox days; I also used a legal pad to write a daily journal so that I could track the withdrawal symptoms. The journal really helped me; I could refer back to days 1–3, and I saw the progress that I was making. Between the journal and the chat rooms, I was able to get through the detox process, but it was one of the toughest things I ever had to do.

Ten days, it took me ten days to rid my body of the poison that controlled me for years. Thank God, I was drug-free. It's funny, everything seemed a little different to me: food tasted different, things smelled different, I could even hear a little better. I had learned a tough life lesson, and I pray that anyone reading this right now that has an addiction, seek help now. It is never too late. "Peace be the journey."

CHAPTER 94

A very strange and very scary thing happened to me after I was detoxed. On one of the nights that I was having hallucinations, I thought I saw a figure standing in front of our barn. It was like four o'clock in the morning, and I could have sworn that I saw a man trying to get into one of the roll-up doors on the barn, but I had convinced myself that it was a hallucination. Something kept telling me that it was real, and I needed to make sure. One day, I sat down in our movie theater, and I played back the security camera feed from that night. Our security system cameras taped twenty-four hours a day, seven days a week, and burned the information onto CDs that erased themselves once a month. The night in question was still on the CD. I scanned the disk in fast forward until something caught my eye; there it was, a man, a strange man trying to get into our barn at 3:45 a.m., just like I had remembered. My whole body froze when I saw the image. What the hell was I going to do? I could not tell Denise because she would not be able to ever sleep again. I could not give police a description of this guy because it was just too grainy of a picture.

I just could not stop replaying a scenario through my head of what it would be like if someone actually broke into my house when we were sleeping. Yes, our security system was top of the line. Yes, the police would be notified and come to our rescue, but what would happen during those moments before the police arrived? I just had no way of defending my family from some psycho.

I decided that I needed to buy some protection, a piece of mind just in case someone tried to hurt my family; I decided to buy a handgun. I went to a local gun shop and told the owner what had happened. This guy was of course progun and was more than happy to lead me in the right direction. I wound out buying a semiautomatic 45 Berretta. The gun was lightweight, easy to use, and had an ammunition clip that held fourteen rounds. I purchased the gun, eight ammunition clips, and a cleaning kit. The gun store owner recommended that I take a class at a gun range that was just down the block from his store. Like everything else in my life, I took things a step further than I probably needed to. I decided to take a concealed weapons class so that I could carry the weapon on me at all times. I am glad I took the class; the instructors were awesome. Safety always came first with these guys, and they made sure that I fully understood how my weapon functioned and what I could expect if, God forbid, I ever had to use it to stop a predator. I passed the class, I purchased several hundred rounds of ammunition, and I made sure that I went to our local outdoor gun range several times a month in order to stay sharp and get used to the gun firing.

At night when I was home, I kept the gun loaded and close to my bed. When I was out of town, I kept the gun in our home safe, once again loaded and ready to go. I showed Denise how the weapon worked: click off the safety, aim, and shoot. I prayed that she would never have to use it, and I don't think she would have the nerve to fire that gun anyway, but at least she knew how to. During the week, I always carried the Berretta in my briefcase; I also carried all eight clips filled with ammunition. Why? I don't know. I guess I wanted to be prepared in case the Japanese ever attacked again. Just kidding.

CHAPTER 95

Let's get back to Global, back to the belly of the beast. The sales that Global was experiencing started to put a strain on the employees. We simply were not used to the nonstop action of data entry, customer service, machine programming, and shipping; every employee was working hard, but one of the biggest restrictions that we had was our warehouse space. The shelves in the warehouse were always filled with new equipment, and the warehouse floor was constantly packed with new programmed equipment ready to go out and old equipment that needed to be repaired and serviced. The only thing that would help us right now was more space. Don't get me wrong. We were getting by for now, but any more volume of incoming and outgoing machinery would definitely put a strain on our infrastructure. I sat down with Carrol and Herb, and we came to the decision that it was time to start looking for a bigger building. I decided that renting space was just a waste of money. We were going to be around for a long time, and we needed to start the implementation of our long-term goals.

I decided that Global would buy a building: a large enough building that we could grow into. So once again, I brought Lenny on board to find me a new facility. Now you would think that this guy would take me out to dinner or something for all the business that I threw his way. I mean, he made several hundred thousand in commissions already from my past purchases and sales, but no, nothing. I am just kidding again. I did not expect anything from anyone at this point of my life. The funny thing is that, once again, I was actually the one to find Global's future home. There was a new complex being built right in Weston, and the construction was to begin in 2004. I sent Lenny there to purchase a thirty-thousand-square-foot building, and once again, Lenny profited from my hard work. I held a company meeting at the end of the week and announced the building purchase and our future plans. Everyone seemed to get excited about our new future building and Global's overall direction.

Right around September of 2003, I received a very promising call from one of Global's larger customers. Rob O was an executive at Bear Sterns up in New York, and he currently owned over fifty Global ATM machines. Rob called me with a request for me to come to New York and meet with him and several Bear Sterns employees; why you ask? Well, Bear Sterns was interested in turning Global into a public company. I could not believe what I was hearing. Rob O made it very clear that Global would need to considerably grow in size, but he felt we were on the right track to initiate this meeting. I thought I was going to die. The only person that I told about the meeting was Carroll. I did not want things to get crazy at Global. People speculate way too much when they here news like this. The guys at Bear Sterns were working in a strict schedule and requested my presence in New York, only two days after our initial phone call. I simply could not get a flight that quickly that did not have two or three transfers or layovers. I can't stand flights that are not nonstop; it just drives me crazy.

I decided to treat myself to my first private charter. I called a local jet charter company and rented a Learjet for the trip; yes, it was expensive, but when you consider why I was going up to New York, it was very easy for me to justify the cost. Okay, for those of you who have never been on a private jet, I can tell you one thing: it doesn't suck. In fact, I could not believe how enjoyable travel was via private plane. The crew was professional, the jet was beautiful, the food that was catered on board was awesome, and we got to New York faster than I ever had gotten there before. No stupid security lines, no waiting anywhere, no hassles, just pure luxury and comfort. I highly recommend the experience. So I actually landed in New Jersey's Teterboro Airport, and Bear Stern had a limo waiting for me to take me into Manhattan, first-class the whole way. Bear Sterns had this insane building right in the middle of the financial district. I could not believe the size and elegance of this place. Security at this place was like Fort Knox; it took me longer to get up to the meeting than it took me to get from New Jersey to New York.

The meeting was held in a conference room that seemed to be larger than my new house. It was a formal get-together; we started by signing disclosures and noncompete forms so that everyone would be protected. I will be honest with you all. I should have brought a lawyer or at least someone a heck of a lot smarter than me. I had no real clue what I was signing. No biggie, these were just precautionary steps just in case this deal went to the next level. I went over Global' s past, present, and how I envisioned its future; the people at Bear Sterns seemed to be very impressed with how quickly we were growing and even more impressed that I planned on having over ten thousand machines operating within the next twenty-four to thirty-six months. Rob O and his crew agreed that if Global could reach that level of operation, then a public offering would be in the books. I agreed to keep them updated quarterly on our progress, and I also signed an agreement that would give them first right of refusal to take Global public. I shook hands with the big boys of Bear Sterns, and we parted ways.

On the limo ride back to the airport, I found myself feeling very proud. I can't explain it. It was not an ego thing, I guess. I just really felt proud that a company the size of Bear Sterns was paying attention to my little Global Vending. I guess you cannot take the little guy out of me because on the ride back to the airport, I asked the limo driver to stop at a local delicatessen. I purchased a six-pack of light beer and a few bags of chips for the flight back to Florida; yes, the plane had food and hard liquor, but you know what, enough was enough. I needed a good old-fashioned beer and a greasy bag of chips. I took my shoes off on the flight back, knocked down a few beers, and ate my chips. I even offered the pilot and copilot a beer, but thank God they were normal, responsible men; they refused. They did laugh, but they refused. Now let's see what I can do about hitting that ten thousand unit mark so I could get stinkin' rich and party with hookers and rock stars.

CHAPTER 96

October 2003 came around, and I was hit with some great news on the location front. Kim W informed me that we needed to do a presentation for a Taco Bell/KFC chain that currently operated over two hundred locations, and they were very interested in our ATM machines. The presentation would take place next week in California at their quarterly co-op meeting. I could tell that Kim W was just getting warmed up with good news. Kim always had a little shit-eating grin that she used to prepare me for big doings. Kim W informed me that she had heard back from one of the dollar store chains that she had been pursuing. Kim slid a letter over to me from one of the country's largest dollar store corporations in America. The letter requested our presence at their annual budget meeting to discuss the placement of ATM machines in all seven thousand plus locations that they operated nationwide. The corporation had already done its due diligence by calling some of our fast-food restaurants to see how we operated as a company. We received high grades across the board, and the dollar store chain felt that our machines would be a great fit for their stores. The letter clearly indicated that they simply needed to discuss the logistics of placing our machines in their stores. In other words, this was seemingly a done deal. The meeting was scheduled for the second week in February of 2004. Somebody please pinch me or slap me. Could this really be happening? Please don't let me be dreaming, please.

I sat down at my desk with Kim and Carrol, and we went over our current ATM numbers: Global had sold a total of 2,700 machines at that point, we had over 1,100 machines already placed and operating in the field, we had just under 800 additional machines either programmed or in the process of being programmed for secured locations (some of these machines were already at their locations waiting to be activated; others were with Brett at his Shawnee, Kansas, warehouse waiting to be installed, and the rest were in Global Vending's warehouse). We still needed to purchase and find locations for an additional 800 machines that we had already sold. I checked Global's bank accounts, and we had enough cash reserve to purchase double that amount. Global's business plan was right on track. The coolest part was that once we signed on the dollar store chain and placed machines in their locations, we would be right at the 10,000-unit mark set by Bear Sterns. I had told Bear Sterns at our meeting to expect that level of operation from us in twenty-four to thirty-six months, yet here we were, preparing to meet that goal in less than two months. I was absolutely freaking out. I made it very clear to Kim W and Carrol that the dollar store news was not to leave my office. If people started to talk, then it would be very possible for one of our competitors to stick their necks into the mix. The dollar store contract would be worth over $35M in equipment sales for Global Vending, not to mention the residual income and a shot at a public offering with Bear Sterns. I put some serious pressure on Herb to get installations and shipping to happen at a faster pace. If Kim W and I were to sign on the two hundred KFC/Taco Bell locations next week, we were going to need some room in the warehouse. I called in our UPS sales rep to help coordinate the effort with Herb, and I authorized Herb to hire as many temp workers as he needed to get things moving.

These moments, this kind of "good pressure" and fast-paced activity, is what I loved the most about running Global: make a decision and stick with it, roll with the punches, and then simply execute. What a rush.

CHAPTER 97

I decided to start to put together a list of Global's customers that were considered to be "heavy hitters," people that I would approach after we signed on the dollar stores to make additional, larger purchases at somewhat discounted prices. Global had several large investors that included doctors, lawyers, entrepreneurs, and financial investment groups. Out of Global' s current three hundred plus investors, I would say that we had fifteen that were heavy hitters, people with the ability to invest a lot more than they currently had invested. Global did not currently have a "re-investment program," so that would be something that I would have to work on. To this point, Global never made it a practice to call old investors to purchase additional equipment; there just was never a shortage of new people looking to buy ATM machines from us.

So I am compiling this list of Global's largest customers when Bruce hit me with a request for help. Bruce had a person that was interested in making a large purchase of ATM machines. Bruce called this guy his first true "whale," a person capable of buying a seriously large number of machines from us. He had several long conversations with this individual, and he just felt that this guy needed to hear from me, the company owner. I usually did not get involved in sales until the customer made the commitment to come down to Global for a visit, but Bruce insisted that I needed to get involved now. Bruce gave me all the information that he had gathered on this kid. Yes, that right, I said kid,. Kent was his name, and he was only in his mid-twenties. Kent lived in Sioux Falls, South Dakota: he owned an arena football team, and his family owned and operated huge banks up in the Dakotas.

I decided to place a call to Kent to see if I could help the sales process move along for Bruce. Kent and I had a very long first conversation; we spoke to each other like we had known each other our entire lives. Kent was an ambitious go-getter that very easily could have just lived off his family's fortunes, but instead, Kent chose to make fortunes of his own. I liked him from day 1. I convinced Kent to come down to Global that week so that we could talk in person and hopefully bring him on as a customer. When Kent arrived at Global with his beautiful wife, and I could not believe how young he looked to me. I mean, yes, he was in his mid-twenties, but Kent looked like a teenager. We decided to go for lunch at my Weston Country Club where we talked business, cracked jokes, and quickly became friends. I will never forget how our day ended. We arrived back at Global after lunch. Kent and his wife were going to be flying back to South Dakota that same evening, so I only had an hour or so to close our business.

> Kent: So, Tom, how many machines does your largest customer currently have in his portfolio?
> Me: 105, why?
> Kent: Well, I decided that I want to be your new largest customer.
> Me: That's great, Kent. I look forward to doing business with you for a very long time. How many machines to you want to purchase?
> Kent: I will need you to drop your machine price to $4,000 each. Is that possible?
> Me: I have never sold a machine for less than $5,000, Kent. You would have to be talking about a large purchase to get that price. I don't want to turn Global into a garage sale. I am sure you understand.
> (Kent broke out a checkbook and wrote a check made out to Global. He slid the check over to me. The check was in the amount of $1.2 million.)

Kent: Three hundred machines to start, and once they are placed, we will talk about a much larger purchase.

Me: Kent, you have yourself a deal. Let me get Bruce to put together the paperwork for you.

Kent: Listen, I have to run. My wife wants to see the beach before we fly out tonight. Just fax the paperwork to my office. I will sign it and fax it back tomorrow. It was nice meeting you, Tom.

Me: Same here. Have a great flight home and welcome aboard.

Now Kent is my type of guy. We shook hands, and that was good enough for him. That is the way I liked to do business. Kent knew he was not simply buying equipment; he was investing in a company, in a concept. Kent was young, but he was old-school business: let's shake hands and leave the details up to others. I wish I had three hundred Kents as customers.

CHAPTER 98

Tell me, folks, tell me how things could have gotten any better for me. My company was exploding at the seams. It would appear that we were heading for greatness, the true American dream, garage operation to an American icon. I wish I could fully explain to you the feelings that I had inside. I wanted to celebrate and live large in the moment. I was a guy that seemingly had it all. Didn't I? The answer to that question unfortunately was no. A large piece of life's puzzle was missing for me. I had no one to truly celebrate with. I mean, Carrol and I were best friends, and we went out often and ate and drank and laughed together, but that was not the kind of celebrating that I am talking about. I needed, I desperately desired, a significant other to share my feelings of joy with. My relationship with Denise was simply not like that. I loved Denise. I always had, and I always will. But Denise and I were more of a comfort couple than a couple that was truly in love. What I mean by that is that we simply were two different people whose lives made sense to stay together, but we would never be soulmates. We had two great kids that we both loved very much, we went out on weekends, we shared good times and laughed together, but at the end of the day, there was still a great distance between us, an almost emptiness. I wanted, no, I needed more than that.

The best comparison that I can make for you in order to explain what I was feeling at this time, and how I reacted to this feeling, would be to compare my situation to that of a music group that had just become famous. Think about it. I am sure you have seen documentaries or read magazine articles or books that discussed the rise and fall of some very famous bands. The story was almost exactly the same with each group that self-imploded: they would scratch and

250

claw their way to the top, simply work their asses off for a lifetime to get to the top, and as soon as they got there, they would become self-destructive and simply fall apart. Some band members would turn to drugs, others would become egomaniacs that no one wanted to work with, and yet others could not handle or manage money, and they would become bankrupt. Whatever path they chose to self-destruct via, the bottom line is that most of these men and women were simply lonely at the top; they almost all expressed the need for someone special to share and help control their success. That is the feeling that I suddenly found myself fighting: I was a successful guy that wanted to share, to celebrate his life with someone special, but I just could not get my special someone to come on board.

I am embarrassed to say that I decided to turn back to my old painkiller friends. You would think after all that I had gone through detoxing myself of that poison that I would never even consider going back to taking pills, but I did. I convinced myself that I could control it this time; I would just take a few on days when I was feeling down or in need of a pick-me-up. Spoken like a true addict. Listen, folks, I am not blaming my drug use on Denise. I was obviously addicted to this shit, and I should have sought out a support group to help me stay off pills. I did not do that. I could have broken up my marriage and gone out in the world and looked for my soulmate or whatever I was seeking at the time, but instead I chose to stay committed to the woman that I married and to my children whom I loved dearly and did not want to hurt. The drugs were just an excuse, an escape, and I was the one who chose to start using again.

CHAPTER 99

I did seem to find a secondary escape in my life to be poker. I continued to play at the Hard Rock, and I also played anytime that I was in Las Vegas. I had developed a real skill for the game. It seemed that while I was playing in a tournament, I was in another world, a fantasy world in which hundreds of people were battling me, and I needed to strategize to defeat each and every one of them. I had accumulated over $60,000 in winnings in 2003, and I kept that money in my home safe in case there was ever a rainy day. (What a stupid line, most people back then did not make $60,000 a year. What kind of a rainy day for God's sake?) I had the money wrapped in casino receipts that showed where, when, and how much money I had received that day; it really looked cool to have that much cash laying around.

Anyway, poker definitely got me through some tough times when I was feeling sad and lonely. Speaking of money, my home safe, and lonely, Denise's mother had suddenly become a steady visitor to our house. Apparently, Lenny had started to drink again, and Denise's mother did not want any part of that. Lenny had been an alcoholic for the majority of his life, but he had sobered up and was alcohol-free for several years until now. Maybe it was all the money that he had made through my real estate deals. Whatever his reasons were, Lenny was boozing it up again, and Ronnie (Denise's mother), wanted no part of that life again. Ronnie started showing up at our house with money that she placed in our home safe. She usually brought over a couple of hundred dollars every week. I have no idea where she was getting the money from, but I do know that she intended to use the money to hire a high-end divorce lawyer and rid herself of Lenny.

Ronnie had almost $10,000 in our safe by November of 2003. Her plan of course was to divorce Lenny and take half of his fortune that was left to him by his mother and father, not to mention the money that he was making as a real estate broker. It was real sneaky shit that she was doing. I would expect no less from her.

Life seemed to be picking up pace, and maybe I should have slowed things down just a little in order to keep things under control, but that just was not and still is not my style. Balls to the wall, full throttle at all times is the way that I have always lived my life.

CHAPTER 100

Kim W and I hit the road for California on our mission to close down these two hundred fast-food locations, get back to Global, and prepare for our 2004 meeting with the dollar store chain. What I did not know at the time was that this particular trip would change my life forever. This trip would change the person that I was. This trip would bring a whole new perspective to the way that I viewed myself and my life as a whole.

We were like a well-oiled machine when it came to our sales presentations. Once I stopped talking, Kim would know to jump right in and take over; when Kim stopped talking, it was my turn to take the ball. We presented ourselves with professionalism and grace. We knew our industry inside and out; the people that we made presentations for appreciated our knowledge and ability to answer any and all questions. We called ourselves the dream team; just try and say no to us, let's see what happens. Kim and I closed the deal in California like true professionals; it almost seemed to be getting a little too easy or something. Just kidding, there is no such thing as too easy in sales. We were kind of like an old married couple on the road. I know that sounds funny, but we had done some serious traveling over the past two years. I made sure that we always stayed in the nicest hotels in whatever town we were in. We always flew first-class, or we would take a private charter whenever it made sense to do so. After work each day on the road, we would either eat together in the hotel, or we would find a nice restaurant to kick back at and unwind. We learned each other's travel habits and knew how much time we each needed to get ready for a meeting or to get up in the morning. It's funny how two people that simply worked together could become so familiar with each other's needs.

On the night that we closed the deal in California, Kim and I decided to celebrate at a highly recommended Italian restaurant. The restaurant was just beautiful. They had great food, great service, a very relaxing atmosphere, and my favorite wine, Pinot Grigio Santa Margarita; yes, I am a simple person when it comes to wine. I could not help but notice a bit of a change in Kim that evening. Kim was really dolled up and more complimentary toward me than she normally was. At one point in the evening, I realized that Kim was dressed different than usual. She had on a long tight skirt that had a nice long slit up the side. She was wearing a silk button-up top that hugged her body and was unbuttoned enough to show off her sexy upper body. I had always thought that Kim was an attractive woman, but it seemed that on this particular evening, she wanted me to realize just how hot she really was. I found myself staring at her, and I found her staring at me. After one particularly awkward moment toward the end of our meal, Kim took things one step forward. Kim placed one of her hands on top of mine and told me that she needed to talk to me. She was having a problem at the office, and I needed to listen to what she had to say. Great, she was going to quit; that was the only thing that I could think of. If she quits, I will kill her. I need this woman and her locating talents.

> Me: Okay, Kim, lay it on me. What seems to be the problem? Obviously it's important because you are holding my hand. Let me have it.
>
> Kim: Listen, Tom, this is not easy for me. I need my job, but there is something that is just eating away at me. Please listen with an open mind. Okay?
>
> Me: I promise, but you are freaking me out right now.
>
> Kim: Are you fooling around with Kim S?
>
> Me: What? That's what you want to talk about? Me and Kim S. Listen, my friend, and listen good. I have told this over and over again

to every person that has thought that Kim S and I were fooling around. It simply is not true. Kim S and I have never touched each other, ever! I have known her for a long time, and she is a good soul. She just needs a lot of attention to help her get through some tough times, and I like to give her that attention. That's it. I will be honest with you though, my friend, I don't see how that would be any of your business anyway. Why would that be a problem for you?

Kim: Because it makes me jealous. I get jealous, Tom. I like you. Don't you know that? Can't you see the way that I am around you?

Me: I like you too, Kim. We have a good thing going for us, and I need you and your talents. You have become a very close person in my life.

Kim: No, Tom, no, you don't get it. I want to be with you. I don't want to be your travel buddy. I want to share myself with you. I want a relationship like I thought you and Kim S were having.

(Man, was I an idiot. This chick wanted to bang my brains lose, and I couldn't see that. What the hell had become of me? Did I turn into a fag at one point and not realize it? How much more does this Southern hottie have to spell it out for me.)

Me: Oh, wow, are you sure? I mean, you're married. I am married. How long have you felt this way?

Kim: Listen, Tom, I have felt like this for quite some time, but you are a tough guy to get through to. I love my husband, and I know you love your wife, but I need more than my husband will give me. We have drifted

apart over the years, and I am lonely. You
seem to be a little lonely yourself.
(Man, did she hit that nail right on the head.
This was the kind of shit that I was used to seeing in movies. I was totally not prepared for this
conversation.)
Me: What do you say we walk back to the hotel
instead of taking a taxi. I need some air.
Kim: That sounds great.

The walk back to the hotel took almost forty-five minutes. It
was fairly brisk out, so I decided to put my sports coat over Kim's
shoulders. Kim decided to wrap her arm around mine and walk arm
in arm with me back to the hotel. I did nothing to discourage her. As
we arrived at the hotel, there were several steps leading to the front
door; Kim took a few quick steps ahead of me and stopped in her
tracks. She turned and faced me. Since she placed herself in front of
me, she was almost eye to eye with me. Kim placed her arms on my
shoulders, closed her eyes, and pulled me toward her until we were
embraced in a kiss: an unbelievable long, sexy, mind-blowing kiss.
Once again, I not only didn't discourage her, but I participated with
extreme passion. Kim and I went up to my room and made love until
the wee hours of the morning. She and I were obviously both starving for attention and affection. It had been such a long time for me,
to be able to fully express my emotions with a woman that wanted
more and more as the night went on. I was sure that this was what a
normal healthy sexual relationship was supposed to feel like.

The next morning, I woke up in an empty bed. Kim had left
a note for me explaining that she had to pack for our flight back
to Florida later that day. The note had a heart at the bottom and a
little love message, "Thank you for such a wonderful evening. It was
everything I had hoped it would be and more. Love, Kim."

I lay there in bed with so many emotions running through my
head. I felt guilty that I had cheated on Denise, but at the same
time, I felt that I had tried my hardest to get her to be that special
someone with me. I was a little worried that Kim might expect us to

become a couple and get divorces. Then I just felt great. My body had never been so relaxed. I had never been at such peace as I was at that moment. I decided to just go with the flow and see how things progressed with Kim. I was not going to get a divorce. I loved Denise, and that was that.

I went to take a shower, I had some packing to do of my own, and I was starving. After only a few minutes in the shower, I heard my room door open and slam shut. Kim announced that she was back. She told me that she had taken my room key so that she could get back in and hoped that was all right with me.

I said, "No problem. I will be out in a few minutes."

Not so fast, Tom, not so fast. Before I knew it, Kim was in the bathroom with a hotel robe on. She stared at me in the shower, dropped the robe, and came into the shower. Kim was not quite done with me yet. We enjoyed each other in the shower like two lovebirds. Kim obviously did not want this relationship to end, and quite frankly, neither did I. We spoke over breakfast, and thank God, Kim was on the same page as I was. Kim did not want to leave her husband, and she certainly did not expect me to leave Denise. She just wanted a man that would take care of her sexual and emotional needs, and she wanted to be the woman to take care of mine. How could I argue with that? It was funny. At no time from that point forward were there any uncomfortable moments with Kim.

We still worked great together, we had no problem when our spouses were around us as a group, and when the time was right, we would both be ready for some emotionally satisfying sex and love. I accepted this for what it was, two lonely people that were being there for each other, nothing more, nothing less. But yes, I was now officially a cheating husband. (Take a few more painkillers, you jackass. That will make things better!)

CHAPTER 101

It was now the middle of November 2003, and the holidays were rapidly approaching. I was in bed one night watching the Local 10 news, when one particular story caught my attention.

The news reporter's name was Diane Magnum, and she was reporting a story about a local Easterseals charity center that had been robbed. Can you believe that? The Broward County Easterseals had collected toy donations for the past several months, and they were going to pass out the toys to all the Easterseals children just before Christmas, and some lowlife pieces of shit decided to break into the Easterseals building and steal all the toys. It made me sick to my stomach.

I called the news station and left a message for someone to call me back. I explained that I had heard the news story about the Easterseals robbery, and I wanted to help. The following day at work, one of the producers for Local 10 News called me and gave me a contact person at Easterseals that I could call and offer my help to. I called the Easterseals location, I found out the ages of the kids that were supposed to be receiving the now stolen toys, and I found out how many children there were. I then told the lady that ran the Broward County Easterseals that I was going to replace all the stolen toys. She was just overjoyed.

We decided that I would deliver the toys on the day of their planned holiday party. I grabbed $10,000 of my poker winnings from my home safe. I grabbed Denise, Bruce, and a few other Global employees, and we took a ride to the local Toys R Us. I have never had so much fun shopping. We filled like thirty shopping carts with toys for both girls and boys. The people at Toys R Us thought we were just out of our minds.

On the day of the Easterseals party, I convinced Bruce to wear a Santa Claus outfit, and Bruce, Denise, and I headed over to the Easterseals party. We were greeted by a Chanel 10 News crew that filmed the entire event. The kids were awesome; they were all just so thankful and happy that Santa was there with presents for them. I received like one hundred hugs and kisses from these little angels, and the director of the charity must have thanked us a dozen times; what a great feeling. That night, much to our surprise, Channel 10 News aired the story. I must have received over two dozen phone calls from family and friends that had seen us on TV. We had done a good thing, and that is what life is all about.

CHAPTER 102

Back at the office, I continued to prepare for a monster 2004. I purchased scanners and software so that Burt and his customer service crew could scan all old documents and place them in our ACT database. I wanted to rid our company of any and all paper documents; there was no need to have dozens of file cabinets full of papers when technology allowed us to store everything on our server. Burt's crew was proceeding at a very slow pace, and that was not acceptable to me. We needed to be prepared for 2004. We needed to be completely caught up with all old business so that we could hit the ground running once the dollar stores came on board. Burt was having trouble with one of his staff members. He was continuously in my office complaining that Nitae was the cause of his slow progress and that she was not following his directions.

Now let me tell you, I had never had a problem with Nitae being productive. Nitae was always more than willing to dig in and help the cause, but Burt insisted time and time again that she was the root of his problems. I hired Burt to manage and supervise a department. I paid Burt a ridiculous amount of money to do that job, and I found myself compelled to accept his judgment when it came to his staff. I did not want to start micromanaging all over again, so I told Burt that he needed to figure things out on his own. I would not get involved. Burt's response to that was he fired Nitae. I can't tell you how much I hated to hear that. Nitae was a single mom, and I know she needed the job, and truth be told, I believe Burt fired Nitae because she was black. Burt always had a problem with black people, and I just could not help thinking that his prejudice was the reason for her firing.

I should have not allowed that to happen; I should have intervened and offered her another position in the company, but I didn't.
To this day, I regret listening to Burt and allowing Nitae to have been
fired. Please accept my apologies, Nitae. You are a good soul.

CHAPTER 103

The year 2003 ended just like the past few years had: I gave out bonuses, we had a great holiday party, and the outlook for the next year once again looked great. Our numbers for 2003 were just off the charts. We had a total of 1,200 operating ATM machines; we had another 1,100 ATM machines ready for installation and/or immediate operation. Our sales for 2004 were over $7M. The 1,200 operating machines were producing over $110,000 per month in residual income. We still needed to purchase and place another 1,000 ATM machines for customers that had purchased during 2003, but that would be taken care of in the first quarter of 2004 when we started placing machines in the dollar stores and the fast-food restaurants that we had not yet gotten equipment to. Global's bank accounts had over $1.2 million to cover future machine purchases. I had over $600,000 in my personal bank accounts, and my retirement account was now valued at over $1 million. I would say that financially, we were doing better than I had ever dreamed. I thanked my lucky stars for my good fortune. I hoped and prayed that our success would continue in 2004.

I do want to make one thing very clear at this point. I realize that I purchased a lot of luxury items over the past few years. I realize that to the average guy, my purchases might even seem excessive, but hey, I was just enjoying the fruits of my labors. I was living my American dream. Numbers-wise, I only spend 18 percent of Global's total income on myself—18 percent, that's it. Eighty-two percent of Global's income went to operations, employees, and of course to our customers. In fact, Global had sold just over $12M worth of ATM machines, and Global customers had already received almost $4M in returns, and that was with only one-third of our sold machines operating. I projected at that time that the average customer would get his entire return on investment in less than three years. That's a great investment no matter what investment you are talking about, and best of all, I had 350 happier-than-shit customers. I guess my point is that I was not being greedy or anything like that. Everyone was reaping the rewards of Global's ATM program: everyone. I really hate to say it. In fact, it hurts me to even think about it, but I must cue the dickhead for the last time: "All good things must come to an end."

weapons. Shit, there were a lot of them. I took aim on the two figures that were closest to me and standing side by side. If I hit one or two of them, maybe the rest would panic and run. Suddenly, I realized that my trigger finger was now flush to the trigger. The safety was no longer in the safe position. It was now or never. Out of the corner of my left eye, I suddenly spotted a man in uniform. What the hell? It was a Broward County sheriff, and he was walking right in the middle of this pack of intruders. Something was not right here. I have no idea what was going on, but I do know that I was not going to shoot a cop.

I backed away from my office door. I hit the button on the Berretta that released the ammunition clip, and I slid back the loading chamber again, which ejected the live shell that was ready to be fired. I put the weapon back in my briefcase, and I stood there for a moment fighting off a fucking heart attack. I needed to go and find out what was really going on here. For God's sake, I almost shot another human being. As I walked out of my office, I raised my voice.

I said, "What the hell is going on out here? Who the hell are you, people? Officer, what's going on?"

My voice prompted the whole crowd to turn toward me. Holy cow, the two intruders closest to me were both woman: I almost shot two fucking women, oh my god.

The first woman said, "I am FBI Special Agent Delano (sorry, name slightly changed due to me being a pussy author), and I have a task force with me to serve search-and-seizure warrants on this premise. Please come with me, Mr. Foley, so that I can explain to you exactly why we are here.

Agent Delano and another woman walked into my office and motioned for me to follow them. How the fuck did this person know my name, and why were they here with a task force and search-and-seizure warrants? God, I hoped this was just a nightmare, and I was going to wake up laughing in a few minutes. Maybe it was the drugs fucking with my brain. Sorry, guys, it was not a nightmare, not going to wake up in a few minutes. Things were only about to get worse, much worse. As I entered my own office, Agent Delano hit me with her first question.

> Agent Delano: Do you have any weapons on the premise?
>
> (In my mind, my answer was, "Yeah, I almost blew your fucking brains out like two minutes ago, moron.")
>
> Me: I have a 45 in my briefcase.
>
> (Agent Delano seemed taken aback by that. She reached into my briefcase and took out the Berretta and all the ammunition clips.)
>
> Agent Delano: Nice piece. Why all the ammo?
>
> Me: Just in case.
>
> Agent Delano: Just in case what? A war breaks out?
>
> (In my mind, I thought, *Hey, that's funny. That is what I used to joke around about. You know, the Japanese might attack again. I will keep that to myself.*)
>
> Me: Listen, I need to know what is going on here. Who are all these people, and what does the FBI want with my company?
>
> (Out in the main sales office, I could see at least two dozen agents now. This was getting crazier by the minute.)
>
> Agent Delano: Those people are a task force from multiple agencies. They are from the FBI, DEA, US Marshals, ice agents, and some Broward County Sherriff's officers. We are here to execute search-and-seizure warrants due to a complaint filed against your company.
>
> Me: This is all because of a complaint? Who complained and about what?
>
> Agent Delano: Look, Mr. Foley, I will be asking the questions here today, and I need you to answer them to the best of your ability.

THE DAY THE FEDS CAME CALLING

Perhaps we can clear this whole mess up. In the meantime, the agents outside are going to run warrant checks on you and all your employees, search the building, and box up all your business files and any other evidence that we find. We will also be making copies of your computer server hard drive and all your individual computer hard drives.

Me: Take my files? What are you talking about? It doesn't sound like we are going to clear this mess up if you are taking my files. We need those files to operate here. We have not put them all into our database yet. This is a freakin' joke.

Agent Delano: (with a whole lot of attitude) This is no joking matter, Mr. Foley. You have been accused of running a multimillion-dollar Ponzi scheme. The files are being confiscated as evidence. We have already seized your personal and your business bank accounts. Now I need you to answer some questions.

Me: You seized my bank accounts? Are you serious? I just wrote out over 350 checks to my customers. They are all going to bounce. Holy shit!

(Then it hit me, a Ponzi scheme! I had only heard that term used once before by Andy, Alan, and scumbag lawyer Andrew Cove. Suddenly, I understood why these people were in my building.)

Agent Delano: The checks that you wrote to your customers will bounce. There will be no more fraudulent checks leaving this company.

Me: There has never been any fraud in this company. Look, Agent Delano, you have been lied to, big-time. Let me guess, the complaint came from Andrew Levinson and Alan Nudelman. Right?

Agent Delano: What makes you think that?

Me: Because they threatened to have my company shut down. They both tried to blackmail me. They promised to make up lies about my company and have this place shut down. I have a signed statement from Andrew Levinson in my home safe along with a tape recording of him admitting to making shit up about my company. He even had a lawyer call me for money. You guys need to believe me. You know what, I want a lawyer here right now. I don't feel comfortable talking to you.

Agent Delano: Sorry. This is a crime scene. You cannot have a lawyer come in here. Besides, if you didn't do anything wrong, what do you need a lawyer for. You aren't under arrest, at least not yet.

Me: This is freakin' crazy.

(There was a knock at my office door, and a male agent walked in. He whispered something into Agent Delano's ear.)

Agent Delano: Mr. Foley, we need you to put the top up on your car.

Me: My car? Why are you messing with my car?

Agent Delano: We have a seizure warrant for your car. It is being confiscated.

(I turned around and looked out of my office window. Sure enough, my pride and joy, my AMG Roadster was already on a flatbed tow truck.

Me: I don't believe this. If I am not under arrest, what gives you the right to take my property?

(Agent Delano got moodier and threw a copy of
the search-and-seizure warrants on my desk.)
Agent Delano: A federal judge gave us the right
to take your car. Oh, and by the way, I need
you to call your wife and tell her to go back
to your home. We have a second task force
waiting there to execute search-and-seizure
warrants on your residence.

Okay, now I was really about to lose it, and I mean big-time. In my mind, I thought, *Let me get this straight. I am going to call Denise: "Hey, honey, how is your day going? That's great. Listen, I need you to do me a small favor. I need you to go home and open the gate and front door for a bunch of FBI agents that are waiting there. No, no, don't worry, they just want to execute search-and-seizure warrants. Everything is fine."* Yeah, right, that was going to go over well. I argued back and forth with this absolute bitch of a person. I offered to go and open the house up myself.

Agent Delano said, "You are not going anywhere right now, Mr. Foley. We still need to run warrant checks, and you still need to answer some questions. Look, it's up to you. Your wife can go back to your residence and open the door for the agents, or the agents can ram your front gate and kick in your front door. Your choice."

What choice did I have? I certainly did not want my front gate rammed open or my front door kicked in. This just did not seem real, but I did it. I made the call to Denise.

Needless to say, Denise freaked out big-time; I can't blame her for that. It's not every day that your husband calls you and asks you to go home and open the front door to your home so that the FBI can search it. I did my best to calm her down, but that was a waste of time. Denise was definitely in shock and was looking for answers that I could not give her yet. After a brief exchange of words, I ordered Denise to go home, and she did.

When I hung up the phone, I went into serious attack mode. I tried over and over again to tell Agent Delano that she had this all wrong and that she had been lied to by Alan and Andy. Agent Delano insisted that her investigation to this point had proven my company to be a fraud. Agent Delano decided to show me her "smoking gun," the evidence that proved that Global was a big fraud. Agent Delano showed me copies of past checks that I had sent to customers. She explained that her team had gone through my bank records with a fine-tooth comb, and the checks memo sections clearly showed that several Global customers were getting paid for the same ATM machines.

She concluded from the filed complaint and the repeating pay-outs that Global was a Ponzi scheme. Global was selling the same machines over and over again and was paying new customers with old customers' investment money. She continued her allegations by saying that I was pocketing the customers' money in order to support my lavish lifestyle.

I could not listen to any more of this garbage. I put up my hand, indicating a stop signal. I gave Agent Delano a very sarcastic chuckle.

I said, "So are you telling me that these customers are the ones that filed the complaint? These customers claimed to have been defrauded?"

Agent Delano replied, "No, I am not saying that. In fact, I have not spoken to any of your victims yet."

I said, "Oh, now they are victims. I didn't think these allegations would have ever come from customers because all of my customers are happy. All my customers know exactly how Global operates. I am not selling the same machines over and over again, and I am certainly not spending my customers' money on any lavish lifestyle. Are you aware that we have a program called the shared location program? Do you know how it works? Silly question, sorry. If you knew about it, you would not be here right now."

I explained the shared location program to Agent Delano and her mute partner. (This other female agent had not yet said even one word.) I told Agent Delano that the two morons that filed the complaint participated in the program while they were with Global.

Agent Delano said, "Sorry, Mr. Foley, I simply don't believe you."

I told here, "Can I show you some of the files in order to prove my point?"

Agent Delano replied, "Sure, enlighten me."

I already fucking hated her.

Agent Delano followed me to the customer service office. On the way to the office, I saw agent after agent lining cardboard boxes up on the floor. My guess was that the boxes were for our files. I also saw an agent with a laptop hooked up to our server, and my guess on that one was that he was copying our hard drive. I could hear a bunch of the other employees in one of the back offices where an agent stood guard at the door. I felt horrible for them. I could just imagine what was going through their heads right now.

When we arrived at the customer service office, I reached into one of the file cabinets and pulled out a file that matched one of the customer checks that Agent Delano had made a copy of. I opened the file and pulled out the customer's signed shared location agreement, which clearly indicated that the customer was aware that he did not yet own any ATM machines and that he was receiving rebates of his own money while he waited for his own locations. Agent Delano read the agreement. Within a few seconds, her little shit-eating grin had disappeared from her face. The really funny part about the agreement that I gave to Agent Delano was that it was signed by Alan Nudelman as Global's authorized representative. I could tell that this just ruined her day. My guess is that when Alan and Andy filed the complaint, Agent Delano thought she had some slam-dunk case. I mean, why would two former Global insiders lie to the FBI? Well, because they were fucking retards; that was why. Anyway, let's just say that things were not so rosy all of a sudden for Agent Delano.

My cell phone began to ring nonstop. I could see from the caller ID that it was Denise, but I could not talk to her yet. I needed to try and get some answers here first. I needed to stop this train wreck from continuing. Yes, I still had this crazy notion that I could reverse what was going on in front of me. I was in complete denial that this could actually be happening.

Another agent came into the office and wanted to speak to Agent Delano. It hit me now; Agent Delano must be the lead agent in charge because everyone wanted to talk to her about developing situations. Agent Delano asked me to follow her and this new male agent to our warehouse. When we got into the warehouse, the male agent pointed at all the boxes that were stacked up from the floor to the ceiling on steel shelves. Our warehouse ceiling was over twenty feet tall, so there was plenty of boxes staring us in the face.

> Male Agent: What is in these boxes?
> Me: Each one of those boxes hold a new ATM machine that is waiting to be programmed. The two hundred plus boxes that are out near our loading dock are brand-new ATM machines that have already been programmed and are waiting to be shipped to locations.
> (I shit you not, folks, God's honest truth, the male agent turned to Agent Delano.)
> Male Agent: Ooppss.

Yeah, ooppss, motherfuckers. We actually buy our customers ATM machines like we promise to. We are a legitimate company, you dumb fucks. No, of course I didn't say that to them, but that was exactly what was going through my mind at the time.

My cell phone rang again. Again, it was Denise. I decided to take the call this time. Denise was hysterically crying. She begged me to come home. There were over twenty agents at the house, and they were taking everything: Denise's car, her SUV, the ATVs, my dirt bike, all her jewelry, and now they wanted the combination to the safe. Fuck this, I had enough.

> Me: You people are sick. You're taking things from my house now? I will not say another word. I will not answer another question. This is horseshit. I have to have some rights. I need to leave and be with my wife. I want a fucking lawyer.
> Agent Delano: (with a smug-ass bitch attitude) So go, go home. Go get a lawyer. Who's stopping you?

Me: You. You told me that I could not leave. You told me that I could not have an attorney here.

Agent Delano: No, Mr. Foley, I told you that your lawyer could not come in the building because this was a crime scene. I never told you you could not have one meet you outside. You chose to voluntarily answer my questions. I told you we just needed to run warrant checks on your employees. We know that you don't have any warrants.

Me: You are so full of shit. How long are you guys going to be here?

Agent Delano: Until we are done.

I walked away without saying another word. Anything else that would have come out of my mouth probably would have gotten me arrested. I saw Carrol, and I asked him if he would stay until the feds left so that he could lock the place up. Carrol informed me that all the employees were just asked to leave the building, but he would wait outside until they were done and then lock up. As I started to walk away from Carrol, he grabbed my arm and looked me in the eyes.

Carrol said, "Everything is going to be all right. We did nothing wrong here."

I really needed to hear that from another individual. I was starting to have some doubts that maybe I missed something. Carrol was such a good guy.

I got to my office, grabbed my briefcase, and left the building. You know, these people were such retards. If I was not such a stable person, I could have freaked out. I could have just reached into my briefcase, pulled out my Berretta, and gone postal on them. But no, I was stable, I was normal, I was a guy who was having an awful day, and I needed to get home to my wife. Wait a minute. How was I going to get home? They took my car. FUCK!

My sister pulled up next to me and told me to get into her car; she would give me a ride home. God bless my sister Paula. She was such a simple person. Paula thought the feds were in my office because of all the pills that I was having delivered there. Yeah, I wish it was that simple. I explained to Paula that I believed that her ex (Alan) and Andy were behind the whole event. Paula immediately started to cry. I guess she felt guilty that her ex-husband had caused me so much trouble, and all I was trying to do was to get Paula down to Florida to be close to the rest of the family. I did not have time to babysit Paula. I asked her to get it together so that I could think.

CHAPTER 105

I decided to call my business attorney, Lisa Daniels, and inform her of what had taken place. Now Lisa was not a scumbag. I was using her last name because she was a great person, and she was good at what she did. I want the whole world to know that there are good attorneys out there, and Lisa was one of them. Lisa had helped me from time to time with business contracts and disclosures. I always had a good working relationship with her, and I trusted her judgment. Lisa was just floored at what I had told her. This was not anywhere near what she was trained to handle, but Lisa did have a very close friend that was a criminal defense attorney down in Miami for over Z5 years. Lisa told me that she would have him call me ASAP. I thanked her, and I told her I would be in contact soon; I knew I was going to need her help at some point.

The next phone call that I made was to my sister-in-law Laura. She was on her way home from Global, and I asked her if she would pick my boys up from school at the end of the day and bring them to her house. I did not want my boys to come home and be surrounded by these pricks. My boys were only four and seven years old at the time, but they were not stupid. I just wanted to protect them. Anyway, Laura's son Antonio went to the same school as my boys, so picking up my kids would not be a problem. I thanked Laura and told her that I would call her later.

As I arrived at my house, I could not believe what I was seeing. There were three flatbed trucks in my driveway with all my vehicles already on board. There were cars everywhere including a few Broward County Sherriff's cars. My front door was wide open. I could see people walking all over my property like this was some sort of flea market or something. I was just sick to my stomach. I got out of my sister's car, thanked her, and asked her to leave. This would not be a good time for her to come in. I knew that Paula understood.

As I walked toward my front door, I was stopped by an agent who wanted to know who I was. After I told him, he walked me into my house. It was a freakin' circus inside. There were agents everywhere, and they were going through everything. I just felt so fucking violated. Once again, the thought of breaking out my Berretta briefly entered my head.

The agent that walked me into my house brought me to meet Agent Doug Willis (yes, slightly changed this prick's name as well). Agent Willis was in charge of the operation at my house, and he was partners with Agent Delano. He told me that they were almost finished and that technically my wife and I were not supposed to be in the house, but if we did not cause any trouble, we could stay. Hey, thanks a lot, shit face. This is my house after all.

I found Denise sitting at the kitchen table; she did not look good at all. I whispered into her ear that everything was going to be all right, and we just needed to let them finish up, and then they would all be gone. Denise had only one thing to say: "They took my wedding ring."

How does one respond to that? I felt just awful. Agent Willis asked me for the combination to my home safe: his paperwork made it very clear that I did not have any choice but to give it to him. I was actually able to make a compromise with Agent Williams. I told him that I would open the safe for them.

As soon as I opened the safe, another agent stepped between me and the safe, which forced me to back up. This guy was such a fucking loser. He immediately saw the cash that I had won playing poker. I had it all nicely stacked up on a shelf with the casino receipts wrapped around each pile. This asswipe yelled out, "Jackpot." I mean, are you kidding me? Grow the fuck up and be a little professional, moron. The agents cleaned out my safe except for one item that they left behind: my passport. Was that an invitation to run away? Were they testing me to see if I was going to stick around to face the music? Of course, I was going to stay. I had done nothing wrong.

The feds had taken everything that they wanted; they had searched every nook and cranny of my house, and as quickly as they had arrived, they were gone. I remember sitting down in a chair in my living room all by myself. I was replaying the day's events through my cluttered mind. I honestly don't know how many people could have survived the day that I just had. Yesterday, I had millions of dollars, nice cars, a successful business, and I was living on top of the world. Today, I was stripped of everything that I had worked for, and I still did not know why. It's funny, I was raised in a country named the United States of America, and in America, individuals were supposedly innocent until proven guilty. How in the hell could all this have taken place with me not even having been charged with a crime? I have never in my life heard of this happening to anyone. Was this legal, and if so, when did that start because this was just not fair? Look, I needed to rally myself and start to figure things out. I had a wife and two small kids that were depending on me. I had a business with employees that were going to be looking for answers, and I had customers that were about to find out that the checks that I had just sent them were all bad checks. This was no time for a pity party; it was time to gather information, regroup, and then fight back with all my might. I was not going to go down like some pussy with no backbone. I wanted my life back. Take some pills and move forward.

CHAPTER 106

I tried my hardest that day to console Denise. I tried to tell her that I would make everything all right and that I needed her support. I needed her to be strong while I figured out what was going on. Denise had very little to say to me. In fact, I received some looks from her that I certainly did not appreciate and I did not deserve. I could tell that Denise was not in my corner at that time, but to be honest with you, I did not expect her to be. Denise already had insecurity issues when it came to finances, and that was when we were living large. Now, well, just forget it. Still, you would think after what had just happened that day that she could pop one of her pills and give me a fucking hug. Anyway, fuck it. Once again, I would be the whipping board and take this thing head-on.

I received a call from Lisa Daniels's defense attorney friend; his name was Scott Sakin. I gave him a brief rundown of what had taken place so far, and he felt that we should meet over the weekend. Scott made it clear that the weekend meeting was a free consultation, but I had better figure out a way to retain a full-time attorney. Scott made it very clear that I was going to need one. That was just great, just freakin' great.

I went on my home computer and decided to check my bank accounts just in case the feds had left some money behind. Yeah, right. My business accounts were both closed; my personal checking account was closed. My kids' college funds were gone. I made a call to the company that was building Global's new office. Sorry, the deposit had been seized by the feds. I called the sales office that was building my penthouse condo in Las Olas. Sorry, feds had already been there. This was just fucking unreal. I don't know why I saved it for last, but I decided to log onto my Charles Schwab retirement account that was being managed by my friend Rob, and wouldn't you know it, the balance was over one million dollars. I could not believe it. Maybe the feds are not allowed to seize retirement accounts? I don't know, but what I did know was that this money could save my business until things were sorted out with the magical disappearing feds.

I called my friend Rob's office and got him on the phone. I told Rob what had happened today and that I would need to get some money from him in order to keep my business afloat until the feds were willing to admit that they made a mistake and give me my assets back. Rob was at a loss for words after I told him the whole story; he advised me that there was a cash balance of $20,000+ in my account, and that money could be withdrawn at any time. The rest of my money was in stocks and bonds that would have to be sold. I told Rob that I would come to his office later that same day to pick up a check for $5,000. Rob told me he would have it ready for me. Well, already things seemed to be getting a little better.

I called Enterprise Rent a Car and asked them to pick me up at my house so that I could rent a car from them. I had used Enterprise before, so they already had my information, and they said they would be by in an hour or so. Enterprise's pickup service is totally awesome.

I decided to update Denise on what I had done so far. I thought that might make her feel better; instead, she went off on this crazy bullshit about us never being able to retire if we used that money. You have got to be kidding. Okay, no more updates for her. I might have a fucking heart attack at this rate.

Not ten minutes after I called Rob's office, I received a call from his company's SEC compliance officer. Who the hell was this guy? I had never spoken to or met this guy during any of my appointments at Rob's office, and now he was calling me. This ought to be good. The compliance officer informed me that I could not pick up a check from their office for at least five working days. He explained to me that since I informed Rob that the feds had seized some of my assets that they could not touch my account until a "cooling off" period took place. This prick told me that I was a distressed investor and that I could not touch my money until five days passed. Distressed, no, I was not distressed. I was fucking livid at this point. I asked this piece of shit to put Rob on the phone, and he refused. Rob, my buddy, my chum, was not allowed to talk to me during the cooling-off period. What a fucking joke. I hung up on the compliance douchebag after I had some choice words about what he should do to his own mother. I came so close to throwing my cell phone at a wall in my house; I mean, I seriously started to have chest pains at this point. I popped a few painkillers, probably around ten, and I relaxed for a moment.

CHAPTER 107

Once I had my shit back together, I decided to call the local Charles Schwab office and talk to a manager. I gave the Schwab employee my account number and advised him that I had a falling out with Rob's company who, up until this point, had handled all my investments through Schwab. I asked the manager if I had the ability to manage my own account, and he advised me that I could at any time make whatever trades I wanted to on my own. I would simply have to come into their office and prove to them that I was the account holder. No problemo there, Schwab. I would be in tomorrow to make some trades. Fuck you, Rob Isbits, you lowlife lying piece of shit. Yes, Rob Isbits, my first Florida friend, the guy who literally begged me for years to invest through his company, had just made it onto the scum-bag list. Congrats.

A guy from Enterprise Rent a Car showed up like they promised and took me back to their office to get a car. I told them I would need a vehicle for around a week. Enterprise did all the paperwork and tried to run my American Express card through to hold a deposit for the rental. Guess what, card denied. Folks, I have had an American Express card since I was in high school. I currently held an American express Black Card, which is not an easy card to get approved for. My average monthly Amex bill over the past two years was around $20,000, and I never ever was even late with a payment, and now my card was being denied. I gave the Enterprise guy my Visa card, and that went through without a problem.

As I drove out of the Enterprise location with my newly rented SUV, I called the American Express customer service department to find out what was going on. Once again, I get hit with a real winner. As of today, American Express viewed me as a risk account. My account had been closed. I must have been transferred at least five times while I was on the phone with Amex. I wanted to hear them tell me why my account had been closed after all the business that I had given them for so many years. Person after person sidestepped the issue. All I was told was that my account was closed, and that was that. It was really funny when the final supervisor that was on the phone with me informed me that I had a $6,400 balance that was due upon the closing of my account. So let me get this straight. You close my account after I had a card for over twenty years, you will not tell me why my account was closed except for the fact that I was suddenly a high-risk client, but you want immediate payment for a balance that should not be due until the end of the month. How's this: kiss my hairy white ass. You give me a reason in writing as to why my account had been closed, and I would pay the fucking bill. Goodbye. Man, this day just kept getting better and better. Wait till I get home. "Oh, honey, by the way, don't use your Amex card. The account's been closed for no apparent reason." If it wasn't happening to me, if someone was to tell me this story, I would not believe them. I would surely think that they were exaggerating or hiding some facts, but no, this was actually happening to me.

When I got home, I gave Denise the keys to the SUV, and I told her that I'd be buying her a new vehicle this weekend, so she needed to find something reasonable that she liked. Laura had called while I was away, and Denise gave her the all clear to bring my kids home. I went into their rooms where they were playing, and I gave them both long hugs; I almost did not let go. I needed to try and protect these innocent kids from as much of this madness as possible. I did not want a four- and seven-year-old to be scared by the events that had taken place and the events that I would be going through in order to end this shit. I sat my young ones down and told them that the ATVs had to go back to the store because people were getting hurt by those things, and until they were made safe, we would not get them back. I also told them that Mommy and Daddy were going to get new cars this weekend, and they could help pick them out. The only thing that upset the boys at all was the fact that my car was gone; they loved getting rides in the Roadster with the top down. They loved the sound when I punched the gas and the engine roared. I promised them that one day I would buy a car like that for them to have rides in, but for now, we were going to get safer, bigger cars. They were so good; they just took what I had to say and went on with their day as if nothing had happened. That really gave me some relief. I told myself over and over again, just keep things as normal as possible for them. I couldn't let this hurt them.

CHAPTER 108

A little later on in the day, people started to come by and check in on us; I guess the word was starting to spread. First, Denise's mother and Lenny came by. Lenny had a spare 1970 Something Diesel Mercedes that blew out black smoke, and he left it for me to use. Hey, by the way, guys, all our money was taken. How about a loan? Yeah, right, they came and left within minutes.

Next my sister Lisa and Burt came over. They made some small talk. It was very shallow talk, no real emotion in anything they said. I figured they came over for some reason other than to see if we were okay, and sure enough, I was right. Burt started in about how much he needed the job at Global, and he wanted to know what was going to happen. Could I make payroll? Was this going to be a long, slow process to get back to normal operation? He just needed to know. I did my best to be understanding, but please, will someone give me a fucking break. I mean, he was there. He worked at Global. He knew my business plan and model. How in the hell would I know how long it would take to convince federal agents that we were legitimate? I told Burt to be at work the next day, and we would talk. Burt then hit me with a showstopper. He told me that Alan had come by his house today to hang out with him and Lisa. Yes, Burt and my sister Lisa were evidently still friendly with Alan the scumbag. After what he did to me at work, after how he treated our sister Paula and her children, these two were still friendly with him. Burt told me that Alan was so happy about what had taken place today because he finally got his revenge on me. Yes, it was confirmed, Alan and Andy were the people that filed a complaint. Hey, Burt Moron, I can't understand why you were so friendly with Alan. He just put you out of work. Why didn't you ask him when he would come clean to the feds so that we could get back to work and you could be put back on the payroll? I saw Burt and Lisa in a completely different light than I had ever seen them before, and I didn't like what I was seeing. These two were clueless about how Alan had just ruined all our lives. I asked them if they would please leave so that Denise and I could spend some time together. That, of course, was just an excuse. I wanted them out of my house.

Next, Carrol called. He wanted to come over and hang out with me. He offered to bring us some dinner or whatever else we needed. I thanked Carrol, but I had had enough for the day. I asked Carrol if he would call all the Global employees and tell them to report to work tomorrow; Carrol, of course, said yes and that he would see me in the morning.

I knew that there was no way that I was going to get any sleep that night. I had so much racing through my mind, and I needed to get more organized. I spent a lot of the early evening playing with my boys like I always did. Once they were in bed, I went into my office/library and got to work. I planned out my entire next day and part of the weekend. I then decided to draft a letter to the Global Vending customers in order to inform them of what had happened; I needed to be proactive with the customers. I needed to be very sensitive of how they were going to initially react to the news. After all, there was a lot of money at stake for them.

After I finished the letter, I faxed it to Lisa Daniels's office for her to review when she got into her office the next day. I then worked on what I was going to tell the employees. I needed them to stand by Global. We needed to keep the ATM machines running and generating revenue for the customers. If we lost customer support, or our ATM locations, the party would be over for Global.

CHAPTER 109

I managed to get a couple of hours of sleep that night. When I woke up, I started my day off like I normally would. I got the kids out of bed, got them dressed and ready for school, and said my goodbyes to them in our garage. The garage suddenly looked different: no shiny cars, no excitement, just a rented SUV and a 1970 shit box Mercedes. The events of yesterday suddenly hit me again.

I pulled my self together, got into the shit box, and drove to Global. My appearance would say a lot on that day, so I needed to stay composed and positive. As I entered Global that morning, I was surprised to find all the employees already there. I was on time, but they were all early; I was greeted with hugs, handshakes, and kisses. It was nice to see this group pull together like a real family; I was suddenly a little more at ease. I gathered my small army of employees in the main sales office and began my speech. I informed everyone what I had learned so far, which unfortunately was not much. I told them that I was meeting with a lawyer over the weekend with the hopes that he would be able to open up the lines of communication with the feds. I told them just how important it was for us to maintain and operate all the equipment in the field and to continue to place more machines in the field as we promised our customers we would. I went on to tell them about the letter that I drafted to the customers and how we were going to be proactive toward letting them know what had happened. The earliest that checks would start to arrive at customers' houses would be Monday, and today was only Friday. Sales would cease until I found out why the feds did not like our shared program or if that was even the real problem. Bruce would be assigned duties that would support customer service and Kim W on locations. I asked the employees not to concentrate on what we did

---

CHAPTER 104

January 15, 2004 was a day that started like any normal day in my life. I wrangled my two sons out of bed and got them ready for school. I said my goodbyes to Denise and my boys in the garage, a kiss for all three, and I waved goodbye as Denise pulled her SUV out of the garage. I fired up the AMG and headed out onto the open road. I loved cruising in that car in the morning with the top down; I just felt so free. I made my usual stops, Starbucks for coffee, and Dunkin' Donuts for a couple of dozen doughnuts for the crew at Global. Just for the record, I hate Dunkin' Donuts coffee.

I arrived at work around 7:30 a.m. The rest of the staff usually started to file in just before 8:00 a.m. I had my normal two cups of heart-pounding coffee in me and probably three or four painkillers to start the day off, and yes, I had some doughnuts. I remember sitting back in my black high-back leather chair and just enjoying the start of a new day; you just never know what is in store for you when you are running your own company. It was approximately 8:30 a.m. when I was taken aback by a very loud bang that came from the reception area. My office shared a wall with the reception area, and it sounded to me like the front door had slammed into that wall. As I rose out of my desk chair, I heard a bloodcurdling scream come from my receptionist Susan, followed by a lot of additional yelling from voices that I did not recognize.

Susan said, "Oh my god! Oh my god, don't shoot!"

I heard unknown voices say, "Don't you move. Don't you dare make a move."

I heard at least four or five different voices yelling commands to other employees who came to the front to see what was going on. It just sounded like total chaos. The only thought that came to my

265

mind was that we were being robbed. We were an ATM company; perhaps someone thought we had large amounts of cash on hand. I don't know. Everything suddenly seemed to be happening in slow motion, except for inside my mind, I was at a loss about what I should do. For some reason, it never dawned on me to call the police; it just didn't. I had often daydreamed while watching the news about what I would do if I found myself in a crises. I mean, you hear about it all the time. One minute you are in line at a bank or a supermarket, and the next thing you know, the place is being robbed. You and your loved ones are suddenly in a potential life-or-death situation, so what do you do? In my daydreams, I always saw myself protecting myself and my loved ones with any means possible. It bothered me to think that about how I would feel if I chose to do nothing and someone I loved was hurt or God forbid was killed. I have always told myself that I would die on my terms, at least trying to protect myself and others around me, but this was different. This was no daydream; this was really happening right here and right now. How would I react?

Before I even realized what I was doing, I had my Berretta out of my briefcase, and I was slamming a fourteen-round clip into the weapon. I grabbed the top of my gun and slid the entire loading chamber back toward me, which loaded a live round into the chamber. *Remember your training, Tom.* That was all that went through my head, over and over again. The voices and commotion were getting closer. Remember your training, Tom. Control your breathing, easy slow deep breaths. I could hear my firearm instructor in my head: "A bullet will not go where you wish it to go. It will go wherever you are aiming your weapon. Never place your hand on the trigger and aim your weapon at another human being unless you are prepared to take a life. Once a bullet leaves your gun, you cannot take it back." My right hand was holding the Berretta, while my left hand acted as a support underneath my right. My trigger finger was running parallel to the gun's barrel, and I had my weapon pointing straight ahead as I approached my office door.

The door to my office was opened a few inches, and I tried my best to peek through it to see what was going on in the main sales area. I saw at least six individuals, all in suits and all brandishing not have but to keep in mind what we did have: we had over 1,200 machines producing over $110,000 per month in residual income. We would use some of that money for operating expenses, but the majority would have to be set aside for the customers. I could tell that the group was worried about getting paid. I understood why. I mean, that was why they were all working for Global in the first place. My decision was to cut everyone's salary in half until Global's legal situation was cleared up. I promised them that upon the resolution of our legal matters, everyone would go back to full salary, and I would pay them for the amount of money that they had not received during the pay cut. I made it clear that I would understand if any of them needed to seek employment elsewhere, but I hoped that would not be the case. I asked one open question that I felt was very important to put out there for my employees to answer: "Does anyone have any doubt at all that Global Vending is operating as a one hundred percent legitimate company? Does anyone feel that our business plan, model, or operations are not being executed with the customers' best interest in mind? I need to know now." Everyone agreed that we were all about customers' success and customer loyalty; there were no doubters in the crowd. Then one at a time, each one of them committed to staying on board. I felt proud. I felt like this group got what life was really all about. Sometimes, you have to take a step backward to move forward. I finished the meeting by asking my group to continue to work as if yesterday had never happened (except for Bruce, of course), and then I left them with something to think about: "And out of the ashes, a phoenix shall rise."

CHAPTER 110

If I had to judge company morale at that point, I would say that we had dropped from an A to a B, but I could not expect much more than that until things started to clear up. It certainly did not take long before more bad issues started to arise.

First, Ron came to my office from technical support with a killer piece of news. Ron informed me that all our hard drives, including our server, were empty. Empty? There was not one customer contact left, not one location contact left, not a customer service note, nothing. It was as if we had just purchased brand-new computers. You have got to be kidding me. The feds took the rest of the hard-copy files, so we basically were driving blind and deaf at that point. I made notes of everything the employees pointed out to me. It would be up to me to come up with solutions, and I mean quick solutions. I informed our receptionist, Susan, to transfer all calls to the proper departments, then instructed all the employees to inform our customers and locations that called in that our computer system was down, and we would not be able to assist them until Monday.

I asked everyone to remain calm, apologize for the inconvenience, and to get off the phones as quickly as possible. I called up our two processing companies in order to get all our location data dumped back into our computers; that would be a quick fix for our missing location database. We still would not have notes or a history of repairs that had taken place at each location but at least would have a list of all locations with contact information.

I decided to inform Bart at ATMS what had taken place; I felt that he was a good person and someone that I could trust with that information. ATMS operated 90 percent of our ATM machines, and I may need some help from him explaining things to our locations once the news got out. Bart was just unbelievable; he took the news in stride. He knew me, and he knew what Global was all about; Bart offered to help in any way possible. I was very grateful for his offer. Our second processor, Nationwide Cash System, was not a company that I would give this information to, at least not at this time. Nationwide was run by two slick willies named Tom Denis and Ben Gonzalez. I did not trust either of them as far as I could throw them. The only reason why I did any business at all with them was because they had sold us thirty ATM machines in fast-food restaurants that were producing good numbers. Ben was constantly trying to charge us for services that we did not need and did not use. I can't even count how many times I had confrontations with him about him shorting our monthly checks; no, Nationwide would find out last.

I decided to rewrite the letter that I had faxed over to Lisa Daniels's office the night before. I included it to say that each customer would need to mail or fax all their Global paperwork to Lisa's office so that she could recreate files that were taken by the feds. I faxed the new draft to Lisa's office, and then I called her. Lisa and I spoke for a while about the situation. Lisa made some changes to the letter, worked out a very reasonable rate that she would charge me to recreate Global's customer files, and we decided that come Monday, all customer phone calls would be rerouted to the law office of Lisa Daniels. This was not an easy decision for me to make. I had committed myself to these customers, I had made promises to them, and I did not want them to think that I was running from them. The decision to have Lisa take all the calls for a while was made in order to give out unified information; everyone needed to hear the same information from the same source. We did not want one customer service rep telling a customer one thing and another to hear something else; I wanted to minimize customer speculation by providing them with a professional to talk to. I informed Lisa to tell the customers that once their file had arrived at her office and was reentered back into Global's system, then they could start to call Global directly again. I felt that would speed up the process of customers sending us back copies of their files.

Lisa faxed the letter back to me with her changes, and I had our customer service staff and Bruce prepare copies of the letters and envelopes to be sent to all our customers. I called my bank representatives at the branches where our two business accounts once existed, and I asked the bank employees if they could make me a copy of all the checks that I had sent out the previous month. The checks that cleared the previous month would all include our customer rebate checks, and those rebate checks had the customers addresses printed right on them. That would give me addresses to send the letters to. The banks agreed to make the copies, and I informed them that Carrol would come by in a little while to pick them up. Now the letters were going out to customers to give them a heads-up of what had happened and what we needed them to do to help us help them. The location information was being emailed to Ron from the processors. It was not pretty, but it was the best I could come up with at the time.

It just kept haunting me as to what a bad situation the feds had left me in. I mean, I had not been charged with any crime, yet they dismantled my company and partially dismantled my personal life. I could not wait to meet with Scott the next day in order to get back on the offensive, but for now, I was in a defensive posture, and I needed to get to the Charles Schwab office and secure my money so that I could finance this whole interim operation. I jumped back into the shit box Mercedes and headed over to Schwab.

The Schwab people were just great to me. They initially tried to keep me as a client, but when I said that it was not in the cards right now, they asked me for instructions of what I wanted them to do. "Liquidate everything." I was informed of the massive losses that I would be taking if I were to liquidate bonds that were not even close to maturing, but I did not care. I wanted my entire account to become available cash for me to use right now. The Schwab representative cut me a check for just over twenty thousand dollars, and I gave him wiring instructions to send my liquidated account to my father's checking account.

I had asked my father if I could send him the funds until Scott had made contact with the feds. I did not know how the feds and seizures worked: would any money that I put in any bank just be taken? Was I allowed to even have a personal bank account at this point? I had no idea. The feds simply took shit and ran; they never gave me any dos or don'ts or instructions of what was expected of me. Sending the money to my father seemed to be a safe way to secure and have access to the money for my operation. I was informed by the Schwab employee that the money would be wired on Monday after all my trades had been settled. If I were to ever get my life back again, I would not hesitate to give Charles Schwab my future investments.

So I left the Schwab office with a cashier's check for just over $20,000. I decided that I had no choice but to test the waters and open up personal and a business checking account. I mean, what was I going to do with that check? How was I going to pay business and personal bills without checking accounts? I opened a personal checking account at a small local bank called Horizon Bank. I deposited the Schwab check there, and I was told that those funds would be available on Monday. I then opened a business checking account at another small bank called Metro Bank. I used a small amount of cash to open that account up. I just wanted to get the ball rolling again and see what, if any, banking obstacles I was going to encounter. So far, as far as opening accounts up, all seemed okay. I was anticipating getting our monthly residual check from each of our two processors sometime during the following week, and now I had a place to deposit those checks and start paying business expenses. One of my biggest concerns that I still had not addressed was how in the hell was I going to pay my mortgage payments. My mortgage was over sixteen thousand dollars each month, and the next payment was due in two weeks; I would have to see how things progressed. I spent the rest of the day with the Global employees, answering questions and preparing for what I called Black Monday. It was now up to Lisa Daniels to keep my customers calm, cool, and collected.

CHAPTER 111

I met Attorney Scott Sakin on Saturday for my free consultation. Truth be told, since Lisa highly recommended this guy, I already had every intention of hiring him to start pursuing the feds and to open up lines of communication with them. Scott was an older gentleman, very soft-spoken and very reserved, not really my type of person, but he was an attorney, and I was not. Scott's office was in downtown Miami, but he lived right in the town of Weston, so we decided to have our first meeting at a Starbucks coffee shop in Weston. It made me pretty pissed off that our initial fifteen minutes or so was spent on Scott probing me for money, how I was going to be able to afford retaining a lawyer like him if the feds had taken all my money. I guess business is business, and believe me, an attorney is definitely a business. I told Scott about the retirement fund that the feds had not touched. I asked him if he had any idea why they would have left that money behind. I mean, Agent Delano made it very clear that she had been through my banking records with a fine-tooth comb, and the monthly checks that I wrote out for my retirement account were the largest checks consistently written out. Scott had no answers for me yet; it was way too early in the game. I pressed Scott to please tell me how in God's name my business and personal assets were taken from me, and yet I had not been charged with any crime. Scott's response just made me sick to my stomach. My assets were taken compliments of "the Patriot Act." That's right, the Patriot Act. So let me get this straight, terrorists attack America on September 11, 2001. As a result, the Patriot Act was enacted to help combat terrorist and their abilities to get funding, but there was also some tiny little section added to the Patriot Act that also allows the United States government to seize assets of not only suspected terrorist but

294

also of anyone else that is suspected of committing any other crime. In other words, any American citizen can have all his or her assets seized if they are being investigated for "possibly" having committed a crime. Let me tell you, folks, I was very attentive when the politicians were discussing the Patriot Act after the September 11 attacks, and I surely don't remember them mentioning that part of the act. No, it was all rah rah rah, America will get these bad terrorist guys. Scott also informed me that the government placed a lien on my house, which would prevent me from selling it or borrowing against it. And are you ready for this one? The Anti-Terrorism and Effective Death Penalty Act of 1996 (AEDPA) allows for such a lien to be used by the government. Okay, so here I am, American Tom, Mr. Nobody, Mr. Never Been in Trouble with the Law Before, and I had just been financially crushed by the Patriot Act and the Anti-Terrorism and effective Death Penalty Act of 1996. Are you fucking kidding me? Scott told me that in order to get some answers, he would have to contact the feds and start asking questions on my behalf. He warned me that nothing happens quickly with the feds. I told Scott that my biggest concern were my customers and the machine assets that were out there operating. I told him what steps Lisa Daniels and I had taken so far to keep my customers informed. I once again was not happy with Scott's response. He simply told me obviously not to sell anything until we could talk to the feds, no problem there, but he also told me that I should consider halting all operations and conserving my money for the battle ahead of me. Thanks for the advice, but no fucking way. No way was I going to bail on my customers or on my employees. Our meeting ended with Scott asking me for a $5,000 retainer if I chose to have him pursue the feds. Scott would bill me at an hourly rate of $200 per hour as he worked on my case. Now I saw why he wanted me to save my money; he wanted it all. Anyway, I used one of my new personal temporary checks, and I paid him his $5,000 and told him to get started. Just like that, I had an attorney, big fucking deal.

CHAPTER 112

I left the meeting with very mixed emotions. I was happy that I had someone in my corner that was going to try and get this mess settled for me, but at the same time, I was not happy that I had to pay someone to defend me when I had not done anything wrong or had not been charged with doing anything wrong. The whole situation just seemed upside down. In fact, it seemed to be staged. I guess I was still living in that dream world of mine where things like this just did not happen to good people. The bottom line was I did not have a choice at this time but to get a pro like Scott to try and help me. So Monday rolled around, and back to work I went. Lisa Daniels called me from time to time with customer updates. Surprisingly, most of the customers were being very cooperative and understanding. Lisa did give me a customer from time to time that she felt needed me to call them, just so that they could hear a familiar voice and fall back into that comfort factor; I gladly made those calls.

As the week progressed, customers received the letters that we sent out, calls came pouring in, and so did the paperwork that Lisa was asking the customers to send her: we were quickly rebuilding our customer database. I received the two checks from our processors that week, and I deposited them into my new business checking account. I immediately started to pay our business operating expenses, and I paid out our first post-fed payroll to the employees. Just for the record, there was no payroll for me. I would not pay myself a dime until my entire legal matter was cleared up, and we were back to business as usual.

One other positive call came into our office that week. The dollar stores had to delay our meeting until late March. I saw that as a positive because there was no way that we would be able to purchase and place seven thousand ATM machines in the condition that we were in at this time. The dollar stores bought us some valuable time, and it showed me that they were still very interested.

I decided that since I now had money to operate the business, I would use some personal money to get vehicles for Denise and myself. Denise had decided that she wanted a Nissan Morano, and I had picked out a Ford Sport Trac, a small pickup truck: both were a far cry from what we were used to driving, but I needed to keep things light and affordable until I knew where the feds were heading with their allegations. The nice part was that I still had perfect credit, so leasing the two vehicles was a piece of cake. Small battles, small victories, that was the best I could do for right now.

I returned the Enterprise rental and Lenny's shit box, and all of a sudden, Denise and I were self-sufficient again. That felt good, but let me tell you something, folks. This was not an easy time in my life. I was juggling so many different things at once, and I did not know how long I could keep this pace up for.

I received some updates from Scott, and I answered as many questions as he could throw at me. I also made it a point to let him know almost every move that I was making business-wise and personally. I could hear some frustrations in Scott's voice: he was trying to get a sit-down with the FBI and the assistant United States attorney that was overseeing my case: they simply had no interest in talking to us. Okay, no charges against me, you take my shit and run, and now you simply don't want to talk about it. How in God's name is this legal?

CHAPTER 113

After weeks of hounding the prosecutor's office, Assistant United States Attorney (AUSA) Larry Barfeld (the man overseeing my case) decided to cave in and set up a meeting. The meeting took place at the Broward County AUSA building. The participants were me, Scott, Larry Bardfeld, Agent Delano, Agent Willis, and an FBI forensic accountant. I was very excited the day of the meeting. Finally I would be heard, and finally I would hear what these clowns decided after looking at my files. I also had this crazy idea that the FBI would be give me a copy of all the shit that they copied off our hard drives. Anyway, Scott made one thing clear to me before the meeting. I was to sit there and shut up. I was not to say a word to these people without whispering to him anything that I had to say. Now that just sounded ridiculous to me, but remember, he was the professional, and I hired him to do a job.

So I entered into the lion's den with high hopes, not realizing just how much I was about to get shit on by these gutless pricks. We all gathered around a large conference table, and introductions were made. Scott shook everyone's hands, and no one, I mean no one, even attempted to shake my hand: I felt like the Antichrist. As I looked around the table at this motley crew, I suddenly realized why I was so willing to initially speak to Agent Delano on the day of the big raid at my office; Agent Delano had a seriously nice set of tits: a bad polyester suit, a shit attitude, but one hell of a nice set of tits. Okay, enough of that. I needed to focus.

Scott started by laying out what our concerns were: the customers, the operating machines, and the employees of Global Vending. Scott asked what the government's intentions were at this point and what they would be willing to do in order to preserve the customers' assets. Scott also asked for some of the business assets to be released while they finished their investigation so that we could continue to place machines out in the field for customers that had already made purchases.

When Scott was finished, I looked around the room, and the feds looked like they had just heard Scott speak in some foreign language. There were some seriously puzzled and annoyed-looking expressions on their faces.

Agent Delano broke the ice for the feds with her usual womanly charm: she explained to Scott that she was sticking by her assessment that Global Vending was a complete fraud, a Ponzi scheme, and they were going to finish their investigation so that Larry Barfeld could prosecute me to the fullest extent of the law. I would say that Agent Delano used the word *fraud* at least one hundred times that day. There would be no assets released, there would be no more machines placed out in the field, and there were no customers, only victims of my fraud. Agent Delano did not give a shit about operating machines that were currently generating over $100,000 per month, Fraud, fraud, fraud—all of it was fraud. I wanted to jump across the table and smack the shit out of her and her nice tits.

I whispered over to Scott, and I asked him to request a receivership be put in place to run Global until the investigation was over. For those of you who do not know what a receivership is, it is a government employee that would step in and run Global to preserve assets. I would step aside and wait to see how the investigation concluded, but in the meantime, the machine revenue would be collected, a small portion would be used to pay a skeleton crew to maintain the machines, but the lion's share of the revenue would go into an escrow account for the customers to receive at a later date. Receiverships are very popular in situations like this. Oh, and just for the record, I offered to pay the receivers salary out of my personal account. I just wanted to preserve my customers' investments.

Once again, no, no, no, no. "We will not promote the operation of a company that is a fraud." I started to chew on my tongue at this point to prevent me from bursting out in profanity. Agent Delano was still doing all the talking. She explained that they were protecting the victims by shutting us down. No one was to blame except for me. I stole their money, and that was that. The forensic accountant then decided to open his retarded mouth.

He said, "Mr. Foley, do you realize that you were paying out almost two times the amount of money than what the machines were bringing in? That is a classic Ponzi scheme. Your company was just about to collapse. That's why we intervened. You were losing money every month and spending the victim's money on all sorts of toys for yourself. This company is an absolute disgrace."

Okay, it was at this moment that I felt like I was seriously spending time with mentally challenged people. I had heard enough. These people obviously had their minds made up, but I was not leaving there without getting into the mix. As I started to talk, Scott told me to shut up. Yeah, he actually told me to shut up.

I told him, "Hey, Scott, you shut up. Don't ever tell me to shut up again."

That seemed to catch everyone off guard.

I said, "Listen, people, you obviously have your opinion about me and my company, and I am telling you right now, for the record, that you are way off on this one. I have great customers who are happy and love my business model. It's the customers who get the final say as to whether they were defrauded, not you. All this bullshit about paying out more than the machines were bringing in is exactly that: bullshit. I did that by design, and I already explained that to Agent Delano when she was at my office. I just don't see how taking our operating funds and running away is going to help your so-called victims. Not one of those people has lost a dime to this point, and they don't have to. You are creating victims if you allow their assets to be shut down. I have read all about Ponzi schemes, and every Ponzi Scheme collapses once new money stops coming in, yet Global is still earning over $110,000 per month, and we have not even turned half of our machines. How do you not see that? I am sorry that Alan Nudelman and Andrew Levinson lied to you. I am sorry that you chose not to properly investigate the situation before you went on your little asset scavenger hunt, but that's your problem. I just want my company and my life back, and I will fight these ridiculous charges until the day I die in order to see justice served. Okay, Scott, now I will shut up."

Scott just kind of shook his head as he looked around the room. He reached into his briefcase and took out a letter that he had drafted for the prosecutor. Scott handed the letter to the prosecutor and explained that it was a letter of intent to self-surrender should charges be brought up against me; in other words, if the feds decided to charge me with a crime and arrest me, Scott had just put them on notice that I would surrender myself to any law enforcement facility that they chose at the time that they chose. Scott and I had discussed this beforehand, but man was that a fucking reality check. Surrender myself. How did I get here?

Well, that was the end of the meeting. I don't think that it could have gone worse. It really made me mad that these people had their blinders on and were not willing to help protect the customers at all. These people were supposed to protect Americans, not cause them loses that were avoidable, but you know what the bottom line was: NO VICTIMS, NO CRIME. The feds came, they took, they realized that they had made a mistake, but there was no turning back for them at that point, at least not in their little pea brains. I just was so lost at this point. This just did not seem real.

CHAPTER 114

I decided to get on as much of an offensive as possible. I also needed to see if perhaps I was the crazy one. Maybe my customers were not on board with Global Vending and my business plan. I put together another letter to my customers along with a list of what the feds had accused me of doing to my customers. I included a checklist that basically outlined Global's business model and the promises that Global had made to the customers. Next to each phase of the business plan, or alleged promise, I placed an "agree/disagree." The letter instructed the customers to read all the allegations and to then read what I believed my customers invested in and to either circle agree or disagree. The letter asked the customers to have the survey notarized and then to send it back to Lisa Daniels's office. The object of these surveys was twofold: (1) to make sure I was not operating in a fantasy world; maybe all the drugs I was taking was clouding my brain, and maybe I was lying to myself; (2) to hopefully show the feds that my customers knew exactly what they had purchased and that they knew exactly where their rebates were coming from.

I planned on getting a survey back from every customer and then have Scott present the surveys to the prosecutor. Scott warned me that this was a double-edged sword; what if the surveys came back in an unfavorable fashion? Are you kidding me, Scott? Damn, brother, you had better start to get used to the fact that you have an innocent client for once in your life. I knew that there would be no way that these surveys would not result in a favorable situation, and you know what, if they did, then I had really fucked things up, and I would need to shut Global down and face the music.

Scott made a few small adjustments to the letters, and then off they went to the customers. "What if they don't come back favorable?" Holy shit, have some faith.

CHAPTER 115

As we waited for the surveys to come back to us, I started to see that the feds were not taking the fact that we were still operating very lightly. First the FBI started to show up in the parking lot of Global on a daily basis. They wore blue slickers with bright-yellow letters on the back that said FBI. Hey, morons, you should try and wear those jackets the next time you raid an office. This way, you may not almost get your fucking heads blown off. Anyway, the FBI would walk from car to car and write down license plate numbers. They were trying their hardest to intimidate us. Then the FBI started to follow each employee home and pull them over at some point. The feds would tell the employees that they were working at a fraudulent business, and if they continued to work there, then they could be charged as coconspirators.

Once again, I just felt awful for my people. All they wanted to do was earn a paycheck and take care of their families; that was it. I will tell you one thing though. Not one employee left the company. Every single one of them knew that we were running a legitimate operation; they would not be scared off.

The next move that the feds made was just a disgusting display of unprofessional behavior. I could not for the life of me figure out why these people were being so vindictive or why they were wasting so much time and so many assets on a nobody like me. I started to receive sporadic calls from some of the operating companies that ran our fast-food restaurant chains. The management told me that the FBI had called them and had told them that Global Vending was a fraudulent company. The FBI also told them that if they continued to allow our machines to operate on their premises, then there would be a chance that their corporation could be charged with conspiracy to promote fraud. Can you fucking believe what these people were doing? Weren't there like threats to our national security that needed to be investigated: for God's sake, I still had not been charged with any crime.

I tried my hardest to explain to the management companies what had been going on, but at the end of the day, these people were in the fast-food business and not the ATM business: some of the locations started to request that we pick up our machinery. This was one of my biggest nightmares starting to come true. The other problem with this shitty situation was that the fast-food industry was a tight-knit group, and soon, the word would spread. I was blown away when I received a call from the dollar stores corporate headquarters. The dollar store chain called to cancel our meeting in March. One of the fast-food chains that I had given to the dollar stores as a reference had called them to advise the dollar stores about the FBI's phone call. Shit on a stick. I can't blame the fast-food people; they were just covering their own butts. Seven thousand locations just got flushed down the toilet. As I thought back to my meeting with the feds, I felt like shooting myself: I was the one that mentioned how I could not afford to lose customer support or operating locations, and here the feds were attacking both. Me and my big fucking mouth. Okay, Scott, I will say it, you were right. I should have kept my mouth shut. I had no choice, so as locations began to cancel, I picked up their machines and stored them in our warehouse. All I could do was to hope that this did not spread any further.

CHAPTER 116

My next stroke of bad news came via a call that I received from Rob. Not Rob my investor scumbag, but Rob O, my customer and big shot over at Bear Sterns. Now I obviously knew that this whole legal clusterfuck was going to kill my chances of ever taking Global public, but Rob O hit me with an even shittier request. Rob had sent his survey back to Lisa Daniels's office; his survey was in complete support of Global Vending and its operating practices. Rob asked me to get the survey back from Lisa and rip it up. What? Why? Well, I will tell you why: Rob had tried to get some information from the feds on his own. He called the FBI and spoke to Agent Delano. After Agent Delano informed Rob of the reason for their investigation, Rob actually went to bat for Global and told Agent Delano that she was greatly mistaken. He also told her that he had just sent in a notarized survey to Lisa Daniels in complete support of Global. Agent Delano informed Rob that I would be charged at some point with fraud and that anyone who signed a survey like the one that Rob had signed would not be entitled to any restitution.

Okay, first of all, for those of you who do not know what restitution is, restitution is the payment that criminals have to make to victims of certain crimes. Restitution is usually funded by the seizure and sale of the criminal's assets.

With that being said, I have not committed any crimes, I have not been charged with any crimes, and it is surely not up to the FBI to discuss restitution with potential victims of a crime. The FBI is simply supposed to be an investigative agency, gather facts, and present them to the attorney general's office; that's it. Now Agent Delano was giving out legal advice. Give me a fucking break.

CHAPTER 117

The FBI at this point were completely out of control, they were completely unprofessional, and they were doing whatever it took to destroy my company and reputation. This was not the country that I believed I lived in. This was not justice; this was just an old-fashioned Salem witch hunt, and I was the one being hunted.

Lisa Daniels had already received over 300 supportive surveys and zero unsupportive surveys; Global had 360 customers in total. Although a few more surveys did still trickle into Lisa's office, it was obvious that the FBI had reached my customers. I had Burt and his crew call the remaining customers that had not sent in their surveys, and the majority had received calls from the feds. Once again, I can't blame the customers for being scared or skeptical of me at this point; who would you listen to, a federal agent or an ATM guy? This was really starting to suck.

Lisa sent the surveys that she had received to Scott so he could decide what to do with them. Regardless, 300 out of 360 was a hell of a statement. A few things now became very obvious to me: the government had no intention of letting Global operate at any level, and at the rate that things were going, my customers could potentially lose the balance of their investments. In fact, that seemed almost inevitable. Sorry, I would not let that happen. I had my father send Lisa Daniels almost $100,000. I needed to get caught up with her fees that she charged me for her hard work. The rest were placed in a trust account by Lisa so that I could implement my next attempt to help my customers.

I also had my sister Paula open a checking account in Weston, and my father transferred half of my funds to her account and the balance to my personal checking account. The personal account funds were needed to help me keep up with my huge mortgage payments and my now mounting legal bills with Scott. The business money would be used for what I named operation whole. I decided to start to offer my customers options to get out of the ATM business since the feds were in the process of destroying that business. I cared about these people more than I can explain, and I did not want them to get hurt any more than they already had been hurt.

Once again, I put together a draft of a letter that I wanted to send to my customers. The draft outlined three buyout options that I would be offering my customers. I sent the letter to Scott for his review, and once again, Scott told me that I was wasting my money and my efforts to help the Global customers. I simply did not see it that way. I needed to make every effort possible to counter the destructive actions of the FBI. Here were the three options that I offered my customers.

Option number 1: I would buy any customer out of the business at a price of $1,000 per machine purchased. Whatever they had already received as returns would be theirs to keep, but I would now send them a check in the amount of $1,000 for each machine that they had purchased from Global. Most people that chose to accept this option would wind out losing money, but at least this would help them recover a portion of their investment, and the checks would go out right away.

Option number 2: This option would have me sending the customer a brand-new ATM machine for each machine that they had purchased, plus I would pay a professional locator's fee that would be used to find a location for each of the ATM machines. The ATM machines would be placed close to the customer's residence so that the customer could now service their own machines. I had three professional locating services that the customers could choose from, and I had an agreement in place for ATMMS to process the transactions directly for the customers. So once again, this option offered customers a machine, a paid professional locator, and processing through ATMS.

Option number 3: This was an option for a full refund plus a 15 percent added return on investment the total return due to my customer would be: their total purchases, plus 15 percent more, minus what they had already received as a return from Global. Whatever that final balance came out to would be paid back to the customer in equal monthly payments over a period of ten years. I chose a ten-year payback period because that was the term of Global's contract with each customer.

These options would be funded with the money that I had from my retirement account, machines that had already been purchased but not placed, and the revenue generated by the remaining operating ATM machines. I set limits on how many people could sign up for each option, and it was a first-come-first-serve basis.

After Scott made a few small changes to my draft, I produced a final letter, and once again, the employees of Global put together a mass mailer to my customers. Let's see who chooses what. It was funny. The initial reaction from the customers to my latest letter was not what I expected. The majority of the phone calls that I received were customers almost begging me not to give up. These people did not want out of the business. I received call after call from customers asking me what they could do to help stop the collapse of Global. It really sucked because I could hear the desperation in some of their voices. Global's ATM program was more than an investment for some of these people; it was a life-changing event. The potential returns that these people saw as a real possibility could have changed their lives for the better, and now that dream was being taken away from them. I had to be honest with them. I wanted nothing more than for Global to explode and move forward as I had planned, but I just knew that the government was not going to let that happen. You know, there is a thing called normality blindness.

Normality blindness is a sort of blinding that one goes through when they just want things to go how they were once going. In other words, the Global customers refused to see that the glory days were over at Global because they wanted their normality back. When people are in this frame of mind, they refuse to acknowledge the reality of what is taking place. I mean, think about it; I had already advised these people that the FBI raided my house and office. The FBI had taken all the company's assets. These people had bounced checks in their hands that were worthless, yet they still wanted to continue on with their investment. It was just a very sad moment in my life. I continued to slap these people and throw water in their faces in hopes that they would come around and help themselves by choosing a buyout option and then moving on with their lives: eventually, that was exactly what started to happen.

CHAPTER 118

Once reality started to set in with the Global customers, buyout paperwork started to roll in. It was a pretty even split at first with customers choosing a combination of all three options. As the paperwork came in, I had the Global employees take the necessary actions to satisfy the orders. Checks in the amount of $1,000 per machine went out immediately, machines and locating fees also went out immediately, and customers that chose a full refund in option number 3 received an amortization schedule that showed when payments would begin and how the payments would progress over the next ten years. I know that this was not how I planned things at Global. I know that this was not what the customers really wanted, but I still felt good that I was not leaving these people high and dry, which I could have easily done. With all things being considered, I felt I had done my best for them.

As things progressed with the buyout paperwork, I started to get paranoid about what steps the FBI might take in order to stop me from retaining customer support as I had done through these buyout options. The only way that I could foresee them making any future waves for me was to once again seize my funding: that would be devastating at this point.

I decided to play it safe and take the majority of my remaining money out of the bank. I had multiple cashier checks in the amount of $40,000 drawn out of one account: I figured that as I needed to fund the buyouts, I could just deposit one cashier check at a time. I started to take cash from the other two accounts, my sister Paula withdrew cash from the account that she was holding, and Denise and I withdrew cash from our personal account.

Now here is the funny part. You would think that if you had $200,000 in a bank account that you could just walk up to the teller, write yourself a check for $200,000, and they would have to cash it. Not that easy, my friends. Just try it someday; in fact, try and cash a check for over $10,000 someday. Most banks will not be able to or be willing to do it. Paula tried to withdraw $25,000, and the bank told her that they do not keep that much cash on hand. Denise tried the same thing, and the bank manager told her she did not feel comfortable letting her leave with that much cash at one time. I am serious. Try it sometime, and you will see the resistance that you will run into, especially at small banks.

Denise asked the manager at Horizon Bank just how much money she could take out each day, and the manager told her that she would be comfortable with an amount of $5,000 to $9,000, so that was what she started to withdraw. I told Paula what had happened with Denise, and she also started to take out amounts of $5,000 to $9,000. I felt that with all that was going on, I was in no position to start trouble with the banks, so we just went along with it.

CHAPTER 119

After a couple of days of receiving option requests back, I received a call from one of my larger customers named Thomas C. Tom was a businessman from up where I grew up on Long Island. I had never spoken to Tom before this day, but he had insisted on talking to me before he chose a buyout. Tom made it very clear to me that he was not happy about the whole buyout program or the fact that the feds had raided my office and were accusing me of fraud. Tom advised me that he was going to accept the $1,000 machine buyout, which would mean that I would be sending him a check for $85,000 for the eighty-five machines that he had purchased. I once again apologized to Tom for the losses that he would be suffering, and I told him I wish that there was something else that could be done, but I just did not see any other avenues at this time. Tom ended our conversation with a threat: "Don't fuck me over with this buyout. I will send you the paperwork today, but I expect the money to be wired to my account the day that you receive my paperwork."

Now I was not happy with his tone, but he was upset, and I could not blame him. I agreed that instead of a check, I would wire him his $85,000. That was how the conversation ended.

A week or so went by, and I had still not received Mr. C's paperwork back. I received yet another call from Mr. C, and this time, he was even more agitated. Mr. C wanted to know where his money was. I explained that I had not yet received his paperwork, and I could not send out his payment without that paperwork. Tom became enraged as he insisted that he sent his paperwork to Lisa Daniels's office a few days after we had spoken. I told him that I would call Lisa's office and get right back to him.

Sure enough, when I got a hold of Lisa, she advised me that she had received Mr. C's paperwork and had forgotten to send me a copy. Great, just great. I quickly called Mr. C back, and I told him what had happened.

I could tell from our phone conversation that Mr. C did not believe what I was telling him. I offered to have Lisa Daniels call him, but he was not interested. I promised him that he would receive a wire transfer in the amount of $85,000 the very next day. That was the best I could do at this point. Mr. C. told me that he would not hold his breath but that I should send the funds tomorrow. Once again, if I were to put myself in his shoes, I would probably be skeptical also. Tomorrow would be a new day, and Mr. C would see that I am a man of my word.

CHAPTER 120

I had a million things going on at work with all the buyout letters coming in, so I asked Denise if she would stop at the bank first thing in the morning in order to deposit two of the $40,000 checks into my account so that I could wire to Mr. C his money. There was already some money in the account to cover the balance I owed him. Denise agreed to help me out.

That next morning, I received a call from Denise around 9:00 a.m. Denise told me that she went to the bank and gave them the deposit, but the computers were down at the bank, and the deposit would not take place until their computers were back online. What else could go wrong with this one stupid buyout?

It took me maybe thirty minutes after I hung up with Denise before I started to get a gut-wrenching feeling that something was wrong. I mean, what were the chances that a bank's entire computer system went down on the one day that I really needed a deposit made? I mean, I had been unlucky for the past few months, but for some reason, this just did not settle well with me. I decided to call the local branch that Denise had been at, and I asked a customer service representative if they were having any computer problems on that morning, and much to my dismay, she said no, no computer issues at their branch. I just got this sick feeling in my stomach. I thought I was actually going to throw up. I hopped in my truck and flew over to the bank.

Once inside, I asked for the branch manager, and I explained to the manager what had happened that morning with my wife. Much to my surprise. the branch manager was not surprised or confused at all. The branch manager just simply handed me a business card from his pocket: it was a card from Agent Delano of the FBI. The manager told me that Agent Delano had stopped in at the bank late yesterday and had instructed the bank to hold any deposits that anyone attempted to make to my account. What the hell was going on? This was like a childish little game that the FBI was playing. If they wanted the money that I had, why in God's name didn't they ask me for it or, even better, order me to give it to them? Do you realize just how frustrating this was? I demanded that the branch manager give me my checks that Denise had left there to be deposited. I gave the manager several choice words that did not go over very well.

The manager appeared frightened. He handed me back my deposit and asked me to leave the bank. It's funny because the bank had absolutely no legal right to hold my checks and to lie to my wife about the computers being down. I guess Agent Delano was cutting corners by asking the bank to hold all deposits to my account so that she did not have to go through the process of getting seizure warrants to confiscate money once it was deposited into the bank. Whatever the reason was, this just was not right. I had no way to get Mr. C his money. (I guess that was the point.)

CHAPTER 121

I went back to my office and called Lisa Daniels's office. I told Lisa what had just taken place, and I asked her to call Mr. C and explain what had happened. I asked Lisa to tell him that the money would be transferred from her office trust account as soon as she could arrange for that to happen. Lisa agreed to help me by calling Mr. C, and I told her I would deposit more money into my trust account the next day. I was quickly getting tired of running into these FBI-related brick walls. I was not trying to do anything but help my customers, and these fucking pricks were dead set against that. How could the FBI possibly say that they were protecting these people? It was a fucking joke.

I called Scott and told him what had happened at the bank: once again, he told me that I was spinning my wheels by trying to help my customers. Great, now I had to listen to a bunch of "I told you sos." Just do your fucking job, Scott, and document this shit. I seriously felt my blood pressure rising as I sat there in my office; this was not good for my health, and neither were the dozens of pills that I was popping each day in order to keep my sanity.

At the end of the day, I grabbed my briefcase that contained the two cashier's checks, and I headed out of the office. As I pulled out of the office complex, I noticed that there was a local Sunrise Police cruiser right behind me. I was very careful to obey every driving law known to mankind, but just before I reached the expressway, the cruiser put on his blue-and-red lights and the siren to go with it. I was being pulled over. Just fucking great. Like I needed this shit on top of my decaying life. I complied by pulling my truck over, and I waited for the officer to arrive at my driver's side door. Officer Goldstein asked me for my license, registration. and insurance card.

I produced all three for him. I asked the officer why he pulled me over. The officer advised me that I had run through a stop sign a few blocks back from where we currently were. I calmly disagreed with the officer, but I was in no mood for this shit. Just give me a ticket and let me get home. The officer then told me that he was originally following me because of the office complex that I had come out of. The officer told me that they had been having a lot of problems with drug dealers and the sale of handguns in my complex. Three years in that complex and I had never seen or heard of any drug problems or gun problems in my office complex; this was class A office space, but once again, who cares? What does this have to do with me? The officer asked me if I had any weapons or drugs in my truck. Thank God I decided to stop carrying my gun since the whole FBI raid mishap; yes, I had a license to carry it, but I was just relieved at that very moment that it was not on me. I advised the officer that I had no weapons and no drugs. The officer asked me for permission to search my vehicle. I suddenly got agitated with this prick.

I said, "Look, if you pulled me over for running a stop sign, then give me a ticket, and I will fight it in court, but you have no reason to search my vehicle. I am having a shitty day, and I don't have the time or the patience for this, so no, you may not search my vehicle."

The officer told me that he was going to run my driver's license and write me a ticket for running the stop sign that I never ran through, but I could give a flying rat's ass at this point. He walked maybe two feet and then quickly returned back to my window. This time, he had his hand on his service revolver.

Officer Goldstein said, "Mr. Foley, I need you to step out of your vehicle."

I said, "Why? What's the problem now?"

The officer replied, "You lied to me, Mr. Foley. I see a weapon in your back seat. That gives me probable cause to search your vehicle. Now get out."

I said, "A weapon? What are you talking about?"

He said, "There is a bat on the floor of your truck. That is a weapon. [Officer Goldstein now visibly tightened his grip on his weapon but still had not taken it out of his holster.] For my safety, I am ordering you out of your vehicle, now."

What the hell was I going to do? I got out of my truck. The last thing I needed was this freak shooting me because I had a softball bat in my truck. Oh, and by the way, I also had my softball glove and cleats in the back seat. Anyway, this prick walked me to the back of my vehicle and told me to sit on the curb. I complied.

The officer then walked to his vehicle and made a call on his cell phone. I figured he was busting my chops for telling him that I was in a rush, but no, I could not have been more wrong about that. In less than two minutes, a dark sedan pulled up behind the cop's car, and out stepped none other than Agents Delano and Willis. You have got to be kidding me. The three amigos walked up to me where I sat on the curb. Officer Goldstein then advised the two FBI agents that I consented to having my vehicle searched. What? I jumped up off the curb and began my protest. I was in mid-sentence when Agent Willis walked to my vehicle, opened the driver's door, opened my briefcase, and took out the two cashier checks.

I said, "What the hell do you think you're doing? You have no right to take those checks."

Agent Willis said, "These checks are part of the fraud you have committed, and I am confiscating them."

I replied, "I told Officer Goldstein, and I told you that you could not search my vehicle. This is bullshit. What happened to the search for guns and drugs? This is such a setup, and you guys say that I am crooked? Take a look in the mirror. I suppose you guys just happened to be in the neighborhood when I ran that imaginary stop sign. Right."

Agent Delano thanked Officer Goldstein for his help; she got in the car with Agent Willis, and they drove away. Just like that. They were on the scene for less than five minutes. Here is the kicker. Officer Goldstein handed me a clipboard and told me to sign a vehicle search consent form. I decided to tell the good officer to go and have sex with his own mother, except I actually said, "Go fuck your mother."

I was escorted back to my vehicle where I sat for a good forty minutes. Officer Goldstein wrote me a ticket for driving through a stop sign. I shit you not, folks, this happened to me just the way I described it. All that just kept running through my head as I drove home that day was that these guys represented the law. These guys were calling me a criminal, yet they completely ignored the law and my rights as a citizen of the United States of America. Yes, I was mad, but to be honest with you, I was more sad that this was the way that my country chose to treat me. Serve and protect, my ass.

CHAPTER 122

The next day, I decided to call Mr. C and told him what had taken place. Once again, I could tell that he thought that I was full of shit. I was in no mood to try and convince him, but at least I did the right thing by calling him. Then Mr. C hit me with a line that explained a whole lot to me.

Mr. C said, "When I called the FBI, they told me that you were going to play games with me."

Mr. C had called the FBI a few days prior. He told them about the buyout options and how my attorney (Lisa Daniels) was making all the arrangements; well, at least now I knew how they found out about the buyout, and now I knew just how far these pricks would go to turn customers against me. Once again, how was this protecting anyone?

I called Scott once again to now inform him of what had taken place at the fake traffic stop, and I could tell that even this seasoned lawyer was taken aback at what the FBI was doing to me at this time. There was still no word on any charges being filed against me or any further communications between Scott and the feds. I was still left in limbo.

I sat outside by my pool that evening trying to get a grip on what my situation really was. Was I just kidding myself into thinking that I could still help my customers? Was the idea of Global getting back into normal operations an unattainable goal? Unfortunately for all parties, the answer to both questions was yes. If the Mr. C buyout was a sign of what I was going to run into with each and every customer, then my efforts would surely fall short. I needed to take another route, a much quicker route to settle with all my customers at one time, but how?

As I sat out in my quiet little haven, I started to jot notes on a legal pad in hopes of coming up with an out-of-the-box solution, something that I had not thought of yet. I found myself listing positives and negatives that were taking place at Global. The positive side of my paper was looking pretty thin. The one positive that stuck out like a sore thumb was the revenue that was still being generated by our operating ATM machines. Despite the FBI's efforts to destroy that revenue stream, the operating machines were still producing over $80,000 per month. I needed to use that money to my customers' advantage before any more damage was done. It finally hit me: a plan that I had not considered before, a plan that could allow Global to continue in operation for a very long time. I could sell the company and give the proceeds to the customers.

I first decided to check with Scott to see if selling Global would be a legal issue for me, but I could not see how this would be an issue for me. I was not charged with any crimes, and I would not personally benefit from the sale of the company. Once again, Scott could not understand why I was wasting my time and efforts, but he did agree that as long as I did not personally benefit from the sale, it should not be a problem.

CHAPTER 123

I decided to bounce the idea of a sale off one of my very first customers, Don M from Pensacola, Florida. Don owned a huge Florida construction company, and he had been purchasing machines on a fairly steady basis. Don had always hinted that I should keep him in mind if anything big ever came along, so here was that something big. Don was extremely cordial on the phone and very receptive to my idea. In fact, Don wanted to meet in person and discuss terms of him buying Global Vending. Don was an extremely smart hands-on businessman that did not like what the feds were doing to me or his Global investment. We decided to meet in Orlando, Florida, in hopes of hashing out a sale that would make sense and benefit all Global customers. Finally, something was heading in a positive direction.

I chose to bring Kim W with me to the Orlando meeting. Kim could help answer any of Don's locating questions, and besides, I sure did need some of Kim's special stress relief. Don brought his business partner with him to Orlando, and the four of us met in Don's huge hotel suite. I mean, you could land an airplane in this freakin' room. I have to admit, I was nervous about the meeting, not because of the business at hand but because this would be the first Global customer that I would be seeing face-to-face since my legal troubles began. As it would turn out, Don greeted me with open arms and nothing but positive feedback and support. I can't even describe how good that made me feel. I guess I had built something special.

After several hours of discussions, brainstorming, and innovative thinking, Don and I came to an agreement how he would purchase Global Vending. The terms were better than anything that I could have dreamed of. Don would retain full ownership of Global Vending Inc., all its assets, and of course the revenue stream from the operating ATM machines that they had purchased. Don would initially pay each Global customer $1,000 for each machine that they had purchased and also would set aside 0.20 per ATM transaction to be distributed to the customers on a monthly basis.

Global had sold almost 3,200 ATM machines, so the 0.20 per transaction would be collected for an entire month and then would be divided by 3,200, then each customer would receive one share of that fund for each ATM machine that they had purchased.

So let's say for argument's sake that the 0.20 fund totaled $32,000 for a particular month, Don would divide that $32,000 by 3,200 shares, making each share worth $10. So if Customer X had purchased ten machines from Global, then they would receive a check in the amount of $100 for that month. Don also agreed to finish placing Global's remaining machines out into the marketplace until he reached the 3,200-unit mark. Global's customers would receive 0.20 per transaction for every machine placed up to and including 3,200 machines. Every customer would receive a full refund this way and then make a nice healthy return. The deal also called for job offers to Kim W for locating services, Ron for technical support, and Kim S for technical support. This was how business was supposed to take place; this was a good piece of cooperation between two businessmen that wanted to do the right thing for everyone. Like I said earlier, Don was a smart businessman. Don made it very clear that he was going to present this deal to his attorneys and contact the feds to let them know of his intentions. Don did not want to get blindsided like I had been. I did not like the fact that the feds were going to be notified of the sale before it happened, but I understood he felt the need to do it. I would just have to wait and see how his attorneys and the feds reacted to our deal.

CHAPTER 124

Don contacted me a few days later to discuss where he was at with the purchase of Global. Don advised me that his attorneys gave him the green light to make the purchase, but the feds left him unsure of what to do. He had contacted Agent Delano and Assistant United States Attorney Larry Barfeld. AUSA Barfeld had very little to say. He made it clear to Don that they had no legal right to stop me from selling Global Vending. Agent Delano offered Don a lot to worry about. Agent Delano told Don that he could do whatever he wanted, but she did not foresee the processors cooperating with him or making payments to him. Why would she say that? Why did she feel that the processing companies would not pay Don like they had been paying me? Don told me that if I got written confirmation and a new processing contract from ATMNS and Nationwide Cash Systems that reflected him as the person to be receiving the ATM monthly revenue, then he would proceed with the purchase as planned.

I first called Nationwide to arrange for the new processing agreement, and I quickly found out why Agent Delano was so sure of herself. Nationwide's CEO and scumbag president, Ben Gonzalez, informed me that Agent Delano had called him and warned him against sending out any further checks to Global Vending. She informed him that if he continued to send out checks, he would be considered a coconspirator of the fraud that I had and was still committing. Scumbag Gonzalez then told me that he placed a stop payment on the last check that he had sent to me and that he reregistered the thirty machines that I had purchased from him back into his company's name. What a fucking piece of shit. Ben actually laughed on the phone and hung up on me. He refused to take any future calls from me. I strongly considered flying out to California and shooting this prick right between the eyes as he begged for his useless life, but of course, I did not do that. I am a good Christian.

Next, I called ATMMS, and I spoke with my friend Bart. He too had just received a call from Agent Delano, and he was also threatened by her not to send out any future checks. Bart was very apologetic to me; he was being placed in a very tough spot here. Bart told me that he contacted his attorney and was advised that since the feds refused to send him written instructions of why he could not send me funds or what to do with the funds that my machines were generating, Bart and his attorney decided that the best thing to do would be to take all the monthly ATM funds that were owed to me and place them in a trust account until my legal battle was settled. I could hear how sorry Bart was that he had to do this, but Bart also had a multimillion-dollar business of his own that he had to protect. I thanked Bart for his efforts, and I told him I would be in contact when this was all settled. Well, folks, that was the end of that; no monthly revenue from the processors, so no deal with Don M. Once again, the feds had managed to destroy an opportunity for the customers of Global Vending Inc. to have received back their investments and make a nice return.

Once again, I sat in my office and scratched my head, wondering just how the feds felt that this was protecting these people. At this point, I was pretty much shot. I had very little wind left in my sails. I mean, how could I possibly help my customers with this kind of resistance?

I contacted Scott and informed him of what the FBI did with my processors and how the sale of Global had just gone down the shitter. Scott once again documented what I had told him, and he all but begged me to stop trying. I have to admit that I was pretty close to giving up.

CHAPTER 125

The straw that broke this camel's back came at the end of March 2004 when I was still in the process of making good on as many buyout options as possible. I received a call from Lisa Daniels's office, who informed me that the feds had not only seized the funds in my trust account but that she had to hire a lawyer for herself because the FBI accused her of laundering money for me. I could not believe what I was hearing; my lawyer needed a lawyer. What the fuck? I had no doubt that I was up shit's creek without a paddle and a hole in my boat.

I called my business and personal banks that day, and both informed me that the feds had seized my accounts. That was the end of that. No more operating funds for buyouts, no more payroll, no more anything. The Feds had finished the job that they had started, yet I still had not been charged with any crime. What a fucking joke. I was too numb to cry and too mad to think very clearly, but I did know that I was finished at Global. My dream had finally ended in a life-changing nightmare.

I walked into the main sales area and asked all the Global employees to gather around. I informed them of what had happened, and then I simply asked them to pack up their belongings; Global Vending Inc. was officially out of business. That moment was one of the saddest moments in my life. I could see the disappointment on my employees' faces. At one time not too long ago, we were larger than life, and now, even though we stuck together as a team and fought for our survival, we were defeated. The whole scene was like that of a funeral. As I said my goodbyes to each employee in private, I realized just how special some of them were and just how fucked up some of them were.

I told Carrol that I would help him find a new office for the photographic vending business. I also asked Carrol to hire my sister Paula to work with him and to use my half of the photo business to payroll her. Carrol gave me a big manly hug and agreed to hire my sister.

My receptionist, Susan, was in tears. We had grown close over the years, and saying goodbye to her was very hard. I promised to email her a reference letter so that she could seek employment elsewhere.

Bruce and I hugged, and I just felt awful for him. He moved his family down from New York and was now unemployed in Florida. Bruce made things easy on me. He told me he would be fine and that I should call him when things were settled. Perhaps we could get into another business at a later date.

Ron and I said our goodbyes, I had been working with Ron for over eight years now, and I would miss him as an employee and as a good all-around guy.

Kim S and I hugged when we said our goodbyes. Yes, there were tears in our eyes, and we promised to stay in contact. I informed Kim S that I would do anything in my powers to help her find another job.

My sister-in-law Laura and I would still be seeing each other of course, but it was still a sort of goodbye. We gave each other a big hug, and Laura made it clear that she would be there for me during my continuing legal fight. I have nothing but good things to say about Laura.

My goodbyes with my brother-in-law Burt was my first look into who the real Burt Blum was. (Yes, add him to the shit list.) I would of course still be seeing him around since he was married to my sister Lisa, but Burt's goodbye concerns were not like anyone else. Burt simply asked me how and when I was going to pay him for his last two days of work. This gutless insensitive prick wanted his paycheck for his last two days of work. I simply laughed at him and asked him to leave my office. What a fucking jerk.

After everyone had left the office, I wandered over to Kim W's office to say my goodbyes to her. This would be a tough one. As I approached Kim's office, I saw that she was busy packing boxes on her desk. I said a quiet hello, and Kim decided to come around her desk and give me a big hug. I apologized to her for what had happened with my company; after all, Kim was another person who moved from a different state to come and work for me. Once again, this was a true life-changing moment for her. This moment with Kim W was very awkward to say the least. I mean, what do you say to a person who had worked for you for several years and whom you had a physical relationship with for several months? As I tried to talk to Kim, I could not help but notice that she continued to pack boxes like the building was on fire. Finally, I asked her what she was packing. Kim told me that she was taking all the location information with her, all the research books that I had purchased to hunt for locations, and all my business contacts that I had developed over the years. At first, I jokingly replied that she could have asked me if it was okay to take that stuff with her, but her reaction caught me off guard. Kim started to go off on how she was too old to restart her life again and how she was entitled to take whatever she wanted from the office. I'm telling you, I had never seen this hostile, arrogant attitude from her before. I asked her to calm down and to please talk to me about how she was feeling, but Kim snapped at me and told me that I should mind my own business. This was not what I was expecting from her. I got pissed off, and I demanded that she stop packing my files. When Kim ignored me, I asked her to leave the office, or maybe I should say that I demanded her to leave. Kim simply looked up at me, told me she did not know why she was acting the way she was, and she left the building in tears. That was the last time I would see or hear from Kim W. What a shitty fucking day.

CHAPTER 126

I was now facing the task of telling Denise what had happened with the company and the remainder of our personal bank accounts. Over the past few weeks, I had been able to withdraw almost $160,000 in cash, and that money was sitting in my home safe. I know that sounds like a lot of money, but with a huge mortgage, mounting legal bills, no income, and an uncertain future, that money did not make me feel secure, so I could just imagine how my already insecure wife was going to feel. I gave her the news just like I was pulling off a Band-Aid: one quick motion and it was all over. Denise asked all the usual questions about our financial future, and I really had no answers for her; we would have to wait out the feds and see what was on their minds.

I called Scott and set up a time to meet with him over the weekend. I had a fire inside me that was growing bigger by the minute, and I wanted these pricks to pay for what they had done to me, my family, my employees, and the customers of Global Vending Inc. When I met with Scott, I definitely got the feeling that he was at a loss of what to do. Scott explained to me that his usual client wanted to hide from the feds, not stir the pot, and hope that they would just disappear, but not me. No, you see, I was innocent, and I wanted justice to be served. My guess was that Scott's usual client was a person who was caught dead to rights committing a crime, so hiding would be the best option. After a brief discussion, Scott advised me that he could file a motion with the courts that would force the government to take action within the next thirty days or so. If Scott filed this motion with the district court, the feds would either have to charge me with a crime or release all my seized assets back to me. I immediately told Scott to file the motion. He again warned me to be careful of what I wished for. I just might get it. Screw it, I wanted this to be resolved; having this unknown bullshit hanging over my head was just leaving me in complete limbo, and that was no way to live. I had a wife and kids to think about, and we were not getting any younger. It was time to enter wasp's nest. Scott filed the motion as I requested, and that set an action date of May 6, 2004: let's see what happens.

CHAPTER 127

I felt funny doing it, but I lied to my children. I felt a need to shelter them from what was taking place. I did not want this to scare them in any way. Perhaps when they were older, I could explain to them what had really happened. I told my children that I had sold my business and that I was going to take a little time off before I started a new company. I tried to fill them with positives, and I made it seem like it was really no big deal. My boys were just great, and they made me feel so good inside. They got so excited when they realized that I would now be able to spend more time with them and that I would not be traveling as much as I used to. My boys and I were always close, and I was going to use as much of my new free time to bond with them and be the dad that I always saw myself being.

Denise decided that she needed to be out of the house more, and since shopping every day was no longer an option, she decided to get a job. Denise was hired by a local retail store that made custom cookies and cookie bouquets. Denise was given retail hours that included weekdays and some weekends. At a whopping $10 per hour, her new job was not going to solve our problems, but at least she was getting herself out of the house and staying busy. I saw that as a very good thing.

I took over the duties of dropping off and picking up the boys from school; I became a regular in the pickup/drop-off line at school, and I was starting to get a feel of what it was like to be a stay-at-home dad: truth be told, I loved every minute of it. I joked with my kids on the way to school. I sometimes took them out to eat on the way home from school, and as soon as we arrived back home, it was either swims in the pool, sports in the yard, or sometimes a movie in our home theater. Within a very short time, we were inseparable. I was making plans for what I was going to do with them for the summer and beyond.

April had gone by in a flash of an eye, and summer was only one month away. I had Scott contact my mortgage company and advise them that I would no longer be able to make payments until my legal issues were resolved. Scott sent them all the seizure paperwork and the papers that showed the government lien. My mortgage company was Washington Mutual, and I only mention their name because of how cooperative they were. My home had tons of equity in it, and the bank knew that my house would not be in a negative situation for a long time.

The only person from Global that contacted me during the entire month of April was Ron from technical support. Ron called and asked me to meet with him and his father-in-law at Global's office so we could talk. I always had Global's rent prepaid for several months in advance, so I was in no rush to move the rest of our inventory to any storage facility. It was weird when I first got to the office. Ron and his father-in-law were waiting for me in a moving truck. Ron's father-in-law was a well-to-do businessman, and he and Ron had a business proposition for me. Ron wanted permission to move all of Global's ATM inventory to a storage facility that he had rented. Ron planned on hooking up with Kim W and placing the remaining ATM machines into the marketplace. I sat and listened to Ron and his father as they laid out their plan of attack; it sounded very unorganized and simplistic to me, but what did I have to lose? Ron promised to make me a silent partner, and once they were established, I would be cut in for some of the profits. I decided to give them what they wanted. Ron, his father-in-law, and I loaded all of Global's ATM machines and parts into their moving van, and off they went. I had no problem giving Ron my inventory. I did not see any real way of selling it off, nor did I have the ambition to do so. If something good came out of Ron's plan, then that would just be a bonus for me at a later date.

CHAPTER 128

May 6, 2004, the last day that the government had to shit or get off the pot: return my assets or charge me with a crime. It was weird the way that this day developed. Denise was the vice president of my kids' parent-teacher association, and she had a meeting at their school that morning. Normally, I would have driven them to school, but since Denise was going there anyway, she took my dropoff and pickup duties for the day. I planned on calling my sister Paula to see if her and Carrol wanted to have lunch that afternoon, and then maybe I would be meeting with Scott to work on a motion for the return of my property.

I slept in that morning and strolled out of bed around 9:00 a.m. I tried to call Paula, but I did not get any answer on her cell phone. I assumed that she and Carrol were busy taking film orders, so I just figured I would pop in and surprise them with lunch later that day. I made myself some coffee, took a shower, and kicked my feet up on my desk in the library as I checked my emails.

Now my office/library faced the front of my house, and I had a perfect view of the other three lots on my block where only one other house was currently under construction. Something caught my eye immediately. There was a dark-blue sedan parked on the lot with two men sitting in the car. Because of the size of my property, and the wall that surrounded my property, I could not make out what these guys looked like or what they were doing in the car. I just know that these were not construction workers because there was no activity on the house that morning. Maybe it was my drug-induced mind, or maybe I was just becoming paranoid, but I started to consider calling the local police to report a suspicious vehicle. I decided to give it a little time and see if they simply left. I played a little poker online that morning, and then I watched the local news.

Around 11:00 a.m., I was almost ready to head out and pick up lunch for Paula and Carrol when I decided to check on that sedan and its occupants. It was still there. I had an idea. I would take my dog for a walk and stroll by to see what these people looked like. Yeah, that was the ticket. Oh, and just in case, I would take my loaded Berretta with me. When I look back at this time in my life, I just can't help but ask myself if I was truly retarded. I have a saying that I use all the time: "What is the worst thing that can happen if you do..." In this case, what was the worst that could have happened if I approached a strange car with my dog and a loaded semiautomatic weapon. Well, things could go down the shitter pretty fucking fast, you moron, but anyway, that was my genius plan.

I put a leash on my trusty shih tzu, Molli; I grabbed my Berretta and slapped a clip in it; and I headed out to the garage.

As the electronic door rolled up on the garage, and I stepped out onto the driveway, I instantly heard a loud air horn sound off from way down the block; it scared the shit out of my dog. Now remember, I live on a cul-de-sac block with no other houses and only one road leading in. Down that road came no less than a dozen dark sedans and marked Broward County sheriff's cars, all with sirens wailing and lights flashing. I froze in my tracks. The two guys that were in the dark sedan on the lot next door started yelling orders at me on a bullhorn. "Don't you fucking move. Get down on the ground, and don't you fucking move." Don't move? Lick my balls, you freak. This is my house, and I will do whatever I damn well please. Oh, and by the way, who the hell are you? You know, things are just not like what you see on television. How about yelling, "Freeze, FBI!" or something simple like that. Anyway, I was drugged up and not thinking like a normal human being.

Anyway, with this huge convoy of cars closing in on my front gate, I decided to head back into my house so that I could calm down my dog who had now officially shit on the driveway. I got into the garage and hit the button to close the electronic door. I unleashed my mutt and headed for the phone to call Scott. My heart was now pounding out of control. This was obviously the government's decision not to return my property. I know, hard to believe. As I got to the phone, it rang, two short rings, one long ring. That was how my phone rang when someone was pressing the security intercom at the front gate.

You know, you have to laugh for a quick minute at this situation. Here they were, the cops and the FBI tearing ass down my block in full force to make the big bust, bullhorns blaring and sirens wailing, and what did they do? They stopped at my gate and pushed the intercom button for me to let them in. I don't know, on TV, they would have rammed through the gate, sparks would fly, and a small army would dismount and rush the house. No, I got a bunch of pussies that rang to be let in. Okay, it wasn't funny at the time, but it is when I look back on that day. Okay, so I picked up the phone.

> Me: Hello?
>
> Officer: Mr. Foley, I am with the Broward County sheriff's office, and I am here with the FBI. We have a warrant for your arrest. Can you please open the front gate.
>
> (Wow, please? This guy was actually being polite to me.)
>
> Me: I have no problem opening the gate for you. I need to secure my dog before I let you in, and I also need to secure my firearm before I let you in.
>
> Officer: I can give you one minute.
>
> Me: No problem.

I hung up the phone, and I swear that I could see my heart beating through my shirt. I was being arrested; I was fucking being arrested. Holy shit. I put my dog in one of the spare bedrooms. I even was able to remember to leave her water and food. I ran across the house to my bedroom. I opened my safe, and I put the Berretta away. I ran to my bathroom, found my painkillers, and downed at least eight of them if not more. That probably was not a good idea, but chances were that I was having a heart attack anyway, so I might as well enjoy the ride.

The phone rang again. Once again, it was the front gate. I picked up the phone and entered the code that opened the front electronic gates. Don't ask me why, but I emptied my pockets right there on the bed where I had answered the phone. Suddenly, I heard several loud bangs at the front door. This was it; this was it. I walked to the front door and opened it. Bang, the door was pushed open so hard that I almost fell flat on my ass. The first one through the door was none other than Special Agent Willis of the FBI, and he was followed by over a dozen other agents and uniformed police officers. My god, you would think that they were arresting a mass murderer or a serial rapist or something. I mean, give me a fucking break. These guys had Ar15s and tactical gear on. Well, Agent Willis forced me against a wall, and I mean forced me against a wall. I was not at all happy with that action. In fact, one of the Broward sheriffs asked Agent Willis to calm down. Agent Willis ignored the officer and started to read me my rights as he was patting me down. The whole time, he still had one arm on the back of my neck, and my face was pressed against the wall with quite a bit of force. I told Agent Willis that I was not going to resist and that he needed to lighten up on my neck. "This is not necessary" was the only thing that I could get out of my mouth with my faced pushed up against the wall. At that moment, Agent Willis decided to force one of his knees between my legs. He got right up into my ear and told me to shut up. Well, maybe those eight or so painkillers kicked in at that moment, or maybe I just had enough of my face being shoved against a wall in my own house, who knows what triggered me, but I had had enough of this bullshit. When Agent Willis's breath disappeared from my neck, I threw my right elbow back, which caught Agent Willis right on his neck. Down went Agent Willis, and then down went Tom Foley. Like a quarterback getting sacked from his blind side, I got crushed by two of the agents. The agents wrestled my arms behind me and placed handcuffs on me so tightly that my arms went almost instantly numb. All I can say is thank God I was flying high on pills because I could not imagine just how much that probably should have hurt me. As the agents lifted me off the ground, I could see Agent Willis getting to his feet; man was he pissed. Agent Willis grabbed me by the throat and started to swear and threaten me with promises of an ass-beating. I should have just shut my mouth and taken his bullshit. I mean, come on, I probably bruised his ego and embarrassed him in front of his coworkers. Instead, I chose option B. I got right back into his face and told him what a pussy he was. I told one of the sheriffs that I would sign a waiver if they let me and Agent Willis fight, mano a mano; the sheriff would have no part in that. I don't know what's wrong with me sometimes. I was just pissed that he decided to get tough now that I was in cuffs and surrounded by his buddies, yet two seconds ago, I leveled him with one shot. Fuck him. Thank God for the Broward County sheriffs; they made sure that cooler heads prevailed. The cop that walked me out to one of the FBI cruisers even joked with me in a very reserved voice, "Nice shot, Foley. Now keep your cool. This guys an asshole, okay?"

I thought that was really cool of him, and it worked. I calmed down.

The local sheriff placed me in one of the FBI's unmarked sedans, and he wished me luck with my legal issues.

I can still remember sitting in the back of that car, staring at my house, my neighborhood, my property, and I could not help but compare my life at that moment and my life just five months earlier; how in God's name did this happen? How do you go from private planes and SL65 Roadsters to handcuffs and a ride to jail? I was wishing that this was a nightmare, and I would wake up with a good laugh, but no, this was real, and it was only just the beginning.

CHAPTER 129

The ride to the Miami FBI headquarters was fairly uneventful. The agents read me my rights in the car since they never got a chance to finish reading me my rights in my house. The only thing that kept running through my mind was the fact that I did not have a chance to let anyone know what was happening. How were people going to figure out that I was arrested and on my way to jail? I also started to replay in my mind the whole scene that took place just a few moments earlier in my house. I could not help but think about how Scott had provided a letter to the feds at our one and only meeting that advised the feds that I would self-surrender to any law enforcement facility if they were going to charge me with a crime. That whole scene at my house could have been averted, but no, these people wanted me to get the full effect of being arrested. They were not going to make any step of this procedure civil or with exception. No, they wanted to instill fear in me; they wanted me to lay down and roll over. Sorry, guys, you have the wrong person for that shit. Self-surrender is a no; AR 15s and tactical gear are a yes. Give me a fucking break.

I loved the movie *Wall Street* with Charlie Sheen playing the power and money-hungry stock broker Bud Fox. I could watch that movie a hundred times and never be bored or disappointed; that is, of course, until the very end. I can't even start to tell you how pissed off I was when Bud Fox gets handcuffed in his office, he is being escorted out by a New York City cop, and all of a sudden, he starts to cry. That just pissed me off something fierce. Bud Fox crumbled as soon as the law came down on him, and all of a sudden, his stoic character was dismantled. I understand why the movie writers chose to show his vulnerable side. I mean, the man was a crook, and he had been caught, but still, I felt he should have taken his hits like a man and cut out the freakin' crying shit.

Anyway, I had been through a lot in my life, and I knew that I had done nothing wrong. There would be no tears from this guy, and there would be no laying down or rolling over either. I saw this moment as game on!

CHAPTER 130

We arrived at the Miami FBI headquarters where I was to be processed and then taken to jail. As I entered into the processing room, I got smacked with yet another shocking scene; there, handcuffed to a desk, was my sister Paula. What the fuck was going on here? Paula had obviously been crying. Her face was red and swollen, and there was a pile of used tissues in front of her. The feds handcuffed me to a table next to her and left us alone. Paula told me that she was arrested early in the morning by Agent Delano. Paula was walking her dog in her pajamas when she was surrounded by FBI agents and handcuffed right there in front of all her neighbors; she was simply a mess. I must have apologized to her a million times, and I tried my hardest to convince her that everything was going to be all right; she did not buy that for a second. Paula just kept crying over and over again that she was supposed to pick her kids up from school that day. Who would pick them up? No one knew that either of us had been arrested. There were so many questions that we needed to have answered; once again, it was the not knowing that really became a heartache. The FBI did not feel compelled to answer any of our questions, and they would not allow us to make any phone calls: they simply told us that we were going to be processed and then transported to the federal detention center in Miami where we would remain until we had a bond hearing. I knew nothing about prison, I knew nothing about bond hearings, and I still had no way of contacting Scott to let him know what had happened. I was getting pretty close to my boiling point.

Paula and I were held at the Miami FBI office for around an hour or so, and then it was off to prison. Lucky me, Agents Delano and Willis personally drove us to the federal detention center in

Miami. This was their victory lap. The ride there was only fifteen or twenty minutes, but it was the ride from hell. Paula cried nonstop and begged the agents to let her make a phone call so that she could arrange to have her children picked up from school. The agents just ignored her. Agent Willis was obviously still boiling over the whole incident at my house, and Agent Delano made sure that he knew that she was aware of what had happened.

I would be lying if I told you that I was not getting nervous as we approached the prison facility. I had no idea of what to expect once we were inside. Like most people in America that have never been arrested by the feds before, I only knew what I had seen on TV, and I had no way of knowing if any of that crap was real.

CHAPTER 131

FDC Miami is accessed through an underground parking facility, and every vehicle is searched inside and out before entrance is approved. As we waited for our car's turn to be searched, Agent Delano finally broke her witch streak and allowed Paula a phone call. Paula gave Agent Delano her ex-husband's phone number (Alan) to dial, and once connected, Agent Delano handed Paula her cell phone. Yes, we were handcuffed, but our cuffs were in front of us at this point, not behind our backs. I heard Paula start to explain to Alan what had happened, and then she suddenly stopped speaking. I could hear Alan laughing through the phone. Alan had already known that we were being arrested on that day; the feds had been keeping him updated. Paula started to cry even harder now. Can you imagine what an evil son of a bitch Alan is? All Paula wanted to do was to make sure that her kids would be taken care of, and Alan laughed at her on the phone; he simply was not a human being. Agent Delano had a huge smile on her face too; this was all a big game to these people and a cruel one at that. I raised my voice to Paula in an attempt to get her back to reality here.

I said, "Enough, enough crying. You need to get through this moment in time, Paula. You need to straighten up and stop getting hysterical. I promise you this will all be over soon, and you will be home with your kids. Now straighten up and chill out."

My little rant seemed to work for the time being. Paula apologized and told me she would do her best; I was steady and firm on the outside, but inside, I just wanted to cry for her. This whole pile of shit had nothing to do with her at all; this was all on me.

We finally got approval to enter the facility. The garage and its surroundings were cold and evil, almost dungeon-like. Paula and I were placed in an elevator that took us up a few floors. Once out of the elevator, prison guards signed paperwork that Agent Delano was carrying, and as they left, Agent Delano told us to enjoy our stay. Someday, Agent Delano, someday. At this point, Paula and I were separated. I gave her a wink as we were led away, but her tears had already started again.

My first stop was to a room where I was stripped off my clothes and searched. That was a moment in time that I would love to forget, but honestly, I will never be able to rid myself of that humiliation. It took three prison guards to do the strip search, three, and if I had to guess, they were all flaming homosexuals. I stood there naked in front of them for at least fifteen minutes as they barked out their commands: open your mouth, lift up your balls, turn around, bend over, cough, lift your feet up one at a time. "Good boy," one of the pricks said. I didn't like it, but I took it. I was in their world now, and for now, I would play their game.

So Elton John, Liberace, and Doogie Howser took turns picking out underwear and a jumpsuit for me, and finally I was able to get dressed. The clothes smelled like shit, and all of it was way too small on me. Once again, big fucking deal. It was going to take more than this to break me down. I had my mug shot taken, fingers were printed, and an ID card was produced for me. I was now officially federal inmate number 70819-004. The guards gave me a medical questionnaire to fill out, a brown paper bag with my dinner in it, and then they placed me in a holding cell.

As I would quickly find out, federal holding cells were generally equipped to hold ten to fifteen inmates at a time, but they were almost always packed with twenty-five to thirty inmates. There was no place to sit, no place to stand, and no place to walk to; the cell was simply packed. The next thing I noticed was the temperature; I would say that it was about fifteen degrees below zero in this cell. Yes, I am exaggerating, but only a little; it was freezing in there. As I looked around for a spot to plant my ass, I could not help but notice the people that I was locked up with. It looked like the entire crew that used to cut my lawn. These guys were all third-world-nation transplants that did not understand the concept of speaking to one another. This group of degenerates yelled at one another in nine different dialects of Spanish, and it sure did appear that they were having a great time. My painkiller high was quickly wearing off, and I was building up a headache that made me feel like my head was going to explode. *Deep breaths, Tom, deep breaths. This is only temporary.*

As if being strip-searched by three fags and then getting locked up with a bunch of Frito Banditos was not bad enough, I suddenly started to hear my nickname being called out. "TJ, TJ, are you around here?" I made my way back to the cell door, and sure enough, directly across the way was Paula, all decked out in her new orange prison attire. What a freakin' nightmare. Paula was crying, of course, and another female inmate was trying to console her. Great, Paula was in prison for just over an hour, and she was already someone's bitch.

I sat in that hellhole of a holding cell for over five hours before a guard finally came to get me so that I could make my one phone call. It was around 8:00 p.m., so I decided to call Denise at home instead of Scott at the office. Denise picked up on the first ring. I couldn't believe it. She had already figured out that I had probably been arrested and told me that when she got home with the kids that day and found Molli locked up in one of the guest rooms, the front door wide open—yes, the feds never even closed the front door—and all my personal items like my phone, wallet keys, and cash on our bed, she figured out that something had gone bad. Denise called Scott, and Scott called the prosecutor, who told him that I had been arrested. Scott called Denise and let her know. Neither of them knew that Paula had been arrested also. Denise told me that I had a bond hearing the very next day, and Scott requested that my entire extended family be there in order to show the judge that I was not a flight risk. She had already arranged the whole thing. For the first time in years, I could hear that Denise had some genuine concern for me in her voice. It was nice to hear that concern from her. Maybe this whole thing would somehow bring us closer together like we used to be. She told my boys that I was away for the night and that I would be back in a day or two. She had no way of knowing how the bond hearing would go. Like I had said earlier, keeping my boys sheltered from the reality of what was taking place was very important to me, and so far, Denise and I managed to keep a lid on things. I eased Denise's concerns, and I let her know that I would be fine and that I would see her in court the next day. We said our goodbyes. I decided to lie to Paula in order to calm her down. I told her that we had a bond hearing the next day and that we would be home by tomorrow afternoon. Paula took the news in, and immediately she was okay. If for some reason we were denied bond the next day, I would have my freakin' hands full with her. I prayed that that would not be the case.

Anyway, back to the holding cell with the mariachi band where I sat and waited until 1:30 a.m. A guard finally came and got me. He issued me a bedroll and took me up to the tenth floor, also known as Fox West. The entire FDC Miami inmate population was locked in their cells at 9:30 p.m., so by the time I arrived at my cell, everyone was locked up and sleeping. Wow, my first prison cell, what a treat: eight feet by twelve feet, white cinder-block walls, a metal-framed bunk bed, a counter with a sink, and a toilet stuck to the wall. The toilets had no seats by the way. I almost threw up. I threw my sheet and blanket on the available top bunk. The man that I was sharing a cell with appeared to be dead. He was definitely in his late seventies or early eighties, and he had underwear hanging on homemade clotheslines all around the cell. What a fucking treat that was. I was exhausted, but no matter how hard I tried, I could not fall asleep. My mind was racing all night trying to figure out just how I had gotten to this point and how in God's name I was going to resolve this. I prayed that night, and I spoke to my mother in heaven; I was simply asking for strength and guidance to get through this mess, strength, and guidance.

CHAPTER 132

At 5:00 a.m., a guard came and woke me up. He advised me that I had a court hearing, and I needed to be ready in fifteen minutes. Get ready? I was still wearing the same damn clothes. In fact, that was all I had. Get ready. Yeah, let me run and take a shower without any soap or towels. Let me run to my closet and change my clothes, maybe a quick cup of coffee and a doughnut. Dick. I was escorted down to a holding cell again just like the night before; sure enough, Paula was in a cell across from me, and boy oh boy did she look like shit; I almost did not recognize her. Paula's face was so swollen that she actually looked like a completely different person. My god, how much can one person cry?

Anyway, at around 8:00 a.m., Agents Delano and Willis came back to pick us up for our court date up in Broward County district court. Don't these two have anything better to do? I mean, god, they were FBI agents, and their biggest task was to act like taxi drivers? Whatever. Nice shiny handcuffs were placed on Paula and me again, and off we went with Frick and Frack to our bond hearing. Within minutes of getting on the road, I could tell that the agents had an agenda. They were either looking for information, or they were looking to torture Paula and I just a little more. Paula just did not know when to shut up sometimes. She kept asking me, "Are you sure that we are being released today? Are you sure?"

Now as I would soon find out, Agent Delano liked to play mind games with people, but to be honest with you, she was not very good at it. What Agent Delano would soon find out was that I could play mind games with the best of them. I played poker with some of the best in the business, and poker is a true mind game. Besides that, I have a way of getting under people's skin quickly, and once there, I do not let up.

Agent Delano said, "Oh, Paula, what makes you think that you are getting out on bond today? I have been doing this job for a very long time, and I have never had anyone get bond on their first hearing. Never."

Of course, Paula took the bait and started to cry like you just could not believe. I told Paula to ignore Agent Delano and not to say a word to her about anything. I then focused on the wicked witch of the south.

I said, "So you like to pick on the weak ones, don't you? That's very professional of you, but you really aren't very good at your job. Anyone can make someone like Paula cry. Why don't you take a shot at me. Let's see what kind of training they really give you at the FBI."

Agent Delano said, "I don't know what you're talking about, Tom. I am just stating a fact to your sister. She should not get her hopes up too high."

Right there, that was what I was looking for, folks. Agent Delano just called me Tom, not Mr. Foley. I read that as a weakness. FBI agents should not try and get personal with suspects, not unless they were looking for information, so I figured I would take a shot.

I said, "It's funny to me. I would think that you guys would at least be trying to get information from me on the case at hand, yet all you seem to be interested in is making Paula cry. I don't get it. I love to talk, and I have nothing to hide from you guys. Don't you want to ask me anything?"

This was my setup. I already had the knife out to cut open her skin and get inside, and she had no clue. I was actually having fun at this point, and Paula had stopped crying. Not bad, aye?

Agent Delano said, "Well, Tom, I thought that since you had an attorney, you would not answer any of my questions, that's all. I would love to ask you some questions."

Okay, now Agent Delano was turned around and facing Paula and me in the back seat. A quick look at her eyes and her posture and I could see that she was excited about the opportunity that I had just presented to her; I needed to pull the reins back just a little.

Me: Okay, I will tell you what. Let's start off light. You ask me a question, and then I get to ask you a question. I have just as many questions as you have. Deal?

Agent Delano: Okay, let's start off light like you said: the prison records from last night state that you have a tattoo on your right hip. What is it a tattoo of?

Me: It's a tattoo of a Ghostbuster, you know that little ghost that the Ghostbusters had on the side of their vehicle with a red line running through it. Well, that's my tattoo. I got it when I was younger.

Agent Delano: (with a smile on her face) Well, that's a first. Okay, what would you like to ask me?

Me: Okay, how big are your tits?

Agent Willis spit his coffee all over the dashboard while he was driving. Paula looked at me like I was out of my fucking mind, and Agent Delano, well, let's just say that smile left her face pretty quickly. She swung her body around and was now no longer facing me, and she grabbed some napkins to start cleaning up Agent Willis's coffee spray.

Agent Delano: I don't think you're funny, Mr. Foley, and you better be very careful not to cross over any lines here.

Me: What are you talking about? You asked me a question, and now I get to ask you a question. Those were the only rules we made, and I want to know just how big your tits are. I mean, I have a general idea. I looked at them quite a bit during our meeting a few months ago, but I should not have to guess. I told you my tattoo was a Ghostbuster. Now give me the scoop on your tits.

Did you notice that I was now back to Mr. Foley? Mission accomplished. I got no answer from Agent Delano. My guess, by the way, is that she has 38C tits, but I don't claim to be an expert. Now that I had this witch under control, it was time to drive in the stake and kill this evil being.

> Me: Okay, fine, don't answer. Hey, Paula, you're a woman, how big do you think her tits are?
>
> Paula: (trying her hardest not to laugh) Would you please stop it.
>
> Me: Fine, I should have figured you women would stick together on this one.
>
> Me: Hey, Agent Willis, how about you? Give me your guess. How big do you think her tits are.
>
> Agent Willis: (also trying not to laugh) That's enough, Mr. Foley.
>
> Me: Fine, but I feel like you guys cheated me. Can you both pretend that you don't know what my tattoo is? That would kind of make things even again.

There was no response from the feds, except for Agent Willis turning on the car radio. I looked at Paula, gave her another one of my patented winks, and enjoyed the rest of the ride to court.

CHAPTER 133

The bond hearing was a joke, but it was also very humiliating. I was led into court in handcuffs, and I was chained to a group of at least twenty other inmates including my sister. I could see my family as I was escorted into court. Their faces were all sad, and some even looked embarrassed. That really bothered me. Scott came over to where I was sitting. He told me that the prosecutor was not going to fight against me being released on bond. That was good to hear. Scott had also entered a temporary appearance on behalf of Paula so that he could represent her at the bond hearing also. He made sure to let me know that I was being charged for Paula's temporary representation also.

Okay, so I was in court, I was arrested yesterday, I spent the night in a shithole prison, I was doing battle with two FBI agents during taxi time, and Scott needed to advise me at that very moment about more fees: I almost choked him out right there.

The judge simply informed me of the conditions of my release on bond. I had to answer a string of yes-or-no questions that made sure I understood the bond conditions, and just like that, I was released. The funny thing is that Paula and I were released in prison clothes. Our street clothes that we were arrested in had been boxed up yesterday and mailed back to our homes. When you get arrested by the feds, you have a choice: you can either mail your clothes back home, or you can donate them to charity.

I thanked everyone for coming down and supporting me in court. I made it short and sweet because all I could think about was getting a few pills in me to settle my nerves and then get in a fucking shower. I just felt so damn dirty. I hugged Paula, and I told her I would take care of this mess. She was just glad to be out of handcuffs.

I reminded her of what Agent Delano had said to her in the car, "No one ever gets bond at their first hearing." It was just the first of many lies to come.

The ride home was filled with questions and concerns from Denise. I could only answer her questions about the prison that I was in, but as far as the future and what would happen, I told her that I had to wait until I met with Scott again: that would be on the upcoming weekend. Now let's get home so I could shower up and get ready to pick my boys up at school, just like nothing had ever happened. I don't want to downplay the level of support that I had received up until this point from my extended and immediate family; it was huge. My father and his wife drove a long way from Palm City to be at that five-minute bond hearing, Denise's sister and husband were there, my sister Lisa and Burt were there, and all these people missed worked or rearranged their schedules to show a judge that I had family ties in south Florida and that I would not be a flight risk. I know that made a huge difference for me and Paula at that hearing.

As far as the conditions of my release, they were pretty simple. I had to report in person to a probation officer (pretrial officer in the feds) once a week. I was required to take random drug tests (that might be a problem), I could not travel outside of the south eastern district of Florida without the court's permission, I had to mail the court financial updates at the end of every month, I had to surrender my passport to the feds, and I had to get rid of my firearm. That was it. I transferred ownership of my beloved Beretta to Lenny the Drunk. He was the only other member of my family that owned and did target practice with handguns. My passport was surrendered, and the rest was up to me.

CHAPTER 134

My meeting with Scott that weekend could not come fast enough. Scott had an attorney friend that allowed him to use an extra office space that he had in Weston, and that helped a lot since the commute down to Miami was awful. Once we were together, Scott decided to first go over the charges that I was indicted on. The first thing that really pissed me off was that the indictment listed me as using an alias name "Thomas Richards." I advised Scott that he could rest assured that I had never used an alias before and that I had no idea what would lead the feds to think that I used an alias; most likely it was another one of Alan Nudelman's lies that the feds bit on. Scott made notes as we went through the indictment together. I was being charged with two counts of mail fraud (counts 1 and 2), both of which listed Tom C as the victim. That's right, the Tom C that I had tried so hard to get money back to, but the FBI stopped that from happening. I wondered if Tom C was ever told by the FBI that they seized the $80,000 that I was trying to get to him; I highly doubt it. The FBI had successfully created a hostile victim. The funny thing about counts 1 and 2 of the indictment was that I was being charged with sending Tom C money under false pretenses, not taking money from him. That just struck me as weird: people can send me money all day, and I could give a shit where that money was coming from. Anyway, counts 3, 4, and 5 were wire fraud charges that listed two other customers as the victims: the customers were Kent V, yes, young man Kent from South Dakota, the rich kid that owned the arena football team, my single largest customer; and the other customer was Dr. Richard W from Michigan. Dr. Richard W was one of my first customers, and he had actually become one of the Global Vending references; I had a great relationship with the good doctor and with Kent. Why in God's name did the feds pick these two guys to specifically list as victims in the indictment? Scott questioned me over and over again as to why I felt the government picked those three customers as victims for the indictment. We pulled out their files that Lisa Daniels had put together, and Scott was just amazed at how well-documented these three accounts were, and that was without our computer records that were a hell of a lot more detailed. I figured that Tom C had gone to the feds after he did not get his eighty grand, but the other two just had me puzzled. Scott told me that the first five counts were the serious charges against me, but he also told me that I had really caught a break because the government only chose to list three customers in the indictment, and that limited my potential prison exposure should I be found guilty. The indictment also had twenty-eight counts of expenditure money laundering and one count of conspiracy to structure money. In a nutshell, expenditure money laundering is the act of using ill-gotten gains (money in my case) to purchase anything. The government's twenty-eight counts included my purchases of my home, cars, jewelry, etc. The last charge of conspiracy to structure money was a total joke. The indictment charged Paula with money structuring, and I was charged with conspiring with her. Money structuring is a crime that most people don't even know exists or how it works. Money structuring occurs when an individual consistently withdraws or deposits cash into or out of a bank in amounts of less than $10,000. This has nothing to do with the IRS or paying taxes. It has to do with the federal government knowing how much cash is in play out on the streets. Anytime that an individual makes a bank deposit or a bank withdrawal of over $10,000, the bank is required to file a form with the feds. The bank customer is not made aware that this form exists and never is advised of this process. The bank is simply advising the feds that money has entered the streets or has been removed from the streets. Money structuring is the crime of purposely preventing the bank from filing that form by keeping the withdrawals and deposits below $10,000. How the hell is someone supposed to know that the form even exists, and what about the fact that Paula, and Denise for that matter, both tried to take out more than $10,000, but the bank

stopped them from doing so. That charge was the least of my worries. Paula would have to be defended on that charge, but I needed to
concentrate on the mail fraud and wire fraud charges: if I am found
not guilty of mail or wire fraud, then all the money laundering would
have to be dismissed; that's the law.

CHAPTER 135

As I scanned through my copy of the indictment, I found my emotions getting the best of me. First I was shocked at what I was reading, then sad, and finally I became infuriated. All the allegations in the indictment came from "confidential informants #1 and #2." That would be Alan and Andy of course. All the hard work that I had done to grow Global Vending was now being made out to be a scam, a fraud, a Ponzi scheme. The blood, sweat, and tears of the Global workforce was being disrespected in the worst of ways. Just reading through the entire indictment was a serious challenge for me. The federal justice system revolves around a set of guidelines that were set up by Congress in order to make sure that federal crimes were punishable in a very consistent mannerism. The crimes that I was being charged with fell under the federal sentencing guidelines titled Fraud. After briefly going over the charges and the indictment, Scott opened up the current federal sentencing guideline manual so that he could figure out what my maximum prison exposure would be if I proceeded to trial and was found guilty on all counts of my indictment.

Scott pointed out that the charges of mail and wire fraud were controlled by the dollar amount of the fraud and the number of people that were victims of the fraud. The higher the amount of fraud in dollars, the higher the prison sentencing level went. The more victims involved in the fraud, the higher the prison exposure, and so on. This was where Scott showed me that I caught my first break. He explained to me that by the government only listing five counts of combined mail and wire fraud, and only listing three customers in those charges, I could only be held accountable for defrauding three people, and the amount of fraud would be limited to the amount of money that those three victims had lost with Global. Had the government listed all 365 customers as victims, I would have been facing a hell of a lot more potential prison time.

As it was, Scott informed me that I was facing a maximum of sixty-three months in prison, just over five years. That was catching a break? (A quick spoiler alert, Scott was 100 percent wrong on my potential prison exposure, and not in my favor of course.) My head was spinning when Scott laid that news on me. I was an honest businessman, I had done nothing wrong, I busted my ass for my customers, and now I was going to be fighting to prevent myself from spending years of my life in a federal prison. Oh, and by the way, that did not include the fact that I would be responsible for paying back the customers their losses if I was found guilty. I needed to keep my cool. I needed to remember that I was innocent, and innocent people do not go to prison. Just be strong and fight. I am not a stupid person. I know that this was basically Scott's sales pitch. He wanted to sell me his services, and as it stood, it would appear that I was in great need of those services. Scott hit me with his proposed fee. Scott explained to me that we were at the very early stages of the legal process and that this process could become very complex and take years to resolve. Scott's proposal was to charge me with a single flat rate, on a large fee that would cover all his legal representations right through trial if it was to come to a trial situation. His fee was $130,000, and that was not including the $30,000 that I had already given him. This really sucked, folks. I mean, what are your options at this point? Your life is on the line here. I advised Scott about the cash that I had in my safe at home. Scott told me that he could accept no more than $30,000 of his fee in cash; the rest would have to come from a traceable source, like checks from friends and relatives. I would have to figure that part out.

But he was not done with the bad news for the day yet. No, he had plenty more for me. First of all, Paula would have to retain a separate attorney. He could not represent the two of us together. Scott gave me a list of other attorneys that he would recommend for Paula, friends of his of course, one big happy fucking family. The next doozy that Scott laid on me was that Global Vending was forced into involuntary bankruptcy by three of Global's investors. What the hell is involuntary bankruptcy, and why would I give a shit at this point? Well, involuntary bankruptcy is when three or more creditors that a company owes $10,000 or more go to the United States Bankruptcy Court and force the company into bankruptcy in order to protect company assets. Scott of course had a very close friend that was a bankruptcy attorney, and he advised Scott that if fraud was involved in a company, the bankruptcy charges could be just as damaging as the criminal charges. That was just great, just perfect. Bankruptcy was a very specialized area, so I would now also need a bankruptcy attorney: more fees would be coming. I told Scott to give his friend my information and to have him contact me to set up an appointment. I agreed to Scott's fees, and I told him I would arrange payment that week; I also told him to pick out one of his friends and have them contact me so I could retain him for Paula. Money was going to quickly become an issue, and of course, I had to deal with Denise.

Last but not least, I was advised by Scott that under no circumstance was I to have any contact with any Global customers or any members of the FBI: I needed to get ready to help him prepare my defense, but more importantly, I needed to keep my big mouth shut. Scott would be filing motions for discovery, which would force the government to provide us with a copy of every piece of information that they were holding in regard to my case. They were not allowed any surprises in the courtroom: somehow I doubt that they would not have surprises for me. How else can you convict an innocent person of a crime that never even happened?

CHAPTER 136

In an interview with writer Lawrence Grobel, the great Al Pacino was asked about a legal battle that he once had with one of the major Hollywood studios that he acted for. Pacino and the studio became entangled in a legal battle, and Pacino's inner circle advised him to seek representation by a trained professional attorney because the studio was sure to have a team of attorneys fighting for them. Pacino hired an attorney who took over the legal battle and told Pacino to keep his mouth shut and to stay out of the conflict. After months of motions and court dates, and mounting legal bills, Pacino had enough. Mr. Pacino told Lawrence Grobel that he simply walked. Yes, he physically walked, over to the studio, and asked to sit down with the studio executives in order to discuss the legal matters at hand. Within thirty minutes, Pacino and the executives of the studio had the conflict resolved, and all lawsuits were dropped. Pacino told Mr. Grobel how the legal process had made him feel inferior to the attorneys and to the legal process itself. He felt like another person that quickly found himself believing in things that he would normally never even entertain. Pacino was made to believe that these "professionals" all knew more than he did, when the simple fact is, no one knew more about him and his life than Pacino himself.

At this point in time, I know exactly how Pacino felt. I felt inferior; I was being told to sit on the sideline and let someone else determine how my future would play out, and that, my friends, is not a Tom Foley trait. But for now, I had to get organized and let Scott get the process started for me.

On my way back home from my first postarrest meeting with Scott, I decided to make a few phone calls to start the process of collecting Scott's fees.

My first call was to my buddy Carrol. As expected, Carrol did not hesitate to offer his help. Carrol told me that he had a $60,000 business line of credit and that he would gladly write out a check to Scott in that amount. I arranged to meet Carrol later that week to give him $60,000 in cash in exchange for his check.

I called my father and my father-in-law, and each offered to help in the amount of $5,000. It was the same deal. I would give them the cash, and they would write out a check to Scott.

My last call was to my cousin up in New York. My cousin John and I grew up around the block from each other in Massapequa. John's mom, my aunt Carol (my father's sister), passed away when John and I were very young: I believe John was around four years old, and I was around ten. My aunt Carol died a slow death from cancer, but to this day, I only have fond memories of her as being one of the most beautiful people that God ever placed on this earth. John's father, my uncle Frank, took her death in the worst of ways. My Uncle Frank unfortunately turned to alcohol as a comfort blanket, and my cousin John was the one that truly suffered the most. With the absence of my Aunt Carol, and my uncle hitting the bottle, John was raised for a good portion of his young life by my mother. The positive that can be spun on that whole chain of events was the fact that John and I were able to spend a lot of our childhood together. It was kind of like having the brother that I never had. John and I had never lost contact even after I moved to Florida. John always showed an interest in my business ventures. John was now a husband and a father of two beautiful young children, and he was working as a Nassau County emergency medical technician. Once again, John did not hesitate to offer his help. John sent a check to cover the balance of Scott's fees, and just like that, my attorney was paid in full, all before I made it home that day. It's amazing sometimes what you can do when you are truly determined to get a job done.

CHAPTER 137

Back on the home front, things would not go as smoothly for me as they had on my quest to get Scott paid. I sat Denise down, I showed her the indictment, and I told her what the government was charging me with. I then told her what I did in order to get Scott paid so that I could defend these bullshit allegations that I was being charged with. To say the least, Denise's response caught me completely off guard. My wife, my high school sweetheart, the mother of my children looked me right in the eyes and said, "Well, you must have done something wrong, or they would not be doing this to you. The FBI does not do this for no reason. You are wasting our savings on this crap, and that's not right."

Really? That was the support that my own wife was going to lay on me? I never heard this woman complaining when she was out shopping every day and spending over $10,000 per month on her American Express card. No, I never heard anything from this woman while she was on vacations or while she was signing our children up for private school, and I certainly never heard a complaint when she was picking out a $60,000 cocktail ring that she just had to have.

I was trapped between throwing up on her and just punching the living shit out of her right there; to this day, I have no idea how I managed to keep my cool and walk away from the situation. Regardless, I can tell you that I would never look at the woman again the same way.

My fire inside to prove my innocence just had gasoline poured on top. I was sick of being accused of wrongdoing, and this was just the beginning. There was no need to check in with Denise anymore about legal decisions and strategy now that she pretty much hung me out to handle this on my own.

I received a call from Scott's bankruptcy attorney friend; his name was Fred Buresh. Fred was one of the nicest guys I had spoken to in a long time. He completely understood my financial problems and offered to bill me at a reasonable hourly rate to handle my involuntary bankruptcy matters. Fred explained to me that a lot of the proceedings would be delayed until my criminal trial was over, or at least more developed. Thank God.

CHAPTER 138

Altogether, the FBI dropped off over twenty boxes of files and other materials that they had collected. Scott and I already had over twenty boxes of our own files, so thing suddenly seemed a little overwhelming, not only to me but also to Scott. I searched the boxes and found a set of twelve computer CD-ROMs that were marked "Global Hard drives." Bingo, payday, that was what I wanted to show Scott. Scott insisted on organizing and starting from the very beginning, which would be the information used to get search-and-seizure warrants for my business and for my house. I was like a little child that was just told that he could not have a toy or a piece of candy or something. To me, nothing else mattered except showing just one person that did not work at Global that Global was a legitimate and viable company. Fuck the rest of this legal shit; it was meaningless to me. I paid Scott a lot of money to do a professional job, so it had to be his way or no way at all. I quickly found myself being a passenger on this ride through hell, and I did not like that feeling at all.

Scott located the affidavits that Agent Delano had presented to a judge in order to obtain search-and-seizure warrants on my business and my home. Scott first read the affidavits and then passed them over to me to see if I saw anything out of the ordinary. He said that they read like standard affidavits, but the personal information about me could be best confirmed by me. Now remember, what I was looking at was a sworn statement made by an FBI agent in order to search and seize my business and personal property. Without a judge approving the warrants, the FBI could not have seized my business or personal assets. I read two paragraphs of the affidavit, and I stopped in pure disbelief of what I had just read. The affidavit initially read just like the indictment; all the facts and information came from confidential informant 1 and 2. Once again, those were my ex-brother-in-law scumbag Alan Nudelman and my ex salesman scumbag extortionist Andrew Levinson. What caught my eye right away were the confidential informants' statements that allowed my house and personal assets to be searched and seized. The statement made by these two losers and presented to a judge under oath could not possibly have been true.

You see, in order for the FBI to be able to search and seize property from my residence, they had to physically tie my business activities to my house. In other words, they had to prove that I was at least partially conducting business from my house. I never ever conducted business from my home. When I left the offices of Global Vending, I left my work there; I did this in order to prevent myself from burning out.

Anyway, Frick and Frack testified under oath that on separate occasions, and on more than one occasion, they each witnessed me place Global Vending documents into my briefcase, leave the Global offices in my Black SL55 Mercedes with my briefcase, and travel to my residence where I removed the Global documents and worked on those Global documents in my home office located at 6225 Stallion Way in Southwest Ranches, Florida. The statement itself claiming that they each witnessed this supposed chain of events was crazy enough. I mean, come on, why would they be tracking my activities? But regardless, that was one of those he said / she said arguments. The real problem with the affidavit statement was that at the time that Alan and Andy worked for Global, or were hanging out with me, I did not own my black SL 55 Mercedes, and even worse, I did not live at my current residence of 6225 Stallion Way. I was driving a white S500 Mercedes and still living in Weston Hills Country Club. Alan and Andy were not in my life at all when I purchased my SL55 Mercedes or the house on Stallion Way. The affidavit was a complete fabrication that was used to seize my personal assets. Chalk up another lie for Alan, Andy, and the FBI. One document checked, one major fabrication unveiled. Nice start. Scott would have to file a pretrial motion in regard to this discovery.

CHAPTER 139

While looking through another box, I found a large manila envelope that contained hundreds of photographs. My heart sunk when I saw that the photographs were pictures of my house on Stallion way, pictures of me driving my car, and pictures of me with my kids playing in our front yard. What the hell was this all about? I saw it as the FBI's way of letting me know that they were watching me and that I would never know exactly when they were watching me. I found it very offensive and disturbing that the FBI felt that there was a need to photograph me playing with my children; I felt even more violated now than I did when the FBI took my assets.

I had had enough for one day. Scott could see that I was upset, so we called it a day. I got permission from Scott to take the computer disks home. I told Scott that I would take the time and scan through a few of the disks and print out some of the material that I knew would help clear my name. Scott agreed that it would be okay, and we parted ways for the day.

Even though the discovery of the photos had upset me, I wanted nothing more than to run home and tell Denise what we had discovered with the false affidavit. Then I remembered that the last time I tried to discuss my case with her, we had a huge blowout, so I decided to keep things to myself. Besides, Scott had warned me not to discuss our findings or our defense with anyone outside of his office. We had enough of a challenge taking on the United States government without letting them know how I would be defended.

When I got home with the disks, I settled myself into my office and popped the first disk into the computer. It was time to seriously help my own defense. Now I may not be an IT tech or a licensed computer software engineer, but I do know computers, how to operate them, and how scan through a CD-ROM. What I found on the disks was just not possible: they were all filled with absolute gibberish, garbage jumbled computer code, and fragments of useless information. Global's files and all our documentation were simply not on these disks. Perhaps it was a mistake. Yeah, right! I was at a complete loss for words. I just kept thinking to myself, *So this is how they do it. This is how the feds get a 98 percent conviction rate.* As if the deck was not already stacked heavily against everyday shmoos like me, these fucks had to lie and destroy evidence. Let's get real here just for one minute: the feds showed up at Global, they supposedly made copies of our hard drives while at Global, and with no one around, from that point forward, all our hard drives were void of any information. Years of entries simply vanished from our system, information that easily proved my innocence was gone, then the feds provided me with a copy of that information so that I could properly defend myself, but as luck would have it, there was no information once again. This was just absolute horseshit. The FBI saw that our hard drive information proved my innocence, and instead of putting their tales between their legs and walking away from the case, they chose to lie, to cheat, to destroy evidence, and then to create victims to help their prosecution of an innocent man: end of story, that was what happened.

I called Scott the next day and advised him of the empty disks. Scott, being an officer of the courts, refused to believe that the government would stoop this low. He insisted that it was a mistake and that he would get us a usable copy of the hard drive information that the feds had seized during their raid. Scott told me he would call the prosecutor and get back to me. I will be honest with you all, after talking to Scott, I started to feel stupid. I felt like maybe this whole ordeal was making me unnecessarily paranoid. What was wrong with me? This is the United States government, you idiot. Why would they go to such evil extents to prove a nobody like me to be guilty of a crime that never happened? Perhaps I had been watching too many movies, or perhaps those damn pills were starting to fry my brain for good. Hopefully Scott would prove me wrong, and I would have my defense material that I so desperately needed.

I received a call from Scott a few hours later. How about this: my case had suddenly been transferred from Broward County down to Miami where I was assigned a new judge by the name of Marcia Cooke. No big deal for me. I did not know who the first judge was, and I did not know this second judge was, so no harm, no foul. Scott then told me that my prosecutor Larry Bardfeld withdrew from my case, and I was reassigned to Prosecutor Bruce Reinhart. Okay, weird, but okay. Then the kicker, Mr. Reinhart informed Scott that the FBI agent that made the copies of the Global hard drives had screwed up while making the copies. The copies were all corrupt: I guess I had a right to be paranoid after all. I was now supposed to believe that a trained FBI agent had screwed up and corrupted CD-ROMs while copying not one computer at Global but twenty-three computers plus our server. That was a hell of a lot of mistakes, don't you think? What made me feel even more uncomfortable was the fact that Scott was even taken aback by this huge "mistake." Once again, we would have to fight this miscarriage of justice in a court of law. What other choice did we have? I could not help but wonder why in God's name the feds just did not tell us from the beginning that the disks were useless. Why give us corrupted disks and wait for us to notice? It was just part of the game, my friends, just part of this game that the feds were playing with my life.

CHAPTER 140

I did not like the way that the month of May was shaping up. The whole disappearing disk scandal was a big hit to my confidence, and now I was about to lose a little more support, but this time, it would be personal support, not legal support.

Carrol asked me if I would meet him on a Saturday for lunch, and of course, I agreed. If there was one thing in my life that was helping me cope with the reality of what was taking place, it was my friendship with Carrol; I could always rely on that big lug's friendly smile and supportive attitude to cheer me up when I was down.

Carrol and I met in town for lunch, and I could immediately sense that he was uncomfortable; he did not have good news for me on this particular day. Carrol and I had always been up-front and honest with each other; that was one of the things that made our friendship so special. On this occasion, there would be no exception to our honesty rule, no beating around the bush. Carrol informed me that he was moving back to South Carolina. Wow, that was not what I wanted to hear. Carrol apologized to me and promised to continue to support me in any way that he could. If I needed him to testify in court, then he would be there. If I needed money, he would be there. And if I needed a guy's night out, he would be there. At first, Carrol told me that he had made this decision so that he could make an attempt to become a part of his kids' lives again. But his kids were already grown up, and even he did not believe that the excuse would fly with me. When push came to shove, he then told me that he just could not take the constant harassment from the FBI. I had no idea that he was being bothered by them; he had never mentioned it. Evidently, the FBI made regular visits to his new office to harass him. They followed him while he drove around town, and worst of all, they were pressuring Carrol to testify against me in court. Carrol would have no part in that, but enough was enough for him. Carrol decided to put some distance between him and the Miami FBI in an attempt to regain somewhat of a normal life again. My insides melted as Carrol told me what he had been going through. I loved him even more as a person for trying to protect me by not telling me of his troubles for the past few months. The man really was watching out for me, and that is a very rare thing nowadays, one human being truly watching out for the well-being of another. I of course made Carrol's decision very easy for him. I did nothing but support his decision and thank him for all that he had done for me and for being my friend.

We finished our lunch, hugged, and said our goodbyes; I was going to miss him terribly, but hopefully once this was all over, we could get right back on track. As a last business decision with Carrol, I decided to give Carrol my half of the photo business. Paula would now be out of a job, but with Carrol moving back to South Carolina and my inability to provide technical support for the photo booths, the business was rightfully his. Even though the photo booth business was now officially a dying dinosaur, Carrol was very appreciative of my decision.

I left lunch that day feeling lower than I had felt in a long time; I could not help but feel like shit about how many people I had let down by allowing these feds to destroy my life and business. I could only do my best to stay focused and turn that sadness into a raging fire so that I could fight back with a vengeance. For now, though, pop a few dozen pain killers and call me in the morning.

Scott interviewed Carrol before he left town. He also interviewed my sister-in-law Laura, Herb from Global's operations department, my brother-in-law Burt from customer service, and Kim W, my locating mistress. I was not allowed to be present during these interviews. Scott did not want any of these people to feel pressured to say things that they did not mean, simply because I was in front of them. That made sense. Scott told me after each interview what he had discovered and who would be testifying on my behalf. Burt, Laura, Carrol, and Herb would all be powerful witnesses on my behalf. It was decided that Kim W would not be asked to testify. No, she did not have anything bad to say about me or Global, but I did disclose to Scott that Kim W and I had an inappropriate affair, and Scott did not want that thrown out in front of a jury. That would suddenly make me appear to be a bad person, and in court, image is everything. Let me tell you what pissed me off something awful about the interviewing of my Global workers; Ron would not allow himself to be interviewed—Ron, the guy whom I knew the longest at Global and before that at Photo Vend. He was my first employee, the guy whom I watched after and helped put through college, the guy who came to me with his father-in-law just a month ago for help in getting back into the ATM business. A guy whom I considered to be a friend would not meet with Scott. No, in fact, Ron's father-in-law hired Ron a lawyer to distance him from me. That hurt; that hurt a lot. Even if Ron had done this because the feds were harassing him, which he never made claim to, the least he could have done would have been to man up and tell me like Carrol did, but no, Ron chose to hide. Fuck him.

CHAPTER 141

As Scott and I met during the month of May 2004, we went through files, created defense exhibits, and continued to scratch our heads over why the feds specifically chose the customers that they listed in the indictment; things just did not add up. Scott was also waiting for the government to supply us with a list of witnesses that they were going to us at trial. He was specifically looking for the person that the feds were going to use as a keeper of records for Global Vending. If the government wanted to present any Global Vending documents in court as evidence, then they were required to have a "keeper of records," a person that could testify that these documents were used at Global Vending on an everyday, or at least on a regular, basis. If there was no keeper of records, then they could not present any documents; their case would not have a leg to stand on. Scott and I were sure that the feds had planned on using Alan and Andy for this purpose, but that would not be possible once we could show that they lied in an affidavit or once we showed that Andy had tried to blackmail me at one time or that Alan lied to the FBI when he initially filed the complaint with the feds. Alan and Andy were just carrying too much baggage to leave this important task in their laps. The government's witness list should clear up just who would be their keeper of records. The only problem at this point was the fact that the government could wait up until the day of trial to present us with a list of witnesses. Scott would have to try and pressure them into providing the list early. Yeah, good luck with that one.

CHAPTER 142

June came around pretty quickly, and I could not have been more excited. I was going to finally spend some real quality time with my boys before the trial of the century started some time toward the end of the year. My oldest son, Thomas, was now eight years old, and he wanted to try an organized sport for the first time. Thomas was not a real sportster, and yes, I will admit it, I bribed him to try a sport. Thomas picked basketball as his first athletic adventure. I headed over to the local YMCA and signed Thomas up for basketball, and I also signed up to be a volunteer coach. I figured that at the very least, I could make sure the kid got some playing time; plus, I always wanted to coach kids. I think organized sports are a very important part of a child's younger years. It builds character. Hell, look what it did for me. Okay, bad example.

Anyway, a few days after I signed Thomas up, I received a call. I was accepted as a coach, and Thomas was on my team. No, I did not mention on the application that I was currently under federal indictment and that there was a good chance that the FBI would be attending most games. I guess I forgot to mention that. Oh, well.

I also made plans with my boys to do some local camping, some fishing, and a lot of time in the old swimming pool. If there was one thing that I was good at, it was being a dad. No, I am not tooting my own horn, but I made that conclusion because my kids actually wanted to spend time with me. I loved that. My kids did ask me questions from time to time about why I was not working. I told them that I decided to take the summer off so that we could have some fun together and that I was planning on playing poker for a living for a while; my boys just thought that was the coolest thing. In fact, my now five-year-old, Jake, was quite a fan of no-limit Texas hold 'em. Anytime that I played in online tournaments, Jake would sit on my lap and help me move my virtual chips around. This kid knew exactly what hand beat what hand. It was pretty cool in my eyes.

Anyway, speaking of poker, I was not lying to them. I started to play tournament poker at the Hard Rock Hotel and Casino in Hollywood, Florida. With Denise working, the boys being off, and me not having a job, poker was a perfect fit. That is, of course, as long as I could develop my skills to a high enough level to actually support a family. Poker was a hell of a lot easier to play when there was no pressure to win, but now, when I lost, it actually meant something. Let's just see how the summer progressed and how my poker skills progressed before any judgment was made. One other positive about playing poker was that I knew that it would just drive the feds crazy. Here was a guy whom they simply dismantled financially, and he chose to play poker for a living. I knew that was not going to sit well with them. Fuck them.

Scott and I were meeting two or three times per week at his new Weston office. We would usually meet at night or on the weekends when Denise would be around to watch the kids.

Things between Denise and I were not good. Our conversations were minimal, and I just could not find a way to get this woman to jump on board and help me fight the good fight. Please don't get me wrong. I love this woman to death, or at least the woman that I used to know. Denise was the mother of my children, and she was very good to them. For now, with all that was going on, that was good enough for me.

CHAPTER 143

On one particular Wednesday night in June, I met with Scott, and unfortunately, Scott once again was the bearer of bad news. There was no way in hell that I could have been prepared for what he was about to tell me, and I had no way of getting around the fact that this news was going to once again forever change my life. Scott sat me down, looked me in the eyes, and told me that the new prosecutor has decided to indict Denise, and the FBI were planning on arresting her the following week. Holy fucking shit, you have got to be kidding me. Denise was already pissed at me. She already was blaming me for ruining our lives, and now she was going to be thrown into the lion's den with me and Paula. How in God's name was I going to tell her this one? Scott told me that Denise was being charged with money structuring just like Paula and that she would need an attorney ASAP. Of course, why not? Let's get another fucking attorney. Oh, and I was sure Scott could recommend one of his friends. This was just too much for any one person to deal with. I mean, think about what I was going through, think about what my friends and family were going through, and it was all on me. No matter how you slice the pie, I was the guy that was at fault here: it did not matter that I was an innocent man; it did not matter that I had helped each and every person in my family millions of times when things were good. The only thing that mattered right now, at least in my mind, was that this was all happening because of events that I set in motion. That was an awful lot of baggage to be carrying around no matter how strong you are mentally.

I drove home slower than I had ever driven in my life. I actually thought some crazy things on the way home: maybe I would just not ever go home again. No, I love those children of mine more than life itself. Maybe I just would not tell Denise and just let the feds arrest her next week. That would buy me at least one more decent week in my life. No, that would be cruel. I had to simply man up and talk to my wife. This was happening no matter what I did, and she needed to be prepared for it. Scott was already contacting another one of his friends to represent Denise. I told Scott to have his friend call me so that I could set up paying him and prewarn him of the absolute nutjob that he was about to get as a client. Sorry, but she was going to be absolutely out of her mind, and people needed to be prewarned of what they were going to be dealing with when it came to Denise.

I arrived home at around 9:30 p.m. Denise had just put the boys to bed, so I stalled by running into their rooms to tell them a good night story. Denise told me she was going to take a shower, so I had a little more time to work up my courage up for the big moment. I also used that time to down ten or so painkillers with a few shots of vodka; hey, fuck you, you try and tell your wife the FBI is going to arrest her while you are sober. Trust me, it's not that easy to do.

Denise finished her shower and eventually came into the living room to watch the local news with me. I had no idea how to ease my way into the conversation about her arrest, but as luck would have it, Denise provided that opening for me. Denise decided to try and make some small talk with me by asking me how my meeting went with Scott. Well…to tell you the truth, Denise, it did not go so good today. I turned the TV off, and I looked her straight in the eyes. Denise immediately knew that something was not right. I did not hesitate at that point. I simply came out and told her what Scott had told me. Denise jumped from the couch in complete disbelief. She actually ran in circles around the couch and started to breathe heavily like she was about to seriously hyperventilate. I stood up and reached out and grabbed her in a bear hug in an attempt to settle her down. I felt just horrible. Denise was not prepared or strong enough mentally to handle this kind of news. She broke free from me and told me to stay away from her. She rambled on and on, repeating the words, "OH MY GOD!" She actually screamed those words several times. I could only ask her to calm down and to try and listen to what else I had to say, but she would have no part of that. She continued on her rampage, yelling that she had done nothing wrong and why would they want to arrest her. She had done nothing wrong. I very easily could have been a scumbag and a wiseass and thrown back in her face the same horrible allegation that she used on me, "Well, you must have done something. The FBI doesn't just arrest people for no reason." But no, I am a much bigger person than that, and besides, like I said earlier, I still cared for her.

After a short while in the bedroom by herself, Denise reemerged with plenty of questions about what was going to happen next. That was a slight relief for me to just see her thinking in a little bit of a rational mannerism. I did my best to answer her questions, and I told Denise that I had already arranged for her to be represented by one of Scott's friends. I begged Denise to just relax and let this mess play itself out. I reminded her just like I reminded myself that she did nothing wrong, and both of us should have nothing to worry about: we needed to let our lawyers do their jobs and fight for our rights. Although Denise finally agreed and went to relax in bed, I could tell that her real anger was focused on me and not on the FBI.

CHAPTER 144

Let me tell you something, folks, I have stuck my neck out on the line many times in the past, and I have become a punching bag because of that many times in the past. When a person has a personality like mine, where they are always the one to take charge of situations, to initiate an action, or to take a chance, that person is loved and adored when things are going well, but that type of person is always going to be the one to take a beating when things go bad. It just comes with the territory; that's why there are so few "true entrepreneurs" in this world. People just do not have the nerve to put themselves on the line or to take a chance that a beating might be coming their way. Most people just fall into complacency, and they just want to survive. Sorry, that's not living to me; that is just existing. I was Denise's punching bag, and that was okay with me. I knew I was strong enough to take any mental beating thrown at me, or at least I thought I was.

The lawyer that Scott referred to me for Denise's representation turned out to be a very sharp tack. I liked Barry from the moment I met him. I did not like Barry's fees, of course, another $18,000 down the drain. Both Paula's and Denise's attorneys agreed to have Scott act as lead counsel, and they would ride on his coattails for most of the pretrial motions and hearings. Barry had managed to arrange something that Scott had tried earlier but failed on my behalf: Barry convinced the FBI and the prosecutor not to come and arrest Denise.

CHAPTER 145

On June 23, 2004, Denise would be allowed to self-surrender to the FBI and be released on a predetermined bond on the very same day; there would be no trip to prison for Denise. That was great relief to me because I did not see Denise as being able to handle even one night in that shithole down in Miami. Denise was of course relieved to hear that she would not be going to prison, but she was still hostile toward me for even being involved in my case. Hey, I was doing the best that I could do for her. I still believe that our whole situation would have gone smoother if we all just simply stuck together and fought as a team. I guess that is easier said than done. After all, I am me, and Paula and Denise were Paula and Denise. I could not expect them to suddenly turn into mini mes, although that would have been nice. Well, now my kids had two parents that were suddenly turned into indicted federal defendants roaming the town on bonds. What a fucking joke. But still, my kids were kept from knowing about any of our legal issues, just like I wanted it.

Barry decided that we needed to hire a private investigator to collect information from the banks that Denise and Paula allegedly structured monetary transactions at. The private investigator went to every bank where Denise and Paula withdrew cash from in order to determine why amounts of just under $10,000 were withdrawn consistently out of their institutions. Now that may sound easy to do, but it's not. The banks were under no obligation to talk to any investigator or lawyer in regard to this case, unless they were ordered to do so in a court of law. If the bank employees were approached in too harsh of a mannerism, or allegations were thrown at them, then the bank employees would most likely clam up, and then Paula and Denise would be heading to trial, not knowing what the bank employees had to say. That would be scary.

Well, evidently, this investigator was a true professional because the bank tellers and managers all spilled their guts to him. The bank employees all agreed that it was the banks and not Paula and Denise that decided on the withdrawal amounts, and more importantly, both banks confirmed that Paula and Denise tried to withdraw more than $10,000 when they first started to withdraw money. According to all three lawyers that were defending us, these bank employee statements would make it nearly impossible to convict Denise and Paula of money structuring, and of course, then I could not be convicted of conspiracy to structure money. No person that wants to structure money would ever try and withdraw more than $10,000. This is in direct conflict of the description of money structuring. For now, Barry and his private eye had done their jobs; the woman should be able to relax from this great news. Unfortunately, Denise and Paula had absolutely no patience at all; they both just kept hounding the lawyers about having the charges dropped now. They would cry every chance that they had when the lawyers would try and explain to them that it was not time yet to let the government know just how weak their case was against Paula and Denise. This was a game that needed to be played with great strategy, and just one slight strategic mistake could prove to be life-changing. Denise and Paula didn't care to hear that. They just kept hounding for instant results. It was quickly driving me to my grave.

Barry did not stop at the private investigator. He wanted to hit the government with a barrage of solid information that would lead the government no choice but to drop the charges against Paula and Denise. Barry arranged for all three of us to take polygraph tests; for those of you who do not watch any television, polygraph tests are lie detectors. Barry arranged for a former FBI agent to issue the tests and to prepare reports based on the results of the tests. Each of us was asked a series of questions about the specific charges that we were facing. We were not asked useless questions like "were we aware of the law, or were our actions mistakes." No, we were asked point-blank why we did what we did and what our overall intentions were each time that we took action. In other words, we were asked questions that if we could prove to be true in a court of law, we would be found innocent. All three of us passed the lie detector tests with flying colors.

Barry and the retired FBI agent prepared a court motion to have the test deemed admissible in court. Barry also sent the prosecutor and the FBI a copy of the polygraph test results and report. Unfortunately, the feds closed their eyes on the results and fought to have the tests results barred from any court proceedings.

CHAPTER 146

The early pretrial motions and hearings turned out to be absolute jokes and wastes of time. You would not believe some of the reasoning that was used by the prosecutor and accepted by the judges. Polygraph tests are used all the time by law enforcement to determine if they are pursuing the right person for a particular crime, yet when a defendant agrees to use a polygraph test in hopes of proving his or her innocence, then all of a sudden, the tests are deemed unreliable and inconsistent by the very people that issue the tests. The prosecutor won his argument, and the judge ruled that not only couldn't we use the test results at trial, but we could not even mention that we took the tests. Now why would we want the truth to come out in court? That just would not make any sense at all now, would it?

The next hearing that we had was a hearing to argue that all my personal property be returned due to the FBI submitting the falsified search-and-seizure affidavit. I was actually looking forward to this hearing. I wanted to see Agent Delano and the prosecutor try and weasel their ways out of an outright lie under oath. Once again, the courts turned out to be part of the deck that was already so heavily stacked against us. Agent Delano got on the stand and played stupid. She was very good at that by the way. When confronted with the allegations of falsifying the affidavit, Agent Delano agreed that it would have been impossible for Alan or Andy to have seen me carry Global documents in a car that I did not yet own, to a house that I did not yet own. She told the judge that she simply relied on sworn witness statements and that whatever was done was done. Basically, she left Alan and Andy to hang out and dry.

As the hearing continued, I begged—no, I freaked out—on Scott to push her and push her hard. There was no way that Agent

Delano did not know that I did not own my SL55 or the house on Stallion Way at the time that Alan and Andy worked with me. Yes, Agent Delano was a complete clusterfuck when it came to her job, but these were very basic circumstances in which anyone that could read a calendar could figure the facts out. The prosecutor argued that it was an unfortunate occurrence that these "mistakes" were not picked up at an earlier time—just an unfortunate occurrence. Holy shit. The judge decided that although the affidavit was not factual, there was no real harm done to me by these affidavit errors. Wait. What? Can you believe this shit? The judge ruled that if I was found to be innocent at trial, then all my property would be returned to me anyway, so no harm, no foul. My property would remain in the custody of the feds pending the outcome of my trial. I almost lost my mind right then and there. I needed to prove myself innocent to receive back my illegally seized property. What the hell was that all about? I thought this country revolved around the theory that people were innocent until proven guilty. The law is the law. The government broke the law in this case, but I was not harmed? Not harmed. What the fuck was this judge talking about? Did I miss something while I was growing up? Did someone rewrite the Constitution while I was high on painkillers? Was this the due process that I was entitled to pursuant to the Constitution of the United States of America? My confidence went from sky-high to absolute shit. Even if I win in court, I lose.

That was also the first time that Scott saw who the true Tom Foley was. Right outside the courtroom, I laid into his ass like I had not laid into another human being in a long time. What pissed me off the most that day was the fact that Scott was not surprised with the outcome. What pissed me off even more was the fact that Scott shook the hand of the prosecutor on the way out of the courtroom. I was sick of this shit. I was sick of this little club that they were all part of, and I was on the outside looking in. I have no problem with not being part of this little club, except for the fact that my life was the only thing being affected by these outrageous decisions. My guess is that Scott had never been called a fucking pussy before because when I used that term on him, he was definitely taken aback. He may have even felt physically threatened. Yes, I was that irate. At one point during my tirade, court security approached and stepped between me and Scott to calm things down. To this day, I have no idea how I did not get locked up right then and there. I am not kidding. I was a madman. I was escorted out of the building, and luckily, cooler heads later prevailed.

I took a short walk to the court's parking garage, and I waited by Scott's car. As Scott approached his car, he once again did not seem prepared to deal with me. I did not apologize to Scott, but I did make it clear that I had calmed down, and I wanted to simply talk. Scott laid out some new ground rules for me and my unpredictable behavior: in a nutshell, I needed to trust him, and I could not let the feds see me getting all crazy. He was right about the last part. I am sure the feds had a good laugh about my emotional outburst, but to tell you the truth, if that was true, then the prosecutor and Agent Delano were two of the most despicable beings in America. They were making a mockery of the United States Constitution and of the judicial system designed to uphold the Constitution. Like I have said before, this was a game to them, and just that alone was sickening.

Anyway, Scott and I spoke calmly for a little while. Scott pointed out to me that Agent Delano had confirmed that Alan and Andy could not be trusted, and that would create a real problem for the government come trial time. How in God's name could the feds call Alan or Andy to the stand now that even the feds deemed them to be liars? Well, they couldn't.

I'm very much aware that the only "sure things" or guarantees in this world is that someday we will all die, but I would have bet my left nut that we would have been victorious in at least one of our pretrial hearings, but as I just told you, we were not. I found myself discouraged with the whole process, and that led me to participating even less in the preparation of my own defense. I mean, I just had a firsthand encounter of the American judicial process, and I did not see how my way of thinking was going to fit into the mix at all. I would let Scott do his job, and I would hope that a jury of my peers would be true Americans like me and would be able to see through the feds' bullshit smoke-and-mirror show.

CHAPTER 147

The government delayed my trial on several different occasions; that was okay with me for now. I was enjoying the time that I was spending with my boys, and I was also enjoying my success at the poker tables. I found myself spending hours upon hours studying some of the poker professionals that played on a regular basis at the Hard Rock. I paid special attention to one player, Mike Mizrachi, whom I had seen play on television several times in the past. Mike lived in Miami and usually showed up for the multi-table tournaments at the Hard Rock. Although it becomes slightly boring after a while, you can learn so much by simply watching great poker players do their thing. I picked up on certain situational plays, percentage reads, and the use of aggression at the right times. Each month, I consistently cashed in at tournaments, and each month, I was able to put cash away for our future or for the next potential rainy day.

Out on the legal battlefront, the bankruptcy trustee decided not to wait for the Global trial to commence before he sprang into action. Bankruptcy laws in the United States are truly the most lopsided laws in the country. I met several times with my bankruptcy lawyer, Fred, and when he told me how bankruptcy laws worked, I almost fell out of my chair. Fred informed me that the bankruptcy trustee would be filing civil lawsuits against me, Paula, Denise, and any other person or company that I had made purchases from. Now check this out. If I was found guilty of committing criminal fraud at my trial, then the bankruptcy trustee was almost guaranteed to be victorious on all his lawsuits. All the trustee would have to prove in court would be the fact that I used money from Global to make purchases; that was it. Now these bankruptcy lawsuits are monetary lawsuits. They do not carry any potential prison time, so the trustee was basically trying to collect money that was supposed to be distributed back to the creditors of Global (my customers). Normally, I would have no problem with that, except for the fact that the trustee would be suing people like my friends that owned the local jewelry store where I purchased all of Denise's jewelry. Talk about a no-win situation for me. These lawsuits in my opinion are just another one of great miscarriages of justice that I have encountered during this whole legal disaster. Here's why: let's say the trustee sues the jewelry store where I purchased over $400,000 in merchandise. All that the trustee has to do in court is to prove that I paid for the jewelry with Global money. That was very easy to do since I used company checks. The trustee won his lawsuit for $400,000. Now the jewelry store had to pay the trustee $400,000. Yes, that was the retail price that I paid for the jewelry, and here is the kicker, the jewelry store does not get the merchandise back. It would be up to the store to sue the United States government for the property, but because the government is seeking to have the jewelry forfeited due to criminal activity, the store cannot win. I could not believe it. The store loses $400,000 plus the products that they sold to me. How unfair is that?

After hearing once again that the deck was stacked against me, I empowered Fred to negotiate plea settlements with the trustee. Paula and Denise each were hit with lawsuits of almost $1 million, but upon my signing a plea deal with the trustee, those lawsuits would be immediately satisfied. In other words, these were simply paper lawsuits in which Paula and Denise would owe nothing. I was hit with a $4 million lawsuit that would extinguish after three years of nonpayment. In other words, if over the next three years, I did not have $4 million to pay the lawsuit, then it would simply disappear. I would not have $4 million anytime in the near future. In return for these "pay nothing lawsuits," I would have to walk the trustee through Global's financing records; that would take minimal effort on my part. Once again, I felt awful for the people being sued by the trustee, but I had absolutely no control over this mess; this was a machine that was placed in motion by the Global customers in an attempt to preserve assets for themselves. You can't blame them for that. I guarantee you one thing though, had the customers of

Global known the true bankruptcy process, they would have taken their chance with me, and they would not have forced Global into involuntary bankruptcy. The sad part is that the trustee and his team of lawyers could give a shit about the Global customers. The trustee's job is to justify his efforts on paper for the court to review, but in the meantime, the trustee and his lawyers were racking up legal fees that ate up almost every dollar that they collected.

Let me give you an example. The bankruptcy trustee and his attorneys started to file motion after motion in the United States district court in order to have Global's main checking account transferred to the bankruptcy court. Yes, the United States (bankruptcy trustee) was now fighting the United States (prosecutors) for assets that were already taken away from me. Government was fighting government for money that was already in their possession. The Global account in question had $1.1 million in it, and the bankruptcy trustee spent over $800,000 in legal fees fighting to get that money transferred. How the hell does that make sense? That $800,000 was paid for by money that the trustee collected in lawsuits, money that was supposed to go back to the Global customers but instead went into the trustee's pocket and his lawyers' pockets.

To make things even worse, the trustee lost the battle; the Global account stayed in the possession of the prosecutor's office. Come on, really? Does that make sense to any of you reading this? Think about it, folks. The prosecutor could have just transferred the money to the trustee for immediate dispersing for the Global customers. If the prosecutor really cared about the "victims," then that was the right thing to do, right? If the trustee really cared about the "victims," then he could have very easily just left the Global checking account where it was and let the prosecutor's office disperse the money after my trial. The truth was that neither could give a shit about my customers; this was a money thing, and the customers lose no matter what.

I wish that I could say that the trustee and his lawyers became more responsible and considerate of the Global customers as time went on, but that would be a lie. Global Vending's assets consisted of over 2,300 ATM machines with an average wholesale price of $1,000 per machine. That was a value of $2.3 million Global's other assets

---

including office furniture, computers, ATM parts, pallets full of ATM paper, and of course, the revenue that was still being generated by the operating machines. At this point in time, more than half of Global's machines had been unplugged, but that's not to say that the unplugged machines could not simply be plugged back in regardless. The operating machines were still producing over $50,000 in net revenue per month. Get ready for this one, folks: the trustee sold Global Vending Inc. and its assets for a whopping $150,000. I was sick to my stomach when I heard that. The trustee could have done the right thing and converted the bankruptcy to a chapter 11 bankruptcy and operated the machines for the "creditors," the global customers, but instead, he decided to liquidate the company for almost nothing.

Wait, of course it gets worse. Here is the part that pissed me off the most: the new owner of Global Vending Inc. was none other than my old friend and technical support man, Ron. That's right, folks. Ron and his father-in-law purchased Global out of bankruptcy for $150,000. I don't have anything else to say about that except that I was of course not made a part of that company as Ron and his father-in-law had promised. No, instead, they simply profited off years of my hard work and sweat. Once again, the customers of Global got the shaft. The last time I checked, the trustee and his lawyers had billed the estate of Global Vending Inc. for nearly $1 million in legal fees, and the customers of Global vending and the rest of its creditors split a onetime disbursement of $200,000: 365 people split $200,000. Are you fucking kidding me? If Global was allowed to operate for two months after the feds showed up, that would have equaled what the customers received. How in God's name do these people have the nerve to call me a criminal?

CHAPTER 148

A firm trial date was set for January 18, 2005, which was rapidly approaching. Paula and Denise became almost unbearable in my presence. The woman wanted me, the guy who used to have all the answers, to end this nightmare for them, but I simply was not given an opportunity to help them: that was of course until the government decided to offer me a plea deal. It was the first week in January, and our trial was just around the corner. Scott gave me a call and told me that the prosecutor had faxed him a plea offer in an attempt to avoid going to trial.

The plea offer included me pleading guilty to one count of mail fraud in which I would be sent to prison for a period of five years. Scott advised me that this plea was of "no benefit" to me (his words). Scott reminded me that according to his calculations of the federal sentencing guidelines, I was facing a maximum of sixty-three months in prison if I were found guilty of all charges at trial. Scott also advised me that the plea deal would force me to give up all the assets that the government had taken from me and pay full restitution to all the Global customers (the estimate was $13 million).

Scott advised me that I might as well take my chances in court and defend myself in front of a jury of my peers. He told me that I really had nothing to lose. I had a better idea. I told Scott to call the prosecutor and tell him that I would accept the plea deal under one condition. The government had to drop the charges against my sister and my wife. Yes, I broke. I was willing to plead guilty to a crime that never happened just to take the pressures off my sister and wife. Scott could not believe what he was hearing, and he insisted on coming over to my house to make sure that this was the route that I wanted to take.

He came over on a Sunday afternoon, and I made sure that my wife and Paula were present. Once again, Scott went over what the government had offered me, and then he repeated that my intentions were to accept the deal as long as the charges were dropped against my sister and my wife. Although both Paula and Denise became emotional when they heard what I was willing to do for them, neither of them tried to stop me making this settlement. I guess you could say that I was expecting at least a little resistance on their parts. I mean, I was giving up my right to defend myself, I was giving up my assets, I was giving up my freedom for the next five years, and worst of all, I would not be around to watch my boys grow up for the next five years. Please give me a little something here, ladies. How about, "Are you sure you want to do this?" I got nothing.

Scott left my house and told me he would call me as soon as he spoke to the prosecutor on Monday, and that was that.

Scott called me on Monday and laid the bad news in my lap: the prosecutor would not drop the charges against Paula and Denise. Scott told me that we were going to trial. I threw my hands up in the air after I hung up with Scott. What else could I do but get into court and defend myself with the one thing that I had going for me, the truth? Yes, the truth will set us all free.

Before I even had time to inform Denise and Paula of the bad news, they found out from their own attorneys. You see, Paula's and Denise's attorneys called each of them to let them know that the prosecutor had offered each of them a separate plea deal. This prosecutor was a true scumbag. He realized that if I was willing to sign a plea deal to get charges dropped from Paula and Denise, then the stage was ripe to get the ladies to sign a plea. The prosecutor would get his convictions without going to trial with Paula and Denise, and he did not have to offer me shit in return.

The plea deals offered to Paula and Denise required them each to plead guilty to one count of money structuring, and in return, the prosecutor would recommend that they each receive two years of supervised release, no prison time. Both Paula and Denise had already signed the deals before I even knew they existed. Just like that, my sister and my wife were convicted felons—convicted felons on charges that even the banks insisted that they did not commit. What a fucking joke. I used to joke around in the past that either my sisters or myself were adopted because I simply come from a different stock. In fact, I come from a different stock than 99 percent of people in this world. Look, my sister and Denise were happy that it was over for them, and I guess I should have been happy for them because that was all that they wanted, but on the other hand, I have such a hard time respecting people that are not willing to fight for what is right. Yes, you will get your ass handed to you when you enter into certain battles, but it's not always about that; it's sometimes about principle and self-respect. I despise cowards, but even more, I despise bullies, and in our case, these federal fucks were just being bullies, and that was simply wrong. With the evidence that the private investigator had collected on Paula and Denise's behalf, the prosecutor should have just dropped the charges against them; that's called justice. By the prosecutor offering them plea deals simply because he knew that they were in distress, he created what I would call a complete miscarriage of justice. The further this whole process went, the more I lost faith in the United States justice system.

I spent a little alone time that night in my backyard, and I was able to reason out that some good did come out of the day's events. What if the worst-case scenario had taken place at trial, and we were all convicted and sent to prison. Who would watch over our children? That would just have been too devastating for me to handle. At the very least, Denise would be free to raise our boys, and Paula would be free to raise her kids: yes, that was a huge positive. The only other plus that I could see was the fact that it would just be me at trial now: me against the thugs that ruined our lives, and believe me, folks, I was not going to go down quietly.

Scott and I spent a lot of hours finalizing my defense that week. We went over exhibits, our order of witnesses, and courtroom mannerism (good luck with that one).

CHAPTER 149

As luck would have it, the feds had one more small surprise for me just before my trial week arrived. This one stung big-time. From the minute that I walked into Scott's office that night, a few days before the trial, I could tell that something was wrong. I sat across from Scott's desk, and he just kept shaking his head from side to side as he looked at a sheet of paper. Then Scott asked me a very strange question. Scott asked me when the last time was that I spoke to my sister Lisa or my brother-in-law Burt. I told Scott that they were over my house a few weeks ago for Christmas dinner, but I had not spoken to them since. Scott handed me the sheet of paper that he had been looking at since I arrived at his office. The paper was from the prosecutor; it was the government's list of witnesses that they would be using at trial to prosecute me. I could not believe my eyes: witness number 1, Burt Blum (my brother-in-law). What? Are you kidding me? Burt had met with Scott on several occasions, and he was supposed to be a witness for my defense. What in the hell was going on here? Scott then told me that Burt was going to be Global's keeper of records for the government; he was going to be the person that would allow the feds to introduce Global Vending documents at trial, my own fucking brother-in-law, my sister's husband.

The most unbelievable part was that this was not a new development. Scott slid another packet of documents over for me to look at: it was an immunity agreement between Burt and the government that was signed months ago. Burt would testify against me in court, and in return, the government waived all rights to prosecute him. This could not be happening. How could this lowlife sack of monkey shit have Christmas dinner at my house knowing he had a plea deal with the government to testify against me? How can a man sit through my defense planning while he was already on board with the government? How could this be legal? To say that I lost my shit would be an understatement. I went off like a rocket: I told Scott that I was going to go to Burt's house and set his ass straight. Scott told me that if I did that, then the government could bring up additional charges for harassing or trying to intimidate a government witness. I did not want to do either. I simply wanted to kick the ever-loving shit out of him and my sister. What kind of people do stuff like this? Who comes to a Christmas dinner and then testifies against that family member in court a few weeks later? How could my own flesh and blood not at least give me a heads-up that her husband was a rat? How could my own flesh and blood stay married to this lowlife piece of shit? I was just beside myself.

When I left Scott's office that night, nothing seemed real anymore. I was lost. I decided to call my sister Paula and my father in order to let them know about Burt. Neither of them believed a word I was saying to them. My sister Lisa was always a self-centered individual, but my father and sister Paula did not believe that even Lisa would stoop this low.

Both Paula and my father called Lisa to see if I was exaggerating or maybe misinformed, but those two theories were discounted once they actually spoke to Lisa. My sister Paula told me that Lisa had no remorse for what was going on. She had no regrets that her own husband was going to try and help the government put her brother in prison. The feds had paid a visit to Lisa and Burt's house several months ago and threatened to take their assets just like they had done to me. Burt jumped on the government band wagon immediately. Hey, I can understand being scared and being placed under pressure. Anyone that saw what I had and saw just how quickly it was all taken from me has every right to be afraid, but give me a break. My own sister couldn't at least have given me a heads-up on what was going on? They did not have to be that secretive and that big of a pair of scumbags as they were. I don't know how to fully describe the feeling of abandonment or the level of disappointment that I was experiencing. I had done nothing but good things for my sister Lisa and her husband, Burt, throughout the years, and now this was my thanks; this was my big reward from them. Thanks a lot, guys. I hope you have both prepared yourselves for your final resting place in hell.

CHAPTER 150

January 18, 2005, was the first day of my trial. Since the trial was now being held in Miami, I had to plan my trip down to the courthouse, keeping in mind that the traffic from Broward County down to Miami Dade County was horrendous during the rush-hour commute. I decided to wake up at 5:00 a.m. every day that I needed to be in court in order to make sure that I made the 9:00 a.m. calendar call. I am not going to lie, I was scared to death to even step foot into a federal courthouse. There was just too much on the line for me not to be nervous. I had already seen firsthand just how far the feds were willing to go to prosecute me, and I was sure that things would only get worse, but what choice did I have? I made sure I dressed respectfully for court. I wore a suit every day, and I tried my hardest to make sure that I did not look flashy or arrogant.

I made the trip down to the courthouse by myself. In fact, Denise had decided not to show up in court at all. To this day, I don't know what to think of that decision. Denise used the kids as an excuse, but our longtime babysitter and friend, Susan, would have been able to help us with the kids. I guess deep down inside, I knew the truth about Denise. She just did not give a shit about me anymore. She was bitter about the way that things had gone downhill for us, and she was holding me responsible for it all.

My cousin John flew down from New York for my trial. I can't tell you how much that meant to me; John's love and support for me was always unconditional, and his presence in the courtroom proved that. My father also drove down for my trial, and he sat right alongside John for the entire trial.

A funny thing happened on the way down to the courthouse on my first day of trial. I was stopped in traffic at a light on the Gratny

Parkway (this road should not be called a parkway; it was a two-lane traffic nightmare), when a man on crutches approached my driver's side window. The man had long curly hair, he was very dirty-looking, and I am sorry to say that he only had one leg. This poor guy knocked on my window and placed his hand out in a sign that he was looking for money. I don't know why, but I rolled down the window, and I started a conversation with this poor soul. As traffic crawled a car or two forward, my new friend hopped right along with me. He insisted on telling me what a terrible life he had been dealt and how he needed me to show him some mercy. The man wanted money for food. I told him about my situation and where I was heading, and the man seemed to actually give a shit. His initial response to me was "Man, that sucks." Yes, my one-legged friend, that does suck. I decided to make the guy a deal. I told him to meet me at the same place every morning, and I would give him some money so he could have a slightly better day. I could not believe this guy's response. My new pal told me that he would accept my help, but only if I updated him each morning on the previous day's trial activity. We shook hands; it was a deal. I decided to give the guy $60 the first day. I told him that he had to get a motel room for the day and take a shower; I told him that I expected a cleaner-looking man. He agreed with a smile. As the one-legged man hopped away from my car, I yelled out to him, "Hey! By the way, my name is Tom!"

He said, "Nice to meet you, Tom. My name is JESUS!"

How about that, folks. I met Jesus on the Gratny Parkway, and he was my new best friend. Maybe this was a sign of good things to come.

CHAPTER 151

My trial was assigned to the sixth floor of the United States District Court House Southern District of Florida. I arrived to the sixth floor early, just like I arrived to everything early in life. The courtroom comprised of dark wood furniture, I would guess red wood, and the floor was covered in a dark-hunter-green carpet. The smell of fresh furniture polish filled the air.

As I stood in the courtroom by myself just looking around, I was approached by two courtroom employees. The first employee was the judge's clerk; his name was Ivan. He asked me if I needed help. In return, I explained to him who I was. Ivan recognized my name immediately. Ivan shook my hand, showed me where I would be sitting during the trial, and he wished me the best of luck. Ivan was an articulate young man, and he seemed to be an all-around nice person. The second courtroom employee was the courts reporter. Robin was an attractive woman with a great smile and a bubbly personality to go with her smile. Robin also shook my hand, and she took time out of her schedule to make small talk with me, which made me a little less nervous. Robin told me that Judge Marcia Cooke was a fair judge and that I was lucky to not have been assigned to some of the stricter judges. As Robin walked away to begin her day, I caught myself taking a good long look at her. I mean, really, Tom, you are about to go through a trial for your freedom and still you are staring at woman. I needed a lot of therapy, but damn she was hot.

One at a time, people started to arrive: Scott, my father, my cousin John, and then the prosecution team. The number of people that arrived with the prosecutor was simply ridiculous. There were four members of the United States Attorney's office and at least six FBI agents. I could not help but sit there and estimate the hourly salary that was being spent to prosecute some nobody like me; it was mind-boggling.

The deep loud voice of the court's bailiff caught me by surprise: "All rise, this court is now in session." Judge Marcia Cooke entered the courtroom and sat upon her elevated perch. Judge Cooke was an African American woman; she was a little larger than the average woman, and she had a fairly pleasant smile. Judge Cooke allowed for all parties to announce their presence in the courtroom and then began the process of jury selection. I was told that I would be judged by a jury of my peers, but I have to respectfully disagree with that statement. I would not consider even one person on my jury to have been one of my peers. I am in no way saying that I am better than anyone on that jury; what I am saying is that none of them were anything like me. The jurors were all hourly employees that worked at places like Publix Supermarket and other menial labor jobs. There was not one business-minded entrepreneurial type in the crowd. Not one of them looked or sounded to have the least bit of ambition in them. Now I know that they were called to jury duty, and 99 percent of America would rather have a rectal exam than go for jury duty, but the poker player in me was reading these people. The best I could hope for would be that they at least listened and then made a fair judgment of my character and of my intentions with Global Vending.

Unfortunately, I could see these simplistic people falling for the smoke-and-mirror show that the feds were going to have to put on in order to convict an innocent person of a crime that never happened. Only time would tell; for now, my jury was ready to hear testimony.

The prosecution started the day with their opening statement. Assistant United States Attorney (AUSA) Bruce Reinhart was the prosecutor, and he made the opening statement. As AUSA Reinhart described his version of Global Vending Inc. and how I ran this huge Ponzi scheme of a company, my blood slowly began to boil. I can't even count how many times Reinhart used the word *fraud* or the word *con man* when he described me. I wanted to knock the ever-loving shit out of him.

Scott had given me a legal pad, and he asked me to write down any comments or questions that I had, and from time to time, he would write down answers for me. My first use of my fresh new legal pad had the words *dickhead* written on it. Scott was not very happy about that.

AUSA Reinhart described Global as a company that was "about" to implode, and he explained how the feds needed to shut us down before we hurt more people. Once again, I almost laughed out loud this time because I could not help but think about how we never had a customer complaint in the history of the company. Every customer had received every dime I promised they would receive, and most of all, this company that was "about to implode" was still up and running and making a profit over a year after the feds shut us down. That's some Ponzi scheme now, isn't it?

Anyway, when it was Scott's turn for an opening statement, he simply asked the jury to disregard what the prosecutor had told them; the truth would come out about what Global was really about, and a verdict of not guilty across the board would be justified. I think Scott was okay during his opening statement, but what rubbed me the wrong way was his lack of enthusiasm. He almost put me to sleep, and my life was on the line here. I could just imagine how the jurors were fighting to stay awake.

Well, the prosecutor sure did make a lot of promises to the jury, and he would need to fulfill those promises during the trial, or Scott would be throwing the prosecutor's short falls right back in his face during closing arguments. Let's see what happens.

The prosecution called its first witness to the stand, and it was none other than my good old brother-in-law Burt Blum. Burt entered the courtroom with his attorney at his side; as Burt made his way to the witness stand, his attorney took a seat behind the prosecutor. That chickenshit motherfucker would not even raise his head and look at me. It took every ounce of self-control for me to not jump over the table that I was sitting at and ring his fucking weasel neck.

Burt was sworn in, and the prosecutor began to present documents and asked Burt questions about those documents. Immediately, there was a problem. Burt was so nervous that he was visibly shaking, and his answers were in such a low volume that the jury had to keep asking Judge Cooke to tell Burt to raise his voice. Each time the proceeding stopped, Burt became more and more distraught. I was glad to see him struggle in that witness stand. I am sure that he noticed my father in the courtroom, and I am sure that my father's presence made this whole ordeal worse for him. As nervous as Burt was and as annoyed as the jury appeared to be with him, Burt had done what the feds needed him to do: Global's documents were entered into evidence, and now the prosecutor could twist and turn these documents any way he chose to. Don't get me wrong, there weren't any incriminating documents entered as evidence, but the fact still remained that if Burt did not agree to be Global's keeper of records, then I would not have been sitting in that courtroom. That is a fact.

It was now Scott's turn to question Burt, and this was when the wheels completely came off Burt's wagon. My guess is that he just lost whatever little concentration he may have had because Burt began to lie on the witness stand, and I am talking about lies that the prosecutor even got annoyed about. Scott asked Burt if he had signed an immunity agreement with the government, and Burt for some reason answered no. Scott disagreed with Burt and informed Burt that he had a copy of Burt's immunity agreement right in front of him. Burt still insisted that he never made any deal with the government. At this point, I could see the prosecutor leaning over to the FBI and shaking his head as they spoke. Scott reminded Burt that he was sworn in to tell the truth, and if Burt was caught lying on purpose, he could be charged with perjury. Burt decided to tell Scott that he refused to answer any further questions. Judge Cooke had had enough of Burt. Judge Cooke castrated Burt and ordered him to answer Scott's questions. Burt agreed to answer. Scott presented Burt's immunity agreement as evidence and showed the agreement to Burt. Scott once again asked Burt if he had an immunity agreement with the government, and Burt simply replied that he signed the paper so that his assets were not taken away from him. I thought the prosecutor was going to have a heart attack.

Scoreboard: one for the defense, zero for the prosecutor.

CHAPTER 152

On the way to the courthouse the second day, I brought my friend Jesus a cup of coffee and some Dunkin' Donuts. Jesus was at the traffic light waiting for me, and yes, he was considerably cleaner. This guy was an absolute trip; he asked me what had happened in court on the first day. I gave him the *Reader's Digest* version, and he told me that he spent the whole night at a local motel and got a great night's sleep. As the traffic started to move a little quicker, I threw him a few dollars and said my goodbyes.

I found myself setting a schedule of sorts in the morning. I guess I was looking for some sort of normality. Wake up, get ready, get breakfast for me and Jesus, get to court early, talk to Ivan and Robin, say my hello to my two supporters when they arrived, and then proceed with trial.

Agent Willis was the government's next witness. Agent Willis was the person that was responsible for having gone through Global's bank records, purchases, and my personal bank records and purchases. I am in no way a fan of Agent Willis. I see him as being one of the people that was trying to ruin the lives that surrounded me, but I will give him on ounce of credit: Agent Willis told the truth on the witness stand. That was a rare thing at my trial. Agent Willis tried his hardest to be a team player for the prosecution. AUSA Reinhart led him along a path, and Agent Willis tried to stay on that path. From what I could gather, Agent Willis's role in this little game was to show the jury that I was using customers' money to live a "lavish" lifestyle rather than purchase ATM machines for the customers. He tried his hardest, but like I said earlier, the truth will set me free.

Under Scott's cross-examination, it became very obvious that Agent Willis did not go over any bank records or purchases in any form of detail. He basically had no idea of what he was talking about. Agent Willis testified that Global had sold 3,000 ATM machines to investors and that Global had only purchased 1,100 ATM machines to date. The biggest mistake that Agent Willis made in his ATM calculations was that he assumed that Global purchased all their ATM machines from ATMMS in Las Vegas (our main processor).

My guess is that Alan had told him that, and like everything else in this clusterfuck, Agent Willis just took Alan's word for it. The problem was that Alan was so uninterested in learning the inner workings of Global that he did not even know where our machines all came from.

Scott pointed out checks written to other companies in amounts as high as $200,000 for ATM machines. Scott showed Agent Willis the invoices from those companies that corresponded with the Global checks. In total, Agent Williams missed over 1,200 ATM machine purchases. More than half of what we had purchased was missed by the FBI. Even Agent Willis seemed surprised at how much he had missed.

You see, that just destroyed the FBI theory that I was spending customers' money on luxury items instead of ATM machines for customers. Global had way more than enough money in its main checking account to purchase the remaining ATM machines, when the time was right. Agent Willis also admitted that he simply overlooked the withdrawals that I had made to set up my retirement account. How do you miss $1 million in withdrawals that took place in $100,000 increments? This admission was also important because the prosecutor's opening statement said that I had tried to hide the money from the FBI after they raided my house, but here was Agent Willis admitting that he did not even know that the money existed.

When all was said and done, Agent Willis made a complete ass out of himself and the FBI. I can only hope that the FBI is more detailed and professional when they are out there in the world looking for terrorists. If not, then we are all dead meat.

Next on the stand was the crème de la crème (I have no fucking idea how to spell that) for the prosecutor: good old Agent Delano. Agent Delano basically testified for Alan and Andy. She was very vague once again: I am sure she did not want to look as stupid as Agent Willis did. Agent Delano had obviously done this before. Her answers were sharp, articulate, and she knew to look at the jury while she answered questions. Agent Delano was also a lying sack of monkey shit on the stand. Agent Delano fell just short of saying that I confessed to her that I was stealing from people. I mean, give me a break. When she first raided the offices of Global Vending, the majority of our conversation was about the shared program that she did not even know existed. Agent Delano tried to plant the thought in the jury's minds that I was at trial due to customer complaints and not a complaint filed by Alan and Andy. I have no idea how she thought she would get away with that, but my only guess was that the prosecutor wanted to plant that seed in the juror's simplistic minds.

On cross-examination, Agent Delano became a completely different person. She suddenly suffered from severe memory loss. Every question that Scott asked her received a reply of, "I don't know" or "I can't remember." At one point, it became so obvious that she was avoiding questions and playing stupid that Judge Cooke stopped the questioning and scolded Agent Delano. I will never forget when Judge Cooke asked Agent Delano point-blank, "Are you really the lead agent on this case because it's hard for even me to believe that you know so little."

I almost pissed in my pants, and I could tell from the jurors' reactions that they felt the same way. Once again, it would appear that the truth was starting to shape up and would be slowly setting me free. The prosecutor handed Agent Delano chart after chart that were all entered as evidence. Most of the government's exhibits and charts were attempts to show the jury that Global was a house of cards that was about to collapse. The problem was that none of the exhibits made any sense at all; they were the worst-thought-out pile of shit that I had ever seen, really.

Let me give you an example. The prosecutor presented a chart on the court's overhead projector that supposedly showed Global's last twenty-four months of cash flow. The chart showed that our ATM machines were producing roughly $100,000 per month in revenue, but I was paying out over $400,000 per month to the customers. The government said that I was using new customer money to pay the old customers, and that was a classic Ponzi scheme according to the prosecutor. Here was the problem with that whole stupid theory. If Global had done $13 million in ATM sales like the government displayed (that number was correct by the way), and I was paying back customers at a rate of $400,000 for the past twenty-four months, then that would mean that the Global customers had already received back $9.6 million in returns over the past two years. At that rate, the customers would be paid in full in less than a year: so where were they being ripped off? How would they lose money? How was this company "about to implode"? The truth was that the government did not think that chart through; every number on that chart was wrong except for the total sales number.

When this was presented by Scott to Agent Delano, she just acted like she did not understand his point, but let me tell you, even a second-grade special ed child could understand that lame-ass math. Chalk another day up for the good guys.

Scoreboard: defense scored runs 2 and 3, prosecution still 0.

CHAPTER 153

As the week progressed, I found myself gaining some confidence that everything was going to be all right. Each morning, I brought Jesus his breakfast, and I even brought him some clean clothes one morning. You know, I purchased things like underwear, T-shirts, sweatpants, and even some basic hygiene items. I made sure that Jesus knew that I was not trying to belittle him with these purchases. I simply wanted to do some good for someone while I was being hit with so much bad. Jesus was very appreciative.

In court, the prosecution team called witness after witness in order to place all my personal purchases on record. This was the smoke-and-mirror show that I was expecting from them: take the jurors' eyes off the real issues at hand and make them almost jealous or mad at me for being able to afford all the glitz that was once a part of my life. People like my old friend Rob, you know, my financial adviser, were called to the stand. I wanted to slap the shit out of Rob when he was testifying. This prick had the nerve to say that he barely knew me and that I was just another one of his clients. I have no idea why he would feel that it was necessary to lie about how well he knew me. Rob pursued me for years to invest with his company; even at his kids' birthday parties, I was pitched by him, and he told the court that he really only knew me on a professional level. What a coward.

I felt sorry for the owner of the jewelry store when she was called to the stand. Tracy from Weston Jewelers was a sweetheart of a woman, and her husband, Ed, was equally as nice. I knew that they were going through hell with the bankruptcy trustee, and I knew that Tracy did not want to be on a witness stand at my trial. When Tracy was finished testifying, she walked by me and gave me one of her patented smiles; that meant a lot to me. You see, folks, the testimony of these retailers did no harm to me; they were not saying anything bad about me. They were just testifying that yes, I did buy jewelry or a car or a house from them. That was all. It was just unfortunate because I would have gladly conceded to all the purchases if they simply asked me to agree that I had made the purchases.

Anyway, Bart, the owner of ATMMS, was called to the stand to discuss my purchases from his company, and I would say that calling him to the stand that day was a big mistake by the prosecutor. Bart decided to vent at one point while he was on the witness stand; he told the jury that doing business with me was a pleasure, and even with everything that was going on right now, he would do business with me again without hesitation. The prosecutor could not wait to get him off the witness stand. When Bart was finished testifying, he walked right up to me and shook my hand. As he was shaking my hand, Bart gave me some nice words of encouragement. He told me to stay strong and to call him when this whole mess was over with. The jury saw and heard the whole exchange. That was some government witness.

Judge Cooke decided to take a fifteen-minute recess after Bart testified; either she had to go to the bathroom, or she could tell that the government needed to regroup. The recess turned out to be fifteen minutes that I will never forget.

CHAPTER 154

As I left the courtroom to go to the men's room, I ran into the government's next witness; much to my surprise, it was Nitae, my old customer service rep that Burt had fired. Now because she was a witness, I was not allowed to approach her or talk to her. Agent Willis was sitting with her in the waiting area. Nitae and I locked eyes, and without warning, she sprung up out of her chair and ran over to me. Nitae gave me one of her huge bear hugs that I had grown to love. I had no idea what to do. Scott was calling for me to get away from her; Agents Willis and Delano were calling Nitae back the waiting area, and Nitae would not let go of me, so I said, "Fuck it," and I hugged her back and lifted her off the ground. Nitae started to ramble that she did not want to be there; she had been summoned to court, and she did not have a choice. Nitae went on that she was only going to tell the jury what a nice person I was and how well I treated her and her son. I tried to calm her down; I told her that I knew where her heart was and that she needed to simply tell the truth, and then nothing bad could ever happen to me. Nitae wanted none of this circus; she even cursed a few times and called the feds a bunch of animals. I did not realize, but the prosecutor was behind us, and he had heard enough. I wanted to laugh my ass off when AUSA Reinhart told Nitae that her testimony would not be needed after all. Nitae smiled and gave me a kiss on the cheek and one last goodbye hug. That was loyalty, my friends. That was what I expected from all my employees and especially from my family; that is what life is all about. Surround me with a few people like Nitae, and I will conquer the world.

After Nitae left the waiting area, I only had a few minutes left before court reconvened, and I still had to take a major piss. I headed into the men's room. The sixth-floor men's room was very small, one urinal, two toilet stalls, and two sinks. As I start taking a piss, the men's room door opened up, and in walked Agent Willis. Now this was one of those uncomfortable moments in time where you really don't know how to act. I mean, here I was taking a piss, and in walked an FBI agent that was trying to put you in prison for a crime that he damn well knew never happened. Here was a guy that helped arrest my sister and my wife, a guy who helped to bankrupt my company that I had worked so hard to build, and a guy whom I had already had a brief physical confrontation with: so what do you do? I decided to keep my cool and say absolutely nothing. I made sure that he knew that I was aware it was him by giving him a look of disgust through the bathroom mirror. Unfortunately, Agent Willis was not smart enough to let the silence be our buffer. No, Agent Willis decided to talk to me.

> Agent Willis: Foley, I just want you to know that none of this is personal. I am just doing my job. I hope you understand that.
>
> Me. (as I shoved the old dick back in my pants and zipped up) Not personal? Are you kidding me? It doesn't get any more personal than this. You do realize that I am a person, right? My wife is a person. My sister is a person. The employees of Global Vending are people, and the customers of Global Vending are people. That makes this whole bullshit trial as personal as it gets, Doug. (Yes, I called him Doug.) I will be honest with you, Doug, if my job was fucking over people like your job is, I would kill myself before I ever went to a day of work. In fact, you should consider killing yourself. At least consider it. Oh, and don't try and small-talk me at this point, Special Agent Willis. I don't talk to cowards like you that hide behind a badge.
>
> Agent Willis: Be careful, Foley. There is such a thing as going too far. I am trying to be civil with you.

Me: Fuck civil. Let me know when you are willing to put the gun and badge away and face
me like a man. Until then, stay the fuck
away from me.

I walked out of the bathroom, but I never took my eyes off that
piece of shit. He was defiantly one of those guys that would suck-
er-punch you; I truly wish he had tried to.

Back in the courtroom, I sat back down next to Scott. I guess my
blood pressure must have been soaring, and my face must have been
bright-red because Scott asked me if I was all right. I just smiled at
Scott and told him that things were just peachy, just freakin' peachy.

Well, that was it. That was the end of the first week of my trial,
and I just kept thinking that could not have gone better. I mean, sure,
I could not be at trial, I could still be rich and traveling the country,
I could still be taking trips with my wife and kids and banging Kim
on the side, but if I had to be at trial, which I did, then things could
not have gone better.

Scott and I spoke several times over the weekend both over the
phone and in person, and he had the same confidence and reactions
that I was having. How in God's name could these people prosecute
me with witnesses that seemingly were on my side? Scott and I did
our best not to get to far ahead of ourselves; the next week would be
the tell-all. The feds had five Global Vending Inc. customers scheduled to testify next week, and I only knew three of them. The jury
was sure to pay special attention to what all five customers had to
say. After all, this trial was all about me supposedly defrauding them.
Let's see what they have to say about that. I tried to spend as much
time with my kids over the weekend. I love spending time with them,
but it was very difficult for me to be my normal cheerful self while
I was going through this trial. I was proud of one thing though: my
boys did not know what was happening to me, and once again, that
was just like I wanted it to be. I found it to be very frustrating while I
was home because Denise never asked how the trial was going; it was
almost as if she was blocking the entire trial out of existence.

CHAPTER 155

The second and third weeks of my trial were shortened due to scheduling conflicts that Judge Cooke was encountering. That was okay with me because these were important witnesses, and I wanted the jury to listen to everything that they had to say.

The first customer called to the witness stand was a man by the name of Eric L. I honestly have no idea why the feds chose this guy out of the 365 customers available to them. Eric had purchased three ATM machines from Global for a total of $16,000. Eric had received about half of his investment back already, and I could not recall having ever had a problem with him as a customer. Eric tried his hardest at first to follow the prosecutor's lead. It quickly became obvious to me that the feds chose him because he was willing to say anything in hopes of getting his money back. Eric testified that he did not know that he was not the owner of the machines that he was getting paid from and that he felt like he was defrauded by Global. That sounded good for the feds, except for the fact that Eric was lying, and it would be easy to prove that.

Upon cross-examination by Scott, Eric quickly folded like an extremely poor poker player. Scott showed Eric the documents that he had signed which very clearly laid out the fact that he was not the owner of any ATM machines at the time the feds raided Global's office. Now I understand that he was willing to say anything that the feds wanted him to say, but why call a guy whose file clearly would prove that he was lying? The feds had a copy of his file; it just did not make any sense to me. Once Scott had Eric against the ropes, Eric really fell apart. He told the court that he would say anything that the government wanted him to say in order to get to the front of the line for the "victims fund." What the fuck is the victims fund?

Scott of course asked Eric this question in a much more politically correct way. He told the court that Agent Delano informed him that all my assets would be sold, and a fund would be developed called the victims fund, and anyone who cooperated with the government's prosecution at trial would be placed first in line for a full refund.

I can't even begin to describe what a crock of bullshit that was. First of all, no one victim of a fraud crime can be given financial preferential treatment over any other victim for any reason. Second, should I be found guilty, the court "may" order restitution, and if they did, there was nowhere near enough money being held to pay back all the customers in full. Agent Delano was just lying once again in order to try and get a conviction of an innocent man. That was just so fucking sad.

Anyway, Scott asked Eric if he would testify that the moon was made of cheese if he could get his money back for saying that, and Eric said, "Absolutely, I would say anything to get my money back." Well, needless to say, this witness should have been called by me rather than by the feds; he was an absolute train wreck for them.

Next up was a customer by the name of Richard M. Richard was a fairly large customer; he had purchased twenty-five machines from Global for just over $125,000. Richard was also one of the customers that had made the mistake of filing papers to help Global get forced into involuntary bankruptcy. Richard had received around 25 percent of his investment back before Global was shut down, so he was out quite a bit of money. Richard's testimony was almost identical to that of Eric's. At first, he was a government parrot that simply repeated the answers that they wanted to hear.

Once again, under cross-examination, Global's documentation of his purchase showed that he was lying for the feds, and once again, Richard talked about Agent Delano's "victims fund" that he was expecting to get paid from.

That was two straight government witnesses that flipped on the government once they were confronted with their own paperwork, and especially once they heard that there was no such thing as a victims fund. I could just see the fire in these customers' eyes. I could not help but think of how every Global customer should have been there in the courtroom to hear these lies and tricks that the feds had played on them: the customers probably would have hung the two FBI agents and the prosecutor right there in court.

Kent V was the next customer called to the stand. I was curious to see what he had to say because Kent did not seem to be the type of person that would lie for anyone, for any reason.

Sure enough, as the questioning began, Kent turned out to be the guy that I thought he was. Remember, Kent was in his twenties; he spent over $1.1 million with my company. He was Global's single largest customer, and he was not a person that liked to be told what he could and could not say. Kent was a businessman, and a good one at that. The feds tried to limit their questions to Kent to consist of the pure size of his purchase and the huge lose that he had taken. They never asked him if he knew that he did not own the ATM machines that he was tracking or if he felt that he had been defrauded.

Scott made sure to ask him those questions. I would say that Kent was my star witness, and I was not even the one to call him to the stand. He made it very clear that he had invested in me, my concepts, and not just in ATM machines. He also told the court that he knew he was not the outright owner of the machines that he was tracking, and no, Kent said he did not feel that I defrauded him. In fact, Kent looked right at me during his testimony and told me to call him when I was finished with this legal crap. Kent wanted to do business with me again. Those were his words, folks, not mine. I shit you not. Upon leaving the witness stand, Kent came over and shook my hand and told me to stay strong. That was the first time during my trial that I almost started to cry; here was a guy that lost over a million dollars when Global was shut down, and he just made it very clear to me that he knew that I was not to be held accountable for his loses. Thank God, I was not crazy after all.

Dr. W from Michigan was next up on the stand. I knew Dr. W fairly well because he had made several purchases from Global over a two-year period. After Dr. W's second purchase, I personally called him to see if he would be a reference for Global Vending, and yes, the good doctor agreed to have a limited number of potential Global customers call him to see what kind of an experience he had when he made his purchases from Global. Dr. W simply asked me to limit the number of people that called him. I mean, after all, he was a doctor, and I was sure that he was a busy man.

Once again, why in God's name would the feds call this guy to the stand? Think about it. Part of the reference process was Dr. W describing how the shared location program worked to potential customers; he obviously knew that he did not own his machines, and that was the big accusation that the feds were making against me: "The customers were deceived. They were defrauded because they think they all own their own machines." Whatever. Dr. W did not tell any of the government's fairy tales. He was upset that he had taken a $70,000 loss, but he was not misled or defrauded—once again, his words, not mine.

The very last customer on the government's witness list was the only one that bothered me when I first saw the list (except for Burt, of course). The customer to testify last was none other than Tom C. That's right, the guy whom I tried to get $85,000 back to as his buy-back option. If you remember, the checks that were taken from me at the bullshit traffic stop by Agent Willis and Agent Delano were supposed to go to Mr. C. Instead of being a customer that was bought out of the ATM business, Mr. C became one pissed-off government witness. And yes, folks, his anger was directed at me.

Mr. C testified with a real vengeance in his voice. He answered the prosecutor's questions with conviction. As far as Mr. C was concerned, I was the Antichrist; I had stolen money from him, I had defrauded him, I had lied to him, and I had deceived him, end of story. He was definitely the government's only damaging witness.

On cross-examination, Mr. C admitted that he had received every monthly check that he was supposed to get during his two years of doing business with Global; he agreed that he was supposed to get an $85,000 buyout check from me but did not know the real reason as to why he never received the funds. Mr. C further admitted that Agent Delano promised him a front spot in the victims fund list, and Mr. C even admitted that had his monthly checks continued to come to him as they had before the feds showed up, he would have been a happy Global customer. When Scott presented paperwork to

Mr. C that documented his acknowledgment in the shared program, Mr. C claimed that he did not ever remember signing the documents presented to him. In fact, Mr. C provided his own set of documents that had all sorts of pencil and ink pen notes written across the forms. In other words, Mr. C had the same documents, but everywhere that the documents referred to the shared location program, there was a cross-out and the words written *not on shared program* in ink or in pencil. Mr. C said that these were his original documents, and he insisted that I must have forged his signature on the documents that we had even though they were notarized. Now I knew that Mr. C was mad at me, and I could even understand his frustrations, but give me a fucking break. The documents that we presented were faxed directly to the law office of Lisa Daniels; her fax header was on each sheet. The documents that Mr. C had in his possession were obviously written on at a much later date. I would even bet my left nut that the ink and pencil scratch-outs were done after the feds heard the other Global customers testify. Mr. C was their bitch, and he was not going to back down. It did not matter what Scott asked this guy; he answered in the same way

Tom C said, "Tom Foley defrauded me. I lost almost $300,000 because of Tom Foley and his fraudulent company."

Toward the end, it became annoying to listen to this fool. I was hoping that the jury would see just how ridiculous these accusations by Mr. C were, especially because he admitted to being promised a front spot in a nonexistent victims fund.

All I can tell you is that for the first time since the trial started, I got this awful empty feeling in my stomach that was telling me that three weeks of positive testimony just went to shit. Scott and I would have to turn this mess back around during our defense presentation. The prosecutor advised Judge Cooke that the government was finished with their prosecution; next, it would be our turn.

Scoreboard upon prosecution completion: defense 7, prosecution 1

CHAPTER 156

It became obvious to Scott and myself that my testimony was the only way to combat the damage that Mr. C's testimony had done. Scott would put a few prep witnesses on the stand first and then let me be the final witness in my own defense. Scott was very worried about me testifying; I guess his worries could be justified because I was a bit of a loose cannon, and I would most likely not respond well to the prosecutor's cross-examination. The only other choice we had would be to rest without putting up a defense, but I made it clear to Scott that I was going to be heard. I was owed that much after all that I had been through. Scott agreed, but he was definitely scared to death to hear what I had to say.

On the first day of our defense, Scott and I drove down to the courthouse together. We needed to pick up a bunch of files and boxes from his office, and we planned on spending that evening working again, so for the first time since my trial started, we were off to court together.

When we arrived at the Gratny Parkway light where I had met Jesus every morning, I made Scott pull over. I got out of the car, and I waved Jesus over to Scott's car. As Jesus crutched his way over to where we had pulled over, Scott had this look on his face that was priceless. He truly felt that his client, who was on trial for his life, had completely lost his mind. Jesus cracked up that morning; as he arrived at Scott's car, he gave the car a once-over (Scott drove a 300 series Mercedes), and he asked Scott why he did not spring for the 500 series. I almost spat my coffee on my man Jesus. I gave Jesus the coffee and bagels that I brought for him, gave him a quick trial update, and then I said my goodbyes. Jesus yelled out that he would be happy to be a character witness for me if we needed one.

I said, "I just might take you up on that one, my brother."

I will never forget how Scott looked at me and asked me a very simple question: "Is there something seriously wrong with you?"

Well, if helping out another human being in his time of need (especially Jesus) can be considered a serious problem, then yes, I have something seriously wrong with me.

Our warmup witnesses were Bruce (my sales rep), Herb (my operations director), and the bankruptcy trustee. Basically, these guys were asked questions about Global's daily operations, about the information that they remember being entered into our computer system, about the number of machines that we had purchased but had not yet had turned on at the time when the feds came in, things like that. Bruce was a great witness because he was able to confirm that the shared program was already in effect when he had been hired at global. The feds claimed that the program had only existed for a couple of months before the raid took place. Bruce also testified that every customer he sold ATM machines to knew that they did not own their ATM machines.

Herb was more of a numbers witness. His testimony helped show that we were a true work in progress, and had the feds not shown up when they did, we would have easily finished the job that we had started.

The trustee was called to testify on the viability of Global Vending. It was the feds' contention that Global was about to collapse at the time of their raid, but the trustee had done a detailed analysis that showed that Global was not only a viable company, but if its growth continued at the same rate as the first five years, Global was destined to be at least a $100-million-per-year operation within the next ten years. I can't even begin to tell you just how sick to my stomach I became when I heard that one. You sold that company for $150,000, you moron.

Anyway, the testimony of Bruce, Herb, and the trustee was good for us, and the prosecutor wisely asked very few questions of each of these witnesses when he did his cross-examination. AUSA Reinhart was a Princeton graduate. He knew when to shut his mouth and when to voice his opinion, and I could tell that he was saving his battleground energy for when I took the stand.

I had a fairly heated argument with Scott later that evening. I had been pushing Scott to summon Alan and Andy to court so that we could show the jury exactly who had started this bullshit and just what type of lying sacks of shit these people were.

My theory on this was simple; the feds did not want them on the stand, so we should be taking a long hard look at bringing them in. I truly felt that it was important for the jury to see the people that made the fraud allegations against me were not customers; they were vindictive scumbags. I felt that would make a difference if this thing came down to the wire.

Scott simply told me that we could not call someone to the stand that would only have bad things to say about me; he called it legal suicide. Yes, he had a point, but just think about how far the feds went in order to not call them to the stand. I was more than willing to roll the dice, but when push came to shove, I let the legal expert win that fight. And no, I was not happy about this decision.

CHAPTER 157

It was time; it was time for me to testify, time for me to finally be heard and to be completely honest. I was scared to death. I was not scared of what I was going to say about my business practices. I have an old saying, "You can't get caught telling a truth," and that was what I had on my side. I was afraid of my temper and the fact that I sometimes (a lot of times) act before I think.

The morning of my testimony was just a mess for me. My stomach was doing flip-flops, I did not sleep well the night before, and of course, it was raining when I finally left for court. I tried to keep to my routine as best I could. I picked up breakfast for me and Jesus, but I did not even touch mine. I drank my coffee in the car, and I found myself downing an unusual amount of good old painkillers. I am not kidding here. By the time I got to Jesus, I probably downed at least twenty pills, and I was just starting to actually calm down. Twenty pills—that's probably enough hydrocodone to kill most people, but I had it for breakfast with coffee. What a moron.

There he was, standing in the rain, waiting for me, good old one-legged Jesus. Jesus was wearing one of the nice clean T-shirts that I had bought him, and he seemed to have a little extra strut to his approach than he normally had. If I didn't know any better, I would say that Jesus was feeling good about himself these days. Good for him, he had been through enough. Once again, Jesus proved to be a rather insightful man: as he reached into my car to grab his breakfast, Jesus looked right into my eyes.

Jesus said, "Holy cow, Tom, are you wasted or what?"

Holy shit! Even one-legged Jesus could tell that I was lit like a candle. I simply looked back at my one-legged friend, I gave him a right-eye wink, and I told him, "Yes, Jesus, yes, I am."

Jesus replied, "Good for you, man. Fucking A. Good for you."

As I drove away, I found myself looking in the rearview mirror to see what I really looked like. I kept telling myself that I did not look any different than I usually looked. I guess that was what people addicted to drugs do the best. We lie to ourselves; that makes things easier. Never fear Southern District of Florida courthouse. Wasted Tom was on his way to testify; this ought to be a real treat for everyone.

I met Scott that morning at the courthouse coffee shop as he had requested. Scott wanted to make sure that I had my shit together and that I understood the order and reason of his questions. I sat down at a small table with Scott. He took one look at me and shook his head.

Scott said, "Have you been drinking, Tom?"

Okay, that was two people in a row that had seen something different in me, but I will be honest again, I was feeling no pain at this point. I was exploding with a sudden rush of confidence. I had myself convinced that I could solve the world's energy and hunger problems right then and there in that little coffeehouse.

I said, "Let's get this shit going, Scott. I got this big-time. This is my day to let it all out."

All Scott could do was to say a prayer and continue on with his prep talk. I don't remember one thing he said at that table, and that was probably because I was not listening, not even for a single moment.

Scott and I arrived at the sixth-floor waiting area, where I spotted my new friend and court reporter Robin typing away on her office computer. Robin was looking A-OK that morning, and I decided that I needed to tell her that. Robin gave me a friendly slap on the shoulder when I mentioned how hot she looked, and Scott gave me a not-so-friendly "Are you fucking kidding me" face. Fuck you, Scott, you fag.

417

CHAPTER 158

Court was now in session. My heart was pumping like a well-oiled sports cars pistons. I was smiling, and I believe I even waved hello to the jury. I was quickly becoming Scott's biggest nightmare, but you know what, he needed to lighten up a little. I was showing no fear of the witness stand, and that should have made him relax a little.

As I took my oath to tell the truth, the whole truth, and nothing but the truth so help me God, I found myself looking over at Agent Delano, and instead of just saying, "I do," I repeated the whole statement back to Agent Delano.

"Yes, I promise to tell the truth, the whole truth, and nothing but the truth so help me God," and I raised my voice just a little at "so help me God."

Agent Delano knew exactly what I was telling her: I would do what you refused to do, tell the truth.

Scott started questioning me about my past, where I grew up, who was in my family, where I attended school, and what kind of work I had done previous to opening Global Vending. I spoke directly to the jury, I smiled a lot, and I threw in an occasional joke, each of which made the jury smile. Scott then went over each of the charges and asked me what my intentions were at each point in time. I then got into how Global came to be, how I operated the company, and how I dealt with my employees and my customers. I tried my hardest to make it sound interesting so that even people like the ones on the jury would be interested in the ATM business. The fireworks started when I started to describe the day of the FBI raid and the days to follow.

The prosecutor was objecting almost every ten seconds, and I knew he was doing it just to get the jury's minds off what I was trying to tell them. I needed the jurors to know just how far the feds had gone to make sure that the customers of Global Vending would lose their investments. The objections were meaningless, and they were all overruled by Judge Cooke, but I could tell by looking at the jury's reaction that they were getting sick of the objections, and that would mean that they would soon be sick of me testifying: no more testimony, no more objections, get it? I reacted to the situation in a way that I was sure that the prosecutor and the judge had never heard or seen before in a courtroom.

> Me: Hey, Reinhart, why don't you shut up already and let the jury hear the truth. What are you so afraid of?
>
> (The jury suddenly found themselves laughing.)
>
> Judge: Mr. Foley, you need to refrain from making comments to the prosecutor.
>
> Me: Well, then can my attorney tell him to shut up?
>
> Judge: No one will tell anyone to shut up in my court. Do you understand?
>
> Me: Not really. Is it actually the words *shut up* that can't be used, or is it the whole concept of implying that someone shut up that is not allowed because to be honest with you, Your Honor, you kind of just told me to shut up.
>
> Judge: Listen, Mr. Foley, you will let me address the prosecutor's objections, and if your counsel has objections, then he is free to voice them, but I have first say when someone objects.
>
> (I could not help it, but Judge Cooke had just left the door wide open for a line straight from the movie *Caddyshack*.
>
> Me: Okay, it's your honor, Your Honor.

419

(Once again, the jury could not help but laugh,
and I mean outright laugh. I thought the prosecutor was going to kill me right then and there in
the courtroom.)
Judge: Mr. Foley, do we understand each other?
Me: Yes, Your Honor, you and I are on the same
    page now.

Well, I tell you, folks, it worked. Scott could give me all the
dirty looks that he wanted to, but the objections suddenly stopped;
maybe they should teach that one in law school. I felt that my testimony was spot-on. The jury was taking notes and looked at me
for the entire first three hours that I was on the stand. When I told
them about the bullshit traffic stop that had taken place the day that
Agents Willis and Delano took the two cashier's checks from me, I
actually saw several of the juror's heads shaking side to side in disgust. Hey, maybe they were a victim in the past of a bullshit traffic
stop, who knows. The point is that I was laying out all the dirty
and sleezy shit that the feds had done to me, my family, and most
importantly, the customers of Global Vending. At one point, I left
the witness stand, and I used an easel with drafting paper to show
the jury just how the Global customers were making money and just
how it would have been impossible for them to have lost even a dime
if Global was simply allowed to continue on the same path. There
was no doubt that I had their attention. Now hopefully they were
understanding the numbers.

Scott and I finished with my testimony with about fifteen minutes left in the day. Judge Cooke decided to leave cross-examination
for the next day, and we were all excused. Scott then asked me to
meet him back at his office after dinner. I figured that was going to
be the case. He needed to read me the Riot Act about tomorrow's
showdown between me and Prosecutor Reinhart. No problemo,
Scott, no problemo.

CHAPTER 159

For those of you who have never had to testify for your life in a federal court, and I hope that that is the majority of you, I need to tell you that it is just an exhausting task. I mean physically and mentally exhausting.

I met with Scott later that evening, and I listened to what he had to say. Scott told me that I had done very well on my first day of testifying, but I really needed to control myself while being cross-examined. I agreed that I was walking a very fine line with my antics, but to be honest, these antics were not planned, and as far as I was concerned, they are not controllable. This is my personality; this is me being me, and you just can't turn that shit off. I had to cut Scott off short that evening. I was exhausted. I am sure it also had something to do with the ridiculous amount of drugs that I had shoved into my poor body. I got home, I kissed my kids good night, and I went to bed.

It was the same routine the next morning. Why mess with success? That's one of my mottos. I took a shower, got dressed, and hammered down a good fifteen or eighteen pills. Heck, at this level of abuse, who's counting anymore? Don't ask me why, but I stopped at an IHOP (International House of Pancakes), and I ordered like twenty pancakes to-go for Jesus.

As a quick regression, I could not help but think about this one ridiculous time when I was growing up in Massapequa, New York. I went to an IHOP with my friends Artie and John. We were simply stoned out of our minds and had an unbelievable case of the munchies. Every time the waitress would bring our check, we would all order another breakfast; we were completely out of control. We wound out running up an $80 bill that morning, and remember, that was around 1980, so $80 was a hell of a lot of money back then. We of course did not have eighty dollars, so we left every dime we had for the waitress as a tip, and we ran out without paying the check. I will never forget that day.

Anyway, I was fairly wasted now, so maybe buying pancakes for Jesus at IHOP was a flashback for me or something. Who the hell knows? What I do know is that Jesus was thankful for the pancakes, and that was all that really mattered at the time.

I arrived at court early as usual, and once again, I was supposed to meet Scott in the coffee shop to go over my attitude. I decided to skip our coffee shop meeting. I was in too good of a mood to listen to any more criticism, no matter how much Scott thought he was helping me. Like I said earlier, you can't just change someone's personality at the drop of a dime. Well, at least I can't. As Popeye always used to say, "I am what I am, and that's all that I am." Holy shit, maybe I am losing it. Now I am quoting a cartoon, not good.

I shot up to the sixth-floor courtroom in an almost-happy mood; I don't really know what was going through my little pea brain, but I was actually happy to be there. Maybe I could sense that the end of the trial was near, and I wanted nothing more than to put this behind me. As I walked past Robin's office door, I could see her hard at work at her computer again. I waved and started to walk toward the courtroom when Robin waved me over to her office. Robin was her normal friendly bubbly self, which was not easy to be this early in the morning, but her attitude definitely made me feel more relaxed than ever. She then broke out a few photos of her "kids," and she handed them to me as she proudly told me all their names. Robin's "kids" were actually dogs: beautiful greyhound dogs that she had rescued from a shelter. It was nice that she felt comfortable enough to share something like that with me. In return, I showed Robin pictures of my two boys and of course my dog, Molli. I can't remember the last time that I showed a "stranger" pictures of my children. I am very protective of them, and you just never know who you are talking to. This is one crazy world that we live in, so you have to be careful. Robin was no threat to me or my family. In fact, if circumstances were different, I could definitely see myself being friends with Robin;

she was just an all-around good-hearted person, and that is rare now-adays. It also did not hurt that she was an attractive woman.

So anyway, Scott eventually showed up at the courtroom with an attitude because I was a no-show down at the coffee shop. I could tell that he wanted to get into it with me, but at the same time, he did not want to get me heated just before the cross-examination started. I put my hand on Scott's shoulder, I told him I was cool and he needed to just sit back and relax, and that was just what he did. What choice did he really have?

My father and cousin John arrived. I hung out with them for a few moments, making some small talk. I could tell from their body language that they were more worried than I was about the upcoming showdown. It's funny, everyone that knew my true personality was worried, and when I think about it, I would say that they definitely had good cause to worry: I was not made to be in a courtroom, a place filled with strict rules and regulations, a place where saying the wrong thing could be a one-way ticket to prison, but you know what, fuck it. I didn't ask to be here, I was forced to be in this room, and I needed to stick to my guns. It is an old sports theory that sometimes the best defense is a good offense, and that was a theory that I was applying in this game of life. Just think about this, my friends: if you want to bring down an empire, you cannot play by their rules. That just would not make sense, and believe me, this prosecution was an empire that needed to be taken down.

CHAPTER 160

The funny thing about being placed in a situation where "rules" rule is that both sides are bound by the rules. In a federal trial, when a witness is being questioned, two things must take place: first of all, the prosecutor has to ask questions, and second, he has to give the witness an opportunity to fully answer the question. AUSA Reinhart tried his hardest to avoid doing both.

The prosecutor started his cross-examination with a small speech in which he described me as being a child that was blaming everyone else for my wrongdoings. He told the jury that I was blaming the FBI, Alan, Andy, and even him for the collapse of Global Vending, when in his reality, I was the one to blame. I would say that he went on for a good three to four minutes before I had heard enough. I could not figure out if Scott was sleeping with his eyes open or if he was just mad about me not showing up at the coffee shop that morning, but Scott never objected to the prosecutor's lack of questions. He just sat there making notes; that is, of course, until I decided to object right in the middle of the prosecutor's little speech:

> Me: I object, Your Honor.
> Judge: You object? I am sorry, Mr. Foley, you can't object. You are represented by counsel. He must object.
> Me: I understand, Your Honor, but I think maybe he is asleep, or he might be mad at me for not meeting him this morning for breakfast. Whatever the case may be, I need to object to this little speech that the prosecutor is giving. I was under the impression

that he had to ask me questions, and I had
to answer them. If he is not going to ask me
questions, then I would like to be dismissed
because he is boring me to death right now.

Judge: Mr. Foley, you are not excused. Mr.
Reinhart, is there a question coming sometime in the near future?

(Like a freakin hammerhead, Scott now decided
to object.)

Scott: I object, Your Honor.

Judge: What is your objection, Mr. Sakin?

Scott: The prosecutor is required to ask questions
and not just simply tell stories.

(No shit, Scott. Hey, that was a great idea, a well-
thought-out objection. What made you think of
that one? Holy cow, I came so close to saying that
to him, but I pulled back on the reins and slowed
down my horses.)

Judge: Objection sustained. (That meant the
judge agreed with the objection.) Mr.
Reinhart, please refrain from long dissipa-
tions, and please start asking the witness
questions.

Me: Nice job, Your Honor. That's what I'm talking
about.

Once again, the jury started to lose it with laughter. Hey, this
sure was not some boring jury duty, I can tell you that. Mr. Reinhart
tried his hardest to throw me off my game. I could read him like a
cheap novel; I knew exactly why he was asking me every question,
and I could almost anticipate what his next question was going to be.
Remember, I was hopped up on painkillers, and I was not trained in
testifying in court, but as I had been saying since the moment these
pricks showed up at my front door, I had the truth on my side: you
can always get caught in a lie, but you cannot get caught in a truth.
I could have testified about Global Vending's operations while I was

high on acid because Global was my life, its business plan was my creation, and my intentions were sincere. I wanted the customers to be just as successful as I was, and that is the truth.

AUSA Reinhart started to get frustrated because I was not falling for his bullshit traps. At one point, I was in the middle of an answer, and Mr. Reinhart tried to cut me off and ask a new question. Once again, I had to object.

> Me: Your Honor, I object again. I know, I know,
> I am not allowed to object, but I would like
> to at least tell my attorney what to object to.
> (Well, you would think that we were at a comedy
> club because the jury and even Robin the court
> reporter started to laugh.)
> Judge: What is it this time, Mr. Foley?
> Me: The prosecutor is not letting me finish my
> answers. I don't want to answer any of these
> questions because most of them are a waste
> of time, but if I have to answer his ques-
> tions, then I would like to have the oppor-
> tunity to give complete answers. I am sorry
> that Mr. Reinhart does not want to hear the
> truth, but if that is the case, then he needs
> to stop asking me questions.
> (This time, Scott did not follow up with his own
> parrot objection. He was definitely embarrassed
> about what I was doing, but tough shit, do your
> fucking job.)
> Judge. Mr. Reinhart, I need to ask you to please
> allow the witness to finish his responses to your
> questions.
> Me: (looking at Mr. Reinhart) That means objec-
> tion sustained.
> Judge: Mr. Foley, last warning for you. Don't get
> carried away.

Me: Sorry, I just wanted that to be on the record.
    It will not happen again.
(Yeah, right.)

I could tell that the prosecutor still had more questions planned for me, or maybe he had more little stories to tell. Whichever the case was, AUSA Reinhart decided to pack it in.

Mr. Reinhart said, "No more questions, Your Honor."

It was kind of like a football game that was stopped in the third quarter. Even to the untrained eye, you could see the frustrations on the face of Mr. Reinhart. The dragon had been slayed.

After everyone had left the courtroom, Scott and I took a few minutes to talk. I know he was mad at me for embarrassing him in court, but that was his problem; I will give credit where credit is due. Scott was professional about the whole thing, and he even managed to tell me that I had done a great job and that he was proud of me. It was almost the making of a Life Savers commercial: well, maybe that's going a bit too far. Tomorrow would be the closing arguments, and then the jury would begin their deliberations. At that very point in time, I felt that I had done the best I could have done defending myself. I would have liked to have called Alan and Andy to the stand, and maybe even some Global customers, but that just did not happen. I told the truth, and I left the courthouse that day with a sense of pride. What more can you ask for?

CHAPTER 161

I cannot tell you what was going through AUSA Reinhart's head when he planned out his closing argument, but I can tell you that it would appear that not one but several screws had come loose in his head. Perhaps it was his previous day's failure while cross-examining me, or maybe he just realized that their case had been presented in a weak, unconvincing manner.

The prosecutor was yelling during his closing argument. He was right in front of the jurors' faces yelling about drug dealers and gunrunners and income tax evaders and how I needed to be treated like all of the above. Scott fired off a flurry of objections, and Judge Cooke quickly reprimanded the prosecutor for implying that I was committing other crimes besides the ones in the indictment. The whole process at that point was a joke. The prosecutor continued his show by telling the jury that Scott had devised my shared location defense and that it was a nonexistent program. Scott lost it at that point: it was bad enough that the prosecutor was throwing bullshit allegations around about me, but now he was attacking Scott's integrity.

This was the first time that I saw fire in Scott's eyes, and I heard it in his voice: sure, it doesn't feel good at all to have people making accusations about you that are not only false, but they are also disrespectful and hurtful. Maybe Scott finally knew what I was feeling and what I was going through.

Scott demanded Judge Cooke pronounce a mistrial due to the prosecutor's misconduct; his request was denied: instead, the judge instructed the jury to forget what they had just heard from the prosecutor and instructed the jury that they could not consider any of his allegations while deliberating. I'm sorry, folks, but do you really think that that is possible for a human being to do? Just forget what you heard, don't consider it, erase it from your thought process. I just don't see that happening. The prosecutor simply made allegations that could not be erased at that point. He knew exactly what he was doing. For three weeks, we had seen a fairly calm, cool, and collected individual, and now we saw his true colors: he was a child that did not play nice when he was losing.

Scott tried his hardest to repair the damage that was done by the out-of-control prosecutor. Scott reminded the jury that they needed to keep their deliberations to the facts that were presented at trial, and if they did just that, then they would have no choice but to find me not guilty on all charges. He also reminded the jury of the prosecutor's opening statements and all the promises that the prosecutor had made and had failed to prove. Scott reminded the jury of the Global customers that testified that they knew exactly what they did and did not own and how they were not defrauded. He went over how the FBI destroyed any chance of the Global customers retrieving their investments, and finally, Scott reminded the jury that for five years, Global Vending ran its operation without ever having a single customer complaint. Global was a viable, well-planned-out business that was shut down for a crime that never happened: not guilty was the only logical verdict.

When closing arguments were finished, the judge read instructions to the jury about the crimes that I was charged with and how they were to deliberate. The jury was given a copy of the indictment and a copy of all the exhibits presented at trial: they were allowed to use any notes that they had taken during the trial during deliberations, and they needed to come up with a unanimous verdict on each count of the indictment, and that was the end of that. The jury was sent to the jury room to deliberate, and I was left with my father and my cousin to wait for a verdict. Scott decided to go back to his office while the jury was deliberating. The clerk of the court would phone Scott if the jury had any requests or if they arrived at a verdict.

CHAPTER 162

Waiting for the jury to come to a verdict was just some of the most painful and grueling time in my life. Time dragged by, and I just prayed for a quick yet favorable verdict. Unfortunately, neither would come for me. Days passed by, and still there was no word from the jury.

Finally, the jury had a request from the judge. Scott was called into court, and once all parties were present, Judge Cooke read out loud a note that the jury had written to her. The jury wanted the court reporter to read them the testimony of Mr. C. Yes, Mr. C (the government's only favorable witness.) Judge Cooke informed the court that federal rules do not allow for testimony to be read back to a jury during deliberations. Request denied. Scott and I agreed that the fact that the jury was taking such a long time to make a decision was a sign that our defense left a lot of doubts in the jurors' minds about my being guilty of fraud. The jury was obviously split, or they would have come to a quick decision.

After day number 3 of deliberations, we found out just how split the jury was. Judge Cooke called all parties back into the courtroom in order to read another note from the jury. The note was short and to the point: they were deadlocked, and they did not feel that a unanimous decision was a possibility. The jury was hung, and they wanted the judge's permission to be dismissed. Once again, Judge Cooke denied the juror's request.

Judge Cooke advised us that she had sent a note back to the jurors asking them to please continue deliberations in good faith and to do their best to come to a unanimous decision. Should the jury be unable to come to a unanimous decision, then there would be a mistrial, and the government would have to decide if they wanted to retry the case.

To me, the whole process was simply exhausting, and it was something that I would not want to go through again. Besides the amount of time, energy, and money that it took to get me through this trial, Scott explained to me that a mistrial was usually not a good thing for a defendant: the government saw what your defense was at the first trial, and they would simply make the adjustments needed to almost guarantee a conviction on the second time around. I was not sure what to think of the whole idea of a mistrial, but I did know that I was looking for closure right now; a not guilty verdict would bring me that much-needed closure.

Everyone was caught completely off guard when the jury sent Judge Cooke a note that they had reached a verdict. It was only two hours after the last note stating that they were hopelessly deadlocked, and now all of a sudden, they had come to a unanimous decision: that just did not sit well with me. With all parties present and accounted for in the courtroom, the jury was brought back in. It took me all but five seconds to realize that something was wrong. For almost four weeks now, I had sat in the same seat, and I watched the same jurors walk into the courtroom. Each time, the jurors entered, eight of the twelve jurors always made it a point to look over in my direction. Maybe they wanted to see what I was wearing, maybe they were trying to get a read on what type of person I was, or maybe it was just curiosity. Whatever the reason was, I took notice that the same jurors always took a look at me. This time, however, the jury entered, and not one of them looked my way. In fact, the majority had their gazes focused on the ground as if they were afraid to step on a land mine or something. It's never good when another human being can't look you in the eyes.

Judge Cooke asked the jury forewoman if they had reached a verdict, and the forewoman replied yes. A verdict sheet was handed to the court bailiff, and then he handed it to Judge Cooke. Judge Cooke silently read the verdict form and then handed it to her clerk, Ivan. Judge Cooke asked me to rise for the reading of the verdict.

There are moments in every person's life that will forever be etched in your memory; this was one of those moments that I will remember until the day I die. I did not imagine this; it was real:

the jury forewoman looked over at the prosecutor and smiled. With God as my witness, this bitch smiled at the prosecutor. It was such an uncomfortable moment in time that even the prosecutor did not know how to react. AUSA Reinhart actually looked over at me to see if I had caught that sudden little smile, and when he saw that I did, he too looked straight down at the ground.

Ivan said, "As to count one of the indictment, guilty. As to count two of the indictment: guilty."

That was about all that I remember as far as the guiltys and not guiltys.

I was found guilty of two counts of mail fraud that had Mr. C's name attached to them. I was found not guilty of the remaining wire fraud charges. I was found not guilty of the money structuring charge: the charges that Denise and Paula pled guilty to. I was found not guilty of obstruction of justice. The two mail fraud counts were identical, so they were grouped together and treated as one charge. Guilty, how in the hell could I have been found guilty of anything? I know that Tom C went off while he was on the stand, but that was one person out of 365 people. That was a far cry from some major Ponzi scheme that the feds claimed I was running.

As I stood there in shock and disbelief, I started to take a look around the courtroom, and that was when I saw the most unreal, the most out-of-the-ordinary atmosphere that I had ever seen. I would compare the courtroom to experiencing a UFO. Nine of the twelve jurors were crying, men and women alike. Crying! Then the court reporter Robin asked Judge Cooke for a recess; she was crying her eyes out. Crying! The clerk and even Judge Cooke started to hand out tissues to jurors and to Robin. Now I was standing there like a man and just absorbing what was going on in front of me. The jury was obviously split among themselves, and unfortunately for me, instead of staying deadlocked or hung as they say in the legal system, the jury made a deal among itself, guilty for defrauding one person, not guilty for the rest. There would be no other reason for crying about their own decision unless that was the case. The jury had no idea what the penalty to me would be; they were never given that privileged information.

As I began to accept the reality of what had taken place, tears came to my eyes. These were not tears of sadness; they were tears of disappointment. I was found guilty of a crime that never happened. The system that I grew up to believe in, the country that I had always been such a patriot of, had let me down. It's funny, I actually found myself feeling sorry for the people that were crying on my behalf. The whole scene was just not real. When was the last time you saw a jury on TV cry after convicting someone of a crime? The answer is never because, in reality, it just does not happen. I know that TV is not real life, but my point is that TV usually tries to portray court-rooms and crime stories in as real a mannerism as possible, and I had never seen a juror cry on one of those crime shows.

CHAPTER 163

Judge Cooke ordered a fifteen-minute recess to let everyone gather their composure. My father and cousin John came over to where I was still standing and gave me big warm hugs and words of encouragement. I found my feelings turning from that of disappointment to that of anger and rage. I should not have looked over, but I did. I saw the FBI agents and the prosecutors shaking hands and exchanging semi smiles; now I say semi smiles because to the government, this was a defeat. They had not convicted me on all charges, and that meant that my sentence could very easily be minimal, so they still had work to do. But still, I saw their celebration as salt being rubbed in my already irritated wounds. These people were scum; they were creating yet another standoff situation in which they "thought" would have no consequences. They lied on the witness stand, they destroyed evidence, they created victims, and now to even consider a celebration in front of a beaten-down man, that was just too much for me to handle.

I said, "Did you get what you wanted? You made a mockery out of the very system that you supposedly represent. Do you feel proud? Is a conviction in your professional file worth destroying a system that a country has worked hundreds of years to develop? Integrity, people, do you even know what that word means?"

As I began to get louder and louder, the court officer called for more help. I did not realize this at the time, but I was in a full-blown frenzy. Scott made a very feeble attempt to walk me out into the waiting area, but all he really did was to bring me physically closer to this pack of shit bags. Agent Willis had placed himself in front of the prosecutor and the rest of the banana squad, like he was going to be their savior.

I said, "What, Doug, what's with the look? You gonna be some hero today? Let me know when you are ready for round two. This time, I won't give you a chance to get up off your sorry ass."

Court security walked me out of the courtroom. My body said kill the mother fucker, get in as many good shots as you can before they are able to stop you, but teach these guys a lesson.

There are consequences, people, when you push any individual too far; there are consequences. It does not matter if you are a federal agent, an average Joe, or even the president of the United States; there are consequences. You need to be careful in life. You never know exactly who you are dealing with. You need to treat people with respect, or one day that quiet little nobody that you bullied and laughed at just might turn around and blow your fucking head off.

CHAPTER 164

When court reconvened, there was an entirely different attitude in the courtroom. Not one member of the prosecution team even dared to look my way. Court security remained in the room, and I would say that that was probably a very good thing. It made me think more than twice about acting up again.

Anyway, Judge Cooke instructed the jury that they were not done with their jury duties. The jury still needed to decide what assets would be forfeited to the United States government. Once again, the prosecutor had an opportunity to give the jury a brief argument on why all my assets should be forfeited, and Scott had a chance to address the jury as well. Something the prosecutor said during his argument struck me the wrong way, and I made Scott aware of it.

The prosecutor told that jury that they had found me guilty of defrauding hundreds of people out of millions of dollars, and that was why all my assets should be forfeited; he even told them how to figure out just how much the customers of Global had lost: "It's easy. Just use the exhibits that we have submitted during trial. You take the amount of money that Global collected from the victims and subtract the amount of money that Global returned to the victims. That is how you find just how much these people have lost. By ordering all of Mr. Foley's and Global's assets to be forfeited, you are helping to repay these people."

What the hell was he talking about? I was found guilty of defrauding one person out of the money that he invested; that was it. Scott told me to relax. He insisted that the prosecutor was just trying to beef up an attempt to have my assets forfeited. Scott argued to the jury that I was not responsible for any more than the investment

436

made by Mr. C. Judge Cooke gave the jury instructions and a list of my personal and business assets, and once again, the jury was sent away to deliberate. Court was now in recess.

It took less than one hour for the jury to make their forfeiture decision. Court was back in session, and Ivan, the clerk of the court, read off a short list of assets to be forfeited. Once again, it was a compromised decision by the jury. A little more than half of my assets were to be forfeited, which meant that I would be receiving back almost $1.5 million in assets. Money was not a primary concern of mine at the time. Yes, making sure that my family would be able to survive while I was in prison (should it come to that) was a very important thing, but I was more concerned with having been found guilty; that was simply unacceptable to me.

Judge Cooke thanked the jury for their hard work and then dismissed them for good. The judge then set a date for the end of March for me to be sentenced. I was reminded that I was still on the same bond conditions and that I was to continue to report to pretrial services each week. Court was now adjourned. I had almost six weeks to prepare for sentencing, but for now, I had to prepare myself for Denise.

Scott spoke to me and my supporters for a few minutes after the courtroom had cleared out. He tried to make me feel like we had been victorious; we had taken on the giant, we did not back down, and we had received a split verdict. In his eyes, thing could have gone worse. Scott told me that he was going to do his best to prepare for my sentencing at the end of March; he would prepare an argument for me to receive a term of probation instead of prison time.

CHAPTER 165

A very important Supreme Court decision had taken place while I was at trial: *United States v. Booker*. In *Booker*, it was decided by the Supreme Court that the United States sentencing guidelines could no longer be mandatory; it was unconstitutional, so the federal guideline system was now "advisory." A sentencing judge was still required to properly figure out a defendant's guideline range, but now, a judge had the ability to depart from the guidelines. For me, a first-time nonviolent offender that received a split verdict on a very weak government prosecution, *Booker* would most likely help me out a lot. Honestly, I could give a shit at that time. I was still stuck on the fact that a jury compromised its integrity in order to reach a verdict, and the government compromised its integrity in order to get a conviction. These things bothered me more than the possibility of prison time, and let's not forget the real people that were suffering from this whole bullshit case. The customers of Global Vending had lost a small fortune. I can't fully explain what was happening inside my brain at this time, but a huge change was taking place. No kidding here, folks, at this very moment, screws were coming loose, and circuits were shorting: I would NEVER be the same person again.

I got to my truck in the court's parking garage, and I sat there for a good forty minutes or so. I had thoughts running through my head that varied from the actual joy that the trial process was over all the way up the range where I strongly considered hunting down Alan and Andy to make them pay for what they had done; everything has consequences, folks, everything. I headed home and decided to call Denise on my way home. I wish to this day that I never made that call because once again, I was about to be disappointed by my other half's reactions.

I informed Denise of the jury's decision, and I informed her of my sentencing date. Denise started to cry, but not for the fact that I was found guilty or because of the fact that I might be going to prison. No, Denise wanted me to tell her just how she was going to survive, how we would restart with two small children to care for and not a dime to our names. I never liked to hear my wife sad. No matter how much we differed as human beings, I still had feelings for this woman, and I would have done anything to make her not be sad. I told Denise that the jury had only ordered half of our assets to be forfeited, and perhaps an appeal would be possible after sentencing. Regardless, no matter what happened to me, her and the boys would not be sent out into the streets penniless. I would say for at least the next ten minutes, she inquired about specific pieces of jewelry and vehicles and bullshit that the government was holding: money, money, money, jewelry, jewelry, jewelry. I could not listen to this bullshit anymore. Hey asswipe, your husband might be going to prison, and your children's father might not be around for a long time. How about a little bit of fucking sympathy. Fake it for Christ's sake. Just stop with the jewelry and the money, please. Once again, I could have been a horrible person, and I could have reminded her that when she pled guilty, she gave up her right s to all the assets that the government was holding. She was not entitled to shit at this point, but no, I am just not like that.

CHAPTER 166

Upon arriving home on verdict day, I found myself hugging my children and not wanting to let go of them. I knew deep down inside that they were the only thing in this world that would keep me sane and stop me from acting on my primal instincts to attack those that had ruined my life. For now, I needed to make sure that my children would not suffer any worse than what could possibly be avoided. Should I be sentenced to prison time, hurt was going to be unavoidable; I was a large part of their lives, and they would miss my presence, just like I would be missing them.

At this point in time, I had no control over whether I would be getting locked up; you can only worry about things that you have control of. It is very easy to kill yourself trying to control the uncontrollable. I was not going to fall into that trap.

The jury decided to give me back half of my assets, but I knew that the feds were not just going to hand that stuff back to me. If I decided to appeal the jury's verdict, then all assets would be frozen anyway, pending that appeal, and that could be for years to come. I needed to concentrate on building up a reserve of cash for Denise and the kids just in case that rainy day turned into a full-blown hurricane.

Finding a job for the next six weeks would be a waste of my efforts. Besides, how much money could I possibly earn at a regular job in that period of time? No, that was not my answer; poker was. I had almost $5,000 remaining in my possession. I had worked for a lifetime, and now with a wife and children depending on me, I had $5,000 left to my name. My biggest fear was that in six weeks, I would face sentencing, and if I was sentenced to prison, then the judge could remand me to prison right there and then; that's right,

440

get sentenced and handcuffed right there in court and shipped off to a federal prison. I had to be prepared for this terrible but likely scenario.

CHAPTER 167

I started to hit the Hard Rock tournaments hard. I stuck to the high-limit single-table tournaments ($1,050 buy-in) and the Hard Rock's multi-table tournaments ($300–$1,100 buy-ins). The best tournament at the Hard Rock was their Wednesday night $1,100 multi-table tournament. This event drew around eighty of the best players in South Florida every week with a payoff of around $28,000. Not bad for eight to ten hours of work. I did not hit first place either of the first two times that I entered, but I did make it to the final table two weeks in a row, which net me just over $12,000: once again, nice money but still too slow for my situation. I decided to go online and see if I could find a larger tournament with bigger payoff possibilities, and that was when I found the yellow brick road.

On March 4, 2005, Harrah's Hotel and Casino in Las Vegas was holding a World Series of Poker Circuit Event. The buy-in was $10,000, and the best players in the world would be there to compete for a first prize estimated to be around $400,000. That was the ticket; it was time to face the pros and go for the big bucks.

There was one major problem with me going to this world series event. I was on bond. I was a convicted felon that was out of prison on bond pending sentencing. I was not to leave South Florida, never mind actually leaving the state of Florida. Like I said earlier, my brain, my way of thinking, my sanity level at this point had changed. I was no longer thinking on even a semi-human scale. I was shot and running around town like a caged animal that had just escaped for the first time. Fuck these guys. I am going. All I need to do was to play this game of life dirty just like they had been doing.

I told Scott that I wanted to go to Las Vegas and look into the housing market. I told him that when this was all over, I wanted to get out of South Florida, and since I planned on playing poker professionally, I needed to start investigating the Vegas scene. Scott did everything in his powers to stop me from asking the court for permission to travel outside of southern Florida. I was going to be sentenced in three weeks, and the last thing I needed was to ask the courts for a favor. Yeah, yeah, yeah, now file the fucking motion for me, or I will do it myself. That got his attention. The motion was filed the next day, and Judge Cooke approved my travel on the very same day.

CHAPTER 168

My good friend Carrol was a master at traveling the country. When you travel for business, you tend to develop little tricks of the traveling trade, little bits of information that the non-frequent flyer would not think of or maybe not be interested in. Over the years of traveling with Carrol, I had become a master of getting what I wanted or what I needed while I was on the road. The feds were looking for me to slip up. They hated the fact that I had started to play poker again because I was building up a bank roll again; these bastards wanted me broke and in prison. I had a pretty good idea that I had been followed on several occasions, and I had no doubt that they did not want me in Vegas for any reason. That was why I did not tell them about the poker tournament; they surely would have fought for my travel motion to be denied if I was going to play poker, but no, I was going to look into a fresh start for my family.

I decided to play the part to the fullest. I booked a first-class flight to Vegas and a suite at the Mandalay Bay Hotel and Casino. If I had the funds, I would have booked a private jet, but that was just not in the cards right now. Anyway, I was on a mission to build a bankroll.

I arrived in Vegas the day before the tournament started. After I settled into my suite, I put my "cover your ass plan" into effect. Like I said, it was the tricks and tips of the travel trade, tips and tricks! The very first thing that Carrol ever told me was that the senior bellman or the senior valet worker at almost any high-end hotel were the people that could make almost anything happen. Alcohol, drugs, hookers, concert tickets, room upgrades, anything, these were the guys that had the true pulse of the hotel and its surroundings. Forget casino hosts and managers; they have rules that they need to stick to.

Bellmen and valet workers, they had only one rule, "pay me." I made contact with the right bellman at the Mandalay Bay, and I informed him of my very strange request. There was no hesitation on his part.

The bellman said, "No problem, Mr. Foley. I would say that $500 should cover it."

I peeled off five crisp $100 bills, and I sent the young man on his way. We would meet again tomorrow. So what did I ask of this bellman, I am sure that you are wondering? None of your business. How does that sound, none of your damn business? At least not right now it's not. I am sure you will find out later.

I was off to register for the poker tournament and get some practice in at the high-limit tables. I paid $10,000 in cash for my entry into the world series event, and I was informed that I was entrant number 85. The organizers of the event were expecting over one hundred people to be playing, and ESPN was there to cover the action.

I decided to check in at home, and much to my surprise, I got a huge boost of support from Denise. After I spoke to my kids, Denise got back on the phone and simply told me to kick their asses the next day. Kick their asses, why the hell weren't you that supportive of me during our entire marriage? I would have owned Microsoft with encouragement like that. I could have run a marathon when I hung the phone up, and I could have bench pressed 500 lbs. I was just that pumped from hearing my Denise tell me to kick someone's ass in a card game. God did I feel good.

I next called my sister Paula to let her know that I arrived in one piece. Paula's son, Jonathon, was always a big fan of mine when I was playing poker, so he thought this was just the coolest thing. I was going to be playing against every poker player ever seen on TV, and he was going to follow the action on his computer: *Card Player* magazine was also doing event coverage, and they did almost real-time updates on their website with pictures, chip counts, and hand-by-hand descriptions when someone was knocked out. Paula and Jonathan wished me good luck, and I was off to bed for the night. Well, almost. You see, I was so pumped up that I could not sleep a wink. I found myself down at one of the hotel bars at 3:00

a.m. doing shots of vodka that were chasing down painkillers; now doesn't that sound like a great way to kill yourself? Well, it did the trick. I stumbled up to my hotel room after half a bottle of sky vodka was in my system. The great part about being addicted to painkillers (if there is a great part) is that you never wake up with a hangover. That is, of course, as long as you had more pills to continue on your happy little journey, and of course, I came well prepared for this trip. A nice long shower, a hand full of pills chased down by a bottle of mini bar wine, and wah la, I was good to go. Yes, I was as messed up as I sound, except I just did not know it at the time, but fuck it.

CHAPTER 169

I felt pumped up beyond pumped up; it was poker time. One of the best parts of poker tournaments are the sponsors. Poker life is all about glitz, glamour, and sex appeal, and my guess is that all three of those things are what originally attracted me to the game. I arrived at the sponsor's registration table, and these totally hot pieces of ass were there manning the table. I had to take a minute to remember my name, but finally it came back to me. One of the knockouts escorted me to my table and seat assignment, and then she handed me a bio package. Almost every major tournament requires that a bio be filled out by every player just in case you do well, and the TV or radio people want to talk about you on air. I filled out my bio, and I answered it honestly:

> Occupation: unemployed convicted felon
> Favorite hobby: taking dozens of painkillers at
>   one time
> Sex: yes, but not as often as I would like

Well, you get the picture. I am sure the people entering that information into their database had a good old time reading it. Anyway, players were arriving at a steady pace. I recognized plenty of the players from magazines and of course from TV. An announcement was made that we had ten minutes before the first hand would be dealt, so I hunted down a waitress, I ordered a Red Bull and SKYY Vodka, I said a prayer, and it was off to the races.

On the first day of the event, I played fairly conservatively. No-limit Texas hold 'em tournaments are about chip management, patience, and picking battles at the most opportune times. At any given time, another player can move all his chips into play at once (called being all in), and if he or she has more chips than you, then you have the potential of being knocked out of the tournament. Ten thousand dollars is a drop in the bucket to a lot of these players, but to a guy that is about to go to prison and has just been cleaned out by the feds, ten grand is everything, and that definitely put a lot more pressure on me. My big break came when an announcement was made that each table was about to be dealt the last hand before a one-hour dinner break. I was the big blind at my table, which meant that most likely I would get to play this hand for a minimal commitment. Each table has a rotating big and small blind. Let's say that the current "blind levels are $25 and $50." That means that the small blind already has $25 committed to the pot, and the big blind already has $50 committed to the pot. Any player that wants to stay in the hand to see the next three cards, "the flop" must put in at least $50 in chips, or he can raise the pot. In general, hands that take place just before a major break have very little raising action because no one really wants to get hurt badly and then have an hour to think about it. In this current hand, everyone at the table folded their cards except for the small blind. The guy sitting directly next to me (the small blind) told me that he would not let me steal the hand just because it was the last hand. He decided to throw in the additional required $25 in order for him to see the next three cards. Remember, he already had $25 in the pot, so $25 more equaled my $50 blind. Now the first two cards that I was dealt face down were the two and three of clubs: if this numb nut would have raised even the minimal raise before the flop was shown, I would have folded my hand and gone to dinner, but no, he was being cute with me and arrogant. I don't like arrogant people at all. Since most people in the room folded their hands for the dinner break, a crowd started to form around me and Mr. Magoo to see why we were still pressing on. Besides the lunch ordeal, me and the small blind were both well above the average chip count for that phase of the tournament, so other players wanted to get a glimpse of how we were playing. The dealer displayed the flop, ace of clubs, four of clubs, five of clubs. Holy shit, I had flopped a straight flush. This is the second best hand in poker, only inferior to the granddaddy of them all, "the royal flush." So the moron to my right started a little needling speech of how I should fold and how he was going to clean me out; I did not know this guy from any magazine or TV exposure, but he was talking out loud to a fairly large group of spectators, and people seemed to know who he was. Moron bet $300 into a pot of $100; that was a minimal bet. I never once looked at him. I was concentrating on my breathing pattern: good players can pick up on changes in your physical posture, hand movements, facial tics, and yes, breathing patterns. Now I was stoned out of my brains from the painkillers and vodka/Red Bulls, but my heart still started to race.

> Me: I can't let you have it. I can't just give up my blind. You have the wrong guy if you think you are going to bully me out of this hand. (That was my setup to get this arrogant son of a bitch on the defensive.)
>
> Moron: Ladies and gentlemen, what you are about to witness is a free lesson in poker and in how to humble a beginner. This young man to my right is about to find out what it feels like to lose $10,000 before dinner.

Okay, now the entire ballroom was surrounding our table, and I seriously may throw up. I knew what I had, but my mind started to play tricks on me. I wanted to look at my hand again, but that would not be a good idea. I could very easily give my strength away. I sat tight, slouched in my seat to show weakness, and said nothing: I simply reached for $300 in chips, and I threw it toward the pot. The dealer dealt the second-to-last card. "The turn," to me it was meaningless; it was the jack of hearts.

The moron said, "Now I don't want to chase you off, so I am only going to bet $5,000. I want to bleed you slowly."

I got worried again. What the hell was he talking about? $5,000 was a huge raise for that size of pot. I replayed the hand in drug-infested brain, and then it hit me, this guy had a strong hand, nowhere near as strong as mine. But he wanted this audience to show off a good hand. I got this guy. He can't lay down his hand even if he wanted to. Let's test the waters.

I said, "I think you're full of shit. You're trying to buy the pot, and I told you, it's not going to work. I call. (I threw in my $5,000.)

Now all of a sudden, there was excitement in the air. This had just turned into a huge pot for this point in the tournament, maybe the largest of the day. The dealer turned over the last card, "the river." Once again, it was meaningless to me, the jack of diamonds. I shook my head from side to side in fake disgust. I was doing the best I could at acting, but I was not sure if anyone was buying it. Fortunately for me, Moron bought it hook, line, and sinker.

Moron said, "Let's put an end to this. I'm hungry. I am all in."

Moron shoved all his remaining chips toward the dealer. The dealer restacked the chips and advised me that he had bet $38,525. I had $38,750 remaining in my chip stack, so if I won the hand, then moron was out of the tournament.

Moron said, "Come on, stop wasting everyone's time and just fold. You have already wasted enough of your chips. Live to fight another day and let this be a lesson to you. (People started to laugh.)

Professional poker players will tell you about this amazing experience that takes place from time to time, in which you not only know that you have the other guy beaten, but you suddenly know what the other guy's hand was without him even showing you his cards.

Professional poker player Daniel Negreanu is one of the best players ever at calling out players' hands before they revealed their cards; he is amazing. It was at this very moment that I realized what this moron's hand was and just how poorly he actually played it.

I said, "Here is the problem with show-offs like you. You get cute, and you forget the basic rules of poker. Rule number one, never slow play aces. [I was letting him know that his two down cards were aces, which meant that as the hand progressed, he went from two aces to three aces to a full-house aces and jacks.] You let me stay in the hand, you got greedy, and now you are going home. I call."

Moron flipped his two hold cards over to reveal two aces, just as I had called it. I flipped my cards over to reveal my straight flush.

The place went absolutely nuts. Moron just sat there with this look of disbelief on his face. I said nothing else to him. I simply restacked my nearly $90,000 in chips and walked away from the table for my dinner break. Moron did not budge an inch. What an unbelievable feeling that was. I can't even start to tell you how many people approached me during dinner to tell me how well I played that hand, including some of the best pros in the business. My cell phone rang about fifteen minutes into my dinner: it was my nephew Jonathan. He read the update online and saw the pictures of what had taken place. Oh, and by the way, I was now in first place.

CHAPTER 170

The session that took place after the dinner break turned out to be profitable for me. There were no other dramatic moments for me that night, but I did play a very relaxed, very consistent game, and when the final hand or day 1 of the tournament was dealt, I sat comfortably in first place with over $110,000 in chips. How do you like them apples?

I called home and told Denise and my boys the good news. My kids did not understand the gravity of the situation, but I could still hear just how proud they were of me. Denise decided to give me a speech about playing it safe the next day, but then she realized who she was talking to, and she changed her tone to the go-kick-some-ass attitude that I so desperately needed to continue to hear from her.

I decided to get totally shit-faced again that night just as I had done the night before. Why mess with success? I last remember seeing the clock on my cell phone at around 4:00 a.m. Man was I a mess. No biggie, the next day, just wake up, pop the old kill pills, and this time, I decided to head over to the hotel spa. I sat in the steam room for a good forty minutes, and I could actually smell the alcohol pouring out of my sweat glands. The smell would probably make the average person sick to their stomachs, but all it did for me was make me thirsty. I headed to one of the hotel's bars and started to drink. Man, this was the life. Could you imagine doing this every day? I bet you I could last at least a year before my body or brain just exploded and I was dead, but wow, what a great year that would be.

It was time to get back to the poker tournament. I had to actually hurry there because I had lost track of time getting hammered at the bar. Upon arriving at my seat, I unbagged my chips that were waiting for me, and I tell you, I had the darndest time trying to stack them.

For the most part, day 2 of the tournament was uneventful. Player after player got knocked out, and although I ran into an occasional buzz saw, my chip stack grew steadily. There were two highlights for me in day number 2: For the first time in my short poker career, I went face-to-face with a recognized poker professional, Andy Bloch, and I knocked him out of the tournament. Andy was a true professional, and a good sport about it. He simply shook my hand and wished me luck. The second highlight for the day was what I was dreaming about for years. It was the announcement that made me puff my chest up and stand taller than I ever had stood before.

The announcer said, "Ladies and gentlemen, we have just reached our final ten players for the tournament. Play will resume tomorrow until only one of these ten survivors will be left standing."

I had done it. I had made the final table of a world series of poker event on my very first try. I was guaranteed at least $20,000 in cash, but I definitely had my eyes on the first place prize of $380,000 in cash and a world series of poker bracelet to go with it. I would be entering the final table in sixth out of tenth place, but the chip counts were so close that no player had a real advantage. This is of course as long as you are not counting experience as an advantage. The pros that were left were Chris "Jesus" Ferguson, JC TRAN, John Pham, and Gavin Smith. Doyle Brunson, Johnny Chan, Phil Ivey, Phil Hellmuth, Annie Duke, Andy Bloch, and many other great names in poker did not make the cut, but Tom Foley did. What a freakin' trip.

Once again, I made my calls home, and I was greeted like a war hero. My kids were just out of their minds when they heard that I had made the final table, and Denise was suddenly my biggest supporter and fan. I also called my sister Paula so that I could check in with my nephew Jonathan, and they too were just at a loss for words that I was able to get this far in the tournament.

When I was alone in my hotel room, I could not help but to stop and think about what led me to this point in time. What a crazy chain of events that led me to be here in Las Vegas, playing at the final table of a World Series of Poker Circuit Event. I tried my hardest not to overthink the reality of what was taking place. I needed to compromise with my own mind, stay in fantasy land, but at the same time realize the gravity of the situation. I mean, this was a life-changing event for my family, but I got there because I was living in this drug-induced fantasy world, and I needed to stay there until this event was over. I know this all sounds crazy, but this is the crazy shit that ran through my head while I was by myself in Las Vegas. That, my friends, is some pretty scary shit. I played most of the tournament wearing an American Flag do-rag on my head. I wanted to show my continued patriotism despite what had taken place over the past two years with the feds.

CHAPTER 171

The next day when I showed up at the final table, I was nowhere near hammered enough to play, so I ran to one of the hotel bars and pounded down some shots of vodka. I jammed a good fifteen pills into my system, and with almost no time to spare, I took my final seat; so much for trying to play sober. What was I thinking with that one?

Within the first two hours of play, two of the remaining ten players had been knocked out. I hated the way that I was playing: I was playing to simply survive and not to win; I was playing scared. This was not my game, and it was not giving me a chance to win this thing. By the time that I realized just how shitty I was playing, it was too late. I had donated almost two-thirds of my chip stack to the pros, and I almost appeared happy to do it. God was I mad at myself. I started to play poker the way I had learned to play poker, aggressive and calculated. I pushed when the odds and percentages told me to push, I started to get a feel for the other players' games and moves, and then it happened: I found myself in a heads-up drawn-out battle with Chris "Jesus" Ferguson. Chris plays with a very deliberate and calculated style. He appears to be in deep thought every time it is his time to make a decision, and he never makes quick moves. At this time in the tournament, Chris was the chip leader, and he was building up a head of steam. Chris made a move on me on the flop of our heads-up battle. I was holding pocket 8s, and the flop had shown no card greater than a seven, yet Chris was pushing hard. My read on him was that he was playing two over cards that he had not yet paired up on, so this would be my opportunity to push back. I decided to raise all in. I pushed my remaining chips into the pot, and I sat motionless. Chris thought long and hard, and finally he gave it a "what the heck," and he called me. My problem at that point was that I did not have enough chips to scare Chris off; it was worth it for him to take a shot at knocking out another player, and if he lost the hand, well, he would still be in the lead, so why not? Chris turned over his cards: the jack and ten of hearts. I had read his hand right, and I had placed my tournament at risk with the best hand in play. I could not ask for any more. Poker is a skill game. You need to be good with percentages, you need to be observant, and you need to be good with psychological warfare, but poker also has a luck factor involved, and there is no professional in the world that can control that part of the game.

The cameras were on me and Chris; the table was waiting for the dealer. The turn card was the ace of spades; I was still in the lead with one more card to go. The river card made Chris a river rat, the ten of hearts. Chris had a pair of tens, and I had a pair of eights: tournament over, at least for me. Chris was a true professional and a good sport. He walked around the table, shook my hand, and told me that he knew that he would be seeing me at another final table someday. I did a quick interview with *Card Player* magazine and with ESPN, and then I was walked up to the casino floor to get paid. My winnings were just over $43,000, not bad for three days' work but not what I was looking for. As I took a moment to reflect on my play, I was happy with what I had done right up to the final table, but once there, I really did not do myself any justice. Bottom of the ninth, two outs bases loaded with a three ball and two-strike count on me. Why the hell did I just sit there and look at strike number 3? That was how I felt at the time.

So it was time to go home. I hunted down my bellman friend, who handed me a legal-size envelope with his completed mission inside. I reviewed the effort that he had done for me, and I was more than happy with his effort. I threw my new friend another $500, and then it was off to the airport for my flight home.

CHAPTER 172

J ust as a point of fact, or maybe it's another one of my life's mottos, I strongly believe in overtipping. I do not tip well when a service is shit, but when a person who works for tips does their job well, or goes above and beyond the call of duty, then I make sure that they know how I feel. You never know when your paths are going to cross again in this crazy world.

I have to tell you a quick funny story now that I have mentioned tipping. Back when Denise and I were first living together up in New York, we went to the Light House Diner for dinner one night. Denise and I both ordered complete dinners, which came with soup and salad. That evening, Denise was not in the mood for soup, and I was in the mood for soup. Denise informed the waitress that I would be eating both soups that night, so if she could please bring both soups and salads at the same time, that would be great. The waitress refused to do so. This witch told me that once I was finished with one soup, she would bring me another one, and Denise could not have her salad until the soups were finished. Seriously, this bitch went on about the diner's policy about sharing food and all this crap. I remember asking her if she thought she was my mother when she was instructing me what I could eat and when I could eat it. Anyway, after a heated exchange, the diner manager stepped in and gave us our order the way we asked for it. I left that rude bitch a $0.16 tip that night just to let her know what her services were worth, and to be honest with you, I overpaid her. Okay, sorry, that was just a funny moment in time.

CHAPTER 173

I arrived back to Florida to a hero's welcome from my children and a "so tell me what happened" from Denise. She was trying to figure out how I screwed up at the final table. Whatever. I placed my winnings in our safe, and I settled back into the reality that I was going to be sentenced in two weeks.

Scott and I had to meet with pretrial services so that a probation officer could interview me. This "independent" employee of the federal government would be creating an "independent" presentence investigation report (PSI) that would be given to Judge Cooke to help determine what kind of sentence I should be given. My PSI would include everything from my upbringing, my family, my education, previous arrests, drug or alcohol addictions, and of course, her version of how the now advisory federal sentencing guidelines should be applied to my case. Now listen, Scott informed me to tell this lady the truth, but he also advised me that this report was going to be used by Judge Cooke to help determine what kind of a threat to society I was, so you read between the lines. I saw it as a very bad thing if Judge Cooke was to suddenly find out that I was addicted to painkillers for over three years and that I was pounding alcohol along with those damn pills; that just sounded like I was and would continue to be a menace to society, so I decided to lie.

The lady that did my PSI interview was a combination of *Sesame Street's* Big Bird and the creature from the movie *Alien*. She was just one big, unattractive, annoying creature. She shot off question after question, and she even started her next question before I was finished answering previous questions. It became obvious to me that she did not want to be there. She hated her job, and in return, she was not listening to a word I said. I denied any drug or alcohol use, and I answered her questions like that of a saint. On paper, Tom Foley was a perfect little angel. The PSI would be sent to Scott by Big Bird Alien before my sentencing day. Scott would have time to review the PSI and file objections to the report via a court motion if needed.

Once the PSI was in Scott's possession, I met with Scott to go over its contents. I should have known right there and then that I was in bigger trouble than I ever knew. The PSI came back recommending that my federal sentencing guideline level be set at a calculated level of 31. What? 31? Scott had told me before trial that if I was convicted of all counts of the indictment, then I was facing a maximum level of 24, which carried a potential prison exposure of 51–63 months. The level 31 recommended by the PSI carried a potential prison exposure of 108–135 months. Now the jury found me not guilty of the majority of the charges. How the hell could my guideline level have increased?

To make things even worse, the government filed objections to the PSI findings; they insisted that my offense level should be a level 38, which carries a prison exposure of 235–298 months in prison. To say that I freaked out would be an understatement. I needed Scott to explain to me how and why these people were coming up with these ridiculous sentencing suggestions. Although he tried to play it cool, I could tell that Scott was taken aback by the calculations in the PSI. Scott told me that he would file objections to the findings and that we would argue this out in front of Judge Cooke; he insisted that the feds were just trying to beef up the sentencing levels in an attempt to downplay the jury's findings. I had no idea what that meant. I had a jury trial, a jury made their decision, and now I had to live with the consequences. Please don't tell me that I still had more to worry about, please.

CHAPTER 174

In preparation for sentencing day, Scott decided to sit me down and have a heart-to-heart talk with me. I kind of felt like he was trying to talk to me like a father would talk to his son. Scott wanted me to know that besides the PSI, Judge Cooke would be considering other factors in determining my sentence, things like my previous involvement with charities, ties that I had made to the South Florida community, my role as a husband and father, and the granddaddy of the all, "Was I willing to accept responsibility for the crimes that I was convicted of?" You have got to be kidding me. Scott asked me if I wanted to have any family members or friends speak to Judge Cooke at my sentencing. I told him that I did not. I had put my friends and family through enough, and I did not need to put more pressure on anyone to try and make this right for me. Besides, I saw that as a retarded waste of the court's time. Scott asked me if I planned on making a statement on my own behalf, and the answer to that question was, "You bet your ass I do. I still have plenty to say about what has taken place."

This was where Scott begged and pleaded with me to not only refrain from attacking the feds at my sentencing, but he also wanted me to admit to my guilt, apologize, and accept responsibility for what had happened at Global. Hmmm, let me think about that for a short moment. Are you fucking kidding me? Are you completely off your rocker? I would rather get the electric chair than to have to get up in front of this judge and admit to committing a crime that I not only did not commit, but it never fucking happened. Man, I have to tell you, I was not happy with my attorney at this point. Did he not learn anything about me over the past year and a half? I mean, with all that these fucks had put me through, there was no way in hell that

460

I would lay down and roll over now. Come on, Scott, get yourself a set of balls and just one ounce of self-pride and dignity. I fully understand what was at stake here, but my life had been compromised enough, and I would not let anyone take away the one thing that I still had control over, my pride, or maybe it was self-respect. Sorry, Scott, no deal, I will be speaking on my own behalf at sentencing, and it will be from my heart; if Judge Cooke saw that as a bad thing, then so be it.

CHAPTER 175

A few days before sentencing, I received a call from Scott who once again had some bad news for me. The government had filed a motion with the court to have my bond revoked and to have me immediately sent to prison pending sentencing. Scott went on to tell me that the government's grounds for requesting my bond being revoked was based on the fact that I had lied to the court about my reasons for having to travel to Las Vegas. The government's motion was filled with pictures of me playing poker at the World Series of Poker event. Scott went on an "I told you so" rampage even though he had no idea that I went to Vegas to play poker. Scott just did not think it was a good idea for me to travel at all. Scott also could not figure out how the feds could have possibly found out about the tournament when it was not even scheduled to air on ESPN for months to come. Scott saw this as a huge problem for me. I would of course have a chance to answer to these allegations, but since it was so close to my sentencing date, that response would have to take place right there in front of Judge Cooke. Scott turned to me for help. He had no idea how he could defend against the obvious. I mean, they had pictures of me and downloads from poker websites, and they even had a copy of the receipt from the casino cage that showed my winnings. Man, oh, man, those FBI agents were hard at work.

> Me: Don't you worry your pretty little self there, Scotty. I will address this little problem when the time is right.
>
> Scott: What the hell are you talking about, Tom? These people are going to take you to prison right there and then. This is not some game.

Me: That's where you are wrong, Scott. This is
the ultimate game that these fucks are playing with my life, and don't you ever forget
one thing. This is my life, not yours. Maybe
they can pull off their little smoke-and-mirror show once, but I want to see how they
feel when someone pulls one off on them.
You just do your job and figure out the sentencing crap. Let me worry about my bond
being revoked. End of conversation.

When I hung up on Scott that day, I actually ran to my bathroom mirror and stood there staring at myself for a good long while. I
had a smile on my face from ear to ear. No, I was not crazy; yes, I had
a ridiculous amount of painkillers in my system. But just remember
one thing, folks. Things are not always as they appear, and if you
are going to be a professional investigator, let's say like an FBI agent
or something, you need to remember never to underestimate your
opponent, and you especially better do your own homework from
time to time. Just because you succeeded while being sloppy and lazy
in the past, it does not mean that sloppy and lazy will work in the
future, especially if your opponent is counting on that.

CHAPTER 176

Sentencing day has arrived for me, and as I get myself ready this morning, I find myself taking long hard looks around my house, my dream-house-turned-nightmare. I did not sleep well at all last night. I was walking through the house making frequent stops at Thomas's and Jake's rooms to just stare at them sleeping. I don't know how I would handle it if Judge Cooke sent me right to prison from court today. I would not have had a chance to explain things to my kids or to say goodbye to them. Reality was smacking me in the face, and it hurt like hell. I did my best to stay positive and to stay focused on the task at hand; that was all that this day really was anyway, just another task that needed to be handled with care, or at least I convinced myself of that.

Denise was not coming to my sentencing. I did not expect her to be there, and to be honest with you, I did not want her to be there. If Denise was present in the courtroom, there would be a good chance that I would not be the outgoing rebel that I felt I needed to be right to the end of this legal challenge. I could not fold and hide in a shell like I did at the final table of my recent poker tournament. No, Judge Cooke needed to see the real Tom Foley and judge the real Tom Foley for what he was, not for what he could pretend to be.

I met Jesus for the final time at the same corner of the Gratny Parkway. I am glad I made that last stop to see him because this one-legged homeless man had a way about him that just made me relax and feel more secure about my situation. Maybe it was the fact that he was homeless. He was in a worse position than I was. I don't know. Maybe it just made me feel good to do what I liked to do best: help others. Jesus said goodbye to me and told me to keep a stiff upper lip while I was talking in front of the judge; that sounded like my type of advice. I shook the hand of Jesus as we said goodbye, and that, my friends, was a special moment. After all, how many people can say they shook the hand of Jesus?

I arrived in court early as usual, except this time, Scott had beaten me there. He looked more nervous than I was. Scott asked me if I had taken care of my personal affairs just in case I was remanded to prison. I handed Scott my car keys and asked him to let Ford Motor Company know where my car was just in case I was sent off to prison. I also handed him my wallet and cash with instructions to give them to my wife if the shit hit the fan today.

With all parties accounted for, the court was now in session. Before a defendant is sentenced, any open motions have to be heard first. The government had two open motions (one to revoke my bond and one to object to the sentencing level in the PSI). Scott had one open motion, and that was our objections to the PSI sentencing level. The first motion to be heard was the motion to revoke my bond. Prosecutor Reinhart went off on me big-time. I was a con man, a thief, a big phony, except this time, I did not steal money. No, this time, I stole the court's integrity by lying about my trip to Las Vegas. The prosecutor told the judge that I never had any intentions of exploring the possibilities of moving my family to Las Vegas. No, Tom Foley lied to you, Your Honor. He cannot be trusted to be out on bond anymore. AUSA Reinhart called Agent Delano to the stand for testimony on my trip to Las Vegas.

Agent Delano said, "Yes, a confidential informant tipped me off to the fact that Tom Foley was playing in a high-stakes poker tournament in Las Vegas. I have dozens of pictures of Mr. Foley at the tournament. Mr. Foley never once made an attempt to look into housing or schools or job markets in Las Vegas as he stated in his motion to travel. No, Tom Foley is a gambling addict that simply lied to this court."

Confidential informant? Hm, I wonder who that could be. Sure enough, I turned around, and sitting in the back of the courtroom was none other than Alan Nudelman. Yes, Alan, my former business partner, my ex-brother-in-law, the man who filed the original complaint with the FBI. Hook, line, and sinker, folks. Hook, line, and sinker. I scanned the courtroom and saw my father, my sister Paula, and my cousin John. I gave them all a big Tom Foley wink. I guess I must have had a smile on my face because Scott asked me under his breath what I was so happy about and then asked me what I wanted him to tell these people. Tighten up, Scott. Tighten up. I got this one.

When the prosecutor was finished questioning Agent Delano, Judge Cooke asked Scott if he wanted to cross-examine the witness. I stood to my feet and informed the judge that I would be questioning this witness. After a brief exchange between Scott, the prosecutor, and Judge Cooke, it was decided that there was nothing legally stopping me from questioning a witness at my own sentencing, so off I went.

> Me: Agent Delano, you claim that you were tipped off about my activities in Las Vegas by a confidential informant. Is that right?
>
> Agent Delano: Yes.
>
> Me: Is that informant in the courtroom today?
>
> Agent Delano: I don't have to answer that question.
>
> Me: Sure you do. It's a simple question. I am not asking you to tell me who the informant is. I am just asking you if that person is in the courtroom. I have a right to face my accusers, don't I?
>
> Judge Cooke: Please answer the question.
>
> Agent Delano: Yes, he is in the courtroom.
>
> Me: I thought so. Seeing that I am sure it is not one of my family members, and it can't be you or Mr. Reinhart, I feel comfortable ruling out the court reporter and Judge Cooke, so let's see who is left. Ohhh, there in the back in the last row, that's Alan Nudelman, the same man who was the original confidential informant in this case. The man who forgot to tell you about the shared location

program, the same man that you yourself told this court had lied in your affidavit in order to get a search-and-seizure warrant on my house. Well, welcome to court, Mr. Nudelman. I am glad you finally crawled out from under your rock. You should be ashamed of yourself, young man.

Agent Delano: Mr. Foley, pictures don't lie. Poker websites and ESPN don't lie. Mr. Nudelman simply told us what you were up to. I made sure that his allegations were real.

Me: Real, yes, but just like your investigation into Global Vending, you were sloppy, lazy, and you did not do a complete investigation. You really should stop relying on Mr. Nudelman's bad tips. They are going to kill your career.

Agent Delano: What are you getting at?

Me: Well, I am glad you asked that question. First of all, Agent Delano, is it against the law to play poker in Las Vegas?

Agent Delano: No, but it is against the law to lie in a motion to the court.

Me: True, but once again, you are assuming things, and you know how that old saying goes. Well, I won't repeat it. Anyway, I repeat my question, is it illegal to play poker in Las Vegas?

Agent Delano: No.

Me: (very, very sarcastically) Thank God because if it was illegal to play poker in Las Vegas, then I would be screwed big-time. Okay, so you saw me playing legal poker in Las Vegas. Did you know that I also ate breakfast, lunch, and dinner each day while I was in Vegas?

Agent Delano: I'm sure you did.

Me: Well, my motion to the court does not say anything about me eating while I was in Vegas, but yet I still had time to eat. Does the court have a problem with me eating in Las Vegas?

Judge Cooke: Mr. Foley, the prosecution is alleging that you lied to this court in order to get permission from me to go to Las Vegas. You listed in your motion that your primary reason for the need to travel was to investigate possibly relocating your family there, not to go there and play poker. The prosecution submits that you never looked into relocating to Las Vegas, and if that is true, then you lied to this court, and your bond will be revoked.

Me: Fair enough, Your Honor. I want you to know that I went to Las Vegas to seriously consider moving my family there. There are just too many bad memories here, and we will all need a fresh start when this is over. My problem here once again is that Agent Delano sucks at her job, and her continuing belief in that lowlife at the back of the courtroom. I will prove to this court that Agent Delano is desperate to make me look bad for this sentencing, and Alan Nudelman is just a vindictive person that cannot be trusted. (At this point, I reached into my briefcase, and I pulled out a file folder which I had marked "Las Vegas" in red marker.) Your Honor, I did play poker while I was in Las Vegas, but that is not the primary reason that I went to Las Vegas. First of all, I would like to show you a copy of my tournament registration form from that Poker event. What you will find is that I was a last-minute walk-in participant. I did not preregister to play. I know that does not tell you very much, but I am testifying to you that this was not planned. Poker helps me to relax, and it is one of the things that I enjoy in life. I have a folder here that contains business cards from the real estate agents that I met with while I was in Vegas. I looked at eight properties in all, and I have the floor plans here along with my notes of what I liked and disliked. I also have information that I picked up from the Las Vegas Chamber of Commerce that discusses the job markets in Las Vegas. I also have information from the two grade schools that I paid visits to so that my wife could research the schools for my children. I even have receipts from meals that I shared with the real estate agents while we were running around town. So I don't know why the hell Agent Delano, the prosecutor, and this piece of shit Alan Nudelman are continuing to try and make me look like a bad person, and I really don't care. I just want you to know that I filed my motion to travel in good faith, and I did what I told you I was going to do while I was there. The rest of these allegations are garbage. I have nothing else to say on this matter.

The courtroom was silent. Scott was even at a loss for words. Agent Delano sat in the witness stand like an ugly beaten stepchild. The prosecutor never looked up.

Judge Cooke looked over my Las Vegas materials.

Judge Cooke said, "I find that Mr. Foley's motion to travel was made in good faith, and the government's request to have his bond revoked is DENIED. You are dismissed, Agent Delano.

Well, it cost me $1,000, but that bellman at the Mandalay Bay Hotel and Casino sure did a good job being me in Las Vegas. He did just as I asked him to do; he went and looked at houses with real estate agents, he collected floor plans, he went to the Chamber of Commerce, and he went to the grade schools and collected information at each stop as requested. The receipts from his meals were his own little added icing on the cake, and I gave him props for that. I hate the fact that I used my nephew Jonathan for my little con, but I knew that he would tell his father exactly what I was doing in Las Vegas, not because he wanted to get me in trouble but because he was really that proud of me. I also knew that Alan was a big enough piece of shit to call the feds on me; add to that the fact that Agent Delano was a lazy piece of shit. I now look like I am being picked on, and I now have Alan in the courtroom looking like the vindictive piece of shit that he really was. Hannibal always used to say on the series *The A-Team*, "I love it when a plan comes together."

CHAPTER 177

Well, with that little bit of excitement out of the way, it was time for the main event. It was time for Scott and the prosecutor to address their concerns about the PSI, and then it would be time for Judge Cooke to sentence me. I hope that none of you reading this ever has to go through this process because it is one of the worst feelings in the world: another human being that knows very little about you is going to decide how your immediate future is going to play out. A federal judge has that power, and after all the debating and pleading are done, the judge has the power to do whatever he or she chooses to do with your life. I am no control freak, but this is my life we are talking about, and the fact that I was at her mercy really sucked. The judge read the PSI and then first asked for the prosecutor to address his concerns.

The prosecutor argued that the PSI underestimated the number of people that were victims and the amount of losses that they suffered. He pointed out a paragraph in the indictment that was boldly titled "Overall scheme to defraud." This paragraph laid claim that I defrauded hundreds of investors out of more than $7 million. The prosecutor claimed that the individual charges listed in the indictment were just vehicles that were used to prove parts of the overall scheme to defraud. According to the prosecutor, by the jury finding me guilty of one count of fraud, the jury was actually agreeing that I had devised and executed this overall scheme to defraud. The prosecutor showed the judge that once you consider every customer to be a victim, and all their investments were now losses, then the guidelines called for a sentencing level 38, and my prison sentence should be over twenty years. Believe me, folks, this is not something that you want a judge to even be considering when it is you that could be slapped with a twenty-year prison term. I went absolutely numb at this point.

Scott argued that the prosecutor was trying to expand the scope of the indictment. He argued that there were five specific charges of fraud in the indictment and three specific victims listed in the indictment. That was all. Scott continued by reminding the judge that I was only found guilty of defrauding one customer and that I could only be held liable for the losses of that one victim. Scott insisted that my sentencing level should reflect one victim and his losses, thus putting me at a sentencing level of 19, which carried a prison exposure of twenty-seven to thirty-two months in prison. Scott then argued that Judge Cooke should depart downward from the level 19 on the grounds that I was a first-time nonviolent offender. I was a family man with strong ties to the South Florida community, I had done extensive work with multiple charities in the past, and I was no threat to society as a whole. Putting me in prison would accomplish nothing.

Judge Cooke made notes during each argument. When both Scott and the prosecutor were finished, Judge Cooke asked me if I had anything to say on my own behalf. I did. I took a few deep breaths as I approached the podium. I knew what I wanted to say, and I hoped and prayed for just a moment in time that I would have the strength to get my thoughts out in a clear and convincing manner.

I started my speech by thanking Judge Cooke's staff for their professionalism and for their kindness throughout my trial. I then started to explain how disappointed I was that a system that I believed so strongly in had let me down. I made it clear to the judge that at no time did I ever have any intent to defraud any customer of Global Vending. I repeated my argument that no customer of Global Vending had to suffer any losses. I went on to describe the hard work and effort that I had put in to get Global Vending to operate at such a high level of profitability and integrity. I slung mud at the FBI and at the prosecutor for their lies and deception before, during, and now after trial. They were a disgrace to the United States of America. I pointed out Alan Nudelman to Judge Cooke once again, and I made it clear to her that only a vindictive person like him would show up on my sentencing day. Alan had lied to the FBI and to the prosecutor, and when the feds realized that he had lied to them, they should have just walked away. Instead, they attacked an innocent man and his family: that was the only crime that took place here. I compared Global Vending to a hospital in which Alan had made claim that I was abusing a dying patient, and when the FBI showed up to shut down my hospital, they quickly realized that my patients were doing just fine. Instead of just leaving my hospital quietly, the FBI decided to shoot each of my patients in the head. Now I was being held liable for their deaths. That sounds extreme, but that was what happened. I told Judge Cooke that I would take responsibility for what took place at Global Vending and for my customers' demise. I was the CEO and president of the company, and the buck stopped with me. I would take responsibility for what happened, but not because I had defrauded anyone. No, I would take responsibility because it was my decision to introduce Alan Nudelman into Global Vending, and that was my one fatal decision that I made at Global.

I said, "Look at me for what I am now but also for what I have been over the course of my lifetime. I am a proud father of two young boys. I am a Christian. I am an American citizen that deserves to be treated better than I have been treated over the past year and a half. I will accept any mercy that you sent my way, Your Honor, but I will not beg for it. I can simply hope and pray that you can see the good that I have inside of me. Thank you for your time.

At this point, there was dead silence in the courtroom. Judge Cooke made note after note on her legal pads; she called over the PSI lady and asked her some questions that we could not hear, and then it was time.

Judge Cooke was ready to sentence me. She asked me to rise for my sentencing; I complied. She started by going over the sentencing guideline arguments that both sides had offered. It was at this point that Judge Cooke showed what I would call a weakness. Judge Cooke could not make a clear decision, so she split the road so to speak. Judge Cooke set my sentencing guideline level at a level 31, which carried a prison exposure of 108–135 months. It was just a coincidence that the PSI had suggested a level 31. Judge Cooke used her own equation to get to this level: she used part of what the jury had decided, part of what the prosecutor had asked for, and part of what Scott had argued for.

Her decision to this point was 100 percent middle-of-the-road compromise, an attempt to appease all parties. I was not appeased at all. Judge Cooke then continued to explain that she now had to consider if there were grounds for her to depart from the suggested sentencing level of 31. Judge Cooke explained to us that for the first time in her extensive legal career, she now found herself in untested waters. She explained that there was a jury verdict in front of her that read "guilty" as to one count of fraud, yet standing in front of her was a man that not only continued to proclaim his innocence, but he also refuses to compromise his integrity by fully accepting responsibility for what had taken place in this case. Judge Cooke made a statement that she felt the jury had made a compromised decision with their partial guilty verdict and that she herself still had some doubts of what had actually taken place at Global. She then reiterated that I had no criminal past, that I was a family man, and that she was taken in by the fact that I was sticking to my guns and not making a last-minute apology to the court. Judge Cooke decided to make a downward departure.

Judge Cooke issued me a prison term of seventy-five months in prison that would be followed by two years of supervised release. There would be a restitution hearing the following week in order to determine how much of the customers' losses I would have to repay. I would not be remanded to prison today. That date would be set after the restitution hearing. Court adjourned.

Seventy-five months in prison, just over six years of my life. I suddenly felt weak in the legs. I sat down in pure disbelief. Crazy thoughts filled my head: my children were now five and eight years old. They would be eleven and fourteen years old by the time I was released; that just did not sit well with me at all. For the second time since this nightmare started, I found myself with tears in my eyes. My sister, father, and cousin gave me hugs and words of encouragement, but there was nothing that they could say or do to take this empty, lost feeling out of the pit of my stomach. This was just not right.

CHAPTER 178

Scott and I decided to meet the next day to discuss the restitution hearing and a possible appeal of my conviction, but for now, I needed some alone time with my family. The news of my sentence did not seem to affect Denise very much; she was sad but certainly not out-of-her-mind sad. Things were still up in the air as to when I would have to report to prison, but one thing was for sure, I would never be the same person again. My life had just changed forever.

For the first time since I had been married to Denise, I actually started to consider that I should get a divorce. I just did not see how our relationship could possibly survive while I was in prison. Out of pure respect for Denise, and love for my children, I decided to leave things the way that they were for now and let her make that decision for us.

Once Scott and I were back together, another piece of good news was laid in my lap (sarcastically speaking, of course): the government had already filed a notice of appeal; they were appealing my sentence and how it was calculated. Can you believe this? These motherfuckers were not happy with me going to prison for "only" six years of my life; no, they wanted more. All I wanted at this time was a little fucking closure on this matter. Was that asking for too much? Now decisions had to be made again. Was I going to cross-appeal my conviction? If so, who would represent me? How would I be able to pay them? Things were just getting worse and worse for me by the day. At the very moment that I felt the walls of life crumbling in around me, the grace of God shined down on me. The Bible says that God will only give you challenges that you are strong enough to handle, and then he will intervene on your behalf. That is, of course, assuming that you truly believe in God. I always have believed in the man upstairs. Heck, I had been buying him doughnuts and coffee for the past month or so.

I feel that I was blessed with God's grace during my restitution hearing. The hearing itself could not have gone worse. The government sent in a restitution and forfeiture special prosecutor named Mr. Beckerleg. This guy was a number 1 prick and a half. The good news for me was that Mr. Reinhart was not in the courtroom at all that day. Mr. Beckerleg assumed full government representation for the day. He ran circles around Scott on the restitution issues at hand. In the end, I was not only ordered to pay every customer back every dime that they invested, but I was also ordered to forfeit the assets that the jury had awarded back to me. So much for my jury verdict. That went down the shitter like it never took place. Anyway, Mr. Beckerleg then argued that I should be evicted from my house immediately and my house should be sold at a government auction. Because I still had appellate rights, and the government had already filled a notice of appeal, evicting me was not a legal option. Judge Cooke ordered that all my assets be frozen until all my appellate rights had been exhausted.

Judge Cooke did however ask me to do the court a "favor" and at least consider letting the government sell my house. Bank fees and unpaid taxes were building up quickly, and my house would soon become a liability rather than an asset. I felt like telling the good judge to shove her favor up her asshole, but that would probably get me a one-way ticket to prison ASAP.

No, I decided instead to negotiate with the court. Everything in life is negotiable, my friends, everything. I told Judge Cooke that I would hire a licensed real estate agent to immediately place my house on the market for a fair price, not some government auction price. I also agreed to let Mr. Beckerleg have the final say on any offer made on my house. In return for this "favor," I asked Judge Cooke to issue me an appeal bond that would keep me out of prison until the appellate process was over. Now just for the record, appeal bonds are almost never issued. The government always fights the issuance of appeal bonds, and they win that argument 99.9 percent of the time. This is not up to the judge though; the government has to argue why I should not be issued an appeal bond, and the problem for the government in my case was that the prosecutor was not present. Mr. Beckerleg had no idea what he was doing; he simply responded, "Sounds fair to me, Your Honor." And just like that, I was issued a new bond that would keep me free until the appeals ended: that could take years. I saw this moment as God intervening on my behalf. I could now continue to raise my young boys, I could help my family financially, and I could get them settled in to a new life without having to worry about getting rushed off to prison. That is, of course, as long as I did not violate the rules of my bond. Not a day goes by that I don't stop for a moment and thank God for that help.

CHAPTER 179

I shopped around with other attorneys to see if I could find one that I could afford to represent me during the government's appeal and also help me file my own appeal, but the fees that were suggested to me were just crazy. I had a long trial and a very complicated case, and potential appellate attorneys would have to spend a lot of time getting caught up on how I got to this point in time. I just did not have anywhere near the money needed.

Scott on the other hand would not need to be brought up to speed. He was there the whole time, and he of course knew exactly how we got to this point in time. I was hesitant to use his services again because I just could not get over the fact that he had misled me on my potential prison exposure at the time that the government offered me a plea deal. Had I known that there was a possibility of me facing twenty plus years in prison, I would have most likely taken the government's plea offer of five years. I am nuts, but I am not that nuts. That is almost a life sentence.

Anyway, Scott said he would handle my appeals for another $60,000. I know that sounds like a lot of money, but that was a third of what other competent attorneys were asking for. I set up a three-payment plan with him, and that was that.

I called my stepfather-in-law, Lenny the Drunk, to see if he wanted to take on the task of selling my house. Lenny not only jumped at the opportunity, but he promised me that he was going to give me and Denise his commission once the house was sold. I had made Lenny a small fortune in commissions in the past, and he felt that was the least he could do for me, his stepdaughter, and his grandchildren. We listed the house at $3.8 million, and if the house sold at that price, Lenny's commission would be almost $100,000.

I also told Lenny to ask potential buyers to purchase the furniture from my house as a completely separate transaction from the house sale. I would discount the house heavily for anyone willing to buy my furniture. I could go as low as $3.2 million and still break even with the mortgage company and tax collector. The furniture money and Lenny's commission would be a hell of a restart for Denise and the boys. For now, I had to start to look for a local rental just in case my house sold quickly, and I also had to look for a job as that was a requirement of my appeal bond.

To say that Prosecutor Reinhart completely lost his shit when he found out about my appeal bond would be a huge understatement; he went ballistic. Mr. Reinhart filed motion after motion objecting to the issuance of my appeal bond, but it was too late for him. A government representative, Mr. Beckerleg, had agreed to the bond, and there was no way of taking that back. Ha ha. Mr. Reinhart went even crazier when he heard that I was being allowed to sell my own house on my own terms.

One day, I received a call from Scott, and he informed me that Mr. Reinhart wanted me out of my house now, and to get me out, he was offering me $150,000 from my assets that were being held. I had a long discussion with Denise and Lenny, and then I decided to turn the prosecutor down on his offer: number 1, I would get more than that once my house sold and my furniture sold; number 2, I was living rent-free right now, and the cheapest Weston rental that I had found was $2,500 per month; and number 3, fuck him, fuck this guy that wanted to see my family thrown out of their home. He was a little piece of shit, and it felt good to see him kicking and screaming like a little child. Don't get me wrong, if I was not getting Lenny's commission or money for my furniture, then I would have jumped at the prosecutor's offer.

CHAPTER 180

I had a pretty strong feeling that Judge Cooke and my probation officer would note considering playing poker to be a full-time job so I would have to play at night and on the weekends, but during the day, I needed a "real job." I decided to open up a commercial swimming pool company that would specialize in chemical delivery. I had done some extensive research on this small niche business, and I saw that it could have huge income potential if it was set up properly. I incorporated under the name Blue Horseshoe. For those of you who saw the original movie *Wall Street*, Blue Horseshoe was the code name that broker "Bud Fox" (Charlie Sheen) used when he called the *Wall Street Journal* to start insider trading in motion action. Remember? He would say, "Blue Horseshoe loves Anacott Steel." Anyway, I used that name for my new company just for kicks.

Some of you might be wondering where I found the strength and drive to start a new company with all that I had been through, and my answer is simple: this is me, this is what I do, this is how I think. I get knocked down, and then I bounce back up looking for more. I just have a relentless drive built into my system that I cannot shut off, nor would I want to shut it off.

I pounded the pavement for several weeks, and I was able to convince some high-end commercial properties to try my chemical delivery service. I also offered these new accounts repair services if they were needed. Within a few short months, I was operating at almost full capacity and making a monthly profit of over $10,000. Now when I say full capacity, keep in mind that I was only working four days per week and about six hours a day. The rest of my time was needed for poker, rest, and my children. Both of my kids were playing in YMCA sports by now, and I was the coach of every team that they played on: football, basketball, baseball. It didn't matter, I wanted to be a part of their lives, and my boys and I continued to do some serious bonding.

Chapter 181

As the summer of 2005 started, I started to take my kids with me while I delivered pool chemicals and did repairs. The three of us made a great team, with the highlight of the day always being lunch at one of our favorite fast-food joints: perhaps someday the pool company would be renamed Foley and Sons.

As luck would have it, my house sold fairly quickly. Lenny found a buyer that not only loved the house, but he also loved the furniture. Lenny went over the specifics of how the furniture needed to be a separate deal from the house, and the new buyer was more than happy to agree to the terms as long as the price of the house was dropped. We settled on $3.4 million for the house and $100,000 for the furniture.

I finally found a very nice house for rent in one of the newest developments in the town of Weston. The rent was $2,600 per month, but it had excellent public schools and lots of kids in the neighborhood for my kids to play with. I could not allow a credit check to be pulled on myself or my wife due to the damage that the feds had done during their siege on my financials, so I paid for the entire year's rent up front.

Denise and I did the move on our own, except for some help of one of Denise's new coworkers and her coworker's husband. We told the boys that we were moving in order to get them closer to where other kids were. My children were obviously upset at first about leaving our monster house, but once they saw the new house and a block full of kids playing in the street, the memories of Stallion Way disappeared quickly. I saw this as a huge step in bringing these innocent children gradually down from one lifestyle to another. My children made the whole process very easy on me; they actually amazed me at how little the material possessions meant to them; me on the other hand, well, this would take some adjusting.

Since Denise had already given up her rights to our house in her plea agreement, I was the only one that had to be at the closing. Lenny was there, the new buyer was there, and Mr. Beckerleg was there to sign for the government. Up until this point in time, I believe that over the past year and a half, I had handled several huge disappointments with grace and dignity. Once again, I would be tested at the house closing. The new buyer decided at the last minute to back out of our furniture deal. Yes, he still wanted the furniture, but instead of paying for it separately, this shmuck had the mortgage company add the price of the furniture into the house so that he could finance it. Not once before the day of closing did he ever suggest that he was going to do this. Mr. Beckerleg obviously knew about the change because he was more than prepared to make me an offer. Mr. Beckerleg would allow a check for $23,000 to be given to me for the sale of the furniture; the rest would be frozen with my remaining assets. I now know why the feds make you give up any and all firearms when you are under indictment: it is because of times like this where I would surely have pulled out my Berretta and shot the whole fuckin' bunch of them.

What pissed me off the most was that Lenny knew about the changes. He had the HUD statement the day before closing, and he chose not to tell me. Lenny pulled me aside and pleaded with me to continue with the closing. He reminded me that his commission was coming my way, and God only knows if we would find another buyer for this size of a house. Once again, I bit my tongue, and I accepted the fucking like a man. I left the closing feeling just about as low as I had felt in a very long time; I was getting tired of this non-stop raping. I realized once again that I could really only trust myself and my abilities to earn a living. It seemed like every time I expected to get money from another source, I would get let down or screwed over. Poker and pools would pull me through, poker and pools.

A week after the closing took place, I had still not heard from Lenny. I figured it would take a day or two for the commission check to clear, and then he would stop by and hand me the funds; well, I was about to realize just how much of a lowlife my wife's stepfather and my mother-in-law were. After asking Denise several times that week if she had heard from her mother or Lenny, Denise broke down and cried in my arms. I had no idea what was wrong, but for Denise to look for comfort from me, there must be something very wrong. Once calmed down, Denise told me that her mother and Lenny moved to Hernando, Florida, which was about seven hours away from where Weston is located. Moved? When? Why? Denise's sister Laura and her husband had moved to Hernando several months earlier for work; now Denise's mother and Lenny had moved there. Denise told me that Lenny and her mother sat her down and told Denise that I was not going to be getting Lenny's commission. Lenny and Denise's mother would hold it for a rainy day. A rainy day? How much more of a rainy day do I need? When the hell was this decided? I lost it. I mean, I lost it. I called Lenny's cell phone to confront him. Lenny would have no part of the conversation. He simply told me that when I went to prison, my family would need a place to stay, and they could come and live with him. This was how he justified me not getting the house commission that was promised to me. When I went off on him, Lenny hung up on me.

Please tell me, what kind of people do this to their own relatives? This was Denise's mother. I mean, she was always a self-centered piece of shit, but this was going above and beyond the call of duty. How many letdowns can one person take without going postal? I would say that it depends on the individual, and I would say that I was displaying superman abilities at this point not to go out and kill.

I had lost most of my respect for my wife. Denise was still a great mother to Thomas and Jake, but she wanted no part of any physical relationship with me. I had already accepted that. But now, just knowing that she knew her mother and Lenny had moved and that they had no intention of giving me the money that I had coming to me, and she chose not to tell me until I pressed her on the issue, well, that was just too much for me to accept. While together, and especially around my children, I would treat her well and be respectful to her, but when I was out on my own, well, let's just say that it was all about me, no more worrying about a woman that obviously did not give a shit about me.

CHAPTER 182

Life as I knew it began to unravel more and more each day. The next defining moment in my life came when my father and I had a fight. I could not believe it, I was talking to my father one day, and he informed me that he was going to my sister Lisa's house for a birthday party. I just could not understand how in the hell my father could go and celebrate my sister's birthday when she was still married to Burt, the man who showed up and testified against me in court. Lisa's husband helped send me to prison, and my father was going to go there and celebrate with them. To top this wonderful event off, Alan was going to be at the party. That's right, Alan Nudelman, the guy who went and lied to the FBI about me. Lisa and Burt were still friends with him, and now my father was going to join them in a nice sweet birthday celebration. Would someone please give me a fucking break here. This was worse than a *90210* episode. Listen, folks, I am a father of two wonderful children, so I can say this with a clear and open conscience. If one of my kids was married to a woman that helped send one of my other kids to prison, I would first kill his wife, and then I would give him a beating that he would never forget. Family is supposed to stick together. We are from the same flesh and blood, yet my father was going to sit in a house and party with two people that basically ruined my life and ripped my family to pieces. That was unacceptable to me, and I made my father know just how I felt. I asked him not to contact me until he was no longer a part of my sister Lisa's life. It hurt me more than I can explain to even get those words out of my mouth, but I did not want my children to know a man that was willing to look the other way when one of his kids were destroying another. I never heard from my father again.

CHAPTER 183

To the average person that knew Denise and me, things appeared to be status quo. We still had Susan and her daughters watch Thomas and Jake on occasion. Denise and I would go out for dinner from time to time and even go to the Hard Rock together every now and then. The truth of the matter was that I was now living a double life. I made my own set of rules when I was away from home, and I quickly realized just how much of an abnormal life I had been living all these years. There was no need for all those years of loneliness. As a whole, people seemed to like being around me, and I enjoyed the company of other people. I was very surprised at how many women approached me now that I had a new attitude about life. Seriously, folks, I am no Brad Pitt when it comes to looks, but looks are not everything. Out of nowhere, I was approached by women that just wanted to meet someone nice. Please don't get me wrong here. These women were not street sluts looking for a quickie, and then off they went. No, these were all-around nice people. I met an older woman in our local public supermarket. She was an Italian sweetheart named Mia. Mia was originally from New York, she had been around the block a few times in her fifty-two years on this planet, but she was in phenomenal shape, and she had such an unbelievable personality. Mia was someone I could call at any time of the day or night, and she was always willing to listen to me, and she never hesitated to ask me over to her house. Mia and I were a great match in bed, and when it was time to say goodbye for the night, there were no hard feelings.

I told every person that I met during this time of my life the truth about me: I was married and obviously having issues with my marriage, I had two great kids that were my driving force, and I was a convicted felon that would most likely be going to prison in the very

486

near future. Mia was only one of six or seven women that I saw on a steady basis. Most of the other women were regulars at the Hard Rock where I spent the majority of my time. I met two young ladies that were originally from Ecuador; their names were Beatrice and Ingrid. Both of them were twenty-two years old, and both of them could have easily been models; they were gorgeous woman. Neither Beatrice nor Ingrid spoke very good English, but that seemed to be part of the fun that we had when we were together; just trying to figure out what the hell they were saying was a good time. My Ecuadorian friends had an apartment ten minutes away from the Hard Rock, and I found myself waking up there naked on plenty of occasions. When I think back about these two beauties, it just amazes me that not only did they like having sex with me, but they insisted on all three of us being together most of the time. The other poker players at the Hard Rock would constantly ask me about them. Sometimes these two would simply watch me play poker for ten hours straight and then party with me until all hours of the night. It was funny, when I first explained to them about me being a felon and the probability that I would be going to prison, they asked me to run away with them back to Ecuador. How's that for an invitation, guys? Run away to Ecuador with two gorgeous women that were half my age or go to prison. Tough decision, but I had kids that I loved more than life itself, and that would never change. I was personally involved with a sweetheart of a bartender at the Hard Rock that probably should have gone back to school to be a psychiatrist. Every time I sat down and spent a night with this woman, she always seemed to always know the right things to say. She just had a gift about herself that should have been used for something more than bartending. I owe her a debt of gratitude for keeping my head on straight and for stopping me from driving home hammered on more than one occasion. I don't want to sound overly proud of my extramarital affairs. I am mentioning them because it was a revelation for me, it changed the way I act around people, and I want anyone out there that is alone or maybe in an abusive relationship to know that there are nice people out there in the world, and there is no need to be lonely.

CHAPTER 184

I probably sound like an idiot when I say this, but I would have given up every one of those women for one normal relationship with Denise. I loved that woman since the day I met her, but at some point, when things are not going your way, you have to move on, and I guess that is what I was doing. No, I did not divorce Denise. I hate to use my children as an excuse, but they were going to be going through enough changes in their lives, and I just did not see the point of putting them through a divorce. Once again, I left that decision in Denise's hands; if she were to come to me and ask for a divorce, then so be it. If not, then I figured I would just ride our relationship out. My pill use and alcohol consumption was at a record pace while I was out at night.

During the day, I was Tom the pool man, and my business was going so well that it was scary. Commercial property after commercial property were referred to me from the customers that I was already servicing, and it got to the point where I started to turn jobs away. The pool industry in South Florida is known for people that do not show up, offer poor service, and have no customer service skills. I offered a great service at ridiculously high prices, but I showed up when I said I would, and I was skilled at what I did. The property managers loved the fact that I took the time to talk to the residents that used the pools, and I offered money-back-guaranteed work.

If I was simply a drunk or a pothead at night, I would never have been able to get my swimming pool work done. I just partied way too hard until way too late at night, but these damn painkillers just made it possible to ignore the night before and to continue on like I had not even gone out in the first place. They really are one of the most dangerous types of drugs in the world. At this point in time, I was beyond addicted to these pills. They were my way of life, and for now, it did not bother me at all. I went balls to the wall with my life, and I decided to start playing in World Series of Poker events in other states. I even played in the 2005 US Poker Championships at the Taj Mahal in Atlantic City, New Jersey. I cashed in several events that year, and in the ones where I did not cash in the official prize pool, I usually made money with side bets with other players. Every major tournament has a "last man standing" unofficial side pool. The last man standing is exactly what it sounds like. The usual entry amount for this side bet is anywhere from $1,000 per man up to as much as $10,000 per man. Let's say, for example, that twenty guys that are playing in a tournament and get together and create a last man standing pool at $1,000 per man. Whichever of those twenty players last the longest in that particular tournament wins the $20,000; it has nothing to do with cashing in with the official prize pool. My poker skills were getting better and better every month that I played. I had a small safe at home that I placed my winnings in, and it was gradually becoming full.

Between my pool business and my poker winnings, I was doing pretty damn good for myself. Denise still had a full-time job at the cookie store, but I never once saw a check of hers. I never once asked her to kick in a few bucks for our living expenses. I knew my wife all too well. She was putting the money away for her and the boys, and that was just fine with me.

So that was my post-conviction routine: pools during the day, sports coaching and quality time with my boys in the early evenings, and during the days on the weekends, poker and woman at night. I did my best to try and put the feds out of my mind.

CHAPTER 185

I checked in with Scott from time to time, and on occasion, I received surprise visits from my probation officer. Time seemed to be flying by as I hung out in limbo. I was very grateful for these precious moments in time that I was able to spend with my children. I was a very active participant in their lives during their younger years, and I could only hope and pray that they would be strong enough to handle my inevitable departure to prison. The year 2005 came to an end, 2006 came and went, 2007 went by without any significant life changes, and still there was no word from the appellate court. Legal delays turned into longer legal delays, and neither side seemed to give a shit anymore. I had this ridiculous thought that perhaps I would just be forgotten.

On January 5, 2008, my sister Paula was married for the second time. Paula had met a nice guy by the name of Chris who, of all things, was an attorney; I decided not to hold that against him. Unfortunately, Paula's wedding became a subject that caused some serious tensions between me and her. Denise, myself, and my boys were all invited to Paula's wedding and dinner celebration, but I declined to go. Paula had recently reconciled with my older sister Lisa, which meant that Lisa and her husband, Burt, would be attending the wedding. I loved my sister Paula very much, and I would have done almost anything to have been there for her special day, but I just did not see this as a possibility. The problem lied within me; I know myself all too well, I know what I am capable of, and I know what I am not capable of. Spending a night in the same room as my sister Lisa and her good-for-nothing husband, Burt, was not something that I was capable of doing. I tried to explain to Paula that I did not want to ruin her special day, and if I were to attend, then her day

490

would surely be a disaster. I have no doubt in my mind that I would have taken the first opportunity possible to stab Burt in the neck with a butter knife—yes, a butter knife. Sorry, folks, but that just does not make for good wedding pictures, at least not where I come from. My sister Paula and my wife, Denise, never had a very good relationship, and I know that Paula placed the blame for me not attending her wedding on Denise. I explained to Paula many times in the past that not only was it my decision not to attend her wedding, but Denise actually was mad at me for not going. Denise and I fought over my decision not to go to Paula's wedding; she insisted that I was being selfish and childish for not being able to control my temper. So one more time for the record, it was 100 percent my decision to miss Paula's wedding; right or wrong, I felt in my heart that I was doing the right thing, and I have to live with that decision.

CHAPTER 186

The year 2008 became progressively shittier for me. I received a call from my dear friend Carrol toward the end of January, and I was simply devastated by what he had to tell me. Carrol was diagnosed with pancreatic cancer. There was a tumor in his pancreas and the surrounding area, and the doctors ruled out any chance of an operation. Carrol was in great pain, and he was immediately placed on morphine to help comfort him, but there would be no possibility of a cure. Carrol was dying. I had been through so much with this man, and I had never seen or heard him cry before, but this time was different. Carroll was afraid and confused about how life could have led him to this point. I did my best to comfort him in his time of need. I begged him to come and live with me in Florida, but Carroll wanted to be close to his children for as long as he could be. I could surely understand that. It's hard to hear someone that you love so dearly be in such pain, especially when they are not in front of you to hold in your arms.

Carrol was a fighter, that's for sure, but in May of 2008, Carrol passed away in his sleep. I received the call from Carrol's daughter Jessica; she wanted me to know that Carrol died in peace, and she wanted me to know just how much I meant to him. I did my best to help Carrol's children sort through his business affairs, and I left an open invitation for them to call me for help. I miss that big lug of a guy. I miss him terribly. Rest in peace, Carrol Jones, rest in peace.

CHAPTER 187

May's downward spiral continued when I received a call from Scott informing me that my appeal had been denied by the Eleventh Circuit. Well, that was putting it lightly. Not only had my conviction been affirmed, but the Eleventh Circuit also ruled in favor of the government's appeal in regard to my sentence and how it was calculated. The Eleventh Circuit ordered my sentence to be vacated, and I was remanded back to District Court for resentencing. Not good, not good at all. You can take my word for what I am about to tell you, or you can do your own homework on the subject, but this is the God's honest truth about what the Eleventh Circuit had decided. It was decided that the charges in which my jury had found me not guilty on contained similar conduct of the charge that I was found guilty of, so the appellate court ruled that my acquitted conduct had to become part of my sentencing guideline calculation. In other words, Judge Cooke was now being ordered to recalculate my advisory sentencing guideline level to include the charges that I was found not guilty on. Every Global customer was to be considered a victim, and every penny invested by these customers was to be considered a loss.

The jury's entire verdict was basically being thrown out the door. The United States Constitution affords a defendant the right to a trial by jury, and I executed my constitutional right for that trial by jury. As far as I knew, NOT GUILTY means exactly that, NOT GUILTY. How in God's name could this decision be legal? How is this possible in America? By adding all the Global customers to the number of victims, and by adding the amount of their losses to the sentencing calculations, it was determined that I was now going to be resentenced based on a level 38, which meant that Judge Cooke could now sentence me to over twenty years in prison, just like the feds had wanted in my first sentencing. You really have to step back for a moment and think about what I just told you. A jury made specific findings based on evidence presented at my trial, but now those findings were being reinterpreted. Scott could try and explain how this could happen a thousand times, but even to this day, I don't see how this could be possible.

I consider myself to be a mentally tough person. I can take a lot in the letdown department, and I believe that up until this point, I had done a good job of not committing suicide or something. Once again, I am not proud of it, but thank God that I was heavily medicated at this time, or there would be a very good chance that I would be dead at this time.

CHAPTER 188

April 25, 2008, my resentencing day, had arrived, and I found myself once again in front of Judge Cooke. I was by myself this time, no dad, no Paula, no cousin John; I asked everyone to stay away. Enough was enough. The courtroom consisted of me, Scott, and an ever-growing prosecution team. Judge Cooke recalculated my sentencing guideline level according to the Eleventh Circuits instructions, and once again, I was asked if I would like to make a statement on my own behalf. Yes, yes, I do.

I made my statement brief. I reminded Judge Cooke that there were no new charges or crimes that caused this sentencing level increase. I pointed out to the good judge that it had been over two years since I had last been in front of her court, and during those two years, I had remained employed, I had not gotten into any trouble with the law, I had continued to raise my two young boys, and I had followed the conditions of my appeal bond. In other words, I was no threat to society, and there was no need for an increase in my sentence.

Judge Cooke then asked the prosecutor if he had anything further for her to consider before she resentenced me. Prosecutor Reinhart told Judge Cooke that he had one new exhibit that he would like her to review before I was sentenced again. Mr. Reinhart gave a copy of this new exhibit to me and Scott, and then he handed a copy of the exhibit to Judge Cooke.

As I reviewed the government's newest propaganda, I slowly but surely became sick to my stomach. I could not believe my own eyes. I became so mad that I seriously wanted to cry. Yes, my frustration level had reached that high of a point. The new exhibit was a color-coded chart that listed all of Global Vending's operating machines individually, and then it listed all the customers that were assigned to each machine. It was just another presentation of the same old theory that the government had presented at trial; Global was a fraud, I assigned multiple people to the same machine and never told the customers, Global was one huge Ponzi scheme, blah blah blah blah blah. What made me so sad, so mad, so frustrated, so infuriated was the fact that for the first time, the government included Global's 2001 customers on their exhibit. The trial never included that group of machines or investors because no machines were assigned to multiple investors at that time. The problem with that little miracle was that I had destroyed Global's 2001 customer files over a year before the feds raided my office. Global's 2001 customer information was the first to have been entered into our ACT database. The only place that this information existed was on the server and hard drives of Global Vending. This proved that the feds had a full access to that information, the information that would have and still could have proved my innocence. The whole story about corrupt disks was absolute bullshit just as I had suspected. The government had full access to our ACT database and notes that proved that Global was not hiding anything from anyone.

Needless to say, I went fucking nuts. Snap, crackle, and pop. I yelled, and I screamed at the prosecutor. I used every four-letter word known to mankind. My physical presence was that of aggression and rage. I was out of control, but I did not give a rat's ass. This court, this prosecution, this whole system was bullshit, and my life was in shambles because of it. I had no respect for any of these people, not even Judge Cooke.

Judge Cooke had seen and heard enough of my antics; she looked me square in the eyes and then hit me with a ten-year sentence. She told me that I was lucky that ten years was all that I was getting. Ten years. Ten fucking years! I had to take a few moments and consider just what this new sentence meant to me. When the feds first raided my home and business back in January of 2004, my boys were four and seven years old. Now I would have to serve a ten-year prison term, and when I do finally get released, Thomas will be twenty-two years old, and Jake will be nineteen years old. Do you have any idea just how hard that was to swallow? On top of that, I could not help but think about the five-year plea deal that I turned down because Scott informed me that I could not get more than sixty-three months in prison if I was found guilty of "all" charges after a trial. If I had taken that plea bargain in 2005, I would have been ready to get out of prison already, and I would have still been a young man. As things stood now, I would be released from prison at the ripe old age of fifty-two years old. I believe that I just added Scott to the list of people that I would kill if I ever decided to go postal.

CHAPTER 189

I was ordered to report to the Federal Prison Camp in Pensacola, Florida, on June 12, 2008. Thank God I was not taken away right there at my resentencing. I needed to get my personal affairs in order, and I needed to put some serious thought into how I was going to break the news to my children.

Denise and I spoke about my new sentence in a very civil manner—civil, unemotional, almost businesslike. Denise decided that she was going to take Lenny up on his bullshit offer and move in with her mother and Lenny. I can't even begin to tell you how much I fought with her to rethink that decision. That household was no place for my children, and Denise's mother and Lenny did not have the values that I wanted instilled into my children. The sad part was that I had no real say in the matter; I was going to prison, so my feelings now meant shit to her. I did not want to fight with Denise because she would be needed to raise our children. She would be my only direct contact with them, so I decided to make this as easy as possible for her. I decided to support her in any way that I could over the next month or so.

The lease was just about up on Denise's SUV, so I asked her to find another vehicle that she wanted to drive for the next few years; Denise picked out a brand-new Jeep Patriot. I went to the Jeep dealer, and I bought Denise the Jeep; I paid for it in full with cash. I also prepaid her auto insurance for an entire year so at least she would not have any real auto expenses to worry about. It was the best I could do for her.

Denise and the boys would have a free place to live, no auto expense, and when the time was right, I would turn over my safe to Denise with all my poker winnings in it. I arranged for a U-Haul truck for the big move, and Denise and I packed the truck on our own. We had a talk with Thomas and Jake about the move, but we still did not mention that I was going to prison. I wanted to continue to ease them into these changes that were taking place in their lives; up until this point, they were completely unaffected by what had taken place with the feds, and I must say that I was very proud of the job that Denise and I did to make that happen.

It was summertime, so school was out, and moving to a new school would be a lot less of a deal than if we had to move during a school year. My kids were a little upset because they were leaving their neighborhood friends, but they were going to be moving very close to Denise's sister Laura; her husband, Fidel; and my nephew Antonio. Antonio was close with Thomas and Jake when he lived in Weston, so hopefully they would bond once again.

I said my goodbyes to the women that I had become so friendly with. Every one of them asked where I would be doing my prison time; every one of them wanted to stay in touch. I thanked each and every one of them for their friendship, love, and support, but I also asked them to just try and forget that I existed. I did not know what prison had in store for me, and I did not want any contact from the nightlife that I loved so much. I was not sure if I would be able to handle hearing from them. Each of them respected my wishes, our goodbyes were sad, but who knows, maybe someday our paths will cross again. For now, I know I made the right decision to try and forget that that lifestyle even existed.

With only a couple of days left before I was to report to prison, I moved my family from the town that I had grown to love, Weston, to the town that I dreaded to even step foot into, Hernando, Florida. My boys were given their own rooms in the house of shame. Denise would also have a nice room to stay in. This area was a very rural and quiet place to live in. There is very little going on in that town, but maybe that was what Denise would need. I agreed with one thing that Denise made clear to me, she would need help raising two young men. I always liked my brother-in-law Fidel; he and I always had a good relationship, and I knew that he would help watch after my two young men when needed. There was very little conversation between

Lenny and I for the short while that I was at their home. He was obviously uncomfortable with what he had done to me. I kept my distance in order to avoid a confrontation. That would have done no one any good at this late hour.

CHAPTER 190

On June 11, 2008, the night before I was to self-surrender to prison, Denise and I finally had our talk with Thomas and Jake. I have done million-dollar presentations in front of CEOs of some of the largest companies in the world, I had squared off in court with the United States of America, I had gone toe to toe with the FBI, I had just buried one of my best friends, and I was on my way to prison for a ten-year stay, but nothing was harder for me than facing those two little men of mine and explaining to them that Daddy was leaving tonight, and he was not coming back for a long while. I explained things to my boys in the simplest of terms possible. I told them that the government did not like the way that Daddy ran his company, so I had to be punished for a while. I never used the word *prison*; instead, I told them that I was going to a camp. I told my boys that once I was settled in there, then they would be able to come and visit me. When Jake asked me how long I had to stay at the camp, I told him that I did not know, but hopefully it would not be for a long time. Once again, I was leading them down this road in stages. I was trying to preserve their innocence during this awful time.

Thomas has always had this mechanism about him: when he is uncomfortable with a situation, he says whatever he has to say to make the situation disappear as quickly as possible. On this occasion, Thomas just yessed Denise and I to death. Yes, he understood what I was telling him. Yes, he was okay. No, he had no questions. I knew that the best thing to do was to let Thomas be. He was twelve years old, and he knew what was going on and how to deal with it in his own little way.

Jake was not okay with me leaving. He sat on my lap and put his arms around me. He cried and cried for what seemed like hours.

I assured Jake that I would be back and that we would pick up right where we left off. Jake made me promise that he could come and visit in the very near future, and Denise promised him that that would happen. I tucked my boys into their beds that night for the very last time, and then it was my turn to cry. I had formed a bond with my two boys, a bond that would make it very tough for me to be separated from them. I would not be there in the morning to rustle them out of bed, I would not be there to coach their sports teams, I would not be there for their birthday parties or to celebrate holidays with them, and I simply would not be in their lives.

I managed to get myself together. I had a heart-to-heart talk with Denise, and I had one simple request for her: if at any point in time she felt the need to move on in her life without me, to please let me know, ask me for a divorce, and I will understand. Just please don't make a fool of me and run around behind my back. I know that sounds funny coming from a guy that was cheating on his wife, but remember, I tried everything possible to make my relationship with Denise work, and she had no idea that I was not true to her. I just felt that at this point, I deserved to be told up front. Denise kind of laughed it off, but I know that she understood what I was getting at. I handed her the keys to the safe, and I told her to try and make it last as long as she could. There was over $50,000 in the safe at the time: 50K, no auto expenses and a place to live rent-free was the best that I could do for my family considering what the feds had done to us.

CHAPTER 191

On June 12, 2008, I woke up at 3:00 a.m. to begin my drive to prison. Denise walked me to the front door and gave me a hug that actually felt genuine. I had trouble letting her go that morning, but I eventually did. I turned and gave her a patented Tom Foley wink, and now it was off to prison. The ride from Hernando to Pensacola was almost nine hours long; I used that time to reflect on what had taken place over the last four years, and I just wished that I could turn back time and start over. Unfortunately, that does not happen in real life. I can't tell you how many pills I ingested that morning; I would guess that it was close to thirty. I had no idea what I was going to do once I got to prison and had to deal with drug withdrawals, so for now, I just ate those damn things like they were candy.

I drove my truck onto the lot of a local Pensacola Ford Dealership. I asked for a sales manager to assist me in turning in a leased truck. The sales manager started to pitch on a replacement vehicle, when I simply slid over a copy of my orders to report to prison. The sales manager was speechless. I started to laugh, and I told him not to worry. I was the one going to prison, not him. I still had a full month left on the lease, but he realized that a missing payment was the least of my worries, and he wrote it off for me. He was a nice enough guy.

The sales manager called me a taxi, shook my hand, and that was the end of my truck. I grabbed a Coke from one of the dealership's vending machines, and I used it to wash down the last ten or so pills that I had in my pocket. I was higher than I had probably ever been in my life, and now I was going to prison. The taxi driver was cool; he must have asked me a million questions about why I was going to prison and how long I would be there. He seemed to be amazed at how relaxed and calm I was, but then again, he did not know that I was drugged out of my mind.

We arrived at the entrance to Saufley Field. The Navy base was where the Pensacola prison camp is located. I paid the taxi driver his fee, and I gave him another $100 as a tip. You are not allowed cash in prison, and I still had the hundred in my pocket, so what the heck, I gave it to the driver. I am sure that tip made his week. A correctional officer met me at the gate and escorted me to the prison's administration building where I would be processed for my prison stay. It was such a sad moment in time for me. How in God's name did I get here? Perhaps someday I will talk about prison in more detail and tell you some of the crazy shit that takes place in federal lockups, but for now, I think I have said enough.

⚜

CHAPTER 192

⚜

I collapsed from drug withdrawals on my second day in prison. I tried to warn the medical staff of my addiction, but prison medical personnel are a bunch of sadistic animals with no regard for human life. Inmates are animals to them, and they are treated as such. I threw up blood while taking a shower that night, and then I simply passed out. I was transported to a local hospital where I lay handcuffed to a bed with the same withdrawal symptoms that I had experienced years before when I quit cold turkey, except this time the withdrawal was worse, and I was not in the comfort of my own home. I completely lost my memory at one point, and I could not remember my name, whether I had a family, or even what state I was in. I was in agonizing pain, and I felt more alone than I had ever felt before. My body and my mind could not handle any more, and all at once, I simply shut down. The shakes stopped, the pain went away, and the room went black.

Something amazing happened as I lay on the hospital bed in complete darkness. I could not feel my body, yet I could feel a presence. I was not alone. No, I am not crazy. I am not even overly religious, but at that moment in time, I believe I met my Maker. I met Jesus Christ himself. No, he was not one-legged. In fact, he was not even a form that could be described; he was a presence above my bed, and he was shaking his head from side to side. I wish I could explain this moment better because I could not see a head or a face, yet I could tell that his head was shaking side to side. I could also tell that he was sad, sad that one of his children had fallen so far from grace. I was at complete ease and comfort; I assumed that I was dead. Without words, Jesus made it clear to me that I was going to be given a second chance at life. I would be forgiven for my sins of the past, but only if I was willing to forgive those that had sinned against me. I needed to forgive those that had hurt me and led me to this point in my life. It would be up to me; only I could decide the future path that I was going to follow. A comforting hand touched my head, and light slowly began to appear to me again. I woke up on the same hospital bed, with the same handcuffs on, except it was now eight hours later. I no longer had any withdrawal symptoms—none. In fact, I felt as strong as an ox. It was just amazing.

I am sure that I could talk about my heavenly experience forever, but for now, I choose not to. My meeting with the Man Upstairs was a very personal affair for me. I was not asked to become a preacher of the Good Book, and to be honest with you, I don't think I ever will be. God has placed all sorts of people on this earth. Some of them are destined to be preachers, some are destined to be followers, and others are his warriors. I would say that I am one of his battle-tested warriors. I have been raised to believe that God exists, and now I have been lucky enough to be shown a better understanding of just who God is and what path I am expected to follow. For whatever reason, my faith was tested by the Man Upstairs, and although on the outside it may seem that I have failed, well, that cannot be further from the truth. I never lost my faith in God, and now I was being given a second chance at life.

CHAPTER 193

The truth of the matter is that prison saved my life. By the Good Lord sending me to prison, I was able to kick my addiction for good. Let's face it, taking that many painkillers along with as much alcohol as I was drinking was surely a one-way ticket to the old dirt bed, but now I would have a fresh start, and it would be up to me to choose the path that I would follow for the rest of my life. I kept my end of the bargain. I wrote letters to Prosecutor Reinhart, Special Agent Kimberly Delano, Alan Nudelman, Denise's mother and Lenny, my sister Lisa and Burt, and of course my father. My letters consisted of an offering of my forgiveness toward them for what had taken place over the past four years, and I asked several of them to please forgive me for my brutal responses. I wrote each of these letters from my heart, and I asked for nothing in return. I just wanted a fresh start in life without carrying around baggage filled with old grudges. I could not believe how good I felt as I wrote these letters from prison. It felt like a huge weight was being lifted off my shoulders as I not only offered my forgiveness on paper but also through my soul.

I never received a response from Mr. Reinhart or from Agent Delano, nor did I expect to. I am at peace with that. Denise's mother and Lenny spoke to me on the phone one day when I called to speak to my boys. The conversation that they offered was fake and shallow, but once again, I had done my part, and I was at peace with my in-laws. In case you are wondering, no, I never saw a dime of the money that was owed to me by Lenny, but once again, that means nothing to me anymore, just another one of life's lessons learned.

My father embraced my letter with open arms. He and his wonderful wife, Sandy, made almost an immediate trip up to Pensacola, which was a very comforting weekend for me. My relationship with my father has never been as strong as it is right now. I hope and pray every day that I will be lucky enough to spend some time with him in the free world before he is called to the heavens.

My sister Lisa wrote me a letter on her and Burt's behalf. It was not a nice letter. Lisa and Burt made it very clear that they feel that they have done nothing wrong to me and that my forgiveness was not welcome. My sister's letter told me that she was not interested in having a relationship with me at that time. Lisa is my flesh and blood, and no matter what, I will always have a place in my heart for her. I know that someday our paths will cross again, and let's just see what happens at that point. Burt, well, he will need to do some soul-searching; he is getting up there in the years, and he needs to get prepared to meet his Maker. My forgiveness is still real for him. I forgave, but I will never forget.

Alan Nudelman chose to write me a fuck-you letter. I did not expect any less from him. Alan is a man (and I use that term very loosely) that still to this day holds a grudge against Paula and me. Alan needs to wake up and smell the roses. He has suffered two heart attacks before the age of forty-five, which should tell him something. You are being warned by the Man Upstairs, Alan. Let your grudges from the past go, live life to its fullest, and you too will feel those weights being lifted off your heart and your shoulders. I am serious; it is a great feeling. Once again, my forgiveness toward Alan was real, but also once again, I will never forget.

CHAPTER 194

It is now the year 2011, and it has been over seven years since the FBI shut down Global Vending. It's funny, isn't it? The feds shut down Global Vending because it was supposedly this huge Ponzi scheme that was about to collapse, yet here we are seven years later, and Global is still operating with huge six-figure annual profits with no "new" money being invested; that's one hell of a Ponzi scheme. Perhaps the "Fumbling Bumbling Idiots" (FBI) can tell the customers of Global Vending exactly when that collapse is going to take place. Too bad my old tech Ron is the only one profiting from all my hard work and all my investors' hard-earned money.

Anyway, Denise divorced me during my very first year in prison, and no, she did not grant me the one favor that I had asked her for. I was made a fool by Denise and her sudden need to chase a man from her far past—high school, to be exact. But to tell you the truth, even that is water under the bridge for me. Denise has been raising our two boys on her own for the three years that I have been in prison. Denise is living in a place of her own and working full-time. I am sure that life has not been easy for her, and I commend her with all my heart for doing such a fine job raising Thomas and Jake. I pray that someday Denise will find it in her heart to forgive me for leaving her to raise our boys on her own, but for now, I am giving her the space that she is asking me for.

I talk to Thomas and Jake on the telephone at least once per week. Thomas is now a high school freshman. He is a straight A student, and he just received his driver's permit. God help us all! Jake is twelve years old, and he is in the sixth grade. Jake plays full-contact football and baseball. He too is close to being a straight A student. I could not be a prouder father than I already am. It would have been very easy for my boys to have used my absence as an excuse to act up and to make bad life decisions, but instead, with the continued guidance of Denise and myself, they have chosen to excel. It hurts like hell to be missing my children growing up. I have missed birthdays, holiday celebrations, and milestones in their lives, which can never be duplicated again. This is the price that I am being asked to pay in order to have a second chance at life. The absence of my children is the one thing that makes life in prison difficult for me. I have no real enemies in prison just like I have no real enemies out in the free world.

I hope and pray every day that the good Lord frees me from my captures before my ten-year sentence is completed, but until that time, I look out of my eleventh-floor window of the Federal Detention Center in Miami. I can see the port of Miami with all of its huge cruise ships setting sail for exotic destinations. I can see South Beach and all the luxury high-rise buildings that line the Atlantic Ocean. I can see the intercoastal waterway alive with speedboats and luxurious yachts. Finally, I can see parts of downtown Miami with its huge business skyscrapers gleaming in the sun. People from around the world pay millions of dollars for this exact view, but for me, well, I get this view for free. So who's better than me?

The answer: just about anyone in the free world. Peace be the journey, my friends. Peace be the journey.

Tom Foley lives in Central Florida with his beautiful wife, Sonia. He is still living the American dream as a proud father of two grown boys and now a proud stepdad to Sonia's three children. Tom and Sonia own a commercial swimming pool company and continue to live life on their own terms. God Bless America.